UIN

PLA

MAY 3 1 2003

WITHDRAWN

ANTON PAVLOVICH CHEKHOV, the son of a former serf, was born in 1860
in Taganrog, a port on the Sea of Azov. He received a classical education at
the Taganrog Gymnasium, then in 1879 went to Moscow, where he entered
the medical faculty of the university, graduating in 1884. During his university
years he supported his family by contributing humorous stories and sketches
to magazines. He published his first volume of stories, *Motley Tales*, in 1886
and a year later his second volume, *In the Twilight*, for which he was awarded
the Pushkin Prize. In 1887 his first full-length play, *Ivanov*, was produced in
Moscow. For five years he lived on his small country estate near Moscow,
practising medicine and writing many of his best stories, but when his health
began to fail he moved to the Crimea. After 1900, the rest of his life was
spent at Yalta, where he met Tolstoy and Gorky. He wrote his best-known
plays in the last years of his life; in 1898 Stanislavsky produced *The Seagull*
at his newly founded Moscow Art Theatre, and it was for him that Chekhov
wrote *Uncle Vanya* (1900), *Three Sisters* (1901) and *The Cherry Orchard*
(1903). In 1901 Chekhov married Olga Knipper, one of the Art Theatre's
leading actresses. He died of consumption in 1904.

PETER CARSON learned Russian during National Service in the Navy at the
Joint Services School for Linguists, Crail and London, and at home – his
mother's family left Russia after the Bolshevik Revolution. His working life
has been spent on the editorial side of London publishing.

RICHARD GILMAN is Professor Emeritus of Playwriting and Dramatic
Literature at Yale University's School of Drama. He has been drama critic
for *Newsweek*, *Commonweal* and the *Nation* and was a contributing editor of
Partisan Review for many years. His latest book is *Chekhov's Plays: An
Opening into Eternity*.

ANTON CHEKHOV

Plays

Ivanov
The Seagull
Uncle Vanya
Three Sisters
The Cherry Orchard

Translated with Notes by PETER CARSON
With an Introduction by RICHARD GILMAN

PENGUIN BOOKS

PENGUIN BOOKS

Published by the Penguin Group
Penguin Books Ltd, 80 Strand, London WC2R ORL, England
Penguin Putnam Inc., 375 Hudson Street, New York, New York 10014, USA
Penguin Books Australia Ltd, 250 Camberwell Road, Camberwell, Victoria 3124, Australia
Penguin Books Canada Ltd, 10 Alcorn Avenue, Toronto, Ontario, Canada M4V 3B2
Penguin Books India (P) Ltd, 11, Community Centre, Panchsheel Park, New Delhi – 110 017, India
Penguin Books (NZ) Ltd, Cnr Rosedale and Airborne Roads, Albany, Auckland, New Zealand
Penguin Books (South Africa) (Pty) Ltd, 24 Sturdee Avenue, Rosebank 2196, South Africa

Penguin Books Ltd, Registered Offices: 80 Strand, London WC2R ORL, England

On the World Wide Web at: www.penguin.com

First published 2002

5

Translation and Notes copyright © Peter Carson, 2002
Introduction copyright © Richard Gilman, 2002
Chronology copyright © Ronald Wilks, 2001
All rights reserved

The moral right of the translator has been asserted

Set in 11/12.5 pt Monotype Fournier
Typeset by Rowland Phototypesetting Ltd, Bury St Edmunds, Suffolk
Printed in England by Clays Ltd, St Ives plc

CONTENTS

INTRODUCTION

'Dissatisfaction with oneself is one of the fundamental qualities
of every true talent.'   — CHEKHOV

In September of 1900 Anton Chekhov wrote from Yalta, a fading
but still rather fashionable Black Sea health resort, to his sister Maria
in Moscow that 'I find it very difficult to write . . . *Three Sisters*,
much more difficult than any other of my plays.' A little later he
wrote to his actress-wife Olga Knipper, for whom he had intended
the important role of Masha, the middle sister, that 'it looks at me
gloomily . . . and I think about it gloomily', and in another letter
told her 'there are a great many characters, it's crowded, I'm afraid
it will turn out obscure or pale.' Even after he'd finished he continued
to fret, telling a friend it was 'dull, verbose and awkward'.

Three Sisters is none of those things; quite the contrary. One of
the greatest dramas in any language since Shakespeare, the play is
animated, often exhilarating, funny and deeply sad by turns, but
never dull; far from being verbose and awkward, it's a masterpiece
of verbal economy and dramaturgical grace. (If you need any more
testimony to Chekhov's courage and mental strength remember that
he wrote this play and another almost equally splendid work — *The
Cherry Orchard* — while suffering through the last agonizing stages of
the tuberculosis (or 'consumption', as it was called then) which would
soon kill him; besides his lungs, the disease had attacked his spinal
cord and intestines. A doctor himself, he strangely refused for years
to acknowledge the severity, or even at first the existence, of his
illness, at times using his literary gifts to disguise, or moderate, the
truth; for example, he once described the sight of blood pouring from

his mouth during a haemorrhage as resembling 'the glow of a distant fire'.)

Olga Knipper, the daughter of a cultivated German-Russian family, had met Chekhov in 1899, when he was already a celebrated writer – of short fiction mostly; his first full-length plays were still making their way into public consciousness – and she was a promising young actress at the theatre with which he would soon become indelibly associated, the recently established Moscow Art Theatre (MAT). They fell in love and quietly married in 1901, but were mostly kept apart by Chekhov's doctors' insistence that, for his health, he must live in Yalta, which he bitterly called his 'warm Siberia'. He wanted Olga to continue her career, though she was more than prepared to abandon it, to help nurse him or simply *be* with him. They built their relationship through occasional meetings, but even more, perhaps, through their many letters, filled with vivid expressions of love, longing, sorrow, frustration, a saving humour, and some equally saving, not wholly serious, quarrels.

Chekhov died in 1904 in a German spa where Olga had taken him, looking for a cure. He was forty-four. She, eight years younger, would outlive him by an astounding fifty-five years, her career launched and sustained by central roles in his plays, but not confined to them. She died in 1959, having never remarried. (It's worth noting that Maria, Chekhov's sister, who for years ran the Yalta house, first as their residence and then, after his death, as a Chekhov museum, also lived to a grand old age, dying at ninety-three in 1957.)

> 'When someone spends the fewest number of motions on a given action, that is grace.'   – CHEKHOV

The difficulty Chekhov experienced with *Three Sisters* was unusual: although he had occasionally proclaimed his unfitness for playwriting, even vowing once or twice to abandon it, this doubtless came largely from anger at what he called the 'conventions' of the theatre, as well as from a modesty which Nathalie Sarraute, the brilliant Russian-French novelist, would later describe as 'fierce'. He was ordinarily a sure-handed, confident dramatist; it was his fiction that sometimes bedevilled him, he once said.

Whatever the truth of this, nothing seems to have given him as much trouble as *Three Sisters*, for a good reason: it was inherently the most difficult artistic enterprise he had attempted, something whose full radical nature he would discover – to his surprise, I think – as the writing progressed.

His artistic task, as he saw it, or at least as we see it now, was to create drama and fiction out of seemingly unpromising materials. A generation or so later Samuel Beckett (with whose work Chekhov's has many affinities) would confront much the same aesthetic task, and assert that he dealt with 'a whole zone of being that has always been set aside by artists as unusable', conditions like 'ignorance and impotence', to which it makes sense to add failure, weakness, apathy, and boredom, previously 'unusable' conditions which Chekhov put to remarkable dramatic use.

'It's only fools and charlatans who know everything and understand everything.'   – CHEKHOV

Almost certainly beyond his full, conscious awareness, Chekhov had for years been creating a new sort of drama. His way of working was painterly: make a starting stroke here, a counterstroke, a thematic strain, perhaps through a relationship between angles and curves, a countertheme, a little blurring, a revelation through juxtapositions, an enigma through loppings-off: the literary equivalents of visual puzzles, bits of emptiness, colours interrogating each other, shapes vying for room.

Chekhov's most daring departure from the conventions of dramaturgical creation was to abandon, as much as possible, the usual linear movement of a play – from a starting-point to exposition and 'development' (which usually meant the 'thickening' of a plot) to a denouement (a climax, the resolution of the play's struggle or dilemma); instead he worked toward the filling in of a dramatic field, an artistic space. This new dramaturgical construction, which began with *Ivanov* and culminated in *Three Sisters*, necessarily affected some of the most solidly rooted traditional elements and procedures of drama: all that had been accepted as its very constituents, and sanctified by centuries of theatrical pieties.

Chekhov as a subversive playwright? A revolutionary? Yes, we have to think of him in that way, in the face of popular and scholarly opinion having fixed him as the charming, conventionally realistic poet of the normal, the domestic and small; the dramatist of 'real', and unusually melancholy, life.

No contemporary playwright has been more widely misinterpreted; none has been more often wrongly directed and performed. The locus classicus of this was the MAT's production of *The Cherry Orchard*, which Stanislavsky directed as a heavy, lugubrious near-tragedy, when Chekhov had taken pains to call it a 'comedy'. Chekhov's categorizing of his own plays is important to keep in mind as we read them. He called *Ivanov* and *Three Sisters* dramas, *The Seagull* and *The Cherry Orchard* comedies, and *Uncle Vanya*, with extreme flatness, 'Scenes from Country Life'. Obviously that last subtitle, together with the designations of *The Seagull* and *The Cherry Orchard* as comedies – when we have been used to regarding them as basically sorrowful works – will engage our attention in the coming pages.

The intention with which Chekhov used subtitles went far beyond conventional practice. In calling *The Seagull* and *The Cherry Orchard* 'comedies' he intended something radically different from our usual meanings; the plays are comedies in the sense of Dante's *La Divina Commedia* and Balzac's ironic secular alternative, *La Comédie humaine*. Neither of these great works is 'funny', full of laughs; in their different ways they are deeply serious, providing us with comedy's truest actions: to liberate, to relieve, to heal. Treplyov's suicide in *The Seagull*, and the loss of the family estate in *The Cherry Orchard*, we might reflexively think, are endings which forbid the use of 'comedy' as ascriptions. But keep in mind that, as we'll see, Chekhov counterbalances Treplyov's death with Nina's exemplary new understanding of the key to productive life. With this in mind we can grasp the play as a comedy in Dante's sense: hope is kept alive, salvation is possible. In *The Cherry Orchard* something similar happens: Anya's maturing wisdom leads the play to an unexpected, potentially 'happy' ending. We shall consider both plays at greater length later on.

Chekhov used his subtitles partly as warnings to readers or audiences or performers or directors not to be trapped by misleading labels, or accurate ones, for that matter. The point he made in *Ivanov* was that labels and tags could be instruments of tyranny; someone expecting a 'serious' drama, upon opening his or her playbill, or programme, for *The Seagull*, or the text itself, and seeing the subtitle 'A Comedy' would have to make some mental adjustments as the play went on to its surely unfunny climax. These adjustments were just what Chekhov wanted from his hypothetical reader or spectator: becoming open to new theatrical experiences, stepping past frozen categories, accepting newness.

'Scenes from Country Life' suggests a pastoral idyll; but of course *Uncle Vanya* is anything but. Why Chekhov decided on that subtitle has, I think, much to do with his sense of the play's being so delicately poised between laughter and tears that the subtitle needed an especially exquisite neutrality to keep the work from toppling over for its audiences or readers into either of Chekhov's main characterizations: drama or comedy. The term 'tragicomic' wasn't in existence in Russia yet, nor would it have been entirely accurate.

'Drama should present not new stories, but new relationships.'
— FRIEDRICH HEBBEL

The European theatre and the Russian stage in particular were at low ebbs in the latter part of the nineteenth century, when Chekhov began writing plays. The stock fare in almost every cultural centre (including Moscow in the 1880s when Chekhov was studying and then practising medicine) were bedroom farces; formulaic, often violent melodramas; light romantic comedies (the whole repertoire mostly translations from the French or based on French models);

vaudevilles; and, very occasionally, productions of classics – the Greeks and Romans, Shakespeare, Molière, Schiller, Racine and Corneille. Here and there in Europe new genius (or at least major talent) had shown itself: Ibsen and Strindberg in Scandinavia, both of whom Chekhov read in translation and admired; Hauptmann in Germany; Zola – primarily a novelist, however – in France; Wilde and Shaw in Britain; Maurice Maeterlinck (with whose aesthetic ideas Chekhov largely agreed) in Belgium; but none gave rise to any movements of consequence or any significant successors. Acting was everywhere florid, declamatory; directing as an art was in its crude infancy; ensemble playing was barely known; costume and stage design were at worst flamboyant, at best uninspired.

> 'We must get the theatre out of the hands of the grocers and into literary hands . . .'
>   – CHEKHOV

With its roots in religious and folk ritual the theatre in Russia had developed much later than in Western Europe. Not until well into the nineteenth century did anything appear that could be called a truly Russian theatre, with native actors, directors, designers and dramatists, instead of French, Italian or German practitioners, as in earlier days. Even so, of the two truly gifted Russian dramatists before Chekhov, Pushkin and Gogol, the former wrote only one full-length play – *Boris Godunov* – and was far more influential as a poet and patriot who incarnated the 'national spirit', while Gogol, who also wrote only one full-length play, *The Government Inspector*, was probably most influential as a satiric fantasist in fiction. Moreover, from its beginnings the Russian theatre was closely associated with the state and thus the court, one consequence being a heavy-handed censorship, something Chekhov continually railed against.

Gogol exerted a strong influence on him, perhaps by his ideas and judgements as much as his formal dramas. Chekhov surely must have read Gogol's famous 1836 denunciation of theatre in Russia during the early nineteenth century and beyond. After deploring the stage's corruption by 'the monster . . . melodrama', Gogol went on to ask 'where is our life, ourselves with our own idiosyncrasies and traits?' (These are almost the same words with which Shaw would praise Ibsen a half century later: 'He gave us ourselves in our own situations.') 'The melodrama is lying most impudently,' Gogol went on. 'Only a great, rare, deep genius can catch what surrounds us daily, what always accompanies us, what is ordinary – while mediocrity grabs with both hands all that is out of rule, what happens only seldom and catches the eye by its ugliness and disharmony . . . The strange has become the subject-matter of our drama. The whole point is to tell a new, strange, unheard-of incident: murder, fire, wild passions . . . poisons. Effects, eternal effects!'

Chekhov would prove to be Gogol's rare, deep genius, although it took a while.

In the summer of 1923 the manuscript of an untitled, previously unknown Chekhov play was found in an old desk in Moscow. It was soon published as *A Play Without a Title in Four Acts*, but wasn't produced until 1954, when a truncated version in Swedish appeared in Stockholm under the title *Poor Don Juan*. Chekhov probably wrote it in 1881 or 1882, which would make it his first full-length play (although rumours persist of earlier high-school epics). Chekhov had shown the manuscript to the prestigious Maly Theatre, which rightly rejected it, for it was an amateurish, if ambitious, piece of work, which was so long that, as far as I know, no complete production has ever been done. Badly or incompletely rendered into English in a number of versions, the play did receive one full workmanlike translation by David Magarshack, who called it *Platonov*, after its central character, a good-looking, womanizing, self-important, quarrelsome yet charming former landowner. Still, nobody has rushed to stage this prehistoric monster.

'A writer must be humane to his fingertips.' — CHEKHOV

Chekhov left behind him many stories, most of them extremely short; a dozen or so one-act plays, or vaudevilles; one non-fiction book – an account of his 1890 journey to the half-Russian, half-Japanese island of Sakhalin off Siberia; the Russian sector was mostly a penal colony, and Chekhov's account of his visit helped bring about some reforms of the atrocious conditions. He also left behind seven full-length plays, five of which, in new translations by Peter Carson, make up the present volume.

Chekhov had begun to write sketches while still a student in Taganrog, a Black Sea port, where his father ran a small grocery store; when his hard-pressed large family – Anton had three brothers and a sister – moved to Moscow in 1876 he stayed behind to go through high school, then joined them after his graduation in 1879. At sixteen he quickly became the chief – sometimes only – economic support of his beloved but improvident family (whose numbers were regularly swelled by relatives paying 'visits' that could last for months) by contributing sketches or stories to the popular journals of the day. At the same time he was earning a medical degree at Moscow University.

The little house on Sadovaya-Kudrinskaya Street in which he first practised medicine is now a museum where among other affecting objects one can see copies of some of the *Punch*-like magazines he first wrote for, often under a pseudonym – Antosha Chekhonte, for instance – his long, narrow bed with its plump comforters, a cane, a pair of pince-nez, and some early medical paraphernalia, including his worn black leather doctor's bag. By all accounts he was a most generous physician, available at all hours to those in need, sometimes treating poor patients without charge and never dunning those who were late in paying him, throwing himself tirelessly, too, into the cause of public health and hygiene.

As good a man as we know him to have been, Chekhov wasn't a saint, the way some of his contemporaries regarded him. After his death a well-meaning friend described him as having looked 'Christ-like', an epithet Chekhov could well have done without. But the chief figure in his near-canonization was most likely Maxim Gorky, who in his *Reminiscences of Tolstoy, Chekhov and Andreyev* wrote this encomium: 'I think that in Anton Chekhov's presence everyone involuntarily felt in himself or herself a desire to be simpler, more truthful, more one's self.'

Gorky, a notorious flatterer (of Josef Stalin among others), compounded the myth-making by extending his sycophancy to Chekhov's writing (some of which he didn't quite get), thereby establishing a view of the stories and plays that has been extremely influential – and almost wholly wrong. Treating Chekhov's work as though it were chiefly a sociological critique, Gorky wrote: 'in front of that dreary grey crowd of helpless people there passed a great, wise and observant man; he looked at all those dreary inhabitants of his country and, with a sad smile, with a tone of gentle but deep reproach, in a beautiful and sincere voice, he said to them: "You live badly, my friends. It is shameful to live like that."' This burst of sombre invention is surely one of the origins of the widely held idea that Chekhov combined the roles of priest and judge, and that his main characters, especially in his great last plays, are, in his eyes and so necessarily in ours, weak, ineffectual, defeated and culpable.

The relation between the main activities of Chekhov's life, doctoring and writing, was sometimes stressful, but he mostly handled it with characteristic humour: 'Medicine is my lawful wife,' he once wrote, 'and literature is my mistress. When I get tired of one I go to the other.' A variant of this concerning his writing is rather more effervescent: 'narrative [fiction] is my legal wife and drama a flamboyant, rowdy, impudent, exhausting mistress.'

Yet in a letter of that period he spoke of the theatre in far less lively terms. 'The atmosphere of the theatre in Russia,' he wrote to a friend shortly before he himself began to help resuscitate it, 'is leaden and oppressive. It is covered inches thick in dust and enveloped in fog and tedium.'

No better source exists for an understanding of Chekhov's thought and character than his large correspondence. Two letters written within a three-month period in the autumn of 1888 and winter of '89, a time when his renown was growing, call particular attention to themselves. The first, to the poet-critic Aleksey Pleshcheyev, is so revelatory of Chekhov's governing values and attitudes that it deserves extensive quotation: 'The people I fear,' Chekhov wrote, 'are the ones who look for tendentiousness between the lines [alongside widespread admiration and esteem, throughout his career Chekhov underwent savage attacks on the political and ideological 'neutrality' of his writing, especially his plays, and on their artistic 'inconclusiveness'] and are determined to see me as either liberal or conservative. I am neither liberal nor conservative, nor gradualist, nor monk . . . I would like to be a free artist and I regret God has not given me the strength to be one. I hate lies and violence in all their forms. Pharisaism, dull-wittedness and tyranny reign not only in merchants' homes and police stations . . . [but] in science, in literature, among the younger generation. That is why I cultivate no predilection for policemen . . . scientists, writers, or the younger generation. I look upon tags and labels as prejudices. My holy of holies is the human body, health, intelligence, talent, inspiration, love, and the most absolute freedom from violence and lies.'

The second letter was to Aleksey Suvorin, his publisher and friend. After writing about the newly finished *Ivanov* Chekhov told Suvorin that he had recently gained 'a sense of personal freedom'; then, out of nowhere, came a tiny, scarcely disguised autobiography. 'Write a story . . . ,' he told Suvorin, 'about a young man, the son of a serf, a former grocery clerk, a choirsinger, a high school pupil and university student, brought up to respect rank, to kiss the hands of priests, to truckle to the ideas of others – a young man who expressed thanks for every piece of bread, who was whipped many times, who went without galoshes to do his tutoring, who used his fists, tortured animals [probably the one untrue statement of the lot], was fond of dining with rich relatives [Anton had one wealthy, generous relative, his father's brother Mitrofan], was a hypocrite in his dealings with God and men, needlessly, solely out of a realization of his own insignificance – write how this young man squeezes the slave out of himself, drop by drop, and how, on awaking one fine morning, he finds that the blood coursing through his veins is no longer that of a slave, but that of a real human being.' (Chekhov was actually the grandson of a slave, or serf, his paternal grandfather having bought the family's freedom in 1840, a generation before the serfs' formal emancipation.)

*

'The plot is unprecedented,' Chekhov wrote to his brother Aleksandr in October 1887, soon after finishing an early draft of *Ivanov*. The assertion was doubly uncharacteristic of Chekhov: first, it was contrary to his innate modesty; and second, it went against his lifelong aversion to aesthetic discussions. The letter went on again in an uncharacteristic way.

'I wanted to be original,' he told his brother. 'I did not portray a single villain or a single angel . . . did not blame nor exculpate anyone.' The subversive effects of this remark would continue to our own day.

Ordinarily Chekhov considered the quest for originality foolish and fruitless; originality was there or it wasn't, but you couldn't pursue it. Yet in *Ivanov*'s case he felt on sure ground. The 'plot' was indeed original. As he'd told Aleksandr, the play had no villains or angels and this marked a drastic break with almost the entire history of drama, and fiction too, for that matter.

From the beginnings of literature, through classic drama, epic poetry, romance and, later, the novel, the literary imagination had been largely propelled by the pitting of good against evil, darkness against light, a Manichaean division from which rose our categories of heroes and villains; both pulp fiction and its various derivatives, and popular plays, which we might call pulp drama (successful lowbrow melodramas), as well as nearly all recent mainstream movies and TV dramas, are built around this tension and struggle between 'good guys' (or gals) and bad, between the forces of light and darkness. Today when a work of drama or fiction or film tries to evade this cops-and-robbers structure it has usually, at best, been damned with the faint praise of 'offbeat'.

The Moscow première of *Ivanov*, badly acted and under-rehearsed, was greeted largely with bafflement, rage, or scorn, with a smattering of praise for the play itself by a few astute critics and a handful of discerning audience members. The loudest complaints, ironically, were precisely that the ostensible hero and villain weren't drawn sharply or accurately enough. How could one find heroic stature in a neurotic, weak figure like Ivanov? And Lvov? Why hadn't Chekhov portrayed him more sympathetically? Even Chekhov's brother

Mikhail asked him to rewrite the two characters to bring them closer to the conventions of drama.

Chekhov naturally refused, as he did Suvorin's plea to depict the character he rightly saw as the implicit villain of the piece, Lvov, even more broadly than Chekhov had drawn him. The public and the literati simply couldn't cope with the absence of the poles of good and evil through which they had always manoeuvred their frail understanding.

Besides its moral-thematic originality, *Ivanov* presented some technical innovations, a few of which had tentatively shown themselves in *Platonov*: dialogue that sometimes wasn't logical or consecutive, characters at times leaving speeches addressed to them unanswered or making irrelevant responses (German has a word for such dialogue, *Aneinandervorbeisprechen*, which can best be translated as 'talking past one another' and which seems to have first appeared on the stage in the 1830s with Georg Büchner's *Danton's Death* and *Woyzeck*); actions that seemed to come from nowhere, and lead nowhere, such as two unnamed characters at the Lebedevs' party crossing the stage in search of refreshments and another character, named Kosykh, mumbling to the empty air about a whist game. There was also some use of pauses, a Chekhov trademark that was really a kind of 'silent speech', a stretch of time during which any number of different mental actions could take place: the preceding speech or action might be tacitly refuted or the coming one undermined; or the characters and audience might simply be given time for reflection, intellectual organization of what has been said and done up to now and what might come. The famous pauses in Beckett or Harold Pinter owe much to Chekhov's example.

Ivanov frustrated its first audiences by its lack of familiar moral structure and resolution. What were they supposed to make of Nikolay's suicide? What, for that matter, were they supposed to think of Nikolay himself, that unprecedented protagonist? And Lvov? Didn't he incarnate goodness, set against Nikolay's evil? Then why do Shabelsky and Anna mock him?

For Chekhov, *Ivanov* seems to have begun as something of a polemic against several contemporary stereotypes, the so-called superfluous man, usually well-educated and well-intentioned, who, suffering from what we might now call an existential crisis, or burn-out, felt left out of society; and the Hamlet figure, a person marked by indecision and mysterious inner struggles. At century's end Russian literature and table-talk were filled with superfluous men and Hamlet types, the two sometimes being combined as they are in Nikolay. They were joined in *Ivanov* by another stereotype, a *narodnik*, a kind of self-righteous, soi-disant saint devoted to abstract words and causes, like the 'people', 'progress' and 'the peasantry'. Lvov is roughly such a figure, as Ivanov is a representative 'superfluous man'.

The first step in grasping Nikolay is to accept that he doesn't know what's wrong with him; he simply doesn't know. The abominable way he treats his wife, for example, is as mysterious to him as it is to everyone else. For before the onset of his malady, he was, and at bottom remains, a good, if bewildered man, as the following desperate, loving speech by Anna attests. In the evenings Nikolay wants to go to the Lebedevs' for amusement and distraction, and Anna heartbreakingly pleads with him: 'Do you know what, Kolya? Try and sing, laugh, get angry, as you once did . . . You stay in, we'll laugh and drink fruit liqueur and we'll drive away your depression in a flash. I'll sing if you like. Or else let's go and sit in the dark in your study as we used to, and you'll tell me about your depression . . . You have such suffering eyes. I'll look into them and cry, and we'll both feel better . . . [*Laughs and cries.*] How does it go, Kolya? The flowers come up again every spring, but joy there is none. Is that it? So go off, go . . .'

For Lvov, the *narodnik*, everything is simple: Nikolay pins him down in his self-righteous cocksureness in an important late scene that widens the play's scope from its local settings and parochial typologies towards more universal ones. Nikolay tells Lvov: 'You think I'm the easiest thing in the world to understand. Right? . . . Man is such a simple and uncomplicated machine,' and goes on: 'we all have too many wheels, screws and valves for us to be able to judge each other . . .' *Ivanov* can now be seen as a play about our destructive need for tags and labels: Mrs Lebedev and Borkin see Nikolay with their mercenary gazes, Sasha with her romantic one;

Lvov with his pious superiority. If it is intelligently performed, *Ivanov* isn't a narrow study of neurosis or perversity but much more a dramatic picture of the harm people do with their types and stereotypes.

In Chekhov's dramaturgy, however, fragments of melodramatic procedure remained, the most blatant being Nikolay's suicide (in an early version Chekhov had him drop dead of a heart attack after Lvov's public tirade!). Almost as egregiously melodramatic is Anna's discovery of Nikolay and Sasha in one another's arms. But even with these disfigurements *Ivanov* still stands as Chekhov's first full, convincing work of dramatic art.

He kept tinkering with it; performances, in St Petersburg now, improved; and, moved by an intelligent review or a discerning friend's recommendation, audiences grew larger and friendlier, until Chekhov had something of a hit on his hands, though he continued to think the play was popular for the wrong reasons, audiences having seized on its melodramatic incidents rather than its intelligent vision; to an extent he was right.

Ivanov had set Chekhov on a course which he would stick to, after one setback, in the major plays that followed. This is a good place to mention Chekhov's main subjects, and examine how he dramatized – which is to say, gave stage life to – these themes, or what I once called, in another context, 'notional presences', ideas adhering to bodies, spirit to corporeality.

Beyond question Chekhov's central themes in these plays are love and work (*Lieben und Arbeit* – Freud's terse reply when asked what was necessary for a complete life). Closely connected to them are time, with a special emphasis on the future, and art, more particularly what being an artist spiritually demands.

Many ways exist for getting Chekhov wrong, so herewith a short guide to avoiding them. Don't look for 'realism' in these plays; don't expect conventional endings, happy or otherwise; be aware of how Chekhov often has one character subvert another's point of view, when it threatens to harden into ideology or melt into sentimentality;

keep alert to the hints and nuances in speeches, along with the literal words; don't look for answers, to your problems or life's dilemmas; throw away any idea you might have that drama is always about 'conflict', or, rather, remember that in these plays conflict is more often internal – within characters – than between them; keep in mind that no single character in any play speaks wholly for Chekhov, the most unbiased and democratic of authors; don't ever regard, admiringly or not, a Chekhov play as an exercise in 'mood' or 'atmosphere' – they're solid works of imagination, not emotional vapours. Here is Virginia Woolf writing in 1920: 'It is, as a rule, when a critic does not wish to commit himself, or to trouble himself, that he speaks of atmosphere.' Don't forget that Chekhov is often very funny, so feel free to laugh, aloud if the impulse strikes you.

The artistic setback I spoke of before was an attempt to write a classical comedy, the kind that ends with lovers united, marriages restored, and a sense of satisfaction, celebration, reigning over everything. Long, complicated, and crowded with incident, *The Wood Demon* was close to being a disaster. Still, Chekhov saw enough in the piece to carry a great many things over – some characters, settings and scenes, even a few swatches of dialogue – to the making of *Uncle Vanya* a few years later, though he obstinately insisted that the two plays were wholly independent, which in spirit they certainly are.

LOVE

Chekhov's notebook contains this rather enigmatic remark about love (as sexual desire or romantic attraction): 'Either it is a remnant of something "degenerating", something which was once immense, or it is a particle of what will in the future develop into something immense, but at present it is unsatisfying, it gives much less than one expects.' In each play that followed *Ivanov* Chekhov made love and sex central concerns, important *notional presences*. Love – erotic or romantic or spiritual – carries a great weight of significance in *The Seagull*, *Uncle Vanya* and *Three Sisters*, before tapering off in *The Cherry Orchard*.

The notebook entry, especially the part about love, or sex, being rather unsatisfying, has been exploited by those commentators who, for various reasons – ignorance, literary envy, feminist theory – want to find Chekhov himself deficient in erotic vigour or enthusiasm. Some argue, absurdly, that because so many of his stories and plays deal with unsuccessful love affairs or marriages, he personally thought dimly of such relationships, seeing them as inherently unsatisfying. One biographer asked the nonsensical rhetorical question: 'What was a woman to him, no matter how desirable, when his life was all pen and paper?' In all the commentary on Chekhov that sentence is, I think, surpassed in foolishness only by some remarks of a scholar who wrote, without any evidence, that Chekhov had a 'gloomy view of heterosexual relationships' and offered the following presumably helpful distinction: 'A full appreciation of Chekhov's work requires . . . a certain degree of involvement, a response intellectual, or, as in the case of his love-stories, emotional.'

Against such an array of unseeing commentators I have space for only one rebuttal. In the best, most illuminating essay on Chekhov's fiction, 'Reality in Chekhov's Stories', Eudora Welty said, simply and sanely, that 'Chekhov wrote of sex with honesty and lack of fuss as he wrote of all human experience . . . Much ahead of its time, and perhaps of ours, in "The Duel" he treated with candour and seriousness a young woman of compelling sexuality. "The Lady with the Little Dog" is a compassionate study of a cynical middle-aged man surprised when, almost against his will and against his belief, his sexual worldliness turns into the honesty and difficulty of belated love.'

In October 1895, Chekhov wrote to Suvorin that he was working on a new long play, his first for several years. Among other things, he continued, the play had the usual 'four acts, a landscape . . . much conversation about literature, little action, and five tons of love.' Chekhov actually wrote *puds*, a *pud* being a unit of about thirty-six pounds. At the end of Act One a major character will exclaim, 'You're all so highly strung . . . And such a lot of love . . .'

The Seagull does indeed contain two or three *puds* of love, if not five – how does one measure such things? – and much talk not only about literature but also about plays and playwrights, art and artists. Love and art, art and love – Chekhov weaves back and forth between these categories of experience and aspiration.

The most ardent lovers in this play of romantic cross-hatchings are the most infected by the practice, or dream, of art – the actresses Nina and Arkadina, the writers Trigorin and Treplyov – and the play they're in is in a sense a drama of selves seeking, or failing, to reconcile the various modes of living.

Chekhov once wrote that 'Nina's part is everything in the play.' The first of Chekhov's heroes of what I call existential sobriety, a person who neither begs for the impossible nor abjectly surrenders to what seems inevitable, but courageously lives through whatever life demands of her, at the same time as it grants her – if she'll seize them – the virtues she needs to survive, to go on: clear understanding, courage, humility, stamina. Sonya in *Uncle Vanya*, all three Prozorov sisters, and Anya, Varya and Mme Ranevskaya in *The Cherry Orchard* will follow in Nina's footsteps.

Against her balanced and hard-earned self-knowledge, her integrity, Chekhov puts Treplyov's immaturity, romanticism and moral weakness. The climactic scene, Nina's unavailing visit to Treplyov, takes its place among the great moments of Chekhovian theatre, and is a workshop in his techniques. I have space for one central example: after Nina says, 'You're a writer, I'm an actress,' she adds, 'I loved you, I dreamed of being famous, but now?' She breaks off and tells him some details of her physical life since she left him, which we know has been bitterly painful. Treplyov's fateful response is to ignore her words and burst out with 'life has been unbearable for me' and 'I call you, I kiss the ground on which you've walked . . .' To this Nina ('bewildered') asks, 'Why is he talking like this?' and repeats the words, which, we quickly see by her use of the impersonal 'he', are not a question but a complex recognition: that Treplyov doesn't so much love as desperately need her, that his emotional immaturity extends to his would-be artist's self; his writing is lifeless because in some deep dimension he himself lacks animation, life.

Before leaving, Nina tells Treplyov what she has learned about being an artist: 'I know now, I understand . . . the most important thing isn't fame or glory or anything I used to dream about – but the ability to endure. To know how to bear your cross and have faith . . . when I think about my vocation I'm not afraid of life.'

Treplyov, who lacks a true vocation, *is* afraid, and his shooting himself is an extreme demonstration of his inability to persevere. A measure of Chekhov's artistic growth is the difference between the suicides with which both *Ivanov* and *The Seagull* end. Nikolay's shooting himself is inorganic and arbitrary, issuing from the stock of melodramatic actions and situations with which Chekhov was familiar. Treplyov's suicide comes from the heart of the play's vision, which itself is seized from actuality in order to be dramatized.

Perhaps the shrewdest comment on the play and its ending was made by someone outside the theatre and academic life. After praising the work, the well-known jurist Anatoly Koni wrote to Chekhov: 'How good the ending is. It is not she, the seagull [who] commits suicide (which a run-of-the-mill playwright, out for his audience's tears, would be sure to have done) but the young man who lives in an abstract future and has no idea of . . . what goes on around him.'

In the '*puds* of love' letter to Suvorin Chekhov wrote: 'I can't say I'm not enjoying writing [the play], though [it would have been more accurate if he'd said 'because'] I'm flagrantly disregarding the basic tenets of the stage . . .'

In his important book *Chekhov the Dramatist* David Magarshack argues that the turning-point in Chekhov's dramaturgy came with *The Seagull*, when he moved from writing plays of 'direct' action – one of the stage's basic tenets – to ones of 'indirect'. Magarshack's theory is too complex and detailed to deal with thoroughly here, but his main point is central to our grasp of Chekhov. Action, especially physical action to the point of violence, had always been at the centre of dramatic practice; language, dialogue primarily, must defer to a play's physical events, or what makes up most of what we call 'plot'. Magarshack implied that plot, bound to or embedded in physical action, was a source of melodrama, which may be defined as drama without 'consciousness'. In turn consciousness can be described as both the recording instrument of our sentient life and the substance of what has been recorded.

The Chekhov scholar Ronald Hingley once made a most astute observation about Chekhov's fiction, which I think it permissible to apply to the plays too: 'The more complex the plot of a Chekhov story, the less artistically successful it's likely to be.'

Why this should be so is a complicated matter. Plot – the twists and turns of the drama's tale, its suspensefulness and surprises, its outcome, its very body or physicality – tends to crowd out consciousness, leaving less room for awareness, insight, perception, contemplation – the basic instruments of our experience of art. Had Chekhov not moved offstage the key elements of Nina's story – her disastrous affair with Trigorin, his abuse of her and desertion, the child she bears who dies young, and her life's effect on her art – Chekhov's play, bursting with intellectual vitality, full of fascinating moral and spiritual dilemmas, would almost certainly have turned into a cautionary tale (talented young girls oughtn't to trust lecherous older writers), or else a spicy love story with twists, but in any case, a melodrama.

WORK

Many, if not most, of the major characters in Chekhov's plays look for salvation, rescue, through love, and learn, to their sorrow, that love isn't the answer; neither is work, to which they most often turn next. The supreme portrayer of what life is really like, the incorruptible artist of the way things are – Beckett's non-contingent *Comment c'est* – Chekhov never allows wishfulness to block out actuality and cannot be tempted away (by audiences' or readers' or critics' shallow or naive yearnings) from what he sees as a writer. Love, sex and marriage are most often grave, painful and difficult in life, and so, too, they are in his writings.

Chekhov, the realist, knows, too, that work is more often dull or painful than fulfilling; something to notice is that women work hardest in the plays (Sonya in *Uncle Vanya*, Olga in *Three Sisters*,

Varya in *The Cherry Orchard*) and men talk about it most often, most abstractly and most romantically: Vershinin and Tuzenbakh, and belatedly Andrey Prozorov, in *Three Sisters*, and Trofimov in *The Cherry Orchard*.

> 'White, wan, slender, and very beautiful in the moonlight, she was expecting tenderness; her constant dreams of happiness and love had exhausted her.'   — CHEKHOV, 'A Visit'.

Irina, the youngest Prozorov sister, is doubly afflicted: she dreams constantly of love, and of work too — until her romantic desire runs up against the hardness of fact, and, after having had at least two jobs, she bitterly deplores their lack of 'poetry'. Meanwhile Olga works hard at her school, and is worn out by her diligence.

The cry 'Work! for we must work!' is heard throughout the last plays. In almost every case the character is speaking out of desperation, not conviction; to claim that the orchard is being lost because the family's ancestors scorned work is both silly and false.

In a masterstroke of Chekhov's artistry in *Three Sisters*, he has Irina accept Tuzenbakh, whom she doesn't love but admires; she then suffers his loss when he is killed in a duel. Chekhov's genius lies in his avoiding the temptations the situation throws out, and which a lesser playwright would have snatched. Such a dramatist would doubtless have portrayed Irina and Tuzenbakh as passionately in love, so that Irina's loss would appear more wrenching. That Chekhov conceived Irina as having matured enough to accept a loveless marriage, after giving up her idle dreams of a lover-to-come in Moscow, the site of potential happiness for Olga and Masha, also makes Tuzenbakh's death all the more poignant.

One of the most heartrending moments in drama is Tuzenbakh and Irina's farewell. In less gifted hands it surely would have been sentimental, even maudlin; in Chekhov it's stringent with the truest feeling. The baron is going off to the duel, which we and all the characters sense will be fatal. As he makes ready to go, they stand irresolute, struggling for words. Finally, he speaks lyrically about the vagaries of life, and notices a dead tree that still sways with the others. So, too, he would still be 'taking part in life', even after his death. She suddenly says, 'I'll come with you', alarming Tuzenbakh into flight.

Then in one of the most piteous speeches in all drama, he turns round and says, 'I didn't have any coffee this morning. Will you ask them to make me some . . .'

The simplicity and matter-of-factness of this utterance, in the face of all the horror we know will come, is exactly what gives the words their extraordinary power to move us. Chekhov takes one more step to ensure that nothing banal or bathetic will occur: he moves the duel so far offstage that the fatal shot can barely be heard.

The play's other affecting – and necessarily ill-fated – love story is Masha and Vershinin's. Chekhov lets their romance develop slowly and rather quietly, with only a few amorous declarations on each side. Their leave-taking is even quieter, with Vershinin simply slipping away after Olga assures him she'll look after Masha and, a lovely note, Vershinin's family too.

Uncle Vanya, the play that followed *The Seagull*, has received the widest range of critical interpretations of all Chekhov's plays. But among the multiplicity of readings, many containing bits of truth, but none entirely satisfying, we can be certain of one thing: the play is NOT a drama about weak, helpless people, 'losers' in our current jargon. David Magarshack's assertion in his pioneering study that *Uncle Vanya*'s principal theme 'is not frustration, but courage and hope' may have overstated the case, but was closer to the truth than all those views of the play as a study of failure, wasted or ruined lives, a picture of disappointment and despair.

Vanya Voynitsky and Dr Astrov are usually considered the heroes of this play, Prof. Serebryakov the villain. Stanislavsky went so far as to proclaim that 'talented people like Vanya . . . and Astrov rot away in dark corners' while Serebryakov 'is shown up as a fraud.'

No such exposure occurs. Vanya labels him a fake but, unpleasant and self-centred as he is, Serebryakov is not shown to be fraudulent.

Similarly, while Astrov may have some talent (he does have considerable charm), Vanya, for all his protestations of having been cheated out of his potential greatness by Serebryakov – 'I might have been a Schopenhauer, a Dostoyevsky' (he names, significantly, a pair of most gloomy giants!), seems entirely talentless, an injustice-collector who seizes on Serebryakov as an excuse for his own emptiness.

The play's neglected heroes are its women, Yelena and Sonya. Yelena, with whom both Vanya and Astrov are smitten, is thoroughly misunderstood both by her would-be lovers and by critics like Eric Bentley, ordinarily so sagacious, but as wrong as possible when he calls her 'artificial, sterile, useless'.

Yelena does complain about being bored and having nothing to do, but this is, I believe, as so often in Chekhov's plays, a defence against revealing deeper or more dangerous feelings and conditions: how uncomfortable she feels in this house, how unhappy she is in her marriage, how insulted by Vanya's and Astrov's amorous importunities.

After the play appeared, an amateur actress named Marianna Pobedimskaya wrote to Chekhov asking if Yelena was 'an intelligent woman . . . thinking and decent . . . or is she an apathetic, idle . . . incapable of thinking or loving? I cannot reconcile myself to [this latter view] . . . I see her as a reasoning, thinking person . . . made unhappy . . . by dissatisfaction with her present life.' Chekhov replied, 'Your opinion of Yelena . . . is completely justified.' Actually, Yelena, the victim of male chauvinism, has a sharp wit, a fine sensitivity and a generous spirit. One of Chekhov's central perceptions is that her decision to stay true to her vows by remaining with her tiresome husband wouldn't be approved of or understood by her fellow characters or the world at large.

As is so often true in these plays, the unmistakable focus of *Uncle Vanya*'s moral and spiritual life is a woman, Sonya. Before looking at her position I need to say something about what I believe to be *Uncle Vanya*'s origin.

In a story of 1887, 'The Enemies', Chekhov wrote of the 'subtle, elusive beauty of human grief, a beauty which would not be understood . . . for a long time . . . Kirilov and his wife [whose small son has just died] were silent; they were not crying. It was as if they were conscious of the lyricism, as well as the burden, of their loss.'

The heaviness and simultaneous beauty of loss or sorrow suffuse Chekhov's last three plays, most pointedly in *Uncle Vanya*, where it presents itself with artistic splendour in Sonya, another figure of existential or ontological sobriety. It should be noticed that from the moment she learns that Astrov doesn't love her she never speaks of love again, never gives the slightest sign of her inward suffering. This isn't simple stoicism, but a mark of her self-control and generosity of spirit: she'll trouble no one with her sorrow.

The play's final moments rank among Chekhov's most memorable. In one production I saw, Sonya cradles Vanya's head in a Pietà-like tableau as she delivers her great last speech. Her words are rightly felt as a prayerful utterance, but I think it a mistake to interpret them as formally religious. Instead, they constitute a kind of spiritual music, the lyricism of grief; what makes up grief's burden is painfully obvious. Magarshack's optimistic reading is, I think, based squarely on Sonya's compassion, her honesty, and her generous heart; she suffers more than any other character, but accepts her joyless future and sustains her poor sad Uncle Vanya as she goes.

TIME

The inherent problem Chekhov faced in *Three Sisters* was, I think, how to write a drama about time, not simply taking place in time – all plays do that – but about how we exist in and with it as though it were a place and a being. Beckett's 'double-headed monster of damnation and salvation', the cradle and ground of all we do, home of our myths, imaginings and actualities. Time as place, place as time, Proustian, Einsteinian, a pact among the tenses, the scene of an appointment for which we're always too early or too late.

Odd as it may sound, *Three Sisters* may be described as a 'replica of time': how it feels to live in it, play with it, spend it, waste it, 'kill' it, trisect it into past, present and future. It is, paradoxically enough, a plotless play with many subplots: the only 'story' we can pluck from it is a negative one – the sisters' failure to get to Moscow. In that regard the writer William Gerhardi wrote in the 1920s a piece of fatally obtuse criticism, a tiny primer for misunderstanding *Three Sisters* and Chekhov: 'Good God! How can there be such people? Why can't people know what they want and get it?' Which is rather like asking, about Hamlet, 'What's wrong with that fellow? Why can't he make up his mind?' or saying about Lear, 'What that chap needs is a sharp estate planner.' Gerhardi's breathtaking insensitivity, his plain dumbness, would, I think, have driven Chekhov, that model of patience, to despair.

Well, why don't the sisters get to Moscow? The simple answer is that they don't get to Moscow because the play they're in is about not getting there. Just as Godot doesn't arrive in Beckett's drama, so Moscow isn't attained in Chekhov's. *Waiting for Godot*'s original French title was *En attendant Godot*, or *While Waiting for Godot*; Beckett himself unfortunately, and unaccountably, left out the *En* in his English translation, thereby considerably reducing the play's complexity from its densely ontological original form – characters like Didi and Gogo, our surrogates, it can be said, are the ones for whom Godot doesn't come – and we are shown how they fill up the time while waiting, ad-libbing for their very lives. In much the same way the Prozorov sisters, who also represent us, are the ones who don't get to Moscow, and we are shown how they live until their illusory dreams of salvation in Moscow are ended, which is the end of the play. If there is a villain in *Three Sisters* it is surely Natasha, who steadily ousts the family from their home. She'll be living there with her cowed husband (and maybe that lovely, unseen fellow Protopopov) when the sisters leave. Incidentally, a very inept critic of the period was named Protopopov.

Very probably *The Cherry Orchard* is Chekhov's best-loved play; it is certainly his most frequently performed. Although far less complex than *Three Sisters*, it's still deep and complicated enough, with some characters who don't easily yield up their truths – Charlotta, Pishchik, Trofimov, and, most important of all, Lopakhin.

Just as Serebryakov and Yelena are the characters in *Uncle Vanya* a misunderstanding of whom is sure to throw the play out of kilter, so Lopakhin is the pivotal figure of *The Cherry Orchard*. To present him unsympathetically, as the capitalistic agent of the family's downfall, is to turn the play into what Chekhov called a 'weepy' drama he could barely recognize as his.

Chekhov usually offered very little detail about his characters (in his Letters he writes, 'Astrov whistles', 'Trigorin wears checked pants') but was lavish with endearing comments about Lopakhin: 'wears a white vest and yellow shoes . . . takes big steps . . . thinks while he walks', and, most essentially, as Chekhov warned Stanislavky, 'he is a decent person in every sense; his behaviour must be entirely proper . . . and free of pettiness and clowning.' In the play he is shown to be generous and kindly; both Lyubov and Pishchik speak highly of him, and, a hugely important point, Varya is still more than willing to marry him after we all learn that he's bought the estate; and indeed, after his seemingly callous and gloating big speech, in which, I think, he speaks out of forgivable momentary elation and pride that he has climbed so far, it's he who tries to comfort Lyubov. Why he doesn't propose to Varya makes up a little comedy of errors, emerging from Chekhov's sense of the way chance affects our lives, the capriciousness of existence: the wrong galoshes, the untimely call to Lopakhin from outside, an inopportune remark about the weather, an errant stick with which Varya whacks Lopakhin on the head; blunders, pauses extended too long, the right moment blurred and then lost, Lopakhin's devotion to Ranevskaya operating as a psychological barrier to intimacy with Varya.

The crux of the play, what makes it a Chekhov comedy, is, as I suggested earlier, Anya's realization that the orchard's beauty is no longer enough to justify their suffocating love for it. Once it was useful, providing the cherries and delicious jam, the recipe for which has been 'forgotten', Firs tells us. It's a fateful word, testifying to the erosions of time, which in one way or another is always at least a partial subject of Chekhov's plays. Trofimov may be a windy ideologue, but he can see that hanging onto the orchard is blocking Lyubov's and Anya's way to a new life. The estate has become more memory and metaphor than actuality, a real place. Chekhov wrote to his wife Olga: 'The central female role is an old woman who lives entirely in the past and has nothing in the present.' This isn't quite right. She has Anya, who has recognized the need to let the orchard go, and her Paris lover, about whom, incidentally, Chekhov is never condemnatory, as he isn't about Masha, Vershinin, Yelena, all adulterers in a technical sense. The play is indeed in part about the decline of one era and the onset of another, but in Chekhov's hands there is no sociological or political inevitability to the process, only the existential pressures of time and fate.

Tolstoy, who became more and more obnoxious as he aged, admired Chekhov's fiction, but detested his plays, largely for their 'immorality', but also for their refusal to be useful. After Chekhov's death he told an interviewer: 'In a dramatic work the author ought to deal with some problem that has yet to be solved and every character ought to solve it according to the idiosyncrasies of his own character. It is like a laboratory experiment. But you won't find anything of the kind in Chekhov.'

No, we won't, and we can be grateful for it.

Richard Gilman

FURTHER READING

Andrew, Joe, *Russian Writers and Society in the Second Half of the Nineteenth Century* (London: Macmillan, 1982)

Bely, Andrey, '*The Cherry Orchard*' in Senelick, below

Benedetti, Jean, ed., *Dear Actress, Dear Writer: The Love Letters of Anton Chekhov and Olga Knipper* (London: Methuen, 1996)

Bentley, Eric, 'Craftsmanship in *Uncle Vanya*' in *In Search of Theater* (New York: Vintage, 1953)

Emeljanow, Victor, ed., *Chekhov: The Critical Heritage* (London: Routledge & Kegan Paul, 1981)

Fergusson, Francis, 'On *The Cherry Orchard*' in *The Idea of a Theater* (Princeton: Princeton University Press, 1949)

Frayn, Michael, *Chekhov: Plays*, Introduction and 'A Note on the Translation' (London: Methuen, 1988)

Friedland, Louis S., ed., *Letters on the Short Story, the Drama, and Other Literary Topics* (New York: Benjamin Blom, 1964)

Gilman, Richard, *Chekhov's Plays: An Opening into Eternity* (New Haven: Yale University Press, 1995)

Jackson, Robert L., ed., *Chekhov: A Collection of Critical Essays* (Englewood Cliffs: Prentice-Hall, 1967)

Karlinsky, Simon, *Anton Chekhov's Life and Thought: Selected Letters and Commentary*, tr. Michael Henry Heim with Simon Karlinsky (New York: Harper & Row, 1973)

Magarshack, David, *Chekhov the Dramatist* (London: John Lehman, 1952)

Rayfield, Donald, *Chekhov: A Life* (London: HarperCollins, 1997)

Senelick, Lawrence, ed. and tr., *Russian Dramatic Theory from Pushkin to the Symbolists* (Austin: University of Texas Press, 1981)

Welty, Eudora, 'Reality in Chekhov's Stories' in *The Eye of the Story: Selected Essays and Reviews* (New York: Random House, 1977)

Yarmolinsky, Avrahm, ed., *Letters of Anton Chekhov* (New York: Viking, 1968)

CHRONOLOGY

1836 Gogol's *The Government Inspector*

1852 Turgenev's *Sketches from a Hunter's Album*

1860 Dostoyevsky's *Notes From the House of the Dead* (1860–61)
      Anton Pavlovich Chekhov born on 17 January at Taganrog, a
      port on the Sea of Azov, the third son of Pavel Yegorovich
      Chekhov, a grocer, and Yevgeniya Yakovlevna, née Morozova

1861 Emancipation of the serfs by Alexander II. Formation of
      revolutionary Land and Liberty Movement

1862 Turgenev's *Fathers and Sons*

1863–4 Polish revolt. Commencement of intensive industrialization;
      spread of the railways; banks established; factories built.
      Elective District Councils (*zemstvos*) set up; judicial reform
      Tolstoy's *The Cossacks* (1863)

1865 *Lady Macbeth of Mtsensk* (1864) by Leskov, a writer much
      admired by Chekhov

1866 Attempted assassination of Alexander II by Karakozov
      Dostoyevsky's *Crime and Punishment*

1867 Emile Zola's *Thérèse Raquin*

1868 Dostoyevsky's *The Idiot*

1868 Chekhov begins to attend Taganrog Gymnasium after wasted
      year at a Greek school

1869 Tolstoy's *War and Peace*

1870 Municipal government reform

1870–71 Franco-Prussian War

1873 Tolstoy's *Anna Karenina* (1873–7)
      Chekhov sees local productions of *Hamlet* and Gogol's *The
      Government Inspector*

1875 Chekhov writes and produces humorous magazine for his brothers in Moscow, *The Stammerer*, containing sketches of life in Taganrog

1876 Chekhov's father declared bankrupt and flees to Moscow, followed by family except Chekhov, who is left in Taganrog to complete schooling. Reads Buckle, Hugo and Schopenhauer

1877–8 War with Turkey

1877 Chekhov's first visit to Moscow; his family living in great hardship

1878 Chekhov writes dramatic juvenilia: full-length drama *Fatherlessness* (MS destroyed), comedy *Diamond Cut Diamond* and vaudeville *Why Hens Cluck* (none published)

1879 Dostoyevsky's *The Brothers Karamazov* (1879–80)
Tolstoy's *Confession* (1879–82)
Chekhov matriculates from Gymnasium with good grades.
Wins scholarship to Moscow University to study medicine
Makes regular contributions to humorous magazine *Alarm Clock*

1880 General Loris-Melikov organizes struggle against terrorism
Guy de Maupassant's *Boule de Suif*
Chekhov introduced by artist brother Nikolay to landscape painter Levitan with whom has lifelong friendship
First short story, 'A Letter from the Don Landowner Vladimirovich N to His Learned Neighbour', published in humorous magazine *Dragonfly*. More stories published in *Dragonfly* under pseudonyms, chiefly Antosha Chekhonte

1881 Assassination of Alexander II; reactionary, stifling regime of Alexander III begins
Sarah Bernhardt visits Moscow (Chekhov calls her acting 'superficial')
Chekhov continues to write very large numbers of humorous sketches for weekly magazines (until 1883). Becomes regular contributor to Nikolay Leykin's *Fragments*, a St Petersburg weekly humorous magazine. Writes (1881–2) play now usually known as *Platonov* (discovered 1923), rejected by Maly Theatre; tries to destroy manuscript

1882   Student riots at St Petersburg and Kazan universities. More discrimination against Jews
       Chekhov is able to support the family with scholarship money and earnings from contributions to humorous weeklies

1883   Tolstoy's *What I Believe*
       Chekhov gains practical experience at Chikino Rural Hospital

1884   Henrik Ibsen's *The Wild Duck*. J.-K. Huysmans' *À Rebours*
       Chekhov graduates and becomes practising physician at Chikino. First signs of his tuberculosis in December
       Six stories about the theatre published as *Fairy-Tales of Melpomene*. His crime novel, *The Shooting Party*, serialized in *Daily News*

1885–6 Tolstoy's *The Death of Ivan Ilyich* (1886)
       On first visit to St Petersburg, Chekhov begins friendship with very influential Aleksey Suvorin (1834–1912), editor of the highly regarded daily newspaper *New Times*. Chekhov has love affairs with Dunya Efros and Natalya Golden (later his sister-in-law). His TB is now unmistakable
       Publishes more than 100 short stories. 'The Requiem' is the first story to appear under own name and his first in *New Times* (February 1886). First collection, *Motley Tales*

1887   Five students hanged for attempted assassination of Tsar; one is Lenin's brother
       Tolstoy's drama *Power of Darkness* (first performed in Paris), for which he was called nihilist and blasphemer by Alexander III
       Chekhov elected member of Literary Fund. Makes trip to Taganrog and Don steppes
       Second book of collected short stories *In the Twilight*. *Ivanov* produced – a disaster

1888   Chekhov meets Stanislavsky. Attends many performances at Maly and Korsh theatres and becomes widely acquainted with actors, stage managers, etc. Meets Tchaikovsky
       Completes 'The Steppe', which marks his 'entry' into serious literature. Wins Pushkin Prize for 'the best literary production distinguished by high artistic value' for *In the Twilight*, presented

by literary division of Academy of Sciences. His one-act farces *The Bear* (highly praised by Tolstoy) and *The Proposal* extremely successful. Begins work on *The Wood Demon* (later *Uncle Vanya*). Radically revises *Ivanov* for St Petersburg performance

1889 Tolstoy's *The Kreutzer Sonata* (at first highly praised by Chekhov)

Chekhov meets Lidiya Avilova, who later claims love affair with him. Tolstoy begins to take an interest in Chekhov, who is elected to Society of Lovers of Russian Literature

'A Dreary Story'. *The Wood Demon* a resounding failure

1890 World weary, Chekhov travels across Siberia by carriage and river boat to Sakhalin to investigate conditions at the penal colony (recorded in *The Island of Sakhalin*). After seven months returns to Moscow (via Hong Kong, Singapore and Ceylon (Sri Lanka))

Collection *Gloomy People* (dedicated to Tchaikovsky). Only two stories published – 'Gusev' and 'Thieves'. Immense amount of preparatory reading for *The Island of Sakhalin*

1891 Severe famine in Volga basin (Chekhov organizes relief)

Chekhov undertakes six-week tour of Western Europe with Suvorin. Intense affair with Lika Mizinova

Works on *The Island of Sakhalin*. 'The Duel' published serially. Works on 'The Grasshopper'

1892 Chekhov buys small estate at Melikhovo, near Moscow; parents and sister live there with him. Gives free medical aid to peasants. Re-reads Turgenev; regards him as inferior to Tolstoy and very critical of his heroines

'Ward No. 6' and 'An Anonymous Story'

1893 *The Island of Sakhalin* completed and published serially

1894 Death of Alexander III; accession of Nicholas II; 1,000 trampled to death at Khodynka Field during coronation celebrations. Strikes in St Petersburg

Chekhov makes another trip to Western Europe

'The Student', 'Teacher of Literature', 'At a Country House' and 'The Black Monk'

1895   'Three Years'. Writes 'Ariadna', 'Murder' and 'Anna Round
       the Neck'. First draft of *The Seagull*

1896   Chekhov agitates personally for projects in rural education
       and transport; helps in building of village school at Talezh;
       makes large donation of books to Taganrog Public Library
       'My Life' published in instalments. *The Seagull* meets with
       hostile reception at Aleksandrinsky Theatre

1897   Chekhov works for national census; builds second rural school.
       Crisis in health with lung haemorrhage; convalesces in Nice
       'Peasants' is strongly attacked by reactionary critics and muti-
       lated by censors. Publishes *Uncle Vanya*, but refuses to allow
       performance (until 1899)

1898   Formation of Social Democrat Party. Dreyfus affair
       Stanislavsky founds Moscow Art Theatre with Nemirovich-
       Danchenko
       Chekhov very indignant over Dreyfus affair and supports Zola;
       conflict with anti-Semitic Suvorin over this. His father dies.
       Travels to Yalta, where he buys land. Friendly with Gorky and
       Bunin (both of whom left interesting memoirs of Chekhov).
       Attracted to Olga Knipper at Moscow Art Theatre rehearsal
       of *The Seagull*, but leaves almost immediately for Yalta. Corre-
       spondence with Gorky
       Trilogy 'Man in a Case', 'Gooseberries' and 'About Love'.
       'Ionych'. *The Seagull* has first performance at Moscow Art
       Theatre and Chekhov is established as a playwright

1899   Widespread student riots
       Tolstoy's *Resurrection* serialized
       Chekhov has rift with Suvorin over student riots. Olga Knipper
       visits Melikhovo. He sells Melikhovo in June and moves with
       mother and sister to Yalta. Awarded Order of St Stanislav for
       educational work
       'Darling', 'New Country Villa' and 'On Official Duty'. Signs
       highly unfavourable contract with A. F. Marks for complete
       edition of his works. Taxing and time-consuming work of
       compiling first two volumes. Moderate success of *Uncle Vanya*
       at Moscow Art Theatre. Publishes one of finest stories, 'The

Lady with the Little Dog'. Completes 'In the Ravine'. Begins serious work on *Three Sisters*; goes to Nice to revise last two acts

1900 Chekhov settles in the house built by him in Yalta. Actors from the Moscow Art Theatre visit Sevastopol and Yalta at his request. Low opinion of Ibsen

Sees *Uncle Vanya* for first time

1901 Formation of Socialist Revolutionary Party. Tolstoy excommunicated by Russian Orthodox Church

Chekhov marries Olga Knipper

Première of *Three Sisters* at Moscow Art Theatre, with Olga Knipper as Masha. Works on 'The Bishop'

1902 Sipyagin, Minister of Interior, assassinated. Gorky excluded from Academy of Sciences by Nicholas II

Gorky's *The Lower Depths* produced at Moscow Art Theatre

Chekhov resigns from Academy of Sciences together with Korolenko in protest at exclusion of Gorky. Awarded Griboyedov Prize by Society of Dramatic Writers and Opera Composers for *Three Sisters*

Completes 'The Bishop'. Begins 'The Bride', his last story. Begins *The Cherry Orchard*

1903 Completion of Trans-Siberian Railway. Massacre of Jews at Kishinev pogrom

Chekhov elected provisional president of Society of Lovers of Russian Literature

Completes 'The Bride' and the first draft of *The Cherry Orchard*. Arrives in Moscow for Art Theatre rehearsal of *The Cherry Orchard*; strong disagreement with Stanislavsky over its interpretation

1904 Assassination of Plehve, Minister of Interior, by Socialist revolutionaries. War with Japan

Chekhov dies of TB on 15 July at Badenweiler in the Black Forest (Germany)

Première of *The Cherry Orchard* at Moscow Art Theatre

TRANSLATOR'S NOTE

The text used for this translation is that of the edition published under the aegis of the Soviet Academy of Sciences, A. P. Chekhov, *Polnoye sobraniye sochineniy i pisem* (*Complete collected works and letters*), vols 12 and 13 (Moscow 1978).

My translation is as exact as I can make it. But though I probably belong to the more literal rather than the freer school of translators, my aim has been that this version can plausibly be spoken as well as read. It is worth saying that the diaereses marked by three full stops in the text are those in the original Russian text to mark a break or pause, which have been retained.

I have almost always left non-Russian words and phrases in the text and translated them in the notes. The originals of Chekhov's many references to and quotations from literature and songs have mostly been tracked down by scholars (even Chekhov could not always give his sources) but I have given a note only for the better known; the details of a forgotten song are not going to be illuminating.

A note on the vexed question of Russian names: all Russian Orthodox (and non-Orthodox) had and have a single first (Christian) name followed by a patronymic deriving from the father's first name. Thus in *Ivanov* Sasha Lebedeva is formally Aleksandra Pavlovna Lebedeva. But Aleksandra can generate a shoal of recognized, often affectionate diminutives: in this play alone, Sasha, Shura, Shurka, Shurochka, Sashenka. Diminutives can be scornful or patronizing too. Patronymics are often abbreviated, so that Sergeyevich, for example, becomes Sergeich. There are the French versions of names, too. I have tended to leave names in the forms Chekhov used. The various alternatives for each character are listed in the appropriate list of characters.

Then there are the 'tears' in stage directions. In a letter of 23 October 1903 to Vladimir Nemirovich-Danchenko, co-founder of the Moscow Art Theatre, Chekhov expresses his concern about Anya in *The Cherry Orchard* being played in a tearful way, making the point that he often uses the phrase '*skvoz' slyozy*' (literally 'through tears' and so 'in tears') in stage directions to indicate mood rather than actual tears. This must go beyond *The Cherry Orchard*. I have translated the phrase throughout as 'with tears in his/her eyes' – leaving it to the reader to determine the precise intention.

A brief Glossary covers currency and units of measurement common to the plays.

For transliteration I have strictly applied the so-called 'British system' now in widespread general use throughout the English-speaking world.

Last – though first – I thank Richard Gilman for some stimulating discussion, and Antony Wood for the knowledge, sensitivity and vigilance exercised in preparing the text for publication.

Peter Carson

GLOSSARY

Desyatina: A unit of land measurement equivalent to 2.7 acres (1.09 hectares).

Pud: A measure of weight, approximately 36 lb (16.33 kg).

Rouble (*rubl'*): Then as now the central Russian unit of currency, divided into 100 kopecks (*kopeyka*). The rouble was stable throughout the period Chekhov was writing, and was worth £ 0.16 or US$ 0.76.

Verst (*versta*): The standard pre-revolutionary measure of distance, *c*. 0.67 miles (1.07 km).

Zolotnik: A measure of weight, *c*. 2.40 drams (4.26 gm).

Ivanov

A Drama in Four Acts

CHARACTERS

NIKOLAY ALEKSEYEVICH IVANOV [*also* KOLYA, NICOLAS, NIKOLASHA], *a permanent member of the Office for Peasant Affairs*

ANNA PETROVNA [*also* ANYA, ANYUTA, SARA], *his wife,* née *Sara Abramson*[1]

COUNT MATVEY SEMYONOVICH SHABELSKY [*also* MATYUSHA], *his maternal uncle*

PAVEL KIRILLYCH LEBEDEV [*also* PASHA, PASHENKA], *chairman of the District Council*[2]

ZINAIDA SAVISHNA [*also* ZYUZYUSHKA], *his wife*

SASHA [*also* ALEKSANDRA PAVLOVNA, SANICHKA, SASHENKA, SHURA, SHURKA, SHUROCHKA], *the Lebedevs' daughter, aged twenty*

YEVGENY KONSTANTINOVICH LVOV, *a young district doctor*

MARFA YEGOROVNA BABAKINA [*also* MARFUSHA, MARFUTKA], *a young widow, a landowner and the daughter of a rich merchant*[3]

DMITRY NIKITICH KOSYKH, *an excise officer*

MIKHAIL MIKHAYLOVICH BORKIN [*also* MISHA], *a distant relative of Ivanov and manager of his estate*

AVDOTYA NAZAROVNA, *an old woman of indeterminate profession*

YEGORUSHKA, *a hanger-on*[4] *of the Lebedevs*

FIRST GUEST

SECOND GUEST

THIRD GUEST

FOURTH GUEST

PYOTR, *a manservant of Ivanov's*

GAVRILA [*also* GAVRYUSHA], *a manservant of the Lebedevs* *Guests of both sexes, servants*

The action takes place in one of the Districts[5] *of central Russia.*

Act One

The garden of Ivanov's country estate. Left, the house façade and terrace. One window is open. In front of the terrace a broad semicircular lawn, from which avenues lead into the garden straight ahead and right. On the right-hand side are garden benches and small tables. On one of the tables a lamp is burning. Evening is coming on. As the curtain rises a piano-cello duet is being practised indoors.

I

[IVANOV *and* BORKIN.]

[IVANOV *is sitting at a table, reading a book.* BORKIN *appears at the end of the garden wearing big boots and carrying a shotgun; he is rather drunk; seeing Ivanov he goes up to him on tiptoe and as he comes level with him takes aim at his face.*]

IVANOV [*seeing Borkin, starts and jumps up*]: Misha, God knows what . . . you frightened me . . . As it is I'm in a state and your silly jokes . . . [*Sits down.*] He gives me a fright and that makes him happy . . .

BORKIN [*laughing loudly*]: There, there . . . I'm sorry, I'm sorry. [*Sits down next to him.*] I won't any more, I won't . . . [*Takes off his cap.*] It's hot. Would you believe it, dear boy, I've done seventeen versts in something like three hours . . . I'm worn out . . . Feel my heart beating . . .

IVANOV [*reading*]: All right, later . . .

BORKIN: No, feel it now. [*Takes Ivanov's hand and puts it to his chest.*] Do you feel it? Boom-boom-boom-boom. There must be something wrong with my heart. I could die any minute. Tell me, will you be sorry if I die?

IVANOV: I'm reading . . . later . . .

BORKIN: No, seriously, will you be sorry if I die suddenly? Nikolay Alekseyevich, will you be sorry if I die?

IVANOV: Stop bothering me!

BORKIN: Just tell me, old man: will you be sorry?

IVANOV: I'm sorry you smell of vodka. That, Misha, is disgusting.

BORKIN [*laughing*]: Do I smell? Surprising . . . Though it's not really surprising. I met the magistrate at Plesniki, and I must confess he and I each put away eight glasses. Tell me, is it bad for one? Is it? Is it?

IVANOV: This is going too far . . . just get it into your head, Misha, that this teasing . . .

BORKIN: There, there . . . sorry, sorry! . . . Good luck to you, sit by yourself . . . [*Gets up and goes off.*] Astonishing people, one can't even talk. [*Coming back.*] Ah, yes! I almost forgot . . . Give me the eighty-two roubles! . . .

IVANOV: What eighty-two roubles?

BORKIN: To pay the workmen tomorrow.

IVANOV: I haven't got it.

BORKIN: I am deeply grateful! [*Imitating him.*] I haven't got it . . . But don't we need to pay the workmen? Don't we?

IVANOV: I don't know. I don't have any money today. Wait till the first of the month when I get my salary.

BORKIN: To have to talk to such people! . . . The workmen will be coming for their money tomorrow morning, not on the first! . . .

IVANOV: So what am I to do now? Just kill me and cut me up in little pieces . . . And why do you have this nasty habit of pestering me just when I'm reading or writing or . . .

BORKIN: I'm asking you this: do we have to pay the workmen or not? Oh why am I talking to you! [*Gesturing with his hand.*] Country gentlemen, devil take them, landowners . . . What a rational enterprise . . . A thousand *desyatinas* of land – and not a kopeck in his pocket . . . A wine-cellar without a corkscrew . . . I'll just take the troika[1] and sell it tomorrow! I really will! . . . I've sold the oats still standing in the fields, and tomorrow I'll go and sell the rye. [*Strides about the stage.*] Do you think I am going to stand on ceremony? Do you? No, I'm not that kind of man . . .

II

[*The same,* SHABELSKY *(offstage) and* ANNA PETROVNA. SHABELSKY's *voice through the window: 'No one can possibly play with you . . . You have less ear than a stuffed pike and your fingering is disgraceful.'*]

ANNA PETROVNA [*appearing in the open window*]: Who was talking here just now? Was it you, Misha? Why are you striding about like that?

BORKIN: Even that won't have got through to your Nicolas-voilà.[2]

ANNA PETROVNA: Listen, Misha, tell them to bring some hay to the croquet lawn.

BORKIN [*gesturing with his hand*]: Let me be, please.

ANNA PETROVNA: Really, what a tone of voice . . . That tone doesn't suit you at all. If you want women to love you, then don't be cross in front of them and don't go all pompous . . . [*To her husband*] Nikolay, let's go and turn somersaults on the hay . . .

IVANOV: Anyuta, it's bad for you to stand by an open window. Please move away . . . [*Shouting*] Uncle, shut the window!

[*The window is shut.*]

BORKIN: Also, don't forget that two days from now you have to pay Lebedev his interest.

IVANOV: I've remembered. Today I'll be at Lebedev's and I'll ask him to wait . . . [*Looks at his watch.*]

BORKIN: When are you going there?

IVANOV: Now.

BORKIN [*animatedly*]: Wait, wait! . . . Isn't today Shurochka's birth-day . . . Tut-tut-tut . . . And I forgot . . . What a memory . . . [*Jumps.*] I'll go too, I'll go . . . [*Sings.*] I will go . . . I'll have a bath, chew some papers,[3] take three drops of ammonia and I'll be ready to begin all over again . . . Sweet Nikolay Alekseyevich, my sunbeam, light of my life, you're a mass of nerves, you're a real whiner, you're in a constant melanchondria,[4] but the Lord above knows what we could do together! For you I'm ready for anything . . . Do you want me to marry Marfusha Babakina – for you? Half the dowry is yours . . . That is, not half, but take the lot! . . .

IVANOV: Will you stop talking nonsense . . .

BORKIN: No, seriously, really, would you like me to marry Marfu-sha? We'll go halves on the dowry . . . But why am I telling you this? Can you understand? [*Imitating him.*] 'Will you stop talking nonsense.' You're a good man, an intelligent man, but you lack that little vein of ambition, do you see, that sweep. To reach out so as to make the imps of hell feel sick . . . You're a mental case, a moaner, but if you were a normal person, you'd make a million in a year. For example, if I now had two thousand three hundred roubles, in two weeks I'd have twenty thousand. Don't you believe me? And you think that's nonsense? No, it's not nonsense . . . Just give me two thousand three hundred roubles and in a week I'll give you twenty thousand. Ovsyanov is selling a strip of land on the other bank of the river, right opposite us, for two thousand three hundred roubles. If we buy that strip, both banks will be ours. And if both banks are ours, then you see we'll have the right to dam the river. Isn't that so? We'll build a mill and as soon as we announce our intention of building a dam, then everyone living down river will kick up a fuss, and we will tell them *Kommen Sie hier*[5] – if you don't want a dam, pay up. Do you see? Zarev's factory will give five thousand, Korolkov three thousand, the monastery will give five thousand . . .

IVANOV: That's sharp practice, Misha . . . If you don't want to quarrel with me, keep it to yourself.

BORKIN [*sitting down at a table*]: Of course! . . . I thought so! . . . You yourself do nothing and you tie my hands.

III

[*The same,* SHABELSKY *and* LVOV.]

SHABELSKY [*coming out of the house with Lvov*]: Doctors are the same as lawyers, the sole difference being that lawyers only rob you, but doctors rob you and kill you too . . . Present company excepted. [*Sits down on a bench.*] Charlatans, exploiters . . . Perhaps in some Arcadia there are exceptions to the general rule but . . . in my lifetime I've got through twenty thousand roubles on treatments and I haven't come across a single doctor who didn't seem to me an outright rogue.

BORKIN [*to Ivanov*]: Yes, you yourself do nothing and you tie my hands. That's why we have no money . . .

SHABELSKY: I repeat, I am not talking of present company . . . Perhaps there are exceptions although I must say . . . [*Yawns.*]

IVANOV [*shutting his book*]: What do you say, doctor?

LVOV [*looking back at the window*]: The same as I was saying this morning: she must go to the sunshine of the Crimea immediately. [*Walks about the stage.*]

SHABELSKY [*bursts out*]: To the Crimea! . . . Misha, why don't you and I become medical men? It's so simple . . . Some little Madame Angot or Ophelia[6] has a tickle in her throat and starts coughing out of boredom, so take a sheet of paper and write a prescription following the rules of the profession: first a young doctor, then a trip to the Crimea, in the Crimea a dashing Tartar . . .

IVANOV [*to the Count*]: Oh stop being a pest! [*To Lvov*] To go to the Crimea one needs money. Even suppose I find it, she still categorically refuses to go . . .

LVOV: Yes, she refuses . . .

[*A pause.*]

BORKIN: Tell me, doctor, is Anna Petrovna really so seriously ill that she has to go to the Crimea? . . .

LVOV [*looking back at the window*]: Yes, it's consumption . . .

BORKIN: Pss! . . . that's bad . . . I long ago saw in her face that she wouldn't last long.

LVOV: But . . . speak more softly . . . you can be heard in the house . . .

[*A pause.*]

BORKIN [*sighing*]: Our life . . . Man's life is like a flower that blooms in its beauty in the field: a goat comes and eats it up and – there's no more flower! . . .

SHABELSKY: All nonsense, nonsense and more nonsense. [*Yawns.*] Nonsense and a swindle.

[*A pause.*]

BORKIN: And, gentlemen, here I am teaching Nikolay Alekseyevich to make money. I gave him a marvellous idea but as usual my powder fell on damp ground. He's unteachable . . . Look at him: melancholy, bitterness, boredom, gloom, depression . . .

SHABELSKY [*getting up and stretching*]: O mind of genius, you think up things for everyone and teach everyone, but why not for once teach me . . . Teach me, great brain, show me the way out . . .

BORKIN [*getting up*]: I'll go and have a swim now . . . Goodbye, gentlemen . . . [*To the Count*] You have twenty ways out . . . In your place I'd have twenty thousand roubles in a week. [*Goes off.*]

SHABELSKY [*going after him*]: How? Come, teach me.

BORKIN: There's nothing to teach. It's very simple . . . [*Coming back.*] Nikolay Alekseyevich, give me a rouble.

[IVANOV *silently gives him the money.*]

Merci. [*To the Count*] You've still got a lot of trumps in your hand.

SHABELSKY [*going after him*]: Which ones?

BORKIN: In your place I'd have thirty thousand in a week, if not more. [*Exit with the Count.*]

IVANOV [*after a pause*]: Superfluous people, superfluous words, having to answer stupid questions – doctor, all this has exhausted me to the point of making me ill. I've become irritable, bad-tempered, unpleasant and petty to the extent that I don't recognize myself. I have a headache for days on end, I can't sleep, there's a noise in my ears . . . And there's absolutely nowhere I can go . . . Nowhere . . .

LVOV: Nikolay Alekseyevich, I must have a serious word with you.

IVANOV: Speak.

LVOV: I must talk to you about Anna Petrovna. [*Sits down.*] She has refused to go to the Crimea but she would go with you.

IVANOV [*thinking*]: For two to go takes money. Also I won't be given any extended leave. I've already taken leave once this year . . .

LVOV: Very well. Now let's go on. The best medicine for consumption is complete rest, and your wife doesn't have a moment's rest. She's constantly upset by your relationship with her. Forgive me, I'm worked up and I must talk frankly. Your behaviour is killing her.

[*A pause.*]

Nikolay Alekseyevich, make me think better of you! . . .

IVANOV: All that is true, true . . . I am probably dreadfully to blame, but my thoughts are confused, my soul is paralysed by some kind of sloth, and I haven't the power to understand myself. I don't understand other people or myself . . . [*Glances at the window.*] We could be overheard here, come, let's go for a walk.

[*They get up.*]

I would tell you the story from the beginning, my friend, but it's a long story and so complicated you wouldn't have got to the end of it by morning.

[*They walk.*]

Anyuta is a remarkable, unusual woman . . . For me she changed her faith, she abandoned her father and mother, gave up wealth, and if I demanded another hundred sacrifices she would make them without blinking. Well, I am wholly unremarkable and have sacrificed nothing. But it's a long story . . . The whole point is, my dear doctor [*hesitates*], that . . . to put it briefly, I married for passionate love and swore to love her for ever, but . . . five years have passed, she still loves me, but I . . . [*Throws up his hands.*] Now you're telling me that she will die soon, but I feel neither love nor pity, just a kind of emptiness, exhaustion. To an outside observer this is probably appalling; I myself don't understand what is happening inside me . . .

[*They walk out down the avenue.*]

IV

[SHABELSKY, *then* ANNA PETROVNA.]

SHABELSKY [*coming in and laughing*]: My word, he's not a crook but a thinker, a virtuoso! We should put up a monument to him. He brings together in his own single person the corruption of today in all its guises: lawyer, doctor, profiteer, accountant. [*Sits down on the bottom step of the terrace.*] And I don't think he has any qualifications, that's what is surprising . . . So what a genius of villainy he would be if he were also a master of culture and the humanities! He says, 'In a week you could have twenty thousand.' He says, 'You also hold the ace of trumps in your hand – your title of count. [*Laughs.*] Any girl would marry you and bring a dowry.'

[ANNA PETROVNA *opens the window and looks down below.*]

He says, 'Do you want me to try and arrange for you to marry Marfusha?' *Qui est-ce que c'est*[7] Marfusha? Oh yes, it's that Balabal-kina . . . Babakalkina . . . the one like a washerwoman.

ANNA PETROVNA: Is that you, Count?

SHABELSKY: What is it?

[ANNA PETROVNA *laughs*.]

[*In a Jewish accent*] Vy are you loffing?

ANNA PETROVNA: I remembered a remark of yours. Do you remember, you were saying at dinner? A thief pardoned, a horse . . . How did it go?

SHABELSKY: A Jew baptized, a thief pardoned, a horse mended — all for the same price.

ANNA PETROVNA [*laughing*]: You can't make a simple joke without an injection of venom. You are a poisonous man. [*In a serious voice*] Joking apart, Count, you're very poisonous. It's hideously boring to live with you. You're always grumpy, complaining, you find everyone bad, good for nothing. Tell me frankly, Count: did you ever speak well of anyone?

SHABELSKY: What kind of a test is this?

ANNA PETROVNA: We've now lived under the same roof for five years, and I've never heard you talk of other people calmly, without bile and without your making fun of them. What harm have people done you? And do you really think that you are better than everyone else?

SHABELSKY: I don't think that at all. I'm like everyone else, another loathsome swine in a skullcap.[8] A vulgarian, a worn-out shoe. I am always criticizing myself. Who am I? What am I? I used to be rich, free, reasonably happy, but now . . . a hanger-on, a sponger, the court jester. I vent my indignation and scorn, and in response to me people laugh: I laugh and they shake their heads at me sadly and say the old man's gone round the bend . . . But more often than not they don't hear me or pay me any attention . . .

ANNA PETROVNA [*quietly*]: It's shrieking again . . .

SHABELSKY: What's shrieking?

ANNA PETROVNA: The owl. It shrieks every evening.

SHABELSKY: Let it shriek. Things can't be worse than they are already. [*Stretches.*] Oh, my dear Sara, if I won a hundred thousand or two hundred thousand, I'd show you a thing or two! . . . I'd be gone in a flash. I would leave this hole where I eat the bread of charity and I wouldn't set foot here again till the Last Judgement . . .

ANNA PETROVNA: But what would you do if you won?

SHABELSKY [*after thinking*]: First I would go to Moscow and listen to the gypsies. Then . . . then I'd go off to Paris. I'd take an apartment there, go to the Russian church . . .

ANNA PETROVNA: And what else?

SHABELSKY: I'd sit for whole days on my wife's grave and think. I'd sit like that on her grave till I dropped dead. My wife is buried in Paris . . .

[*A pause.*]

ANNA PETROVNA: It's dreadfully boring. Shall we play another duet?

SHABELSKY: All right. Set out the music.

[ANNA PETROVNA *goes off.*]

V

[SHABELSKY, IVANOV *and* LVOV.]

IVANOV [*appearing with Lvov in the avenue*]: You only qualified last year, my dear friend, you're still young and confident, but I am thirty-five. I have the right to give you some advice. Don't marry a Jew or a psychopath or a bluestocking but choose yourself someone ordinary, someone a shade of grey, with no bright colours and no superfluous noises. In general, construct your whole life on a conventional pattern. The greyer, the more monotonous the background, the better. My dear fellow, don't do battle against thousands all on your own, don't tilt against windmills, don't beat your head against walls . . . And may God preserve you from all kinds of rational farming, new fangled schools, fiery speeches . . . Shut yourself in your shell and do your little God-given business . . . It's snugger, healthier and more honest. But the life I have lived – how exhausting it's been! Oh how exhausting! . . . How many mistakes, injustices, how much folly . . . [*Seeing the Count, irritably*] Uncle, you're always in the way, you don't let anyone talk undisturbed!

SHABELSKY [*in a plaintive voice*]: To hell with me, there's no refuge anywhere. [*Jumps up and goes into the house.*]

IVANOV [*shouting after him*]: Oh I'm sorry, I'm sorry! [*To Lvov*] What made me offend him? No, decidedly, I've lost my self-control . . . I must do something about myself. I must . . .

LVOV [*becoming agitated*]: Nikolay Alekseyevich, I've listened to you and . . . forgive me, I'll speak frankly, without mincing my words. In your voice, in your tone, not to speak of your actual words, there is so much heartless egoism, so much cold callousness . . . A person close to you is dying because of that closeness, her days are numbered, but you . . . you can be without love for her, you can go about giving advice and showing off . . . I can't express it all to you, I haven't the gift of words, but . . . but I find you deeply antipathetic.

IVANOV: Maybe, maybe . . . You can see more clearly from outside . . . It's very possible that you understand me . . . I am probably very, very much to blame . . . [*Listens.*] I think they've brought the horses. I'll go and dress . . . [*Goes towards the house and stops.*] Doctor, you don't like me and you don't conceal it. That does your heart honour . . . [*Goes into the house.*]

LVOV [*alone*]: My accursed character . . . Again I've missed the opportunity and haven't spoken to him as I should have . . . I can't talk to him calmly. As soon as I open my mouth and say one word, I feel something start to constrict me here [*points to his chest*], I feel it churning and my tongue sticks to my throat. I hate this Tartuffe,[9] this pompous scoundrel, with all my heart . . . Now he's going off . . . His unhappy wife's entire happiness lies in his being near her, he is the air she breathes. She begs him to spend just one evening with her, but he . . . he cannot . . . Because, you see, he finds the atmosphere at home so heavy and suffocating. If he spends a single evening at home, he'll put a bullet into his forehead out of boredom. Wretched fellow . . . he needs space to do some new bit of villainy . . . Oh, I know why you drive over every evening to those Lebedevs. I know!

VI

[LVOV, IVANOV *(in a hat and overcoat)*, SHABELSKY *and* ANNA PETROVNA.]

SHABELSKY [*coming out of the house with* IVANOV *and* ANNA PETROVNA]: Nicolas,[10] this is just inhuman! . . . You yourself go out every evening and we stay here by ourselves. We go to bed at eight out of boredom. This is a horror, not a life! And why can you go while we can't? Why?

ANNA PETROVNA: Count, let him be. Let him go, let him . . .

IVANOV [*to his wife*]: Well, where would you be going with your illness? You are ill and mustn't be in the open air after sunset . . . Ask the doctor here. You're not a child, Anyuta, you must use your reason . . . [*To the Count*] And why would you go there?

SHABELSKY: I'd go into the flames of hell, into the jaws of the crocodile, just so as not to stay here. I am bored. I've become dulled from boredom. I've got on everyone's nerves. You leave me at home so she isn't bored alone, but I've made her life hell, I've eaten her up!

ANNA PETROVNA: Leave him alone, Count, leave him. Let him go if he enjoys it there.

IVANOV: Anya, why this tone? You know I don't go there for pleasure. I have to talk about the promissory note.

ANNA PETROVNA: I don't understand why you're justifying yourself. Go! Who's keeping you?

IVANOV: My friends, let's not devour one another! Do we have to?

SHABELSKY [*in a plaintive voice*]: Nicolas my dear, I ask you, take me with you. I'll have a look there at the crooks and fools, and perhaps I'll be entertained. You know I haven't been anywhere since Easter.

IVANOV [*crossly*]: Very well, we'll go together. I'm so fed up with you all!

SHABELSKY: We'll go? So *merci, merci* . . . [*Gaily takes Ivanov's arm and leads him aside.*] May I wear your straw hat?

IVANOV: You may, only hurry up please.

[*The Count runs into the house.*]

I'm so fed up with all of you! But what am I saying to you? My tone when I talk to you is impossible. That never used to happen to me before. Well, goodbye, Anya, I shall be back towards one.

ANNA PETROVNA: Kolya, my dearest, stay at home.

IVANOV [*with emotion*]: My love, my unhappy darling, I beg you, don't stop me going out in the evenings. It's cruel and unjust on my part, but let me commit that injustice. It's an agony for me at home. As soon as the sun disappears, my spirit begins to be weighed down by depression. What depression! Don't ask why. I myself don't know. I swear by God's truth I don't know. Here I'm in anguish, I go to the Lebedevs and there it's still worse; I return from there and here it's depression again, and so all night . . . Simply despair! . . .

ANNA PETROVNA: Kolya, why don't you stay! We will talk as we used to . . . We'll have supper together, we'll read . . . I and the old grouch have been practising a lot of duets for you . . . [*Embraces him.*] Stay! . . .

[*A pause.*]

I don't understand you. It's been going on for a whole year. Why have you changed?

IVANOV: I don't know, I don't know . . .

ANNA PETROVNA: And why don't you want me to go out with you in the evenings?

IVANOV: If you must have it, well, I'll tell you. It's a bit cruel to say it, but better so . . . When I'm really depressed, I . . . I begin to stop loving you. Also I then avoid you. Very simply, I have to leave the house.

ANNA PETROVNA: When you're depressed? I understand, I understand . . . Do you know what, Kolya? Try and sing, laugh, get angry, as you once did . . . You stay in, we'll laugh and drink fruit liqueur and we'll drive away your depression in a flash. I'll sing if you like. Or else let's go and sit in the dark in your study as we used to, and you'll tell me about your depression . . . You have such suffering eyes. I'll look into them and cry, and we'll both feel better . . . [*Laughs and cries.*] How does it go, Kolya? The flowers come up again every spring, but joy there is none. Is that it? So go off, go . . .

IVANOV: Pray to God for me, Anya. [*Goes off, stops and thinks.*] No, I can't. [*Exit.*]

ANNA PETROVNA: Go . . . [*Sits down by a table.*]

LVOV [*walking about the stage*]: Anna Petrovna, make yourself a rule: as soon as it strikes six o'clock you must go to your rooms and not come out till the next morning. The evening damp is bad for you.

ANNA PETROVNA: Yes, sir.[11]

LVOV: What's this 'yes, sir'! I am being serious.

ANNA PETROVNA: But I don't want to be serious. [*Coughs.*]

LVOV: You see now – you're already coughing . . .

VII

[LVOV, ANNA PETROVNA *and* SHABELSKY.]

SHABELSKY [*coming out of the house in hat and coat*]: Where's Nikolay? Have they brought round the horses? [*Quickly goes and kisses Anna Petrovna's hand.*] Goot night, my angel. [*He makes a face.*] Gevalt![12] Egsguse me, plees! [*Quickly goes out.*]

LVOV: What a clown.

[*A pause: the distant sounds of a harmonica can be heard.*]

ANNA PETROVNA: What boredom! . . . The stables and kitchen are having a dance and I . . . I feel abandoned . . . Yevgeny Kostantinovich, where you are striding off to? Come here, sit down! . . .

LVOV: I can't sit still.

[*A pause.*]

ANNA PETROVNA: They're playing 'Birdy' in the kitchen. [*Sings*] 'Birdy, birdy, where'd you go? Drinking vodka high and low.'

[*A pause.*]

Doctor, do you have a father and mother?

LVOV: My father's dead but I have a mother.

ANNA PETROVNA: Do you miss your mother?

LVOV: I have no time to miss her.

ANNA PETROVNA: The flowers come up again every spring, but joy there is none. Who said that sentence to me? God help me remember . . . I think Nikolay himself said it. [*Listens.*] The owl is shrieking again.

LVOV: So let it shriek . . .

ANNA PETROVNA: I am beginning to think, doctor, that fate has cheated me. The majority of people, who maybe are no better than I am, are happy and pay nothing for that happiness. I have paid for everything, absolutely everything! . . . And how dearly! Why have I paid such terrible interest? . . . My dear, you are all so careful with me, so full of tact, you're frightened of telling the truth, but do you think I don't know what is wrong with me? I know perfectly well. But it's boring to talk about that . . . [*In a Jewish accent*] Egsguse me, plees! Can you tell funny stories?

LVOV: No, I can't.

ANNA PETROVNA: Nikolay can. And I'm also beginning to be surprised at people's lack of justice: why is love not met with love, and why is truth paid for with lies? Tell me: how long will my father and mother hate me? They live fifty versts from here and I feel their hatred day and night, even in my dreams. And how do you think I should take Nikolay's depression? He says he loses his love for me only in the evenings when the depression comes over him. That I understand and tolerate, but suppose he's completely stopped loving me. Of course that's impossible, but just suppose . . . No, no, I mustn't even think of that. [*Sings*] 'Birdy, birdy, where'd you go?' [*Shudders.*] What frightening thoughts I have! . . . You don't have a family, doctor, and you can't understand much of this . . .

LVOV: You are surprised . . . [*Sits down next to her.*] No, I . . . I am surprised, I am surprised at you. Now explain, give me an account of how it is that you, an intelligent, honest, almost saintly woman, have allowed yourself to be so brazenly deceived, to be dragged into this owl's nest. Why are you here? What have you in common with this cold, heartless . . . but let's forget your husband – what do you have in common with this empty vulgar milieu? Lord God above! . . . That perpetually grumpy, crazy Count, Misha, that sly old crook of crooks, with that hateful face of his . . . Explain to me what's the point of your being here. How did you get here? . . .

ANNA PETROVNA [*laughing*]: That's exactly how he once used to talk . . . Word for word . . . But his eyes are bigger, and when he began to talk heatedly about something, then they would glow like coals . . . Talk, talk! . . .

LVOV [*getting up and gesturing with his hand*]: What should I talk about? Go to your rooms . . .

ANNA PETROVNA: You say that Nikolay is this and that, one thing and another. How have you come to know him? Can one get to know a man in half a year? Doctor, he's a remarkable man and I'm sorry you didn't know him two or three years ago. Now he's gloomy and silent and does nothing, but then . . . What charm! . . . I fell in love with him at first sight. [*Laughing*] I just looked at him and the mousetrap went snap! He said, let's go . . . I cut off everything from me, just as, you know, you cut off withered leaves with scissors, and I went . . .

[*A pause.*]

And now it's different . . . Now he goes to the Lebedevs' to amuse himself with other women, and I . . . sit in the garden and listen to the cry of the owl . . .

[*The knock of the watchman.*[13]]

Doctor, do you have brothers?
LVOV: No.

[ANNA PETROVNA *groans.*]

What now? What's the matter?
ANNA PETROVNA [*getting up*]: I can't stand it, doctor, I will go there . . .
LVOV: Where?
ANNA PETROVNA: Where he is . . . I will go . . . Tell them to harness the horses . . . [*Goes towards the house.*]
LVOV: You mustn't go . . .
ANNA PETROVNA: Leave me alone, it's none of your business . . . I can't stand it, I'm going . . . Tell them to bring the horses . . . [*Runs into the house.*]
LVOV: No, I absolutely refuse to be a doctor in these conditions. It's not just that they don't pay me a kopeck, they also turn my feelings upside down . . . No, I refuse. I've had enough. [*Goes into the house.*]

[*Curtain.*]

Act Two

A reception room in the Lebedevs' house; doors opening directly into the garden, and doors right and left. Valuable antique furniture. The chandelier, candelabra and pictures are all under covers.[1]

I

[ZINAIDA SAVISHNA, FIRST GUEST, SECOND GUEST, THIRD GUEST, KOSYKH, AVDOTYA NAZAROVNA, YEGO-RUSHKA, GAVRILA, *a maid, old lady guests, young ladies,* BABAKINA.]

[ZINAIDA SAVISHNA *is sitting on a sofa. On either side of her are old ladies in armchairs; the young people are on chairs. Backstage, by the door to the garden, a game of cards is in progress; among the players are* KOSYKH, AVDOTYA NAZAROVNA *and* YEGO-RUSHKA. GAVRILA *is standing by the right-hand door; a maid is offering sweetmeats on a tray. Guests are circulating from the garden, through the right-hand door and back again throughout the whole act.* BABAKINA *comes through the right-hand door and moves towards Zinaida Savishna.*]

ZINAIDA SAVISHNA [*gaily*]: Marfa Yegorovna, my love . . .
BABAKINA: Good evening, Zinaida Savishna. May I have the honour of congratulating you on the birthday . . .

[*They kiss.*]

God grant . . .

ZINAIDA SAVISHNA: Thank you, my love, I am so pleased . . .
How are you? . . .

BABAKINA: Thank you very much indeed. [*Sits down by her on the
sofa.*] Good evening, young people . . .

[*The guests rise and bow.*]

FIRST GUEST [*laughing*]: Young people . . . but you aren't old?

BABAKINA [*sighing*]: How can we pass as young . . .

FIRST GUEST [*laughing politely*]: Now come . . . You may be a
widow in name, but you can give any girl a handicap of ten.

[GAVRILA *offers Babakina tea.*]

ZINAIDA SAVISHNA [*to Gavrila*]: Why are you serving it like
that? You should have brought some jam. Gooseberry or
something . . .

BABAKINA: Don't worry. Thank you very much indeed . . .

[*A pause.*]

FIRST GUEST: Marfa Yegorovna, did you come by Mushkino? . . .

BABAKINA: No, by Zaymishche. The road's better that way.

FIRST GUEST: Really.

KOSYKH: Two spades.

YEGORUSHKA: Pass.

AVDOTYA NAZAROVNA: Pass.

SECOND GUEST: Pass.

BABAKINA: Dearest Zinaida Savishna, the Government lottery
issues[2] have again gone up very quickly. I've never seen anything
like it: the first issue is already two-seventy and the second almost
two-fifty . . . That's never happened before . . .

ZINAIDA SAVISHNA [*sighing*]: It's nice for those who have a lot of
them . . .

BABAKINA: Don't say that, my love; although their price is high, it doesn't pay to keep one's capital in them. The insurance alone will kill me.

ZINAIDA SAVISHNA: That may be, but still, my dear, you must have hopes . . . [*Sighs.*] God is merciful . . .

THIRD GUEST: As I see it, *mesdames*, I reason thus, that at the present time it is very unprofitable to have capital. Bonds give a very small dividend, and it is exceptionally risky to put money into circulation. I am of this understanding, *mesdames*, that a man who has capital at the present time is in a more critical situation, *mesdames*, than one who . . .

BABAKINA [*sighing*]: That's true.

[FIRST GUEST *yawns.*]

How can you yawn in front of ladies.

FIRST GUEST: *Pardon, mesdames.* I didn't mean to.

[ZINAIDA SAVISHNA *gets up and goes out by the right-hand door; a prolonged silence.*]

YEGORUSHKA: Two diamonds.

AVDOTYA NAZAROVNA: Pass.

SECOND GUEST: Pass.

KOSYKH: Pass.

BABAKINA [*aside*]: Lord, what boredom. I could die!

II

[*The same*, ZINAIDA SAVISHNA *and* LEBEDEV.]

ZINAIDA SAVISHNA [*coming through the right-hand door with Lebedev, quietly*]: What are you doing settling down in there? What a prima donna! Sit with the guests. [*Sits down in her previous place.*]

LEBEDEV [*yawning*]: Oh, our sins weigh heavy! [*Seeing Babakina*]

Lord, the pot of jam is sitting there! Our Turkish delight! [*Greets her.*] How is your most precious health? . . .

BABAKINA: Thank you very much indeed.

LEBEDEV: Well, thank God! . . . Thank God! . . . [*Sits down in an armchair.*] So . . . so . . . Gavrila!

[GAVRILA *brings him a glass of vodka and a tumbler of water; he drinks the vodka and washes it down with some water.*]

FIRST GUEST: Your good health!

LEBEDEV: What good health? . . . I'm not yet a corpse, and for that thanks. [*To his wife*] Zyuzyushka, where's our birthday girl?

KOSYKH [*plaintively*]: For God's sake tell me why we haven't taken the trick? [*He jumps up.*] Why the devil have we lost?

AVDOTYA NAZAROVNA [*jumping up, angrily*]: Because, my friend, if you can't play, you shouldn't sit down at the table. What absolute right do you have to follow someone else's suit? So you've been left with that pickled ace! . . .

[*Both run forward from the table.*]

KOSYKH [*in a tearful voice*]: Excuse me, ladies and gentlemen . . . I have in diamonds ace, king, queen and a sequence of eight, the ace of spades and one, just one, little heart, but she, devil knows why, couldn't declare a little slam! . . . I said no trumps . . .

AVDOTYA NAZAROVNA [*interrupting*]: I said no trumps! You said two no trumps . . .

KOSYKH: This is disgraceful! . . . Excuse me . . . you have . . . I have . . . you have . . . [*To Lebedev*] You be the judge, Pavel Kirillych . . . I have in diamonds ace, king, queen and a sequence of eight . . .

LEBEDEV [*blocking his ears*]: Leave me alone, do me that favour . . . leave me alone . . .

AVDOTYA NAZAROVNA [*shrieking*]: I said no trumps!

KOSYKH [*furiously*]: You can label me a criminal and excommunicate me if I ever again sit down to play with that old sturgeon! [*Quickly goes out into the garden.*]

[*The* SECOND GUEST *follows him,* YEGORUSHKA *remains at the table.*]

AVDOTYA NAZAROVNA: Ouf! . . . He's given me a fever . . . Old sturgeon! . . . Old sturgeon yourself! . . .

BABAKINA: But you were angry, granny . . .

AVDOTYA NAZAROVNA [*seeing Babakina, throws up her hands*]: My treasure, my beauty! . . . She is here and, blind as a bat, I didn't see her . . . My dove . . . [*Kisses her on the shoulder, and sits down by her.*] What joy! Let me look at you, my white swan! . . . [*Spits three times.*] That's against the evil eye . . .

LEBEDEV: Oh you do go on . . . Better find her a husband . . .

AVDOTYA NAZAROVNA: I will! I won't go to my grave, sinner that I am, before I've seen her and Sanichka married! . . . I won't go to my grave . . . [*A sigh.*] The point is, where can one find a bridegroom today? There they sit, our bridegrooms, feathers all ruffled like wet cockerels! . . .

THIRD GUEST: Not a very successful comparison. As I see it, *mesdames*, if today's young men prefer the bachelor life, one must blame social conditions, so to speak . . .

LEBEDEV: Now, now . . . don't theorize, I don't like it.

III

[*The same and* SASHA.]

SASHA [*coming in and going to her father*]: Such magnificent weather, and you're all sitting in here in this fug.

ZINAIDA SAVISHNA: Sashenka, don't you see that Marfa Yegorovna is with us?

SASHA: I'm sorry. [*Goes to Babakina and greets her.*]

BABAKINA: You've got too grand, Sanichka, you've got too grand, you might have come to see me just once. [*Kissing her.*] Happy birthday, my love . . .

SASHA: Thank you. [*Sits down beside her father.*]

LEBEDEV: Yes, Avdotya Nazarovna, there's a problem now with bridegrooms. And not just bridegrooms – you can't get decent ushers anywhere. The young people of today, I don't say it to insult them, are, Lord help them, kind of sour and overcooked . . . No dancing, no conversation, no intelligent drinking . . .

AVDOTYA NAZAROVNA: Well, they're all masters of drinking, just put it in front of them . . .

LEBEDEV: It's no great thing to drink – a horse too can drink . . . No, one must drink intelligently . . . In our time we used to struggle with lectures all day, but as soon as evening came we went straight off somewhere where the lights were shining and spun like tops till dawn . . . And we would dance and entertain the young ladies, and look after this. [*Flicks his throat with a finger.*³] We would talk nonsense and philosophy till our tongues went numb . . . But today's lot . . . [*Waves his hand.*] I don't understand . . . They wouldn't make God a candle or the Devil a poker. In the whole district there's only one worthwhile young fellow, and he's married [*sighs*] and I think he's now started to go crazy . . .

BABAKINA: Who is that?

LEBEDEV: Nikolasha Ivanov.

BABAKINA: Yes, he's a good man [*making a face*], only an unhappy one! . . .

ZINAIDA SAVISHNA: How could he be happy, my love. [*Sighing*] What a mistake he made, poor thing . . . He married his little Jewish girl and the poor man calculated that her father and mother would give mountains of gold with her, but it turned out the opposite . . . Ever since she changed her faith, her father and mother have refused to see her and curse her . . . So he hasn't received a kopeck. Now he's sorry, but it's too late . . .

SASHA: Mama, that's not true.

BABAKINA [*heatedly*]: Shurochka, how is it not true? Everyone knows it. If he didn't have that in mind, why would he marry a Jew? Aren't there enough Russians? He made a mistake, my love, he made a mistake . . . [*Animatedly*] Lord, and she's getting it from him now! What a farce. He comes home from somewhere and rushes in to her: 'Your father and mother tricked me! Get out of my house!' But where is she to go? Her father and mother won't take her in; she could become a servant, but she's not trained to work . . . He goes at her and he goes at her until the Count stands up for her. If it weren't for the Count, he'd have sent her to her grave long ago . . .

AVDOTYA NAZAROVNA: He used to lock her in the cellar and tell her, 'Just eat up that garlic, you so-and-so' . . . She'd eat and eat until it was coming out of her ears.

[*Laughter.*]

SASHA: Papa, these are lies!

LEBEDEV: So what! Let them have their fill of gossip . . . Gavrila!

[GAVRILA *brings him vodka and water.*]

ZINAIDA SAVISHNA: That's why he was ruined, poor man. His affairs collapsed, my love . . . If Borkin hadn't been looking after the estate, he and the Jewess wouldn't have had anything to eat. [*Sighing*] And how we have suffered because of him, my love! . . . Such suffering as only God can see! Would you believe it, dear, he's owed us nine thousand for three years!

BABAKINA [*with horror*]: Nine thousand! . . .

ZINAIDA SAVISHNA: Yes . . . my dear Pashenka made the arrangements for lending him that. He doesn't distinguish between people you can lend to and those to whom you can't. I'm not talking about the capital – who cares – but if he could only pay the interest on time! . . .

SASHA [*heatedly*]: We've talked about this a thousand times!

ZINAIDA SAVISHNA: What's it to do with you? Why are you standing up for him?

SASHA [*getting up*]: But what drives you to say all this about a man who has done you no harm? Well, what has he done to you?

THIRD GUEST: Aleksandra Pavlovna, allow me to say two words. I have a respect for Nikolay Alekseyevich and always counted that an honour, but, speaking *entre nous*,[4] he seems to me an adventurer.

SASHA: And I congratulate you for thinking that.

THIRD GUEST: In proof I will adduce the following fact which was communicated to me by his aide, his so to speak cicerone, Borkin. Two years ago, at the time of the cattle epidemic, he bought some cattle, insured them . . .

ZINAIDA SAVISHNA: Yes, yes, yes! I remember the case. I was told about it too.

THIRD GUEST: Insured them, note, then infected them with the disease and collected the money.

SASHA: Oh, this is all nonsense. No one bought and infected cattle. Borkin himself concocted a plan like that and boasted about it everywhere. When Ivanov learnt about it, Borkin was asking his forgiveness for two weeks afterwards. Ivanov is only guilty of having a weak character and lacking the guts to kick that Borkin out of his house, and guilty of having too much trust in people! Everything he had has been pilfered and stolen; anyone who wanted to has made money from his generous ventures.

LEBEDEV: Temper! That will do.

SASHA: Why do they all talk nonsense? Oh, this is all so boring, boring! Ivanov, Ivanov, Ivanov – and there are no other subjects of conversation. [*Goes to the door and comes back*.] I am astonished! [*To the young men*] I am absolutely astonished at your patience, gentlemen! Are you really not bored sitting like that? The air has set thick from boredom. Say something, amuse the young ladies. If you have no other subjects of conversation but Ivanov, then laugh, drink, dance or something . . .

LEBEDEV [*laughing*]: Give it to them, really give it to them!

SASHA: Listen, do me this favour! If you don't want to dance, laugh or sing, if all that bores you, then I ask you, I beg you for just once in your lives, just for fun, to astonish us or make us laugh, summon up your energy and all together think up something witty or brilliant, say something which even if it's rude or vulgar, at least is funny and fresh. Or all of you together do something small, something we might hardly notice, but which has some tiny resemblance to a serious exploit, so that the young ladies for once in their lives, looking at you, might say 'Ah!' Listen, you want to please, don't you, but why don't you try to please? Oh gentlemen! All of you are hopeless, hopeless, hopeless! Looking at you, flies would die and lamps begin to smoke. Hopeless, hopeless! . . . I've told you a thousand times and will always tell you that you are all hopeless, hopeless! . . .

IV

[*The same*, IVANOV *and* SHABELSKY.]

SHABELSKY [*entering with Ivanov by the right-hand door*]: Who is making a speech here? Is it you, Shurochka? [*Laughs loudly and shakes her hand.*] Happy birthday, my angel, God grant you to die a little later and no reincarnation . . .

ZINAIDA SAVISHNA [*joyously*]: Nikolay Alekseyevich, Count! . . .

LEBEDEV: Well, well! Who do I see . . . Count! [*Goes to meet them.*]

SHABELSKY [*seeing Zinaida Savishna and Babakina, stretches out his arms towards them*]: Two moneybags on one sofa! . . . A sight for sore eyes! [*He greets them. To Zinaida Savishna*] Good evening, Zyuzyushka! [*To Babakina*] Good evening, Pompom! . . .

ZINAIDA SAVISHNA: I am so glad, Count – you're so seldom our guest. [*Shouting*] Gavrila, tea! Sit down, please. [*She gets up, goes out of the right-hand door and returns at once looking very worried.*]

[SASHA *sits down in her previous place*, IVANOV *silently greets everyone.*]

LEBEDEV [*to Shabelsky*]: Where have you come from? What forces brought you here? What a surprise, may God punish me . . . [*Kisses him.*] Count, you're an old pirate! Decent people don't behave like that. [*Leading him by the arm towards the footlights.*] Why don't you visit us? Are you cross or something?

SHABELSKY: How can I get to you? Riding a stick? I haven't my own horses and Nikolay doesn't bring me with him but tells me to stay with Sara so she isn't bored. Send your own horses for me, then I'll come . . .

LEBEDEV [*gesturing with his hand*]: Well . . . Zyuzyushka would sooner burst than give up her horses. My dear old friend, you know that for me you are nearer and dearer than anyone. You and I are the only survivors of the old-timers. 'In you I love the pains I knew of yore, and my dead youth . . .'⁵ I'm joking, but you can see I'm almost crying. [*Kisses the Count.*]

SHABELSKY: Let me go, let me go! You smell like a wine cellar . . .

LEBEDEV: My dear friend, you cannot imagine how bored I am without my friends. I'm ready to hang myself from boredom . . . [*In a low voice*] Zyuzyushka with her loan bank has driven away all the decent people, and as you see only the barbarians are left . . . these Dudkins and Budkins . . . Well, have some tea.

[GAVRILA *offers the Count tea.*]

ZINAIDA SAVISHNA [*to Gavrila, anxiously*]: Look, how are you serving it? You should have brought some jam . . . Gooseberry or something . . .

SHABELSKY [*laughs loudly; to Ivanov*]: What did I say to you? [*To Lebedev*] I had a bet with him on the way that as soon as we arrived Zyuzyushka would at once begin to offer us gooseberry jam . . .

ZINAIDA SAVISHNA: Count, you are still just as sarcastic . . . [*Sits down.*]

LEBEDEV: They've made twenty barrels of it, so what can we do with it?

SHABELSKY [*sitting down by the table*]: Are you still hoarding, Zyuzyushka? Well, do you have your little million yet?

ZINAIDA SAVISHNA [*with a sigh*]: Yes, seen from the outside, there's no one richer than us, but where would we be getting the money from? It's just talk . . .

SHABELSKY: Oh yes, yes! . . . We know! . . . We know how badly you play your game . . . [*To Lebedev*] Pasha, tell me honestly, have you saved a million?

LEBEDEV: God, I don't know. Ask Zyuzyushka that . . .

SHABELSKY [*to Babakina*]: And our fat little Pompom will soon have her little million! Goodness, she gets prettier and plumper[6] not by the day but by the hour! That means a lot of dough . . .

BABAKINA: Thank you very much indeed, Your Highness,[7] only I don't like mockery.

SHABELSKY: My dear moneybags, is that mockery? It's just a cry of the heart, my lips are uttering from an excess of feeling . . . my love for you and Zyuzyushka is boundless . . . [*Gaily*] Rapture! . . . Ecstasy! . . . I cannot see you both without being moved . . .

ZINAIDA SAVISHNA: You're still just the same as you were. [*To Yegorushka*] Yegorushka, put out the candles. Why let them burn uselessly if you're not playing?

[YEGORUSHKA *comes to with a start, puts out the candles and sits down.*]

[*To Ivanov*] Nikolay Alekseyevich, how is your wife's health?

IVANOV: Bad. Today the doctor said she definitely has consumption . . .

ZINAIDA SAVISHNA: Really? What a tragedy! . . . [*Sighs.*] And we're all so fond of her . . .

SHABELSKY: Nonsense, nonsense and more nonsense! . . . There is no consumption, it's doctor's quackery, hocus-pocus. He wants to loaf around playing Aesculapius,[8] so he's dreamt up consumption. It's a good thing her husband isn't jealous. [IVANOV *makes an impatient movement.*] As for Sara, I don't trust one word of hers, not a single movement. I have never in my life trusted doctors or lawyers or women. Nonsense, nonsense, quackery and hocus-pocus.

LEBEDEV [*to Shabelsky*]: You're an amazing character, Matvey . . . You've assumed some kind of misanthropy and traipse around with it like a broody hen. You look like anyone else but as soon as you open your mouth, it's as if you had a boil on your tongue or chronic catarrh . . .

SHABELSKY: What am I meant to do, kiss every crook and rogue or something?

LEBEDEV: Where do you see crooks and rogues?

SHABELSKY: I'm not talking of present company of course, but . . .

LEBEDEV: So much for but . . . It's all put on.

SHABELSKY: Put on . . . It's a good thing you have no world-view of your own.

LEBEDEV: What is my world-view? I sit and wait for the grim reaper every minute. That is my philosophy. You and I haven't got time to think about philosophy, old man. So . . . [*Shouts*] Gavrila!

SHABELSKY: You've had too much Gavrila as it is . . . Look at your nose, it's all lit up.

LEBEDEV [*drinking*]: Don't worry, my love . . . I don't have to go to my wedding.

ZINAIDA SAVISHNA: It's a long time since Dr Lvov came to us. He's quite forgotten us.

SASHA: My pet aversion. Honesty on legs. He can't ask for water or light a cigarette without displaying his exceptional honesty. Whether he's walking or talking, his forehead has 'I am an honest man' written on it! It's boring to be with him.

SHABELSKY: A narrow-minded, one-directional physician! [*Imitating him*] 'The road to honest labour!' He squawks like a parrot at every step and thinks he really is a second Dobrolyubov.[9] Anyone who doesn't squawk is a criminal. His views are amazingly profound. If a peasant is prosperous and lives like a human being, then he must be a crook and an exploiting kulak.[10] I wear a velvet jacket and a manservant dresses me – I am a crook and a supporter of serfdom.[11] He's so honest, so honest he's bursting with honesty. He doesn't know where to put himself. I'm even frightened of him . . . I really am! . . . I'm afraid he might hit me on the snout or treat me like a crook out of a sense of duty.

IVANOV: He's worn me out dreadfully, but I like him all the same; he has a lot of sincerity.

SHABELSKY: Sincerity is nice! He comes up to me yesterday evening, and for no reason at all: 'Count, I find you deeply antipathetic.'

Thank you very much! And none of this is straightforward, it has a message; and the voice trembles and the eyes flash and the knees shake . . . To hell with his wooden honesty! So, he finds me repellent, vile, that's natural . . . I recognize it myself, but why say it to my face? I am a worthless person, but be that as it may, I do have grey hairs . . . This honesty is without talent, without pity!

LEBEDEV: There, there, there! . . . You yourself were young, weren't you, and can understand.

SHABELSKY: Yes, I've been young and foolish, in my time I've played Chatsky[12] and exposed rogues and swindlers, but I've never in my life called thieves thieves to their face or talked of the rope in a hanged man's house. I was properly brought up. But your dim-witted doctor here would feel himself equal to his task and in a seventh heaven if fate, in the name of principle and the common ideals of mankind, gave him the opportunity to get me by the throat and wallop me publicly on the snout.

LEBEDEV: Young people are all temperamental. My uncle was a Hegelian[13] . . . so he used to have his house full of guests, get up on a chair and begin: 'You're all ignoramuses! You're a dark force! The dawn of a new life!' Ta-ta, ta-ta, ta-ta . . . He really kept on giving it to them . . .

SASHA: And what did the guests do?

LEBEDEV: Nothing . . . They listened and drank. But once I challenged him to a duel . . . my own uncle. It was over Francis Bacon.[14] I remember, I was sitting, God help my memory, just as Matvey is now, and my uncle was standing with the late Gerasim Nilych just here, more or less, where Nikolasha is . . . Well, my friend, Gerasim Nilych asks the question . . .

[*Enter* BORKIN.]

V

[*The same and* BORKIN. *He enters by the right-hand door, dressed very smartly, with a package in his hands, jumping up and down and singing. A buzz of approbation.*]

[*All together:*]

YOUNG LADIES: Mikhail Mikhaylovich!

LEBEDEV: Michel Michelich![15] Talk of the devil . . .

SHABELSKY: The life and soul of the party!

BORKIN: And here I am! [*Runs up to Sasha.*] Noble signorina, I make so bold as to congratulate the universe on the birth of so marvellous a flower as you . . . As tribute of my rapture, I venture to present [*gives her the package*] fireworks and Bengal lights of my own manufacture. May they illuminate the night as you lighten the gloom of the kingdom of darkness. [*Bows theatrically.*]

SASHA: Thank you.

LEBEDEV [*laughing, to Ivanov*]: Why don't you fire that Judas!

BORKIN: [*to Lebedev*] Pavel Kirillych! [*To Ivanov*] Master . . . [*Sings*] Nicolas-voilà, ho-hi-ho! [*He goes round everyone.*] Most esteemed Zinaida Savishna . . . Divine Marfa Yegorovna . . . Most ancient Avdotya Nazarovna . . . Most serene Count . . .

SHABELSKY [*laughing loudly*]: The life and soul of the party . . . Immediately he came in, the atmosphere loosened up. Did you notice?

BORKIN: Ouf, I'm exhausted . . . I think I've greeted everyone. Well, ladies and gentlemen, what's new? Is there nothing special, nothing that hits you in the face? [*To Zinaida Savishna, animatedly*] Oh, listen, mother . . . I was driving to you just now . . . [*To Gavrila*] Gavryusha, give me some tea, only no gooseberry jam! [*To Zinaida Savishna*] I was driving to you just now and the peasants were stripping the willows on your river. Why don't you farm out the willows?

LEBEDEV [*to Ivanov*]: Why don't you fire that Judas?

ZINAIDA SAVISHNA [*alarmedly*]: Yes, that's true, it never came into my head . . .

BORKIN [*performing gymnastics with his arms*]: I've got to be moving . . . Mother, what could we put on that's special? Marfa Yego-rovna, I'm feeling on top of the world . . . I'm in a state of exaltation. [*Sings*] 'Afresh before thee I . . .'

ZINAIDA SAVISHNA: Do organize something, we're all bored.

BORKIN: Ladies and gentlemen, why are you so glum? Sitting there like a jury after it's been sworn in! . . . Let's think up something. What would you like? Forfeits, tug of war, catch, dancing, fireworks?

YOUNG LADIES [*clapping their hands*]: Fireworks, fireworks! [*They run into the garden.*]

SASHA [*to Ivanov*]: Why are you so boring today?

IVANOV: I've got a headache, Shurochka, and I'm bored . . .

SASHA: Let's go into the drawing-room.

[*They go out of the right-hand door; everyone else goes out into the garden except ZINAIDA SAVISHNA and LEBEDEV.*]

ZINAIDA SAVISHNA: Now there's my idea of a young man: he's only been here a minute and he's cheered everyone up. [*Turns down the big lamp.*] While they're all in the garden there's no point in the candles burning uselessly. [*Puts out the candles.*]

LEBEDEV [*walking behind her*]: Zyuzyushka, we must give our guests something to eat . . .

ZINAIDA SAVISHNA: Oh what a lot of candles . . . that's why people think we're rich. [*Puts them out.*]

LEBEDEV: Zyuzyushka, really you should give people something to eat . . . They're young, and probably hungry, poor things . . . Zyuzyushka . . .

ZINAIDA SAVISHNA: The Count didn't finish his glass of tea. The sugar's just been wasted. [*She goes out by the left-hand door.*]

[*LEBEDEV spits contemptuously and goes out into the garden.*]

VI

[*Enter* IVANOV *and* SASHA.]

SASHA [*entering with Ivanov by the right-hand door*]: Everyone's gone
out into the garden.

IVANOV: That's how it is, Shurochka. Once I worked hard and
thought a lot but I never got tired; now I do nothing and think of
nothing, but I'm tired in body and spirit. My conscience aches
day and night, I feel deeply guilty but I don't understand where I
am actually at fault. And add to that my wife's illness, my lack of
money, the constant bickering, gossip, unnecessary conversations,
that stupid Borkin . . . My home has become loathsome to me
and I find living there worse than torture. I'll tell you frankly,
Sasha, I can't even stand the company of my wife who loves me.
You are my old friend and you won't be angry at my openness. I
came to your house to find entertainment, but I'm bored here too,
and I want to go home again. Forgive me, I'll now quietly go
away.

SASHA: Nikolay Alekseyevich, I understand you. Your unhappiness
lies in the fact that you're lonely. You need someone by you to
love and understand you. Only love can renew you.

IVANOV: A great idea, Shurochka. It only remains for this sodden
old rooster to strike up a new romance! God keep me from such
a misfortune! No, my clever young thing, it's not a question of
romance. I say as before God that I will endure everything –
depression and mental illness and ruin and the loss of my wife
and premature old age and loneliness – but I cannot tolerate,
cannot endure being ridiculous in my own eyes. I'm dying of
shame at the thought that I, a healthy, strong man, have turned
into some sort of Hamlet or Manfred,[16] some sort of 'superfluous
man'[17] . . . devil knows precisely what! There are pitiful people
who are flattered by being called Hamlet or superfluous men, but
for me it's a disgrace! It stirs up my pride, I'm overcome by shame
and I suffer . . .

SASHA [*laughing but with tears in her eyes*]: Nikolay Alekseyevich, let's run off to America.

IVANOV: I feel too lazy to get to that door, and you're talking about America . . . [*They go towards the doors to the garden.*] Shurochka, your life here is really difficult. When I look at the people around you, I'm afraid: who could you marry here? There's only the hope that some passing subaltern or student will steal you and carry you off . . .

VII

[*The same and* ZINAIDA SAVISHNA.]

[*Enter* ZINAIDA SAVISHNA *by the left-hand door with a pot of jam.*]

IVANOV: I'm sorry, Shurochka, I'll catch up with you . . .

[SASHA *goes out into the garden.*]

Zinaida Savishna, I have a request to make of you . . .

ZINAIDA SAVISHNA: What do you want, Nikolay Alekseyevich?

IVANOV [*stuttering*]: You see, the fact is, the day after tomorrow is the payment date of my promissory note. You would oblige me extremely if you granted a deferment or allowed me to add the interest to the capital sum. At the moment I have absolutely no money . . .

ZINAIDA SAVISHNA [*in a panic*]: Nikolay Alekseyevich, how can you? What a way to behave! No, don't argue, for God's sake, don't torment an unhappy creature . . .

IVANOV: I'm sorry, I'm sorry . . . [*Goes out into the garden.*]

ZINAIDA SAVISHNA: Lord how he frightened me! . . . I'm all of a tremble . . . all of a tremble . . . [*Goes out by the right-hand door.*]

VIII

[KOSYKH.]

KOSYKH [*enters by the left-hand door and crosses the stage*]: I had in diamonds ace, king, queen and a sequence of eight, the ace of spades and one . . . one little heart, and devil take the woman, she couldn't declare a little slam! [*Goes out by the right-hand door.*]

IX

[AVDOTYA NAZAROVNA *and* FIRST GUEST.]

AVDOTYA NAZAROVNA [*coming out of the garden with the First Guest*]: I'd like to tear her to pieces, the old skinflint . . . I'd just like to tear her up! It's no joke, I've been sitting here since five o'clock and she hasn't even offered me a bit of elderly herring! . . . What a house! . . . What a household! . . .

FIRST GUEST: It's so frightfully boring that I'd simply like to run off and bang my head on a wall! And the Lord have mercy on us! . . . You could howl like a wolf and start to devour people from sheer boredom and hunger . . .

AVDOTYA NAZAROVNA: Sinner that I am, I'd like to tear her to pieces.

FIRST GUEST: I'll have a drink, my old dear, and then – off home! I don't need your brides. To hell with it, what kind of love is there to feel here if one hasn't been offered a glass of vodka since dinner?

AVDOTYA NAZAROVNA: Let's go and have a look, shall we . . .

FIRST GUEST: Shh! . . . Quietly. I think there's some schnapps in the dining-room, it's standing on the sideboard. We'll get hold of Yegorushka . . . Shh! . . .

[*They go out by the left-hand door.*]

X

[ANNA PETROVNA *and* LVOV *enter by the right-hand door.*]

ANNA PETROVNA: Don't worry, they'll be pleased to see us. There isn't anyone. They must be in the garden.

LVOV: Now why, I ask, have you brought me here to these birds of prey? This is not a place for you and me. Honest people ought not to have any knowledge of this atmosphere!

ANNA PETROVNA: Listen, Mr Honesty! It is impolite to escort a lady and to spend the whole journey talking to her solely about your own honesty! It may be honest, but at the very least it's boring. Never talk to women about your own good qualities. Let them find out for themselves. When he was your age, my Nikolay, in the company of women, only used to sing songs and tell stories, but at the same time every woman knew what kind of a man he was.

LVOV: Oh don't talk to me about your Nikolay, I understand him very well!

ANNA PETROVNA: You are a good man, but you understand nothing. Let's go into the garden. He never used expressions like: 'I am honest. This atmosphere oppresses me. Birds of prey. Owl's nest. Crocodiles.' He left the menagerie out of it, but when he got angry, then I only used to hear from him 'Oh how unfair I was today!' or 'Anyuta, I'm sorry for that man.' That's how he was, but you . . .

[*They go out.*]

XI

[AVDOTYA NAZAROVNA *and* FIRST GUEST.]

FIRST GUEST [*coming out of the left-hand door*]: It's not in the dining-room, so it must be somewhere in the larder. We must get it out of Yegorushka. Let's go through the drawing-room.
AVDOTYA NAZAROVNA: I'd just like to tear her to pieces! . . .

[*They go out by the right-hand door.*]

XII

[BABAKINA, BORKIN *and* SHABELSKY.]

[BABAKINA *and* BORKIN *run in from the garden, laughing;* SHABELSKY *minces in after them laughing and rubbing his hands.*]

BABAKINA: It's so boring! [*Laughs loudly.*] So boring! They're all walking about and sitting bolt upright as if they'd swallowed a ruler! All their bones have become stiff from boredom. [*Jumps.*] I must loosen up! . . .

[BORKIN *takes her by the waist and kisses her on the cheek.*]

SHABELSKY [*laughing and snapping his fingers*]: The devil! [*Grunts.*] In a sort of way . . .
BABAKINA: Let go, let go of my arms, you shameless man, or Lord knows what the Count will think. Get off! . . .
BORKIN: Angel of my soul, carbuncle of my heart! . . . [*Kisses her.*] Lend me two thousand three hundred roubles . . .
BABAKINA: N-n-no . . . Whatever you like, but as far as money is concerned – thank you very much . . . No, no, no! . . . Oh let go of my arms! . . .

SHABELSKY [*mincing about beside them*]: The little Pompom . . . She has her charms . . .

BORKIN [*seriously*]: That's enough. Let's talk business and have a straightforward commercial discussion. Answer me directly, without fancy words and without any tricks: yes or no? Listen. [*Points at the Count.*] He needs money, at least three thousand per annum. You need a husband. Do you want to be a countess?

SHABELSKY [*laughing loudly*]: What an amazing cynic!

BORKIN: Do you want to be a countess? Yes or no?

BABAKINA [*agitatedly*]: You're making things up, Misha, really . . . And these things aren't done like that, with a bang and a thump . . . If the Count wants to, he can himself and . . . and I don't see that so suddenly, all at once . . .

BORKIN: Well, he'll confuse the issue. It's a business matter . . . Yes or no?

SHABELSKY [*laughing and rubbing his hands*]: Is it actually happening? What the devil, are we really setting up this filthy business for me? Really? Little Pompom . . . [*Kisses Babakina on the cheek.*] My delicious creature! . . . My little pickle! . . .

BABAKINA: Stop, stop, you've got me all frightened . . . Go away, go away! . . . No, don't go away! . . .

BORKIN: Quick! Yes or no? We haven't time . . .

BABAKINA: Do you know what, Count? You come and stay with me for a few days . . . In my house we have fun, not like here . . . Come tomorrow . . . [*To Borkin*] You aren't saying all this as a joke, are you?

BORKIN [*crossly*]: Who would joke about serious matters?

BABAKINA: Stop, stop! . . . Oh, I feel faint! I feel faint! Countess . . . I feel faint! I'm falling . . .

[BORKIN *and* SHABELSKY, *laughing, take her arms and lead her out by the right-hand door, kissing her cheeks.*]

XIII

[IVANOV, SASHA, *then* ANNA PETROVNA. *Ivanov and Sasha run in from the garden.*]

IVANOV [*clutching his head in despair*]: Impossible! You mustn't, you mustn't, Shurochka! . . . Oh, you mustn't! . . .

SASHA [*with exhilaration*]: I love you madly . . . There's no sense in my life without you, no happiness, no joy! You are everything to me . . .

IVANOV: Why, why! Oh God, I understand nothing . . . Shurochka, you mustn't! . . .

SASHA: When I was a child you were my only joy; I loved you and your spirit as I loved myself, and now . . . I love you, Nikolay Alekseyevich . . . I'll go with you to the ends of the earth or wherever you want, even to the grave, only let it be quickly, for God's sake, or else I'll suffocate . . .

IVANOV [*bursting into happy laughter*]: What's all this? Do you mean, to begin life again? Do you, Shurochka? . . . My happiness! [*Draws her to him.*] My youth, my freshness . . .

[ANNA PETROVNA *enters from the garden and seeing her husband and Sasha stops transfixed.*]

Do you mean, to live? Do you? To go back to our task?

[*They kiss. After the kiss* IVANOV *and* SASHA *look round and see Anna Petrovna.*]

[*Appalled.*] Sara!

[*Curtain.*]

Act Three

Ivanov's study. A desk with a clutter of papers, books, bundles of documents, knick-knacks, revolvers; by the papers are a lamp, a decanter of vodka and a plate with herring, pieces of bread and pickled gherkins. On the walls are maps, pictures, rifles, pistols, reaping-hooks, whips, etc. Midday.

I

[SHABELSKY, LEBEDEV, BORKIN *and* PYOTR. SHABELSKY *and* LEBEDEV *are sitting on either side of the desk.* BORKIN *is midstage, astride a chair.* PYOTR *is standing by the door.*]

LEBEDEV: France has a clear and defined policy . . . The French know what they want. They just want to wipe out the Krauts, finish, but Germany, my friend, is playing a very different tune. Germany has many more birds in her sights than just France . . .[1]

SHABELSKY: Nonsense! . . . In my view the Germans are cowards and the French are cowards . . . They're just thumbing their noses at each other. Believe me, things will stop there. They won't fight.

BORKIN: And as I see it, why fight? What's the point of these armaments, congresses, expenditures? You know what I'd do? I'd gather together dogs from all over the country, give them a good dose of rabies[2] and let them loose in enemy country. In a month all my enemies would be running rabid.

LEBEDEV [*laughing*]: Look at him, he has a small head, but it's teeming with great ideas like the ocean with fish.

SHABELSKY: Genius!

LEBEDEV: Good luck to you and your jokes, Michel Michelich! [*Stopping laughing.*] So, gentlemen, 'Jomini, Jomini, but not a tiny word about vodka.'[3] *Repetatur!*[4]
[*Pours three glasses.*] Our good health . . .

[*They drink and eat.*]

Mother herring is the queen of all *zakuski.*[5]

SHABELSKY: Actually, no, gherkins are better . . . Scientists have been thinking since the creation of the world and they have invented nothing more brilliant than the gherkin in brine. [*To Pyotr*] Pyotr, go and bring some more gherkins and tell them in the kitchen to cook four little onion pies. Hot ones.

[PYOTR *goes out.*]

LEBEDEV: And it's a good idea to send vodka down with some caviare. But caviare done how? Here you need some intelligence . . . Take a quarter of pressed caviare, two heads of spring onion, olive oil, mix everything together, and just, you know, a squeeze of lemon over the lot . . . It's to die for! You'll go crazy from just the aroma.

BORKIN: And it's nice to have a bite of fried gudgeon after the vodka. Only you must know how to fry them. You need to clean them, then roll them in dry breadcrumbs and fry them quite hard so they crunch between the teeth . . . cr-cr-crunch . . .

SHABELSKY: Yesterday we had an excellent *zakuska* at Babakina's – white mushrooms.

LEBEDEV: Really . . .

SHABELSKY: Only they were prepared in a special way. You know, with onion, bay leaf and all kinds of spices. When they opened the saucepan, the steam from it, the aroma . . . just ecstasy!

LEBEDEV: So? *Repetatur*, gentlemen!

[*They drink.*]

Our good health ... [*Looks at his watch*.] I suppose I'll miss Nikolasha. It's time for me to go. You say mushrooms were served at Babakina's, but we haven't seen any yet at home. Tell me please, why the devil have you started visiting Marfutka?

SHABELSKY [*nodding at Borkin*]: He wants to marry me off to her ...

LEBEDEV: Marry? ... How old are you?

SHABELSKY: Sixty-two.

LEBEDEV: The perfect age to get married. And Marfutka is just the partner for you.

BORKIN: It's not a question of Marfutka but of Marfutka's cash.

LEBEDEV: So that's what you want – Marfutka's cash ... Wouldn't you like all the tea in China too?

BORKIN: But when our man is married and has his pockets full, then you'll see some tea. You'll be licking your lips.

SHABELSKY: God, he really is talking seriously. This genius is sure that I will listen to him and marry ...

BORKIN: What? Aren't you sure now?

SHABELSKY: You're out of your mind ... When was I sure? Huh ...

BORKIN: Thanks ... Thanks very much! So does this mean you want to let me down? Now I'll get married, now I won't ... the devil himself couldn't tell which, while I've given my word! So you won't marry?

SHABELSKY [*shaking his shoulders*]: He seriously ... An amazing man!

BORKIN [*getting angry*]: In that case why stir up an honest woman? She's gone crazy over the title, she doesn't sleep, she doesn't eat ... Is that something to make a joke about? ... Is that honest?

SHABELSKY [*clicking his fingers*]: But why in fact don't I set up the whole filthy business for myself? Why not? To spite everyone! I'll go and arrange it. My word of honour ... That'll be fun!

[*Enter* LVOV.]

II

[*The same and* LVOV.]

LEBEDEV: To Aesculapius[6] our most humble greetings . . . [*Gives Lvov his hand and sings*] 'Doctor, doctor, save me, I'm frightened to death of death . . .'
LVOV: Hasn't Nikolay Alekseyevich come yet?
LEBEDEV: No, I've been waiting for him for over an hour myself.

[LVOV *strides impatiently about the stage.*]

Well, dear chap, how is Anna Petrovna's health?
LVOV: Not good.
LEBEDEV [*sighing*]: Can one go and pay one's respects?
LVOV: No, please don't go. I think she's sleeping . . .

[*A pause.*]

LEBEDEV: She's so nice, so sweet . . . [*Sighs.*] On Shurochka's birthday, when she fainted at our house, I looked at her face and I knew then that the poor thing didn't have long to live. I don't understand why she felt unwell then. I ran in and looked, she was lying on the floor, very pale; Nikolasha was by her on his knees, he was pale too; Shurochka was all in tears. After that happened Shurochka and I went about for a week as if we were demented.
SHABELSKY [*to Lvov*]: Tell me, esteemed priest of science, what man of learning discovered that in cases of chest illness it is beneficial for ladies to have the frequent visits of a young doctor? It's a great discovery. A great one! Is it allopathy or homeopathy?

[LVOV *is about to answer but makes a contemptuous gesture with his hand and goes out.*]

What an devastating look.

LEBEDEV: The devil's really got hold of your tongue. Why did you offend him?

SHABELSKY [*angrily*]: But why does he tell lies? Consumption, no hope, she'll die . . . He's lying! I can't tolerate it!

LEBEDEV: Why do you think he's lying?

SHABELSKY [*standing up and walking about*]: I can't admit the notion that a living human being suddenly dies for no good reason. Let's stop this conversation.

III

[LEBEDEV, SHABELSKY, BORKIN *and* KOSYKH.]

KOSYKH [*running in out of breath*]: Is Nikolay Alekseyevich at home? Good afternoon. [*Quickly shakes everyone's hand.*] Is he at home?

BORKIN: He isn't here.

KOSYKH [*sitting down and jumping up again*]: In that case goodbye. [*Drinks a glass of vodka and has a quick bite of food.*] I'll drive on . . . Business . . . I'm worn out . . . I can hardly stand on my legs . . .

LEBEDEV: Where have you blown in from?

KOSYKH: From Barabanov's. We played whist[7] all night, we've only just stopped . . . I lost my lot . . . That Barabanov plays dreadfully! [*Plaintively*] Listen: I'm holding hearts the whole time . . . [*Turns to Borkin, who starts away from him.*] He leads with diamonds, I play hearts again, he plays diamonds . . . Well, we don't win a trick. [*To Lebedev*] We play four clubs, I have in my hand ace, queen and six, in spades ace, ten and three . . .

LEBEDEV [*blocking his ears*]: Spare us, spare us, for Christ's sake, spare us!

KOSYKH [*to the Count*]: You understand, in clubs ace, queen and six, in spades ace, ten and three . . .

SHABELSKY [*pushing him away with his hands*]: Go away, I don't want to listen!

KOSYKH: And suddenly, disaster: the ace of spades is taken in the first hand . . .

SHABELSKY [*grabbing a revolver from the desk*]: Go away, I'll shoot! . . .

KOSYKH [*throwing up his hand*]: What the hell . . . Is there really no one even to talk to? We might as well be living in Australia: no common interests, no solidarity . . . Everyone lives separate lives . . . But I must go . . . it's time. [*Takes his cap.*] Time is precious . . . [*Gives Lebedev his hand.*] I pass! . . .

[*Laughter.*]

[KOSYKH *goes out and in the doorway collides with Avdotya Nazarovna.*]

IV

[SHABELSKY, LEBEDEV, BORKIN *and* AVDOTYA NAZAROVNA.]

AVDOTYA NAZAROVNA [*shrieking*]: Drat you – knocking me over!

ALL: Aha-a-a! . . . One can't get away from her! . . .

ADVOTYA NAZAROVNA: There they are, and I've been looking all over the house. Good day, my masters, greetings . . . [*Greets them.*]

LEBEDEV: Why have you come here?

AVDOTYA NAZAROVNA: On a matter of business, sir. [*To the Count*] Business concerning you, Your Highness. [*Bows.*] She asked me to greet you and enquire after your health . . . and my little pet asked me to say that if you don't come by this evening, she will cry her pretty eyes out. The dear girl said, take him aside and whisper privately in his ear. But why privately? Here we're all among friends. And in this business matter we're not stealing chickens, we're acting by law and by love, by mutual consent. For my sins, I never drink, but on such an occasion I will have a drink!

LEBEDEV: And I'll have one. [*Pours.*] And you, my old starling, you're everlasting. I've known you as an old woman for thirty years now . . .

AVDOTYA NAZAROVNA: And I've lost count of the years. I've buried two husbands and I'd have still gone for a third, but nobody wants to take you without a dowry. There were eight children . . . [*Takes a glass.*] Well, God willing we've started something good, God willing we'll complete it! They will live happily ever after and we will look at them and be glad. We'll give them our advice and our love . . . [*Drinks.*] This is some vodka!

SHABELSKY [*laughing loudly, to Lebedev*]: But you see, what is strangest of all is that they seriously think that I . . . Amazing! [*Gets up.*] Pasha, but why in fact don't I do the filthy deed myself? To spite everyone . . . There, he says, you old dog, eat! How about it, Pasha? Really . . .

LEBEDEV: You're talking nonsense, Count. You and I, my friend, should be thinking about meeting our maker, the Marfutkas and their cash have left us behind long ago . . . Our time has passed.

SHABELSKY: No, I will arrange it. I will, word of honour!

[*Enter* IVANOV *and* LVOV.]

V

[*The same,* IVANOV *and* LVOV.]

LVOV: I ask you to find me just five minutes.

LEBEDEV: Nikolasha! [*Goes to meet Ivanov and kisses him.*] How are you, old chap? . . . I've been waiting for you a whole hour.

AVDOTYA NAZAROVNA [*bowing*]: Good day, sir.

IVANOV [*bitterly*]: Gentlemen, you've again set up a drinking shop in my study . . . I have asked each and every one of you a thousand times not to do that . . . [*Goes to the desk.*] Look now, you've spilt vodka on a paper . . . and there are crumbs . . . and gherkins . . . It's disgusting!

LEBEDEV: I'm sorry, Nikolasha, I'm sorry . . . Forgive me. I need a word with you, my friend, on something very important . . .

BORKIN: So do I.

LVOV: Nikolay Alekseyevich, can I speak to you?

IVANOV [*pointing at Lebedev*]: He wants me too. Wait, you next . . . [*To Lebedev*] What do you want?

LEBEDEV: Gentlemen, I want to speak privately. Please . . .

[THE COUNT *goes out with* AVDOTYA NAZAROVNA, *followed by* BORKIN, *then* LVOV.]

IVANOV: Pasha, you yourself can drink as much as you like, that is your illness, but I do ask you not to make a drunk of my uncle. He used never to drink in my house. It's bad for him.

LEBEDEV [*sounding alarmed*]: My dear chap, I didn't know . . . I didn't pay any attention . . .

IVANOV: If that old boy dies, God forbid, it won't be your loss but mine . . . What do you want? . . .

[*A pause.*]

LEBEDEV: You see, my dear friend . . . I don't know how to begin so it doesn't seem so outrageous . . . Nikolasha, I'm ashamed, I'm blushing, I'm tongue-tied, but enter into my situation, old chap, and understand that I'm not my own master but just a Negro slave, an old rag . . . Forgive me . . .

IVANOV: What is the problem?

LEBEDEV: My wife sent me . . . Do me a favour, be a friend and pay her the interest. Believe me, she's driven me crazy, she's worn me out and made my life hell! For God's sake, get free of her! . . .

IVANOV: Pasha, you know that at the moment I have no money.

LEBEDEV: I know, I know, but what am I to do? She won't wait. If she calls in the promissory note, how will I and Shurochka be able to look you in the face?

IVANOV: I'm ashamed myself, Pasha, I'd like the earth to swallow me up, but . . . but where am I to find it? Tell me, where? One course remains: wait till the autumn when I sell the corn.

LEBEDEV [*shouting*]: She won't wait!

[*A pause.*]

IVANOV: Your situation is delicate and unpleasant, but mine is even worse. [*Walks about thinking.*] And I can't come up with anything . . . There's nothing to sell . . .

LEBEDEV: You could go to Milbakh and ask, he owes you sixteen thousand roubles . . .

[IVANOV *desperately gestures with his hand.*]

Look, Nikolasha . . . I know, you're going to swear, but think kindly of an old drunk! As a friend . . . Look on me as a friend . . . You and I were students, liberals . . . We have common ideas and common interests . . . We were both at Moscow University . . . Our *alma mater*[8] . . . [*Takes out his wallet.*] I've got this private nest-egg, not a soul at home knows about it. Take it as a loan . . . [*Puts the money on the table.*] Swallow your pride and look on me as a friend . . . I'd take it from you, I promise . . .

[*A pause.*]

There it is on the table, one thousand one hundred. Go to her today and give it to her yourself. There you are, Zinaida Savishna, you'll say, now choke on it! Only, God alive, be careful not to give any hint that you borrowed from me! Otherwise I'll really get it from old Gooseberry Jam! [*Looks closely at Ivanov's expression.*] Well, well, you don't have to! [*Quickly takes the money from the table and hides it in his pocket.*] You don't have to! I was joking . . . For Christ's sake, I'm sorry!

[*A pause.*]

Do you feel sick at heart?

[IVANOV *gestures with his hand.*]

Yes, things . . . [*Sighs.*] A time has come of sorrow and sadness for you. Man, my dear friend, is like a samovar. It doesn't always stand on a shelf in the chill but sometimes they put hot coals in it and it goes psh . . . psh! This comparison is worthless but you won't think up a cleverer one . . . [*Sighs.*] Misfortunes harden the soul. I'm not sorry for you. You'll come out of this trouble, Nikolasha, it'll all be all right in the end, but I'm offended, old chap, and saddened by people . . . Tell me, please do, where this gossip comes from. There is so much gossip about you going round the district that any minute you'll have a visit from the Deputy Public Prosecutor . . . You're a murderer and a vampire and a thief and an adulterer . . .

IVANOV: That's all nonsense, now I've got a headache.

LEBEDEV: All because you think a lot.

IVANOV: I don't think at all.

LEBEDEV: Nikolasha, spit on it all and come and see us. Shurochka loves you, understands you and appreciates you. Nikolasha, she's an honest, good person. She doesn't take after either her father or her mother, but it must be after the proverbial knight passing by . . . I sometimes look, my friend, and do not believe that such a treasure can belong to me, to this bloated-nosed drunk. Come and visit, talk to her about intelligent things and – relax. She is a loyal, sincere human being.

[*A pause.*]

IVANOV: Pasha, dear chap, leave me on my own . . .

LEBEDEV: I understand, I understand . . . [*Quickly looks at his watch.*] I do understand. [*Kisses Ivanov.*] Goodbye. I still have to go to the consecration of a school. [*Goes to the door and stops.*] She is clever . . . Yesterday Shurochka and I started talking about the gossip. [*Laughs.*] And she fired off an aphorism: 'Papa,' she said, 'fireflies only shine at night so that the night birds can see them more clearly and eat them, and good people exist so that slander and gossip have something to eat.' What do you think of that? A genius! A George Sand!⁹ . . .

IVANOV: Pasha! [*Stops him.*] What's the matter with me?

LEBEDEV: I wanted to ask you that myself but I confess I held back. I don't know, old friend. On the one hand I thought you were being overwhelmed by various misfortunes, on the other you're not the kind of man to let that . . . Trouble won't bring you down. It's something else, Nikolasha, but what – I don't understand.

IVANOV: I myself don't understand. I think, either . . . but no!

[*A pause.*]

You see, this is what I wanted to say. I had a workman, Semyon, whom you will remember. Once at threshing time he wanted to show off his strength before the girls, he heaved two sacks of rye up on to his back and overstrained himself. He died soon after. I think I must have overstrained myself too. The Gymnasium,¹⁰ university, then running the estate, schools, projects . . . My religious beliefs weren't like everyone else's, nor was my marriage, I became excited, I took risks, I threw my money right and left, as you yourself know, I've been happy and I've suffered like no one else in the entire district. All that, Pasha, is my two sacks of rye . . . I heaved the load up on to my back and my back broke. At twenty we are all heroes, we take on everything, we can do everything, and at thirty we're already worn out, we're good for nothing. How, how do you explain this tendency to exhaustion? But perhaps it's not that . . . Not that at all! . . . Go, Pasha, bless you, I've been a nuisance to you.

LEBEDEV [*animatedly*]: Do you know what? You've got depressed by your environment, my friend.

IVANOV: That's silly, Pasha, and it's been said before. On your way!

LEBEDEV: Indeed it's silly! I see now myself that it's silly. I'm going, I'm going! . . . [*Exit.*]

VI

[IVANOV, *then* LVOV.]

IVANOV [*alone*]: I am a bad, pathetic and worthless individual. One needs to be pathetic too, worn out and drained by drink, like Pasha, to be still fond of me and to respect me. My God, how I despise myself! I so deeply loathe my voice, my walk, my hands, these clothes, my thoughts. Well, isn't that funny, isn't that shocking? Less than a year ago I was healthy and strong, I was cheerful, tireless, passionate, I worked with these very hands, I could speak to move even Philistines to tears, I could cry when I saw grief, I became indignant when I encountered evil. I knew inspiration, I knew the charm and poetry of quiet nights when from dusk to dawn you sit at your desk or indulge your mind with dreams. I believed, I looked into the future as into the eyes of my own mother . . . And now, my God, I am exhausted, I do not believe, I spend my days and nights in idleness. I can't control my brain, my hands, my legs. The estate is going to the dogs, the woods are crashing down before the axe. [*Weeps.*] My land looks at me like an orphan. I have nothing to look forward to, nothing moves me to pity, my soul trembles with fear of tomorrow . . . And my story with Sara? I swore eternal love, I prophesied our happiness, I opened before her eyes a future such as she had not seen even in her dreams. She believed me. In the whole five years I have only seen her fade under the weight of her sacrifices, seen her worn out by her struggle with conscience, but, as God can see, not a sideways glance at me, not a word of reproach! . . . And what did I do? I stopped loving her . . . How? Why? What for? I do not understand. There she is suffering, her days are numbered, and like the worst of cowards I flee from her pale face and sunken chest and pleading eyes . . . I'm ashamed, ashamed!

[*A pause.*]

A young girl, Sasha, is touched by my misfortunes. She declares her love for me – for someone who is virtually an old man[11] – and I am intoxicated, I forget everything in the world, I feel a spell like music's, and I cry, 'A new life! Happiness!' And the next day I believe in that life and that happiness as little as I do in the house goblin[12] . . . What is the matter with me? Into what abyss am I driving my life? What is wrong with my nerves? It only takes a sick wife to prick my self-esteem, or if a maid fails to please or a gun misfires, then I become rude, foul-tempered and unlike myself . . .

[*A pause.*]

I don't understand, I don't understand, I do not understand! Why don't I just put a bullet through my forehead! . . .

LVOV [*entering*]: I need to have a candid talk with you, Nikolay Alekseyevich.

IVANOV: Doctor, if we're going to have a candid talk every day, I haven't the strength for it.

LVOV: Would you be good enough to hear me out?

IVANOV: Every day I hear you out and I still fail to understand what actually it is you want from me.

LVOV: I speak clearly and precisely, and only someone without a heart could fail to understand me . . .

IVANOV: That my wife is close to death – I know; that I am irreparably guilty before her – I also know; that you are an honest, straight man – I know too! What more do you want?

LVOV: I am indignant at human cruelty . . . A woman is dying. She has a father and a mother whom she loves and whom she would like to see before she dies; they know very well that she will die soon and that she still loves them, but – damnable cruelty – it's as if they want to amaze Jehovah with their religious rigour: they still curse her! You, a man for whom she sacrificed everything – her faith, her own home, tranquillity of conscience – you in the most obvious way and with the most obvious intentions drive over every day to those Lebedevs!

IVANOV: Ah, I haven't been there now for two weeks . . .

LVOV [*not listening to him*]: With people like you one needs to speak directly, with no beating about the bush, and if you don't feel like listening to me, then don't! I'm accustomed to calling things by their proper name . . . You need this death to achieve new feats of valour; maybe you do, but could you really not wait? If you let her die in the natural way of things and didn't go on breaking her with your arrant cynicism, would Lebedeva with her dowry really leave you? If not now, then in a year or in two years you would have time, you amazing hypocrite, to turn the girl's head and get hold of her dowry just as effectively as now . . . Why are you in a hurry? Why do you need your wife to die now and not in a month, in a year? . . .

IVANOV: This is torment. Doctor, you're a very bad physician if you assume a man can restrain himself for ever. It costs me a terrible effort not to reply to your insults.

LVOV: Enough. Who do you want to fool? Drop that mask.

IVANOV: You clever man, just reflect. You think I'm the easiest thing in the world to understand. Right? I married Anna to get a large dowry . . . They gave me no dowry, I made a mistake and now I am hounding her from this world to marry another woman and take her dowry . . . Yes? How easy and straightforward . . . Man is such a simple and uncomplicated machine . . . No, doctor, we all have too many wheels, screws and valves for us to be able to judge each other by first impressions or from two or three external indications. I don't understand you, you don't understand me, and we don't understand ourselves. One can be an excellent doctor – and at the same time have absolutely no knowledge of people. Drop your self-assurance and agree with that.

LVOV: Do you really think you are so opaque and I have so little brain that I can't distinguish wrong-doing from honesty?

IVANOV: We are clearly never going to see eye to eye . . . For the last time I ask, and please give an answer without preamble, what actually do you want from me? What are you aiming for? [*Irritatedly*] And whom do I have the honour of addressing – my prosecutor, or my wife's doctor?

LVOV: I am a doctor and as a doctor I demand that you alter your behaviour . . . It is killing Anna Petrovna.

IVANOV: But what am I to do? What? If you understand me better than I understand myself, speak frankly: What am I to do?

LVOV: At the very least, don't act so publicly.

IVANOV: Oh, my God! Do you really understand yourself? [*Drinks some water.*] Leave me. I am a thousand times guilty, I will answer before God, but no one authorized you to torture me every day . . .

LVOV: But who authorized you to insult the truth in me? You have poisoned my spirit and made me suffer. Until I ended up in this district, I assumed there were fools, lunatics, people who had affairs, but I never believed that there were criminal persons who deliberately and consciously directed their will towards evil . . . I respected and loved human beings, but when I saw you . . .

IVANOV: I've heard all this already!

LVOV: Have you? [*Sees* SASHA *coming in; she is wearing a riding habit.*] Now, I hope, we understand one another very well! [*Shrugs his shoulders and goes out.*]

VII

[IVANOV *and* SASHA.]

IVANOV [*alarmed*]: Shura, you here?

SASHA: Yes, me. How are you? Didn't you expect me? Why haven't you been to see us for so long?

IVANOV: Shura, for God's sake, this is risky! Your coming here could have a terrible effect on my wife.

SASHA: She won't see me. I came in by the back door. I'll leave at once. I'm worried: are you all right? Why haven't you come for so long?

IVANOV: As it is, my wife has already been deeply hurt, she's almost dying, and you come here. Shura, Shura, this is thoughtless and inhuman!

SASHA: What was I to do? You haven't been to see us for two weeks, you haven't answered my letters. I'm worn out, I thought you must be suffering here unbearably, that you were ill, that you were dead. I haven't had a single night's calm sleep. I'll go away now . . . At least tell me if you are well.

IVANOV: No, I've worn myself out, people never stop plaguing me . . . I simply don't have the strength. And you're still here! What unhealthy and abnormal behaviour! Shura, I'm so much to blame, so much to blame . . .

SASHA: How you love saying fearsome and pathetic things! So you're to blame? Are you? To blame? Well, tell me then, for what?

IVANOV: I don't know, I don't know . . .

SASHA: That's not an answer. Every sinner must know his sin. Have you been forging banknotes or something?

IVANOV: That's not funny!

SASHA: Are you to blame for having stopped loving your wife? Perhaps, but a man is not master of his feelings, you didn't want to stop loving her. Are you to blame that she saw me declare my love to you? No, you didn't want her to see that . . .

IVANOV [*interrupting*]: And so on, and so on . . . Fell in love, fell out of love, not master of his feelings – these are all commonplaces, hackneyed phrases, and they don't help . . .

SASHA: It's exhausting talking to you. [*Looks at a picture.*] How well that dog is drawn. Is it from life?

IVANOV: Yes, from life. And this whole romance of ours is commonplace and trite: he lost heart, and he lost his way. She came along, strong and brave in spirit, and gave him a helping hand. That's all very well and plausible in novels, but in life . . .

SASHA: In life it's the same.

IVANOV: I see you have a fine understanding of life! My whining inspires a holy awe in you, you imagine you've discovered a second Hamlet in me, but in my view my psychopathic character, with all its baggage, can only serve as a good object for ridicule, and nothing more! You should howl with laughter at my affectations till you drop, but instead you sound the alarm! You want to save me, to perform a heroic feat! I feel so bitter today towards myself! I feel that my tension today will be ended by something . . . Either I'll break something, or . . .

SASHA: Now that's exactly what you need. Break something, smash it or shout. You're angry with me, I was stupid in deciding to come here. So lose your temper, shout at me, stamp your feet. Why not? Start getting angry . . .

[*A pause.*]

Why not?

IVANOV: You are being funny.

SASHA: Excellent. I think we're smiling. Please be so kind as to smile once more!

IVANOV [*laughing*]: I've noticed something: when you start to rescue me and teach me common sense, then your expression becomes very, very naive and the pupils of your eyes become wide as if you were looking at a comet. Wait, your shoulder's covered in dust. [*Brushes the dust from her shoulder.*] A naive man is a fool. But you women are clever enough to be naive so that it comes out in you as engaging and healthy and warm, and not so silly as it might seem. Only why do you all behave like this? While a man is healthy and strong and in good spirits, you pay him no attention, but as soon as he rolls down the slippery slope and starts complaining about his woes, you hang on his neck. Is it really worse to be the wife of a strong and courageous man than to be the nurse of some snivelling failure?

SASHA: Yes, it's worse!

IVANOV: Why? [*Laughs.*] Darwin knew nothing about this, otherwise he'd have told you off! You're spoiling the human race. Thanks to the likes of you there'll soon be only whiners and psychopaths born into the world.

SASHA: Men don't understand a lot of things. Every young girl is going to be drawn more to a failure than to a successful man, because they're all attracted by the notion of active love . . . Do you understand? Active. Men are busy with their work, and therefore for them love is something right in the background. A conversation with the wife, a stroll with her in the garden, a nice time, a cry on her grave – that's all. But for us love is life. I love you, that means that I dream of how I'll cure you of your depression, of how I'll go with you to the ends of the earth . . . When you're up, so am I; when you're down, so am I. For example, it would be a great happiness for me to spend all night copying out your papers or watching that no one woke you, or to walk a hundred versts with you. I remember once, three years ago, at threshing time, you came to us all covered with dust, sunburnt and exhausted, and asked for a drink. I brought you a glass but you were already lying on the sofa and sleeping like the dead. You slept in our house for twelve hours and the whole time I stood guard outside your door so that no one came in. And I felt so happy! The more work there is, the better love is – that is, the more strongly love is felt, do you see.

IVANOV: Active love . . . Hm . . . It blights everything, a young girl's philosophy, or perhaps that's the way things ought to be . . . [*Shrugs his shoulders.*] The devil only knows! [*Cheerfully*] Shura, I swear, I'm a decent man! . . . Think about this: I have always liked to philosophize, but I've never in my life said, 'Our women are depraved' or 'Woman has set out on the wrong road.' I've just been grateful and nothing more! That's all. My dear, beautiful girl, how entertaining you are! And what a ridiculous idiot I am! I embarrass God-fearing people, I spend whole days being sorry for myself. [*Laughs.*] Boo-hoo! Boo-hoo! [*Quickly moves away.*] But go away, Sasha! We've forgotten ourselves . . .

SASHA: Yes, it's time for me to go. Goodbye! I'm afraid your honest doctor might report my presence here to Anna Petrovna out of a sense of duty. Listen to me: go now to your wife and stay with her, stay, stay . . . If you have to stay a year – then stay for a year. If ten years – then stay for ten years. Do your duty. Grieve and ask her forgiveness and weep – all that just as it should be. But most of all don't forget your task in life.

IVANOV: Again I feel as if I've been gorging on toadstools. Again!

SASHA: Well, God preserve you! You needn't think of me at all. In two weeks you can scribble me a line – and I'll be grateful even for that. And I will write to you . . .

[BORKIN *looks in through the doorway*.]

VIII

[*The same and* BORKIN.]

BORKIN: Nikolay Alekseyevich, may I? [*Seeing Sasha*] I'm sorry, I hadn't seen you . . . [*Enters*.] *Bonjour!* [*Bows*.]

SASHA [*embarrassed*]: How are you? . . .

BORKIN: You've become a little plumper and prettier.

SASHA [*to Ivanov*]: Well, I'm going, Nikolay Alekseyevich . . . I'm going. [*Goes out*.]

BORKIN: What a wonderful vision! I came for prose and found poetry . . . [*Sings*] 'Thou cam'st like a bird to the light.'

[IVANOV *agitatedly walks about the stage*.]

[BORKIN *sits down*.] And, Nicolas, she has something, a sort of something which other women lack. Doesn't she? Something special . . . dreamlike . . . [*Sighs*.] In fact, she's the richest bride in the whole district, but her Mama's such a nightmare that no one wants the connection. After her death everything will go to Shurochka, but before her death she'll give her ten thousand, a flatiron and another iron for goffering, and she'll make her kiss her feet for that. [*Rummages in his pockets*.] I'll smoke a De los Majoros. Would you like one? [*Offers him his cigar case*.] They're good. A man can smoke them.

IVANOV [*going up to Borkin, choking with rage*]: Get out of my house this minute! This minute!

[BORKIN *half-rises and drops his cigar*.]

Get out this minute!

BORKIN: Nicolas, what does this mean? Why are you angry?

IVANOV: Why? And where do you get these cigars from? And do you think that I don't know where you take the old fellow every day, and what for?

BORKIN [*shrugging his shoulders*]: What's it to you?

IVANOV: What a scoundrel you are! Your dirty projects which you've scattered over the district have made me a dishonest man in people's eyes! We have nothing in common and I ask you to leave my house this minute! [*Walks about quickly.*]

BORKIN: I know you're saying all this out of irritation and so I'm not getting angry with you. Insult me as much as you want . . . [*Picks up his cigar.*] But it's time to drop the melancholy. You're not a schoolboy . . .

IVANOV: What did I say to you? [*Trembling*] Are you making fun of me!

[*Enter* ANNA PETROVNA.]

IX

[*The same and* ANNA PETROVNA.]

BORKIN: Well, Anna Petrovna has come . . . I shall go. [*Goes out.*]

[IVANOV *stops by the desk and stands with bowed head.*]

ANNA PETROVNA [*after a pause*]: Why did she come here just now?

[*A pause.*]

I'm asking you: why did she come here?

IVANOV: Don't ask me, Anyuta . . .

[*A pause.*]

I am deeply at fault. Think up whatever punishment you want, I shall endure it, but . . . don't ask . . . I haven't the strength to talk.

ANNA PETROVNA [*angrily*]: Why was she here?

[*A pause.*]

Ah, so that's what you're like! Now I understand you. At last I see what kind of a man you are. Low and dishonourable . . . Do you remember, you came to me and lied to me that you loved me . . . I believed you and abandoned my father, my mother, my faith, and followed you . . . You told me lies about truth, about good, about your honourable plans, I believed every word . . .

IVANOV: Anyuta, I never lied to you . . .

ANNA PETROVNA: I've lived with you for five years, tormented and made ill by the thought that I betrayed my faith, but I've loved you and never left you for a single moment . . . You were my idol . . . And what happened? All this time you've been deceiving me in the most brazen way . . .

IVANOV: Anyuta, don't tell untruths. I've made mistakes, yes, but I've never once told a lie in my life . . . Don't dare to reproach me for that . . .

ANNA PETROVNA: I can understand it all now . . . You married me and thought that my father and mother would forgive me, would give me money . . . You thought that . . .

IVANOV: Oh my God! Anyuta, don't try my patience like this . . . [*Weeps.*]

ANNA PETROVNA: Be quiet! When you saw there was no money, you started a new game . . . Now I remember, I understand everything. [*Weeps.*] You never loved me and were true to me . . . Never! . . .

IVANOV: Sara, that's a lie! . . . Say what you will, but don't insult me with a lie . . .

ANNA PETROVNA: Low and dishonourable . . . You owe Lebedev money and now, to wriggle out of your debt, you're planning to turn his daughter's head, to deceive her as you have me. Is that a lie?

IVANOV [*choking*]: Stop, for God's sake! I can't answer for myself
. . . I'm choking with anger and I . . . I could insult you . . .

ANNA PETROVNA: You've always brazenly deceived me, and not
only me . . . You've laid all your dishonest actions on to Borkin,
but now I know whose they were . . .

IVANOV: Sara, stop, go away, or my tongue will let slip some word!
I'm just aching to say something terrible to you, something really
insulting . . . [*Shouts*] Shut your mouth, Yid! . . .

ANNA PETROVNA: I will not stop . . . You've deceived me too long
for me to be able to say nothing . . .

IVANOV: So you won't stop? [*Struggles with himself.*] For God's
sake . . .

ANNA PETROVNA: Now go and deceive Lebedeva . . .

IVANOV: Well then, you should know that you . . . will die soon
. . . The doctor told me you will die soon . . .

ANNA PETROVNA [*sitting down, in a weak voice*]: When did he say
that?

[*A pause.*]

IVANOV [*clutching his head*]: How guilty I am! God, how guilty!
[*Sobs.*]

[*Curtain.*]

[*About a year passes between Acts Three and Four.*]

Act Four

One of the drawing-rooms in Lebedev's house. In front is an arch dividing the drawing-room from a ballroom, right and left are doors. Antique bronzes, family portraits. Festive decorations. An upright piano, on it a violin, and beside them a cello. Throughout the whole act guests in evening dress are walking up and down the ballroom.

I

[LVOV.]

LVOV [*coming in and looking at his watch*]: After four. The blessing[1] should be beginning very soon . . . The blessing will take place and they'll be taken off to be married. Here is the triumph of virtue and truth! He didn't succeed in robbing Sara, he wore her out and laid her in her coffin, now he's found another one. He'll act a part in front of this one too till he has robbed her and having done so put her where poor Sara now lies. The old story of exploitation . . .

[*A pause.*]

He's in his seventh heaven, he'll live very well to a ripe old age and he'll die with an untroubled conscience. No, I shall expose you! When I rip that cursed mask from your face and when everyone sees what kind of a bird you are, I'll see you fly down head first from that seventh heaven into an abyss so deep that even the powers of darkness won't be able to drag you out! I am an honest man, it is my task to intervene and open the eyes of the blind. I shall fulfil my duty and tomorrow get out of this accursed district! [*Sinks into thought.*] But what should I do? Explain everything to the Lebedevs – a useless task. Challenge him to a duel? Create a scene? My God, I'm as nervous as a small boy, and I've quite lost the faculty of reason. What should I do? Fight a duel?

II

[LVOV *and* KOSYKH.]

KOSYKH [*entering, joyously to Lvov*]: Yesterday I declared a little slam in clubs but took a grand slam. Only that Barabanov spoilt everything for me again. We're playing. I say no trumps. He passes. Two clubs. He passes. I say two diamonds . . . three clubs . . . and imagine, just imagine: I declare a slam and he doesn't show his ace. If the wretched creature had shown his ace, I'd have declared a grand slam in no-trumps . . .

LVOV: Forgive me, I don't play cards and so I can't share your excitement. Will the blessing be soon?

KOSYKH: It must be soon. They've just brought Zyuzyushka round. She's bawling her head off, she's upset about the dowry.

LVOV: Not about her daughter?

KOSYKH: The dowry. And it is a problem. He's getting married, it means he won't repay the debt. You can't call in your son-in-law's promissory notes.

*

III

[*The same and* BABAKINA.]

BABAKINA [*all dressed up, sweeps across the stage past Lvov and Kosykh; the latter snorts with laughter into his hand; she looks round*]: Stupid!

[KOSYKH *touches her waist with a finger and laughs loudly.*]

Peasant! [*Goes out.*]

KOSYKH [*laughing*]: The woman's gone quite off her head. Until she had ideas about being a countess, she was just an ordinary woman, but now you can't get near her. [*Imitating her.*] Peasant!

LVOV [*getting worked up*]: Listen, tell me frankly: what's your opinion of Ivanov?

KOSYKH: He's no good. He plays like a cobbler. Last year during Lent we had this. We sit down to play – the Count, Borkin, him and me. I'm dealing . . .

LVOV [*interrupting*]: Is he a good man?

KOSYKH: Him? He's a terrible rogue! An old fox who's seen everything. He and the Count are two of a kind. They sniff out where there's a weak spot. He got hold of his Jewess, was swindled, and now he's trying to get into Zyuzyushka's coffers. I'll lay a bet, may I be three times cursed, that in a year's time he'll have reduced Zyuzyushka to beggary. He'll do that to Zyuzyushka, and the Count the same to Babakina. They'll make off with the money and live happily ever after. Doctor, why are you so pale today? You look awful.

LVOV: It's nothing, just one of those things. Yesterday I drank too much.

IV

[*The same,* LEBEDEV *and* SASHA.]

LEBEDEV [*entering with Sasha*]: Let's talk here. [*To Lvov and Kosykh*] Out, wild men, into the ballroom to the young ladies. We need to talk privately.

KOSYKH [*going past Sasha, enthusiastically snaps his fingers*]: What a picture! The queen of trumps!

LEBEDEV: Get out, caveman, get out!

[LVOV *and* KOSYKH *go out.*]

Sit down, Shurochka, so . . . [*Sits down and looks round.*] Do listen attentively and with proper respect. The thing is this: your mother told me to convey to you what I'm about to say . . . Do you understand? I am not going to be speaking for myself, but following your mother's instructions.

SASHA: Papa, do be more brief!

LEBEDEV: Your dowry is fixed at fifteen thousand silver roubles. Yes . . . Look, so there are no arguments later! Wait, be quiet! That's just the blossom, but there'll be berries too. Your dowry is fixed at fifteen thousand, but taking into account that Nikolay Alekseyevich owes your mother nine thousand, a deduction is being made from your dowry . . . Well, but later, apart from that . . .

SASHA: Why are you telling me this?

LEBEDEV: Your mother told me to!

SASHA: Leave me in peace! If you had some small respect for me and for yourself, you wouldn't allow yourself to talk to me in such a way. I don't need your dowry! I didn't ask for it and I won't ask for it!

LEBEDEV: Why are you attacking me? In Gogol the two rats sniffed around first and then went off, but with all your emancipation you've gone into the attack without even a sniff at what I have to say.[2]

SASHA: Leave me in peace, don't insult my ears with your petty calculations.

LEBEDEV [*losing his temper and spitting*]: The lot of you will either make me stick a knife into myself or else murder someone! One shouts and screeches day in day out, buzzes and nags, counts the kopecks, while the other, intelligent, a humanist and, devil take it, an emancipated woman, can't understand her own father! I insult your ears! And before I came here to insult your ears, in there [*points to the door*] I was being drawn and quartered. She can't understand! She's had her head turned and lost her senses . . . to hell with you! [*Goes to the door and stops.*] I don't like it, I don't like anything about any of you!

SASHA: What don't you like?

LEBEDEV: Everything! Everything!

SASHA: What do you mean, everything?

LEBEDEV: Look, I'm going to sit myself down in front of you and tell you. I don't like anything, and I can't even bear to look at your marriage! [*Comes up near to Sasha and speaks affectionately.*] You must forgive me, Shurochka, maybe your marriage is intelligent, honest, sublime, principled, but something there is not quite right, not right! It's not like other marriages. You are young, fresh, clean as a piece of glass, beautiful, and he is a widower, he's frayed, he's worn himself out. And I don't understand him, God help him. [*Kisses his daughter.*] Shurochka, forgive me but something is not quite right. Already people are talking a great deal. For some reason that Sara died on him, then somehow for some reason he suddenly wanted to marry you . . . [*Animatedly*] But I'm being an old woman, an old woman. I've become as feminine as a crinoline. Don't listen to me. Don't listen to anyone, only to yourself.

SASHA: Papa, I too myself feel that something's wrong . . . Wrong, wrong, wrong. If you knew how low I feel! It's unbearable! It's awkward and frightening to admit it. Papa, darling, raise my spirits . . . teach me what to do.

LEBEDEV: What do you mean? What?

SASHA: I'm so frightened, as never before. [*Looks round.*] I feel that

I don't understand him and that I never will understand him. Over the whole time of our engagement he has never smiled once, he has never once looked me straight in the eye. It's nothing but complaints, repentance for something or other, hints at some kind of guilt, trembling . . . I'm worn out. There are even moments when I think that I . . . I don't love him as strongly as I should. And when he comes over to us or talks to me, I get bored. Papa dear, what does all this mean? I'm frightened!

LEBEDEV: My darling, my only child, listen to your old father. Give him up!

SASHA [*fearfully*]: What are you saying, what are you saying?

LEBEDEV: Really, Shurochka. There'll be a scandal, the tongues of the whole district will buzz with gossip, but it's better to go through a scandal, isn't it, than to destroy yourself for your whole life.

SASHA: Don't say it, don't say it, Papa! I don't want to listen. One must fight gloomy thoughts. He's a good, unhappy, misunderstood man; I shall love him and understand him and set him on his feet. I'll do my duty. I've decided!

LEBEDEV: That's not duty, it's psychopathology.

SASHA: That's enough. I've confessed to you what I wasn't prepared to admit even to myself. Don't tell anyone. We'll forget it.

LEBEDEV: I don't understand anything. Either I've become dull from old age or all of you have become very clever, but seriously, I'm the only one who doesn't understand anything.

V

[*The same and* SHABELSKY.]

SHABELSKY [*entering*]: To hell with the lot, myself included! It's disgraceful.

LEBEDEV: What's the matter with you?

SHABELSKY: No, seriously, I've absolutely got to involve myself in something abominable and vile – so I disgust not just myself but everyone. And I will. I promise! I've already told Borkin to announce my engagement to be married today. [*Laughs.*] Everyone is vile and I shall be vile.

LEBEDEV: I'm fed up with you! Listen, Matvey, you'll talk yourself out to a point when – forgive me for saying it – they'll take you off to the yellow house.[3]

SHABELSKY: And in what way is the yellow house worse than any white or red house? Do me the favour, why not take me there right away. Do me the favour. Every little human being is vile, mean, worthless, without talent, I am loathsome to my own self, I don't believe a single one of my own words . . .

LEBEDEV: Do you know what, old friend. Stick some wadding in your mouth, light it and breathe over people. Or better still: take your hat and go home. There's a wedding here, everyone's having a good time, while you go *kra-kra* like a raven. Yes, really . . .

[SHABELSKY *leans over the piano and sobs.*]

Heavens! . . . Matvey! . . . Count! . . . What's the matter with you? Matyusha, dear friend . . . friend of my heart . . . Have I hurt you? Well, forgive me, an old dog . . . Forgive an old drunk . . . Have some water . . .

SHABELSKY: I don't need any. [*Lifts his head.*]

LEBEDEV: Why are you crying?

SHABELSKY: It's nothing, just . . .

LEBEDEV: No, Matyusha, don't lie . . . why? What's the reason?

SHABELSKY: Just now I looked at this cello and . . . and I remembered the little Jewess . . .

LEBEDEV: What a time you've found to remember her! The kingdom of heaven to her, and peace eternal, but it isn't the moment to remember . . .

SHABELSKY: We used to play duets together . . . A wonderful, superior woman!

[SASHA *sobs.*]

LEBEDEV: Now what are you doing? That's enough! God, both of them are wailing and I . . . I . . . At least go out of here, the guests will see!

SHABELSKY: Pasha, when the sun shines even a cemetery is cheerful. When there's hope even old age is good. But I haven't a single hope, not one!

LEBEDEV: Yes, things are really quite bad for you . . . You have no children, no money, nothing to keep you occupied . . . Well, what can you do! [*To Sasha*] And why are you crying?

SHABELSKY: Pasha, give me some money. We'll settle up in the next world. I'll go to Paris and have a look at my wife's grave. I've given away a lot in my life, I've handed out half of what I owned and so I have the right to ask. Besides, I'm asking a friend . . .

LEBEDEV [*confused*]: Dear chap, I haven't got a kopeck! However, all right, all right! That is, I don't promise, but you see . . . very well, very well! [*Aside*] They've worn me out!

VI

[*The same,* BABAKINA *and then* ZINAIDA SAVISHNA.]

BABAKINA [*entering*]: Where is my gentleman? Count, how dare you leave me on my own? Oo, you nasty man! [*Taps his arm with her fan.*]

SHABELSKY [*in disgust*]: Leave me in peace! I loathe you!

BABAKINA [*dumbfounded*]: What? . . . What? . . .

SHABELSKY: Get away!

BABAKINA [*falling into an armchair*]: Oh! [*Cries.*]

ZINAIDA SAVISHNA [*coming in weeping*]: Someone's arrived . . . I think it's the best man. It's time for the blessing . . . [*Sobs.*]

SASHA [*beseechingly*]: Mama!

LEBEDEV: Well now, they've all started up! A quartet! Haven't you had enough of making everything damp? Matvey! . . . Marfa Yegorovna! . . . In that case I . . . I too will start crying . . . [*Cries.*] Heavens above!

ZINAIDA SAVISHNA: If you don't need your mother, if you won't obey . . . I'll do you the kindness and give you my blessing . . .

[*Enter* IVANOV, *wearing a tail-coat and gloves.*]

VII

[*The same and* IVANOV.]

LEBEDEV: It only needed this! What are you doing?

SASHA: Why have you come?

IVANOV: I'm sorry, my friends, let me speak with Sasha alone.

LEBEDEV: It's breaking the rules to come to the bride's house before the ceremony! It's time for you to go to the church!

IVANOV: Pasha, I ask this favour . . .

[LEBEDEV *shrugs his shoulders; goes out with* ZINAIDA SAV-ISHNA, *the* COUNT *and* BABAKINA.]

VIII

[IVANOV *and* SASHA.]

SASHA [*sternly*]: What do you want?

IVANOV: I'm choking with rage, but I can speak calmly. Listen. I was dressing just now for the wedding, I looked at myself in the mirror, and on my temples . . . were grey hairs. Shura, you mustn't! While it's not too late, you must stop this stupid comedy . . . You are young, pure, you have your life ahead, while I . . .

SASHA: None of this is new, I've heard it now a thousand times and I've had enough! Go off to the church, don't keep people waiting.

IVANOV: I'll go home right away, but tell your family that there will be no wedding. Explain to them somehow. It's time to be sensible. I've been playing Hamlet, and you the maiden of high ideals – enough of that.

SASHA [*getting angry*]: What kind of tone is that? I'm not listening.

IVANOV: But I am speaking and I will go on speaking.

SASHA: Why have you come? Your whining is turning into mockery.

IVANOV: No, I'm not whining any more. Mockery? Yes, I am mocking. And if I could mock myself a thousand times more forcefully and make the whole world burst out laughing, then I would do it! I looked at myself in the mirror – and it was as if the core of my conscience burst! I laughed at myself and almost went out of my mind from shame. [*Laughs.*] Melancholy! Noble depression! Unaccountable sorrow! It only remains for me to write poetry. To whine, to be sorry for myself, to bore people, to realize that my vital energy is gone for ever, that I've rusted up, had my day . . . that I've lost my will and got mired up to my ears in this vile melancholy – to realize this when the sun is shining brightly, when even the ant carries its load and is content – no, thank you very much. To see that some think you a charlatan, others are sorry for you, others offer a helping hand, and yet others – worst of all – listen to your sighs with reverence, look at you as a second Mohammed and wait for you to reveal a new religion to them at any moment . . . No, thank God, I still have pride and a conscience! I was driving here, laughing at myself, and I thought the birds were laughing at me, the trees were laughing . . .

SASHA: This is not rage but madness!

IVANOV: Do you think that? No, I am not mad. I now see things in their real light, and my thoughts are as pure as your conscience. We love one another, but our marriage is not to be! I myself can rage and be bilious as much as I choose, but I don't have the right to destroy others! With my whining I poisoned the last year of my wife's life. While you've been engaged to me, you've forgotten how to laugh and you've aged five years. Your father, for whom everything in life used to be clear and simple, no longer understands people, thanks to my good services. If I go to a gathering, if I pay a visit or go shooting, wherever I go, everywhere I bring boredom, despair, discontent. Stop, don't interrupt! I'm being cutting and violent, but, forgive me, my rage is choking me and I can't speak otherwise. I have never lied or abused life before, but in becoming this whiner, I involuntarily abuse life and I rail against fate and complain without noticing it myself, and anyone hearing me is infected with revulsion from life and starts to abuse it too. And what a tone of voice! As if I'm doing nature a favour by living. To hell with me!

SASHA: Stop . . . From what you said just now it follows that you've had enough of whining and it's time to begin a new life! . . . That's excellent! . . .

IVANOV: I see nothing excellent in it. And what new life is there? I am destroyed irrevocably! It's time we both understood that. A new life!

SASHA: Nikolay, pull yourself together! From what point of view are you destroyed? What kind of cynicism is this? No, I don't want to talk or to listen . . . Drive to the church!

IVANOV: I am destroyed!

SASHA: Don't shout like that, the guests will hear!

IVANOV: If an intelligent, educated and healthy man for no obvious reason starts to sing a song of woe and slides down the slope, nothing will stop that slide and there is no salvation for him! So, where is my salvation? In what does it lie? I can't drink – wine gives me a headache; I am incapable of writing bad verse, I cannot worship my own spiritual sloth and see something elevated in it. Sloth remains sloth, weakness remains weakness – I have no other names for them. I am destroyed, destroyed – and there can be no question about that! [*Looks round.*] We might be disturbed. Listen. If you love me, then help me. Give me up this minute, at once! Now . . .

SASHA: Oh, Nikolay, if you knew how you've exhausted me! How you've worn out my spirit! You're a kind and intelligent man, so consider this: can you really create such problems? Every day there's a problem, each one worse than the last . . . I wanted an active love but this is a martyrdom of love!

IVANOV: And when you become my wife, the problems will be even more complicated. Give me up! Understand this: it's not love that

speaks in you but the obstinacy of an honest nature. You set
yourself a goal to resurrect, to save the human being in me at all
costs, it flattered you that you were carrying out a heroic deed
. . . Now you are ready to step back but you're stopped by a false
feeling. Just understand that!

SASHA: What strange, wild logic! So, can I give you up? How will
I give you up? You have no mother, no sister, no friends . . . You
are ruined, they've pilfered your estate, there's slanderous gossip
about you on every front . . .

IVANOV: I did a foolish thing in coming here. I should have acted
as I intended . . .

[*Enter* LEBEDEV.]

IX

[*The same and* LEBEDEV.]

SASHA [*running towards her father*]: Papa, for God's sake, he's rushed
in here like a madman, and he's tormenting me! He's demanding
that I reject him because he doesn't want to ruin me. Tell him
that I don't want his generosity! I know what I'm doing.

LEBEDEV: I don't understand anything . . . What generosity?

IVANOV: There will be no wedding!

SASHA: There will! Papa, tell him that there will be a wedding!

LEBEDEV: Wait, wait a minute! . . . Why don't you want there to
be a wedding?

IVANOV: I've explained to her why, but she doesn't want to understand.

LEBEDEV: No, you explain it to me, not to her, and explain it so
that I can understand! Oh, Nikolay Alekseyevich! God is your
judge! What a fog you've released into our life, so I feel I'm in a
Hall of Wonders: I look and I understand nothing . . . It's pure
punishment . . . Well, what do you want this old man to do with
you? Challenge you to a duel or something?

IVANOV: There's no need for any duel. You only need a head on your shoulders and to understand the Russian language.

SASHA [*walking about the stage in emotion*]: This is terrible, terrible! Just like a child!

LEBEDEV: One can only throw up one's hands, and that's it. Listen, Nikolay! In your view all that you're doing is intelligent, refined, in accordance with all the rules of psychology, but in mine it's a scandal and a misery. Hear this old man out for the last time! I will tell you this: calm your mind! Look at things simply, as everyone looks at them! In this world everything is simple. The ceiling is white, boots are black, sugar is sweet. You love Sasha, she loves you. If you love her, stay, if you don't, leave, we won't hold it against you. It's so simple! You are both healthy, intelligent, moral people, and well fed, thank God, and clothed . . . What more do you want? You have no money? What of that! Happiness doesn't lie in money . . . Of course, I understand . . . your estate is mortgaged, you have nothing to pay the interest with, but I am her father, I understand . . . Mother can do what she wants: if she won't give money – it's not needed. Shurka says she doesn't need a dowry. Principles, Schopenhauer[4] . . . All that's nonsense . . . I have ten thousand hidden away in the bank . . . [*Looks around.*] Not a soul in the house knows about it . . . It was from Granny . . . It's for you both . . . Take it, on one condition: give two thousand to Matvey . . .

[*The guests are assembling in the ballroom.*]

IVANOV: Pasha, this talk is beside the point. I am acting as my conscience tells me.

SASHA: And I am acting as my conscience tells me. You can say whatever you want, I won't release you. Papa, let's have the blessing right away! I'll go and call Mama. [*Goes out.*]

X

[IVANOV *and* LEBEDEV.]

LEBEDEV: I don't understand anything . . .

IVANOV: Listen, my poor friend . . . I'm not going to explain to you who I am – honest or corrupt, sane or psychopath. You'd never understand. I was young, full of fire, sincere, no fool; I loved, I hated and I believed, but not like other men, I worked and I had hopes for ten, I tilted at windmills and beat my head against walls; without measuring my strength, without proper consideration, with no knowledge of life, I took a burden on my back which at once made it crack and my sinews stretch; I hurried to expend all I had on my youth alone, I got drunk, I became excited, I worked; I knew no middle way. And tell me: could it have been otherwise? There are so few of us, and so much, so much to do! God, how much to do! And now the life against which I struggled is taking this cruel vengeance on me! I've worn myself out! I was already hung-over and old at thirty, I'd already put on my dressing-gown. With a heavy head, with a slothful spirit, exhausted, overstretched, broken, without faith, without love, without a goal, I roam like a shadow among men and I don't know who I am, why I'm alive, what I want. And I now think that love is nonsense, that embraces are cloying, that there's no sense in work, that song and passionate speeches are vulgar and outmoded. And everywhere I take with me depression, chill boredom, dissatisfaction, revulsion from life . . . I am destroyed, irretrievably! Before you stands a man already worn out at thirty-five, disillusioned and crushed by his worthless achievements; he is consumed with shame, mocks his own weakness . . . Oh, what indignation in my pride, what rage is choking me! [*Staggers.*] God, how I've worn myself out! I'm even staggering . . . I'm feeling weak. Where is Matvey? Tell him to take me home.

VOICES IN THE BALLROOM: The groom's best man[5] has arrived!

XI

[*The same,* SHABELSKY, BORKIN *and then* LVOV *and* SASHA.]

SHABELSKY [*entering*]: Wearing someone else's worn tail-coat . . . without gloves . . . and for that how many mocking looks, silly remarks, mean smiles . . . Disgusting little people!

BORKIN [*coming in hurriedly with a bouquet; he is wearing tails, with a best man's buttonhole*]: Ouf! Where is he then? [*To Ivanov*] They've been waiting for you in the church for ages, while you've been lecturing on philosophy here. What a comedian! Yes, comedian! You're not meant to drive with the bride, but separately with me, and I'll come for the bride from the church. Don't you even know that? Decidedly a comedian!

LVOV [*entering, to Ivanov*]: Ah, you here? [*Loudly*] Nikolay Alekseyevich Ivanov, I declare for all to hear that you are evil!

IVANOV [*coldly*]: I thank you most humbly.

[*General consternation.*]

BORKIN [*to Lvov*]: Sir, that is very low! I ask you to fight!

LVOV: Mr Borkin, I consider it degrading for me not just to fight with you but even to talk with you! But Mr Ivanov can have satisfaction whenever he wants.

SHABELSKY: Sir, I will fight with you!

SASHA [*to Lvov*]: Why? Why have you insulted him? Gentlemen, please, let him tell me why.

LVOV: Aleksandra Pavlovna, I did not insult him gratuitously. I came here as an honest man to open your eyes, and I ask you to hear me out.

SASHA: What can you say? That you're an honest man? The whole world knows that! You'd do better to tell me in all conscience, do you know yourself or not! You came in here just now, as an honest man, and made him a terrible insult, which almost killed me; and when you pursued him like a shadow and got in the way of his life, you were convinced that you were fulfilling your duty, that you were an honest man. You interfered in his private life, you slandered him and sat in judgement on him wherever you could, you showered me and all our friends with anonymous letters – and all the time you thought yourself an honest man. You, a doctor, did not even spare his sick wife, thinking it honest, and gave her no rest with your suspicions. And whatever violence, whatever acts of cruelty and meanness you commit, you would always consider yourself an exceptionally honest and progressive man!

IVANOV [*laughing*]: Not a wedding but a parliamentary debate! Bravo, bravo! . . .

SASHA [*to Lvov*]: So just think now, do you know yourself or not? Stupid, heartless people! [*Takes Ivanov by the hand.*] Let's go from here, Nikolay! Father, let's go!

IVANOV: Where shall we go? Wait a minute, I'll make an end of all this right away! My youth has woken in me, the old Ivanov has spoken! [*Takes out a revolver.*]

SASHA [*crying out*]: I know what he wants to do! Nikolay, for God's sake!

IVANOV: I've gone downhill for a long time, enough! It's time to go! Keep away! Thank you, Sasha!

SASHA [*shouting*]: Nikolay, for God's sake! Hold him!

IVANOV: Leave me alone! [*Runs to one side and shoots himself.*]

[*Curtain.*]

The Seagull

A Comedy in Four Acts

CHARACTERS

IRINA NIKOLAYEVNA ARKADINA, *by marriage Treplyova, an actress*

KONSTANTIN GAVRILOVICH TREPLYOV [*also* KOSTYA], *her son, a young man*

PYOTR NIKOLAYEVICH SORIN [*also* PETRUSHA], *Arkadina's brother*

NINA MIKHAYLOVNA ZARECHNAYA, *a young girl, the daughter of a rich landowner*

ILYA AFANASYEVICH SHAMRAYEV, *a retired lieutenant, Sorin's estate manager*

POLINA ANDREYEVNA, *his wife*

MASHA [*also* MARYA ILYINICHNA, MASHENKA], *his daughter*

BORIS ALEKSEYEVICH TRIGORIN, *a novelist*

YEVGENY SERGEYEVICH DORN, *a doctor*

SEMYON SEMYONOVICH MEDVEDENKO, *a schoolmaster*

YAKOV, *a workman*

A COOK

A MAID

The action takes place in Sorin's country house. Two years pass between Acts Three and Four.

Act One

Part of the park of Sorin's estate. A broad avenue leading towards a lake in the distance is blocked by a stage hastily put up for private theatricals, so the lake cannot be seen at all. To left and right of the stage are shrubberies. Some chairs, a small table.

[*The sun has only just set. On the stage behind the lowered curtain* YAKOV *and other workmen; there is coughing and hammering. Enter from the left* MASHA *and* MEDVEDENKO, *who are returning from a walk.*]

MEDVEDENKO: Why do you always wear black?

MASHA: I'm in mourning for my life. I am unhappy.

MEDVEDENKO: Why? [*Hesitantly*] I don't understand . . . You are healthy, your father, though not rich, is comfortably off. My life is much more difficult than yours. I get twenty-three roubles a month all told, with pension contributions taken out of that, and still I don't wear mourning.

[*They sit.*]

MASHA: It's not a question of money. Even a pauper can be happy.

MEDVEDENKO: In theory yes, but the reality is this: there's myself and my mother and two sisters and a little brother, and my total salary is twenty-three roubles. We have to eat and drink, don't we? And buy tea and sugar. And tobacco. So try and manage on that.

MASHA [*looking at the stage*]: The play will begin soon.

MEDVEDENKO: Yes. Nina will be acting and Konstantin Gavrilovich has written the play. They're in love with each other and today their souls will be united as they aspire to give the same dramatic effect. But my soul and yours have no common points of contact. I love you and because of that longing I can't sit at home, every day I walk six versts here and six versts back and I just get indifference from you. I understand it. I am poor, I have a large family . . . How can you want to marry a man who has nothing to eat?

MASHA: Nonsense. [*Takes snuff.*] I am touched by your love but I can't feel the same, that's all. [*Offers him her snuffbox.*] Help yourself.

MEDVEDENKO: I don't want any.

MASHA: It's heavy, there'll be a storm tonight. You're always philosophizing or talking of money. In your eyes there's no greater misfortune than poverty, but in mine it's a thousand times easier to go in rags and live by begging than to . . . But you won't understand that . . .

[*Enter* SORIN *and* TREPLYOV, *right.*]

SORIN [*leaning on a cane*]: The country's not really for me, old man, and of course I'll never get accustomed to life here. Yesterday I went to bed at ten and this morning I woke at nine feeling as if my brain had kind of stuck to my skull from a long sleep and so on and so on. [*Laughs.*] And after lunch, without meaning to I again went to sleep and now I'm quite shattered, as if I'd had a nightmare, at the end of the day . . .

TREPLYOV: Yes, you should live in the city. [*Seeing Masha and Medvedenko.*] My friends, when it starts you'll be called but you shouldn't be here now. Go away please.

SORIN [*to Masha*]: Marya Ilyinichna, be kind enough to ask your papa to let the dog off its chain, otherwise it'll bark. My sister again didn't sleep all night.

MASHA: Speak to my father yourself, I won't. Please don't ask me to. [*To Medvedenko*] Let's go.

MEDVEDENKO [*to Treplyov*]: You'll send someone to tell us before it starts.

[*They both go out.*]

SORIN: That means the dog will howl all night again. It's a funny thing, I've never lived in the country as I wanted to. I used to take four weeks' leave and come here to relax and so on and so on, but they'd get at you here with all sorts of nonsense so that you wanted out on the very first day . . . [*Laughs.*] I always left here with pleasure . . . Well, and now I'm retired, at the end of the day there's nowhere to put myself. Whether you want to or not, you have to live . . .

YAKOV [*to Treplyov*]: Konstantin Gavrilych, we're going for a swim.

TREPLYOV: All right, only be in your places in ten minutes. [*Looks at his watch.*] It'll start soon.

YAKOV: Yes, sir. [*Goes out.*]

TREPLYOV [*looking round the stage*]: Here's a theatre for you. The curtain, then the first pair of wings, then the second, and then empty space. No sets. You look straight at the lake and the horizon. We'll raise the curtain at half past eight on the dot. When the moon rises.

SORIN: Splendid.

TREPLYOV: If Nina is late, then of course the whole effect will be lost. It's already time for her to be here. Her father and stepmother watch over her, and escaping home is as hard for her as escaping from a prison. [*Straightens his uncle's tie.*] Your hair and beard are ruffled. Shouldn't you have a haircut?

SORIN [*combing his beard*]: The tragedy of my life. Even when I was young I looked like a drunk – and so on and so on. Women never loved me. [*Sitting down.*] Why's your mother in a bad mood?

TREPLYOV: Why? She's bored. [*Sitting down next to him.*] She's jealous. She's against me and now she's against the performance and against my play because she is not in it and Nina is. She doesn't know my play but she hates it already . . .

SORIN [*laughing*]: You're really imagining things . . .

TREPLYOV: Now she's put out because it'll be Nina having a success on this little stage rather than herself. [*Looking at his watch.*] A psychological curiosity, my mother. Unquestionably talented, clever, capable of crying over a book, she'll declaim all of Nekrasov[1] for you from memory, she looks after the sick like an angel; but you just try and praise Duse[2] in front of her. O-ho-ho! One must have praise only for her, one must write about her, shout and go into ecstasies about her exceptional performance in *La Dame aux Camélias*[3] or *Life's Hell*,[4] but since there are none of those drugs here in the country, she turns bored and nasty, and we are all her enemies, we are all to blame. Then she is superstitious, she sees death in three lit candles, she's scared of the thirteenth of the month. She's stingy. She has seventy thousand in the bank in Odessa – that I know for sure. But ask her for a loan. She'll start crying.

SORIN: You've imagined that your mother doesn't like your play and now you're getting all upset, and so on and so on. Calm down, your mother worships you.

TREPLYOV [*pulling off the petals of a flower*]: She loves me – she loves me not, she loves me – she loves me not, she loves me – she loves me not. [*Laughs.*] See, my mother doesn't love me. Of course not! She wants to live, to love, to wear bright-coloured blouses, but I am already twenty-five and I remind her that she's no longer young. When I'm not there she's only thirty-two. When I am she's forty-three, and for that she hates me. She also knows that I have no respect for the theatre. She loves the theatre, she thinks that she serves mankind, serves a sacred art, but I think the modern theatre is just cliché and prejudice. When the curtain goes up and there in a three-walled room with three walls, lit for the evening, these great talents, priests of the sacred art, show how people eat, drink, love, walk, wear their jackets; when out of these trite images and phrases they try to fish out a moral – a little moral, one easy to understand, useful in the home; when I am offered a thousand variants of the same thing – then I run and run as Maupassant[5] ran away from the Eiffel Tower, which crushed his mind with its vulgarity.

SORIN: We can't do without the theatre.

TREPLYOV: We need new forms. We need new forms, but if there aren't any, it's better to have nothing. [*Looks at his watch.*] I love my mother, I love her very much; but she leads a pointless life, she's always carrying on with this novelist, her name is perpetually coming up in the papers – and it exhausts me. Sometimes it's just the egoism of an ordinary mortal that comes out in me; I'm sorry that my mother is a famous actress and I think I would be happier if she were an ordinary woman. Uncle, what can be sadder and sillier than my situation; she usually entertains no one but celebrities, actors and writers, and there am I, the only nobody among them and am only tolerated because I'm her son. What am I? What am I? I left the third year of university in circumstances, as they say, which are outside the editor's control. I have no talents, not a kopeck to my name, and on my passport I'm a petty bourgeois from Kiev.⁶ My father was a Kiev petty bourgeois even though he was also a famous actor. So when all those actors and writers in her drawing-room used to give me their gracious attention, it seemed to me their eyes were measuring my nothingness – I read their thoughts and had agonies of humiliation . . .

SORIN: By the way, tell me please what sort of man this writer is. You can't make him out. He never speaks.

TREPLYOV: He's an intelligent man, simple, a little – you know, melancholy. Very decent. He's a long way short of forty but he's already famous, and well-fed . . . His writing, well – what should I tell you? Pleasant, talented, but . . . after Tolstoy⁷ and Zola⁸ you wouldn't want to read Trigorin.

SORIN: Ah, the literary world, I love it, old boy. I used to want two things passionately: I wanted to marry and I wanted to become a writer, but I didn't succeed in either aim. How nice it would be to be even a second-class writer, at the end of the day.

TREPLYOV [*listening*]: I can hear footsteps . . . [*Hugs his uncle.*] I can't live without her . . . Even the sound of her footsteps is beautiful . . . I'm madly happy. [*Quickly goes to meet* NINA ZARECHNAYA, *who enters.*] Enchantress, my dream . . .

NINA [*anxiously*]: I'm not late . . . Of course I'm not late . . .

TREPLYOV [*kissing her hands*]: No, no, no.

NINA: I was worried all day, I was so frightened. I was afraid my father wouldn't let me go . . . But he went out just now with my stepmother. A lovely sky, the moon was beginning to rise, and I drove the horse hard, hard. [*Laughs.*] But I'm glad. [*Firmly shakes Sorin's hand.*]

SORIN [*laughing*]: I think your little eyes have had tears . . . Ha-ha! That's no good.

NINA: No, no . . . You see how out of breath I am. I'm going in half an hour, we must hurry. I have to, I have to, you mustn't keep me, for God's sake. My father doesn't know I'm here.

TREPLYOV: Yes, it's now time to begin. We must go and call everyone.

SORIN: I'll go and get them. This minute. [*Goes right and sings.*] 'To France two grenadiers . . .'⁹ [*Looks round.*] Once I started singing like that and the Deputy Public Prosecutor said to me, 'What a powerful voice Your Excellency has . . .' Then he thought a moment and added, 'But . . . not a pleasing one.' [*Laughs and goes out.*]

NINA: My father and his wife won't let me come here. They say you're bohemians . . . they're afraid I might become an actress . . . But I'm drawn here to the lake like a seagull . . . My heart is full of you. [*Looks around.*]

TREPLYOV: We're alone.

NINA: I think someone's there . . .

TREPLYOV: No one. [*They kiss.*]

NINA: What kind of tree is that?

TREPLYOV: An elm.

NINA: Why is it so dark?

TREPLYOV: Now it's evening, all objects are dark. Don't leave early, I beg you.

NINA: You mustn't beg me.

TREPLYOV: But what if I come to you, Nina? I shall stand in the garden all night and look at your window.

NINA: You mustn't, the watchman will see you. And Trésor isn't accustomed to you and he'll bark.

TREPLYOV: I love you.

NINA: Shh . . .

TREPLYOV [*hearing steps*]: Who's there? Is that you, Yakov?

YAKOV [*behind the stage*]: It is.

TREPLYOV: Get in your places. It's time. Is the moon rising?

YAKOV: It is.

TREPLYOV: Have we got the spirit? Have we got the sulphur? When the red eyes appear we need a smell of sulphur. [*To Nina*] Go, everything is ready in there. Are you nervous? . . .

NINA: Yes, very. Your mama – that doesn't matter, I'm not frightened of her, but Trigorin is here . . . I'm scared and feel awkward acting in front of him . . . A famous writer . . . Is he young?

TREPLYOV: Yes.

NINA: How wonderful his stories are.

TREPLYOV [*coldly*]: I wouldn't know, I haven't read them.

NINA: It's difficult to act in your play. It has no living characters.

TREPLYOV: Living characters! Life should be shown not as it is, and not as it ought to be, but as it appears in dreams.

NINA: Your play doesn't have much action, only speeches. And I think a play should definitely have some love interest . . .

[*Both go behind the stage.*]

[*Enter* POLINA ANDREYEVNA *and* DORN.]

POLINA ANDREYEVNA: It's getting damp. Go back and put on your galoshes.

DORN: I'm hot.

POLINA ANDREYEVNA: You don't look after yourself. It's stubbornness. You're a doctor and know very well that damp air is bad for you, but you want me to suffer; yesterday you deliberately sat out on the terrace the whole evening . . .

DORN [*sings*]: 'Say not that youth's destroyed.'

POLINA ANDREYEVNA: You were so carried away talking to Irina Nikolayevna . . . you didn't notice the cold. Admit it, you find her attractive . . .

DORN: I'm fifty-five.

POLINA ANDREYEVNA: Nonsense, for men that's not old. You've really kept your looks and you're still attractive to women . . .

DORN: So what can I do for you?

POLINA ANDREYEVNA: You're all ready to fall on your faces before an actress. All of you!

DORN [*sings*]: 'Afresh before thee I . . .' If society loves actors and treats them differently from, say, shopkeepers, that is in the order of things. It's idealism.

POLINA ANDREYEVNA: Women have always fallen in love with you and hung on your neck. Is that idealism too?

DORN [*shrugging his shoulders*]: So? There was a lot that was good in women's feelings for me. They chiefly loved the first-class doctor in me. Ten or fifteen years ago, you remember, I was the only decent obstetrician in the whole province. And I always behaved honourably.

POLINA ANDREYEVNA [*seizing his hand*]: My dearest!

DORN: Quiet. They're coming.

[*Enter* ARKADINA *on* SORIN*'s arm,* TRIGORIN, SHAMRAYEV, MEDVEDENKO *and* MASHA.]

SHAMRAYEV: She gave an amazing performance at the Poltava fair in 'seventy-three. Pure ecstasy! She played wonderfully. Would you also happen to know where Pavel Semyonych Chadin, the comedian, is now? He was inimitable as Rasplyuyev,[10] better than Sadovsky, I swear to you, dear lady. Where is he now?

ARKADINA: You're always asking about some has-been. How would I know? [*Sits down.*]

SHAMRAYEV [*sighing*]: Pashka Chadin! There are none like him now. The stage has declined, Irina Nikolayevna! Once there were mighty oaks but now we can only see stumps.

DORN: There are few brilliant talents now, that's true, but the quality of the average actor has gone up a lot . . .

SHAMRAYEV: I cannot agree with you. But it's a matter of taste. *De gustibus aut bene, aut nihil.*[11]

[TREPLYOV *comes out from behind the stage.*]

ARKADINA [*to her son*]: My dear son, when does it begin?

TREPLYOV: In a minute. Patience please.

ARKADINA [*quoting from* Hamlet]: 'O Hamlet, speak no more!
Thou turn'st mine eyes into my very soul,
And there I see such black and grained spots
As will not leave their tinct.'

TREPLYOV [*quoting from* Hamlet]: 'Nay, but to live
In the rank sweat of an enseamed bed,
Stew'd in corruption, honeying and making love
Over the nasty sty . . .'[12]

[*A horn sounds behind the stage.*]

Ladies and gentlemen, it's beginning. Your attention please.

[*A pause.*]

I am starting. [*Knocks with a stick and speaks loudly.*]

O you honoured ancient shades, who are borne at night over this lake, put us to sleep and let us dream of what will be in two hundred thousand years!

SORIN: In two hundred thousand years there will be nothing.

TREPLYOV: So let us be shown that nothing.

ARKADINA: Yes indeed. We are sleeping.

[*The curtain rises to reveal a view of the lake, the moon on the horizon, its reflection in the water;* NINA ZARECHNAYA *is sitting on a large rock, all in white.*]

NINA: Men, lions, eagles and partridges, antlered deer, geese, spiders, silent fish which live in the water, starfish and organisms invisible to the eye – in short, all life, all life, all life has been extinguished after completing its sad cycle . . . For thousands of centuries the earth has not borne a single living being, and this poor moon lights her lantern to no purpose. In the meadow the cranes give their waking cry no more and in May the cockchafers are no longer heard in the lime groves. It is cold, cold, cold. It is empty, empty, empty. It is frightening, frightening, frightening.

[*A pause.*]

The bodies of living beings have turned into dust and eternal matter has changed them into stones, into water, into clouds, and all their spirits have merged into one. I . . . I am that universal spirit . . . In me is the spirit of Alexander the Great and Caesar and Shakespeare and Napoleon, and that of the meanest leech. In me human consciousness has merged with animal instinct, and I remember everything, everything, and every life I live out in myself anew.

[*Marsh lights appear on the lake.*]

ARKADINA [*quietly*]: This is a bit of Decadent theatre.
TREPLYOV [*pleading and reproachful*]: Mama!
NINA: I am lonely. Once in a hundred years I open my mouth to speak, and my voice sounds dolefully in this emptiness and no one hears . . . And you, pale lights, do not hear me . . . Towards dawn the decaying marsh spawns you and you roam till dawn, but without thought, without will, without tremor of life. Afraid that life might begin in you, the father of eternal matter, the devil, changes your atoms every instant, like those of the rocks and the water, and you continuously change. Only one spirit in the universe remains constant and immutable.

[*A pause.*]

Like a prisoner cast into an empty deep well, I do not know where I am and what awaits me. It is only revealed to me that in the unyielding cruel fight with the devil, the principle of the forces of matter, I am destined to conquer, and thereafter matter and spirit will blend in a beautiful harmony and there will come the kingdom of universal will. But this will only be when little by little, over a long sequence of millennia, the moon and bright Sirius and the earth will have turned to dust . . . But till then horror, horror . . .

[*A pause; two red points appear against the lake.*]

My mighty enemy, the devil, approaches. I see his fearsome crimson eyes . . .

ARKADINA: I smell sulphur. Is that intentional?

TREPLYOV: Yes.

ARKADINA [*laughing*]: Yes, it's effective.

TREPLYOV: Mama!

NINA: He is lonely without man . . .

POLINA ANDREYEVNA [*to Dorn*]: You've taken off your hat. Put it on or you'll catch cold.

ARKADINA: The Doctor has taken off his hat to the devil, the father of eternal matter.

TREPLYOV [*losing his temper, loudly*]: The play is over! That's enough! Curtain!

ARKADINA: Why are you angry!

TREPLYOV: Enough! Curtain! Lower the curtain! [*Stamping his foot.*] Curtain!

[*The curtain falls.*]

I'm sorry. I lost sight of the fact that only a select few can write plays and act on the stage. I broke the monopoly! For me . . . I . . . [*Wants to say something more but throws up his hand and goes off left.*]

ARKADINA: What's the matter with him?

SORIN: Irina my dear, you mustn't treat a young man's pride like that.

ARKADINA: What did I say to him?

SORIN: You offended him.

ARKADINA: He warned us it was a joke, and I treated his play like a joke.

SORIN: Still . . .

ARKADINA: Now it turns out that he has written a great work. What next! He must have arranged this performance with its smell of sulphur not as a joke but as a demonstration. He wanted to teach us how to write and what to perform. In the end it gets boring. His constant attacks on me, his needling would try anybody! A capricious, self-obsessed boy.

SORIN: He wanted to please you.

ARKADINA: Really? However, he didn't choose some ordinary play but made us listen to these decadent ravings. As a joke I am prepared to listen to raving, but here we have claims to new forms, to a new age in art. And in my opinion there are no new forms here but simply bad behaviour.

TRIGORIN: Everyone writes as he wants and as he is able to.

ARKADINA: Let him write as he wants and as he is able to, only let him leave me in peace.

DORN: Jove, thou art angry . . .

ARKADINA: I am not Jove but a woman. [Lights a cigarette.] I'm not angry, only vexed that a young man spends his time so tediously. I didn't want to offend him.

MEDVEDENKO: No one has grounds for separating spirit from matter since it is possible that spirit itself is the combination of atoms of matter. [Animatedly, to Trigorin] But just think, how about describing in a play and then performing on the stage the existence of yours truly – a schoolmaster. It's a hard, hard life!

ARKADINA: Fair enough, but we won't talk of plays or atoms. It's such a lovely evening. Do you hear, my friends – the singing? [Listens.] Doesn't it feel good?

POLINA ANDREYEVNA: It's from the far shore.

[A pause.]

ARKADINA [to Trigorin]: Sit by me. Ten, fifteen years ago here on the lake we heard constant music and singing almost every night. There are six estates on this shore. I remember there was laughter, noise, shooting, and romance, romance ... The *jeune premier*[13] and idol of these six houses was then – I present [*she points to Dorn*] Doctor Yevgeny Sergeich. Even now he is enchanting but then he was irresistible. However, my conscience is beginning to bother me. Why did I offend my poor boy? I am troubled. [*Loudly*] Kostya! My boy! Kostya!

MASHA: I'll go and look for him.

ARKADINA: Please, dear.

MASHA [*goes left*]: Hallo! Konstantin Gavrilovich! ... Hallo! [*Exit.*]

NINA [*coming out from behind the stage*]: Since it's clearly not going on, I can come out now ... Good evening! [*Kisses Arkadina and Polina Andreyevna.*]

SORIN: Bravo! Bravo!

ARKADINA: Bravo! Bravo! We were full of admiration. Looking as you do, with such a wonderful voice, you mustn't sit in the country, it's a sin. You've clearly got a talent. Do you hear? You have to go on the stage.

NINA: Oh, it's my dream. [*Sighing*] But it won't ever come true.

ARKADINA: Who knows! Can I introduce to you Boris Alekseyevich Trigorin.

NINA: Oh, I am so pleased ... [*Embarrassed*] I always read you ...

ARKADINA [*sitting Nina next to her*]: Don't be embarrassed, my dear. He's a celebrity but he has a simple soul. You see, he himself is embarrassed.

DORN: I think we can raise the curtain now, or it feels odd.

SHAMRAYEV [*loudly*]: Yakov, old chap, raise the curtain!

[*The curtain rises.*]

NINA [*to Trigorin*]: Wasn't that a strange play?

TRIGORIN: I understood nothing. But I watched with pleasure. You acted with such sincerity. And the set was lovely.

[*A pause.*]

There must be a lot of fish in this lake.

NINA: Yes, there are.

TRIGORIN: I love to fish. There's no greater pleasure for me than sitting on the bank and watching my float.

NINA: But I imagine, after experiencing the pleasures of creativity, no other pleasures exist any more . . .

ARKADINA [*laughing*]: Don't talk like that. When people say nice things to him, he shrivels up.

SHAMRAYEV: I remember once in Moscow at the Opera the famous Silva hit bottom *C*. And sitting in the gallery at the same time, just as if it was planned, was a bass from one of our church choirs, and suddenly, you can imagine our extreme surprise, we hear from up in the gallery 'Bravo, Silva!', a whole octave lower . . . Like this [*forcing a low bass*]: Bravo, Silva! . . . The audience froze.

[*A pause.*]

DORN: An angel just passed . . .

NINA: And I must go. Goodbye.

ARKADINA: Where? Where are you going so early? We won't let you.

NINA: Papa is waiting for me.

ARKADINA: That father . . .

[*They kiss.*]

Well, there we are. I'm sorry, sorry to let you go.

NINA: If you knew how hard it is for me to leave!

ARKADINA: Someone could go with you, my lamb.

NINA [*frightened*]: Oh no, no!

SORIN [*pleading with her*]: Stay.

NINA: I can't, Pyotr Nikolayevich.

SORIN: Stay for just one hour, and so on and so on. Well . . .

NINA [*after thinking, with tears in her eyes*]: I can't! [*Shakes his hand and quickly leaves.*]

ARKADINA: An unfortunate girl really. They say her dead mother left all her huge estate to her husband, down to the last kopeck, and now this girl has nothing, as her father has already left everything to his second wife. It's shocking.

DORN: Yes, her papa is a real swine, one has to give him full credit for that.

SORIN [*rubbing his chilly hands*]: Let's go in too, ladies and gentlemen, or it'll be getting damp. My legs are aching.

ARKADINA: They're barely moving, as if they were made of wood. Well, come on, you poor old thing. [*Takes his arm.*]

SHAMRAYEV [*giving his arm to his wife*]: Madame?

SORIN: I can hear the dog howling again. [*To Shamrayev*] Ilya Afanasyevich, be so kind as to tell them to unchain it.

SHAMRAYEV: I can't, Pyotr Nikolayevich, I'm afraid thieves will get into the barn. I've got millet in there. [*To Medvedenko who is walking beside him*] Yes, a whole octave lower: 'Bravo, Silva!' And not a professional singer, a simple fellow from a church choir.

MEDVEDENKO: And how much is a church chorister paid?

[*All go out, except* DORN.]

DORN [*alone*]: I don't know, perhaps I understand nothing or I've gone out of my mind, but I liked the play. There's something there. When the girl spoke of loneliness and then when the red eyes of the devil appeared, my hands shook from emotion. Fresh, simple . . . I want to say a lot of nice things to him.

TREPLYOV [*entering*]: There's no one left.

DORN: I'm here.

TREPLYOV: Mashenka is looking for me all over the park. She's just intolerable.

DORN: Konstantin Gavrilovich, I really liked your play. It's a little strange and I didn't see the end, and still it made a strong impression. You're a gifted man, and must go on.

[TREPLYOV *vigorously shakes his hand and impulsively hugs him.*]

Ouf, you're a nervous chap. Tears in your eyes . . . What do I mean? You've taken a theme from the realm of abstract ideas. Rightly so, because a work of art absolutely needs to express some great thought. Beauty only lies in what is serious. How pale you are.

TREPLYOV: So you're telling me – to carry on?

DORN: Yes . . . But only depict what is important and eternal. You know, I have lived a varied life, I've enjoyed it, I am content, but if I ever came to feel the upsurge of spirit which artists have at the moment of creation, I would scorn my material shell and all that belongs to it, and I would be carried up, up from earth.

TREPLYOV: Excuse me, where is Nina?

DORN: And something else. A work must contain clear, defined thought. You must know the object of your writing, otherwise, if you go down that picturesque road without a definite aim, you will lose your way and your talent will destroy you.

TREPLYOV [*impatiently*]: Where is Nina?

DORN: She's gone home.

TREPLYOV [*in despair*]: What am I to do? I want to see her . . . It is essential I see her . . . I will go . . .

[*Enter* MASHA.]

DORN [*to Treplyov*]: Calm down, my friend.

TREPLYOV: But I will go. I must go to her.

MASHA: Go into the house, Konstantin Gavrilovich. Your mama is waiting for you. She's worried.

TREPLYOV: Tell her I've gone. And I beg you all, leave me in peace. Leave me. Don't follow me.

DORN: But, but, but, my dear fellow . . . you mustn't . . . It's not right.

TREPLYOV [*with tears in his eyes*]: Goodbye, doctor. I'm grateful . . . [*Exit.*]

DORN [*sighing*]: Youth, youth!

MASHA: When there's nothing more to say, people say youth, youth . . . [*Takes snuff.*]

DORN [*taking her snuffbox from her and throwing it into the bushes*]: That's nasty!

[*A pause.*]

I think they're playing indoors. We must go.

MASHA: Wait a moment.

DORN: What?

MASHA: I want to tell you something else. I want to talk ... [*Nervously*] I don't love my father ... but my heart goes out to you. For some reason I feel with all my soul that you are close to me ... Help me. Help me, or I'll do something foolish, I'll make a mockery of my life, I'll spoil it ... I can't any longer ...

DORN: What? Help you in what?

MASHA: I'm so unhappy. No one, no one knows how unhappy I am. [*Laying her head on his breast, quietly*] I love Konstantin.

DORN: You're all so highly strung. So highly strung. And such a lot of love ... O enchanted lake! [*Affectionately*] But what can I do, my child? What, what can I do?

[*Curtain.*]

Act Two

A croquet lawn. Backstage on the right the house, with a big terrace, on the left the lake with the sun's reflection shining on it. Flowerbeds. Midday. It is hot. To one side of the croquet lawn, in the shade of an old lime, ARKADINA, DORN *and* MASHA *are sitting on a bench. On Dorn's knees is an open book.*

ARKADINA [*to Masha*]: Let's stand up.

[*They both get up.*]

Let's stand side by side. You are twenty-two and I am almost twice that. Yevgeny Sergeich, which of us looks younger?

DORN: You, of course.

ARKADINA: So . . . And why is that? Because I work, I feel, I am constantly busy, but you are always sitting in one place, you don't live . . . And I have a rule: don't look into the future. I never think of old age or death. What will be will be.

MASHA: And I feel as if I'd been born long, long ago; I carry my life about with me, like the endless train of a dress . . . And often I have no urge to live. [*Sits down.*] Of course this is all nonsense. I must pull myself together, get rid of it all.

DORN [*sings softly*]: 'Tell her, flowers mine . . .'[1]

ARKADINA: Then, I am correct as an Englishman. My dear, I keep myself, as they say, in training, and my clothes and hair are always *comme il faut*.[2] Would I let myself go out of the house, even just into the garden here, in a house-coat or without doing my hair? Never. I have lasted because I have never been slovenly, I have never let myself go, like some. [*Walks across the croquet lawn with arms akimbo.*] There – like a young bird. I could play a girl of fifteen.

DORN: Well, I'll go on anyway. [*Takes up the book.*] We stopped at the corn chandler and the rats . . .

ARKADINA: And the rats. Read on. [*Sits down.*] No, give it to me, I'll read. My turn. [*Takes the book and searches through it.*] And the rats . . . Here it is . . . [*Reads*] 'And of course it is just as risky for fashionable folk to pamper novelists and take them to their bosoms as it is for a corn chandler to breed rats in his barns. But they love them. And so, when a woman has chosen the writer whom she wants to snare, she lays siege to him with compliments, favours and treats . . .' Well, maybe the French do, but we have nothing like that, nothing so programmatic. Here a woman, before she sets out to capture a writer, is usually – excuse me – head over heels in love herself. Without going very far – take me and Trigorin . . .

[*Enter* SORIN *leaning on a stick, and with him* NINA; MEDVED-ENKO *follows pushing an empty wheelchair.*]

SORIN [*in the tone people use to make up to children*]: Well? Are we happy? Are we cheerful at last today? [*To his sister*] We are happy. Father and stepmother have gone to Tver, and we are free now for three whole days.

NINA [*sitting down by Arkadina and embracing her*]: I *am* happy. I'm one of you now.

SORIN [*sitting in his wheelchair*]: She's rather pretty today.

ARKADINA: Elegant, attractive . . . You're a clever girl. [*Kisses Nina.*] But we mustn't praise you too much or we'll bring bad luck. Where's Boris Alekseyevich?

NINA: He's fishing at the bathing place.

ARKADINA: Why doesn't he get bored? [*Settles to resume her reading.*]

NINA: What are you reading?

ARKADINA: Maupassant's *Sur l'eau*,³ dear. [*Reads a few lines to herself.*] Well, it gets uninteresting and false. [*Shuts the book.*] My heart is anxious. Tell me, what is the matter with my son? Why is he so boring and grim? He spends whole days on the lake and I hardly see him at all.

MASHA: He's depressed. [*To Nina, shyly*] Please, read from his play.

NINA [*shrugging her shoulders*]: Do you want me to? It's so uninteresting.

MASHA [*controlling her feelings*]: When he reads something himself, his eyes burn and his face turns pale. He has a beautiful, melancholy voice; and the manner of a poet.

[SORIN *can be heard snoring.*]

DORN: Good night!

ARKADINA: Petrusha!

SORIN: Ah!

ARKADINA: Did you go to sleep?

SORIN: Certainly not.

[*A pause.*]

ARKADINA: You're not having any medical treatment, and that's bad, brother.

SORIN: I'd be glad to, but Doctor here doesn't want me to have any.

DORN: Prescriptions for a sixty-year-old!

SORIN: Even at sixty one wants to live.

DORN [*crossly*]: Oh! Well, take valerian drops.[4]

ARKADINA: I think it would be good for him to go somewhere and take the waters.

DORN: Well? He can go. Or not go.

ARKADINA: So try and understand.

DORN: There's nothing to understand. Everything is clear.

[*A pause.*]

MEDVEDENKO: Pyotr Nikolayevich ought to give up smoking.

SORIN: Rubbish.

DORN: No, not rubbish. Alcohol and tobacco take away your personality. After a cigar or a glass of vodka you are no longer Pyotr Nikolayevich but Pyotr Nikolayevich plus someone else; your 'I' dissolves and you relate to yourself like a third person – 'he'.

SORIN [*laughing*]: It's all very well for you to argue. You've had a good life, but what about me? I served twenty-eight years in the Department of Justice, but never began to live. I finished without any experience of life, and understandably I very much want to live. You are well fed, things don't matter to you and so you are inclined towards philosophy; I want to live and so I drink sherry at dinner and smoke cigars and so on and so on. You know.

DORN: One must have a serious attitude to life, and to go for medical treatment aged sixty, to regret not having had much pleasure in youth is – forgive me – silly.

MASHA [*getting up*]: It must be time to have lunch. [*Walks with slow, slack steps.*] My leg's gone to sleep . . . [*Exit.*]

DORN: She'll go and put down two glasses before lunch.

SORIN: The poor thing has no personal happiness.

DORN: Empty words, Your Excellency.[5]

SORIN: You're arguing like a well-fed man.

ARKADINA: Oh, what can be more boring than this nice rural tedium. It's hot, it's quiet, everyone talks philosophy . . . It's good to be with you, my friends, pleasant to listen to you, but . . . to sit in a hotel room and learn a part is so much better.

NINA [*ecstatically*]: Splendid! I understand you.

SORIN: Of course it's better in town. You sit in your study, your man lets no one in without announcing them, there's the telephone . . . there are cabs on the street and so on and so on . . .

DORN [*singing*]: 'Tell her, flowers mine . . .'

[*Enter* SHAMRAYEV *followed by* POLINA ANDREYEVNA.]

SHAMRAYEV: Here they are. Good afternoon. [*Kisses Arkadina's hand, then Nina's.*] I'm so glad to see you in good health. [*To Arkadina*] My wife says you're planning to go together to town today.

ARKADINA: Yes, that's the plan.

SHAMRAYEV: Hm . . . That's splendid, but what will you go in, dear lady? We're bringing in the rye today, all the men are taken up. And may I ask you what horses you will use?

ARKADINA: What horses? How do I know what horses!

SORIN: We have the carriage horses.

SHAMRAYEV [*getting agitated*]: The carriage horses? And where will I get harnesses? Where will I get harnesses? This is astonishing! Beyond comprehension! My dear lady! Excuse me, I worship your talent, I'm ready to give ten years of my life for you, but I cannot give you horses!

ARKADINA: But what if I have to go? A strange business!

SHAMRAYEV: Dear lady! You do not know what farming means!

ARKADINA [*losing her temper*]: An old story! In that case I am leaving for Moscow today. Get them to take horses for me in the village or I'll walk to the station on foot!

SHAMRAYEV [*losing his temper*]: In that case I resign! Find yourself another manager! [*Exit.*]

ARKADINA: Every summer is like this, every summer I am insulted! I won't set foot here again! [*Goes out left, where the bathing place must be; in a minute she is seen passing to the house followed by* TRIGORIN *with fishing rods and a bucket.*]

SORIN [*losing his temper*]: Impertinence! What the hell! At the end of the day I've had enough. Bring all the horses out here at once!

NINA [*to Polina Andreyevna*]: To refuse Irina Nikolayevna, the famous actress! Is not her every wish, even caprice, more important than your farming? Just unthinkable!

POLINA ANDREYEVNA [*in despair*]: What can I do? Put yourself in my position: what can I do?

SORIN [*to Nina*]: Let's go to my sister . . . We will all beg her not to leave. All right? [*Looking in the direction where* SHAMRAYEV *went off.*] Intolerable man! A tyrant!

NINA [*preventing him from standing up*]: Sit down, sit . . . We will take you. [*She and* MEDVEDENKO *wheel the chair.*] Oh how awful this is!

SORIN: Yes, yes, it's awful. But he won't leave. I shall speak to him right away.

[*Exeunt; only* DORN *and* POLINA ANDREYEVNA *are left.*]

DORN: People are boring. Really your husband should be thrown out of here on his ear, but it will all end with that old woman Pyotr Nikolayevich and his sister begging his pardon. You'll see.

POLINA ANDREYEVNA: He sent out the carriage horses into the fields too. And every day there are misunderstandings like this. If you knew how it upsets me! I get ill; do you see, I am trembling . . . I can't stand his rudeness. [*Imploringly*] Yevgeny, my dear, my beloved, take me into your home . . . Our time is passing, we are no longer young, and if only, at the end of our lives, we could just stop concealing and lying . . .

[*A pause.*]

DORN: I am fifty-five, it's too late now to change my life.

POLINA ANDREYEVNA: I know, you're refusing me because there are other women besides me who are close to you. You can't take them all in. I understand. Forgive me, I get on your nerves.

[NINA *appears near the house; she is picking flowers.*]

DORN: No, not at all.

POLINA ANDREYEVNA: I suffer from jealousy. Of course you are a doctor, you can't avoid women. I understand . . .

DORN [*to* NINA, *who comes up*]: How is it in there?

NINA: Irina Nikolayevna is crying and Pyotr Nikolayevich has asthma.

DORN [*getting up*]: Let's go and give both of them valerian drops.

NINA [*giving him the flowers*]: Here!

DORN: *Merci bien.* [*Goes towards the house.*]

POLINA ANDREYEVNA [*going with him*]: What pretty flowers! [*By the house, in a low voice*] Give me those flowers! Give me those flowers! [*Having got the flowers, she pulls them apart and throws them aside; both go into the house.*]

NINA [*alone*]: How strange to see a famous actress crying, and for such a silly reason! And strange that a famous writer – the darling of the public, stories about him in all the papers, his picture for sale, translated into foreign languages – spends all day fishing and is delighted to have caught a couple of chub. I thought famous people were proud and unapproachable, that they despised the world and that through their fame, through the glory of their name, they as it were took their revenge on the world for valuing high birth and wealth above all else. But here they cry, fish, play cards and get angry, like everyone else . . .

TREPLYOV [*enters without a hat, carrying a gun and a dead seagull*]: Are you alone here?

NINA: Yes, alone.

[TREPLYOV *lays the seagull at her feet.*]

What does that mean?

TREPLYOV: I was a brute and killed this seagull today. I lay it at your feet.

NINA: What's the matter with you? [*Picks up the seagull and looks at it.*]

TREPLYOV [*after a pause*]: Soon I'll kill myself like this.

NINA: I don't recognize you.

TREPLYOV: Yes, since I stopped recognizing you. You've changed towards me, your eyes are cold, my presence embarrasses you.

NINA: You've become irritable recently, you express yourself incomprehensibly, in some kind of symbolic language. And this seagull is clearly a symbol but, forgive me, I don't understand . . . [*Puts the seagull on the bench.*] I'm too simple to understand you.

TREPLYOV: It started on the evening of my play's stupid failure. Women don't forgive failure. I burnt the lot, to the last scrap of paper. If you only knew how unhappy I am! Your coldness is frightening, incredible, as if I woke up and saw that this lake had suddenly dried up or flowed into the ground. You've just said that you're too simple to understand me. Oh, what is there to understand here? My play failed to please, you despise my inspiration, you now think I'm commonplace, worthless, like many others ... [*Stamping his foot.*] How well I understand that, how I understand! It's as if I had a nail driven into my brain — damn it and my pride, which sucks my blood, sucks it like a serpent ... [*Seeing* TRIGORIN *who is walking reading a notebook.*] Here comes the true talent; he steps like Hamlet, and with a book too. [*Mockingly*] 'Words, words, words ...'⁶ This sun hasn't yet reached you, but you're already smiling, your gaze has melted in his beams. I won't get in your way. [*Goes out quickly.*]

TRIGORIN [*writing in his notebook*]: Takes snuff and vodka ... Always wears black. The schoolmaster's in love with her ...

NINA: Good afternoon, Boris Alekseyevich.

TRIGORIN: Good afternoon. I think we're leaving today, unexpectedly. We probably won't see each other again. A pity. I don't often get to meet young girls, young and interesting girls. I've now forgotten and can't clearly imagine what it feels like to be eighteen or nineteen, and so in my novels and stories the girls are usually false. I would like to be in your place just for an hour to find out how you think ... and generally what kind of little thing you are.

NINA: And I would like to be in your place.

TRIGORIN: Why?

NINA: To learn how a famous and talented writer feels. What does being famous feel like? How do you sense that you're famous?

TRIGORIN: How? Of course, I don't. I've never thought about that. [*Thinking*] It's one of two things: either you're exaggerating my fame, or else it can't be felt at all.

NINA: And if you read about yourself in the papers?

TRIGORIN: It's pleasant when it's praise, and when it's abuse you feel out of sorts for a couple of days.

NINA: It's a wonderful world! How I envy you, if only you knew! People's lots are very different. Some barely drag out their tedious, unnoticed existence, each of them just like the others, all of them unhappy; others, like you for instance, are given a life that is interesting, bright, full of meaning ... you're happy ...

TRIGORIN: I'm happy? [*Shrugging his shoulders.*] Hm ... you're talking now about fame, happiness, some bright, interesting existence, but I'm sorry, I find all these good words just like jelly, which I never eat. You are very young and very kind.

NINA: Your life is splendid.

TRIGORIN: What is special about it? [*Looking at his watch.*] I must go now and write. Forgive me, I have no time ... [*Laughs.*] You've trodden, so to speak, on my very favourite corn, and I begin to get upset and a little cross. But let us talk. We'll talk of my splendid, bright existence ... Well, where shall we begin? [*After thinking a little.*] You can have a compulsive imagination, when for example you think day and night of nothing but the moon, and I have my own moon like that. I am held day and night by one obsessive thought: I must write, I must write, I must ... I've no sooner finished a story than I'm already driven by something to write another, then a third, after that a fourth ... I write with no breaks, as if I were travelling with relays of post-horses,[7] and I can't do otherwise. What, I ask you, is there here that is splendid or bright? Oh, what an absurd life! I am here with you, I'm getting worked up, but meanwhile every single moment I remember that I have an unfinished story waiting for me. Over there I see a cloud like a grand piano. I think, somewhere in the story I should mention a cloud that looked like a piano. I can smell heliotrope. I quickly make a mental note: sickly sweet scent, widow's colour, bring in when describing a summer evening. I catch my and your every sentence, every word, and quickly lock all these sentences and words into my literary storeroom – in case they come in useful. When I finish my work, I run off to the theatre or to fish; then you'd think I might be able to rest or forget, but no, that heavy iron piece of shot is rolling round in my head – a new plot, and I'm drawn to my desk and I must rush again to write and write. And so it remains always, always, and I have no rest from myself, and I feel that I'm devouring my own life, that in order to make the honey which I give away to someone out there, I rob my best flowers of their pollen, I tear apart the flowers themselves and trample their roots.

Am I not a madman? Do my friends and dear ones treat me as a healthy human being? 'What little thing are you writing? What treat are you going to give us?' Always the same, the same, and I think this attention from my friends, these compliments and praises – it's all lies, they tell you lies like a sick man, and I'm sometimes afraid they'll creep up on me from behind and grab me and carry me off like Gogol's Poprishchin[8] to a lunatic asylum. And in the years when I was starting, my young years, my best years, my work was sheer agony. A young writer feels clumsy, awkward, out of place, especially when things are not going his way, his nerves are strained, in shreds; he hangs around close to those involved in literature and art, without recognition or acknowledgement, nervous of looking them straight in the eye, like a passionate gambler without any money. I couldn't see my readers but somehow I imagined them as unfriendly, mistrustful. I was afraid of the public, to me they were terrifying, and when I had to put on a new play, every time I felt dark hair give out signs of hostility and fair hair chilly indifference. Oh how awful it was! What torment!

NINA: But, excuse me, don't inspiration and the actual process of creation give you some elevated, happy moments?

TRIGORIN: Yes. When I'm writing something it feels good. And reading proofs feels good but – I can't bear it when it's just published and I see that it's wrong, a mistake, that it shouldn't have been written at all, and I feel irritated and low in spirit . . . [*Laughing*] And the public reads it, 'Yes, pleasing, talented, but a long way from Tolstoy', or 'A beautiful thing, but Turgenev's *Fathers and Sons*[9] is better.' And to the tomb everything will remain just nice and talented, nice and talented – nothing more, and when I die my friends will say walking past my grave, 'Here lies Trigorin. He was a good writer, but not as good as Turgenev.'

NINA: I'm sorry, I don't want to understand you. You're simply spoiled by success.

TRIGORIN: What success? I never liked myself. I don't admire myself as a writer. Worst of all, I live in a kind of daze and don't understand what I write . . . I love this water, the trees, the sky, I feel nature, which stirs a passion in me, an irresistible desire to write. But I'm not just a landscape artist, I am also a citizen, I love my country, the people, I feel that if I am a writer it is my duty to talk about the people, their sufferings, their future, to talk about science, the rights of man and so on, and so on, and I talk about everything, I hurry, people bear down on me from every direction, they get angry, I dart from side to side like a fox trapped by hounds, I see life and science advancing ever onward, and I get left further and further behind like a peasant who's missed his train, and in the end I feel that I can only write about landscape, and that in everything else I am false – false to the marrow of my bones.

NINA: You're overworked, and you've neither the time nor the will to recognize your own value. You may be dissatisfied with yourself but to others you are great and noble. If I were a writer like you, I would give up my whole life to the people, but I would know that its happiness only lay in rising to my level, and the crowd would carry me along in a chariot.

TRIGORIN: Hm, in a chariot . . . Am I Agamemnon or someone?

[*Both smile.*]

NINA: For the happiness of being a writer or an actress I would bear family hostility, poverty, disappointment, I would live in an attic and eat only rye bread, I would suffer from dissatisfaction with myself, from the consciousness of my imperfections, but in return I would demand fame – real, noisy fame . . . [*Covers her face with her hands.*] My head is spinning . . . Ouf!

[*The voice of* ARKADINA *from the house:* '*Boris Alekseyevich!*']

TRIGORIN: I'm being called . . . probably to pack. But I don't want to leave. [*Turning to look at the lake*] What blessedness . . . So beautiful!

NINA: Do you see the house and garden on the far shore?

TRIGORIN: Yes.

NINA: That's my dead mother's house. I was born there. I've spent my entire life by this lake and know every little island on it.

TRIGORIN: You have a fine place here. [*He sees the seagull.*] But what's this?

NINA: A seagull. Konstantin Gavrilych killed it.

TRIGORIN: A beautiful bird. I really don't want to go. Persuade Irina Nikolayevna to stay.

[*Writes in his notebook.*]

NINA: What are you writing?

TRIGORIN: I'm making a note . . . A plot flashed through my mind . . . [*Putting away the notebook.*] A plot for a short story: a young girl has lived since childhood on the shores of a lake, a girl like you; she loves the lake, like a seagull, and is happy and free, like a seagull. But a man comes along, sees her and idly kills her — like this seagull.

[*A pause.*]

[ARKADINA *appears in a window.*]

ARKADINA: Boris Alekseyevich, where are you?

TRIGORIN: Coming! [*Goes, and looks round at Nina; by the window, to Arkadina*] What is it?

ARKADINA: We're staying.

[TRIGORIN *goes into the house.*]

NINA [*coming towards the footlights; after some thought*]: It's a dream!

[*Curtain.*]

Act Three

The dining-room in Sorin's house. Doors to right and left. A sideboard. A cupboard with medicines. A table in the middle of the room. A trunk and cardboard boxes, preparations for departure are in evidence. TRIGORIN *is having lunch.* MASHA *is standing by the table.*

MASHA: I'm telling you all this as a writer. You can use it. I tell you frankly: if he'd wounded himself seriously, I couldn't have lived a moment longer. But I'm brave. I went and decided: I'm going to rip this love from my heart, rip it out by the roots.

TRIGORIN: How?

MASHA: I'm getting married. To Medvedenko.

TRIGORIN: To the schoolmaster?

MASHA: Yes.

TRIGORIN: I don't understand the need.

MASHA: To live without hope, to wait for something for years on end . . . But when I get married there won't be any time for love, new cares will wipe out all the past. And anyway, you know, it'll be a change. Shall we have another?

TRIGORIN: Won't that be too much?

MASHA: Here you are, now. [*Pours them each a glass.*] Don't look at me like that. Women drink more often than you think. A few drink openly like me, but most do it in secret. Yes. And they all drink vodka or brandy. [*Clinks his glass.*] Your good health. You're a straightforward man, I'm sorry to say goodbye.

[*They drink.*]

TRIGORIN: I don't want to go.

MASHA: Why don't you ask her to stay.

TRIGORIN: No, now she won't stay. Her son is behaving extraordinarily tactlessly. First he tries to shoot himself, and now I've heard he's going to challenge me to a duel. And what for? He sulks, snorts, preaches new art forms . . . But there's enough space for all, new and old – why do we have to wrestle?

MASHA: Well, jealousy. But it's none of my business.

[*A pause.* YAKOV *walks through from left to right carrying a trunk;* NINA *enters and stays by the window.*]

My schoolmaster isn't very clever, he's poor, but he's a good man and he loves me very much. I'm sorry for him. And I'm sorry for his old mother. Well, I wish you all the best. Remember me kindly. [*Shakes his hand vigorously.*] I'm very grateful to you for being kind to me. Send me your books, inscribed please. Only please don't write 'To my dear friend', but just 'To Marya, parentage forgotten, purpose of existence in this world unknown.' Goodbye. [*Exit.*]

NINA [*holding out a fist towards Trigorin*]: Odd or even?

TRIGORIN: Even.

NINA [*sighing*]: No. I've only one pea in my hand. I asked my fortune – should I become an actress or not? I wish someone would give me some advice.

TRIGORIN: One can't give advice about that.

[*A pause.*]

NINA: We're saying goodbye and . . . probably won't see each other any more. Please accept this little medallion from me as a memento. I've had your initials engraved . . . and on this side the title of your book *Days and Nights*.

TRIGORIN: How graceful. [*Kisses the medallion.*] A charming present.

NINA: Remember me sometimes.

TRIGORIN: I will. I will remember you as you were on that bright day – do you remember? – a week ago, when you wore a light-coloured dress . . . We talked . . . there was a white seagull lying on the bench.

NINA [*pensively*]: Yes, the seagull . . .

[*A pause.*]

We can't talk any more, they're coming . . . before you go give me two minutes, I beg you . . . [*Goes off left; simultaneously* ARKADINA *enters right, with* SORIN *wearing a frock-coat and a decoration,*[1] *then* YAKOV *busy with the packing.*]

ARKADINA: Stay at home, old thing. With your rheumatism ought you to be going about visiting? [*To Trigorin*] Who went out just now? Nina?

TRIGORIN: Yes.

ARKADINA: *Pardon,* we're in the way . . . [*Sits down.*] I think I've packed everything. I'm worn out.

TRIGORIN [*reading from the medallion*]: '*Days and Nights,* page 121, lines 11 and 12.'

YAKOV [*clearing the table*]: Do you want the fishing rods packed too?

TRIGORIN: Yes, I'll be needing them again. But give the books away to someone.

YAKOV: Yes, sir.

TRIGORIN [*to himself*]: 'Page 121, lines 11 and 12.' What do those lines say? [*To Arkadina*] Are there any of my books in the house?

ARKADINA: In my brother's study, in the corner cupboard.

TRIGORIN: 'Page 121 . . .' [*Exit.*]

ARKADINA: Really, Petrusha, stay at home . . .

SORIN: You're leaving, it'll be hard for me at home without you.

ARKADINA: And what will be going on in town?

SORIN: Nothing in particular, but all the same. [*Laughs.*] There'll be the laying of the foundation stone of the Zemstvo[2] council house and things like that . . . I want to jump out of this mudfish existence for just an hour or two, and I've got very stale, like an old cigarette-holder. I've asked for the horses to be brought at one, we'll leave at the same time.

ARKADINA [*after a pause*]: Stay here, don't mope, don't catch cold. Keep an eye on my son. Look after him. Advise him.

[*A pause.*]

I shall leave and still I won't know why Konstantin tried to shoot himself. I think the main reason was jealousy, and the sooner I take Trigorin from here the better.

SORIN: How shall I tell you? There were other reasons. One can understand, a young man, clever, lives in the country, in the back of beyond, no money, no position, no future. No occupation. He's ashamed and frightened of his idleness. I am exceptionally fond of him and he is attached to me, but in the end he thinks he's an extra in the house, a sponger, a useless dependant. Understandably, pride . . .

ARKADINA: The trouble he brings me! [*Thinking*] Should he go into government service . . .

SORIN [*whistles, then, irresolutely*]: I think it would be better if you . . . gave him a little money. First he should dress like a human being, and so on and so on. Look at him, he's been wearing the same old jacket for three years, he goes about without an overcoat . . . [*Laughs.*] And a few wild oats wouldn't come amiss . . . Let him go abroad or something . . . It's not expensive.

ARKADINA: Still . . . I can probably go as far as a suit, but abroad . . . No, at present, I can't even manage a suit. [*Firmly*] I have no money.

[SORIN *laughs.*]

No money!

SORIN [*whistling*]: So. I'm sorry, my dear, don't get cross. I believe you . . . You are a noble, fine woman.

ARKADINA [*with tears in her eyes*]: I have no money!

SORIN: If I had money, of course I'd give him some myself, but I have nothing, not a five-kopeck piece. [*Laughs.*] My estate manager takes all my pension and spends it on farming, cattle, beekeeping, and my money vanishes, to no purpose. The bees die, the cows die, I can't ever have horses . . .

ARKADINA: Yes, I do have money, but I am an actress; my clothes alone have quite ruined me.

SORIN: You are kind, my dear . . . I respect you . . . Yes . . . But there's something the matter with me again . . . [*Staggers.*] My head's spinning. [*Holds on to the table.*] I feel quite ill, and so on and so on.

ARKADINA [*in a frightened voice*]: Petrusha! [*Trying to support him.*] Petrusha, my darling! [*Shouting*] Help me! Help!

[*Enter* TREPLYOV, *with a bandage on his head, and* MEDVEDENKO.]

He feels ill.

SORIN: It's nothing, nothing . . . [*Smiles and drinks some water.*] It's over now . . . and so on and so on . . .

TREPLYOV [*to his mother*]: Don't get frightened, Mama, it's nothing dangerous. Uncle often has this now. [*To his uncle*] Uncle, you should lie down.

SORIN: Yes, for a little . . . But I'll still go to town . . . I'll lie down and then go . . . of course I'll go . . . [*Walks leaning on his stick.*]

MEDVEDENKO [*leading him by the arm*]: A riddle: four legs in the morning, two legs at midday, three in the evening . . .

SORIN [*laughing*]: Quite so. And at night flat on its back. Thank you. I can walk by myself . . .

MEDVEDENKO: Come, don't be polite! . . . [*He and* SORIN *go out.*]

ARKADINA: He frightened me!

TREPLYOV: It's not healthy for him to live in the country. He gets depressed. Mama, if you could show some sudden generosity and lend him fifteen hundred or two thousand roubles, he could live all year in town.

ARKADINA: I have no money. I am an actress, not a banker.

[*A pause.*]

TREPLYOV: Mama, change my bandage. You do it so well.

ARKADINA [*getting iodoform and a box with bandage material from the first-aid cupboard*]: And the doctor's late.

TREPLYOV: He promised to be here towards ten, and it's now midday.

ARKADINA: Sit down. [*Takes the bandage from his head.*] It's like a turban on you. Yesterday a caller in the kitchen asked what nationality you were. But it's almost healed. There's next to nothing there. [*Kisses him on the head.*] And when we've left you won't go bang-bang again, will you?

TREPLYOV: No, Mama. It was a moment of crazy despair, when I couldn't control myself. It won't happen again. [*Kisses her hand.*] You have magic hands. I remember long, long ago when you were still working in state theatres –I was little then – there was a fight in our courtyard and the laundress who lived in the building was badly beaten up. Do you remember? They brought her in unconscious . . . You went to look after her, took her medicines, washed her children in the tub. Don't you remember?

ARKADINA: No. [*Puts on a new bandage.*]

TREPLYOV: There were two ballet-dancers who lived then in the same building as us . . . They used to come to have coffee with you . . .

ARKADINA: That I remember.

TREPLYOV: They were so religious.

[*A pause.*]

Recently, these last days, I've felt a love for you as tender and total as in my childhood. I now have no one left but you. Only, why, why do you give in to the influence of that man?

ARKADINA: You don't understand him, Konstantin. He's a most noble person . . .

TREPLYOV: However, when he was told that I was planning to challenge him to a duel, his nobility didn't prevent him playing the coward. He's going away. Shameful flight!

ARKADINA: What nonsense! I myself asked him to leave here.

TREPLYOV: A most noble person! Here we are virtually quarrelling because of him, and he's now somewhere in the drawing-room or garden laughing at us . . . he's working on Nina's development, trying to convince her once and for all that he is a genius.

ARKADINA: You find pleasure in saying nasty things to me. I admire that man and I beg you not to speak badly of him in front of me.

TREPLYOV: And I don't admire him. You want me too to think him a genius, but I'm sorry, I can't lie, his books make me feel sick.

ARKADINA: It's jealousy. People with aspirations but no talent have nothing left but to criticize genuine talent. What a consolation for them!

TREPLYOV [*with irony*]: Genuine talent! [*Angrily*] If it comes to that, I'm more talented than all of you! [*Rips the bandage off his head.*] You slaves of convention have grabbed the prime places in the arts and you only recognize your own activities as legitimate and real, and everything else you crush and stifle. I do not recognize any of you. I don't recognize either you or him.

ARKADINA: Young decadent!

TREPLYOV: Go off to your darling theatre and act there in pathetic, talentless plays!

ARKADINA: I have never appeared in plays like that. Leave me alone! You're not capable of writing even a wretched little vaudeville sketch. Kiev bourgeois! Parasite!

TREPLYOV: Skinflint!

ARKADINA: Dirty tramp!

[TREPLYOV *sits down and quietly weeps.*]

Worthless creature! [*Walks to and fro, upset.*] Don't cry. You mustn't cry . . . [*Weeps.*] You mustn't . . . [*Kisses him on the forehead, cheeks and head.*] My darling child, forgive me . . . Forgive your wicked mother. Forgive me, I'm unhappy.

TREPLYOV [*embracing her*]: If you knew! I've lost everything. She doesn't love me. I can't write any more, all my hopes are gone . . .

ARKADINA: Don't despair . . . Everything will be all right. He'll go away now, she will love you again. [*Wiping away his tears.*] Stop it. We've now made up.

TREPLYOV [*kissing her hand*]: Yes, Mama.

ARKADINA [*affectionately*]: Make your peace with him too. You mustn't have a duel . . . Must you?

TREPLYOV: Very well . . . Only, Mama, don't let me see him. It's hard for me . . . more than I can stand . . .

[*Enter* TRIGORIN.]

Here he is . . . I'll go out. [*Quickly puts the medicines away in the cupboard.*] And the doctor will do the bandage later . . .

TRIGORIN [*looking in a book*]: Page 121 . . . lines 11 and 12 . . . Here it is . . . [*Reads*] 'If ever you need my life, come and take it.'

[TREPLYOV *picks up the bandage from the floor and goes out.*]

ARKADINA [*glancing at the clock*]: They'll bring the horses soon.

TRIGORIN [*to himself*]: If ever you need my life, come and take it.

ARKADINA: I hope all your things are packed now.

TRIGORIN [*impatiently*]: Yes, yes. [*Musing*] Why do I hear sadness in this appeal from a pure spirit, why is my heart so painfully constricted? . . . If ever you need my life, come and take it. [*To Arkadina*] Let's stay one more day.

[ARKADINA *shakes her head.*]

Let's stay!

ARKADINA: My dear, I know what's holding you here. But control yourself. You've got a little tipsy, sober up.

TRIGORIN: You too must be sober, must be intelligent and show good sense; I beg you, just take a look at all of this as a real friend . . . [*Presses her hand.*] You're capable of sacrifices. Be my friend, release me . . .

ARKADINA [*with strong emotion*]: Are you so infatuated?

TRIGORIN: I am called to her! Perhaps it is just what I need.

ARKADINA: The love of a provincial girl? Oh, how little you know yourself!

TRIGORIN: Sometimes people sleep on their feet, so while I'm talking to you it's as if I'm sleeping and seeing her in a dream . . . I am overcome by sweet, wondrous dreams . . . Let me go . . .

ARKADINA [*trembling*]: No, no . . . I am an ordinary woman, you mustn't talk to me like that . . . Don't torment me, Boris . . . I'm afraid . . .

TRIGORIN: If you want, you can rise above the ordinary. Young, beautiful, poetic love that transports us into the world of dreams – that's the only thing on earth that can give happiness! I've never felt such love . . . When I was young I had no time, I was hanging round the doors of publishers, struggling with poverty . . . Now this love has come, at last, it summons me . . . What sense is there in running away from it?

ARKADINA [*in anger*]: You're out of your mind.

TRIGORIN: Well?

ARKADINA: Today you have all conspired to torment me! [*Weeps.*]

TRIGORIN [*putting his head in his hands*]: She doesn't understand. She doesn't want to understand.

ARKADINA: Am I really now so old and ugly that you can talk to me of other women with no shame? [*Hugs and kisses him.*] Oh, you have gone mad! My beautiful, wonderful man! . . . The last page of my life! [*Falls on her knees.*] If you leave me even for a single hour I won't survive. I shall go out of my mind, my marvellous, magnificent man, my conqueror . . .

TRIGORIN: Someone might come in. [*Helps her get up.*]

ARKADINA: Let them, I am not ashamed of my love for you. [*Kisses his hands.*] My treasure, my wild man, you want to behave like a lunatic, but I don't want you to, I won't let you . . . [*Laughing*] You are mine . . . you are mine . . . This forehead is mine, and these eyes are mine, and this beautiful silky hair is mine too . . . You are all mine. You are so talented, so wise, the best of all writers today, you are Russia's one hope . . . You have such reserves of sincerity, simplicity, freshness, sane humour . . . In a single line you can convey the essence of a person or a landscape, your characters are alive. Oh, no one can read you without going into ecstasy! Do you think this praise is absurd? Am I a flatterer? Come, look into my eyes . . . look here . . . Do I look like a liar? You see, only I can appreciate you; only I tell you the truth, my dearest, wonderful friend . . . Will you come? You will? You won't abandon me? . . .

TRIGORIN: I have no will of my own . . . I never had a will of my own . . . Feeble, flabby, always giving in – can that really appeal to a woman? Take me, carry me off, but just don't let me one step away from you . . .

ARKADINA [to herself]: Now he's mine. [Lightly, as if nothing had happened] But if you want to you can stay. I myself will go off and you'll come on later, in a week's time. In fact, what's the hurry?

TRIGORIN: No, let's leave together.

ARKADINA: As you like. Together it is . . .

[A pause. TRIGORIN writes in his notebook.]

What are you doing?

TRIGORIN: This morning I heard a good phrase, 'the virgins' wood' . . . It'll come in handy. [Stretches.] So, we are leaving? Back to railway carriages, stations, buffets, chops, conversations with strangers . . .

SHAMRAYEV [entering]: I have the melancholy honour of announcing that the horses are ready. It is now time, dear lady, to leave for the station; the train arrives at five minutes past two. Irina Nikolayevna, be so kind as not to forget to make a little inquiry: where is the actor Suzdaltsev now? Is he alive? Is he well? Once upon a time we used to drink together . . . He gave an inimitable performance in *The Post Office Robbery*[3] . . . I remember the tragedian Izmaylov worked with him in Yelizavetgrad – another remarkable personality . . . Do not hurry, dear lady, you can have another five minutes. They were once playing two conspirators in a melodrama, and when they were suddenly discovered, the words were 'We have fallen into a trap', but Izmaylov said, 'We have fallen into a prat.' [Laughs noisily.] Prat! . . .

[*While he is speaking,* YAKOV *is busy by the trunks, the maid brings Arkadina her hat, coat, parasol and gloves; they all help Arkadina to dress. The* COOK *looks in at the left-hand door and after a moment comes in awkwardly.* POLINA ANDREYEVNA *enters, then* SORIN *and* MEDVEDENKO.]

POLINA ANDREYEVNA [*holding a little basket*]: Here are some plums for your journey . . . They're very sweet. Perhaps you'll feel like a little treat.

ARKADINA: You are very kind, Polina Andreyevna.

POLINA ANDREYEVNA: Goodbye, my dear. If anything wasn't quite right, forgive me. [*Cries.*]

ARKADINA [*embracing her*]: Everything was all right, everything was all right. Only you mustn't cry.

POLINA ANDREYEVNA: Our time is passing.

ARKADINA: What can we do!

SORIN [*wearing an overcoat with a cape and a hat, and carrying a stick, comes in at the left-hand door; walking across the room*]: Sister, it's time, we mustn't be late after all that. I'm going to get in the carriage. [*Exit.*]

MEDVEDENKO: And I'll walk to the station . . . to see you off. I'll walk fast. [*Exit.*]

ARKADINA: Goodbye, my dears . . . If we're alive and well, we'll meet again next summer . . .

[*The maid,* YAKOV *and the* COOK *kiss her hand.*]

Don't forget me. [*Gives the cook a rouble.*] Here's a rouble for the three of you.

COOK: Our humble thanks, my lady. Have a good journey. We're very grateful to you.

YAKOV: God bless you!

SHAMRAYEV: Cheer us up with a little letter. Goodbye, Boris Alekseyevich.

ARKADINA: Where's Konstantin? Tell him I'm leaving. We must say goodbye. Well, think of me kindly. [*To Yakov*] I gave a rouble to the cook. That's for the three of you.

[*All go out at right. The stage is empty. Offstage there is the usual noise of people saying goodbye. The maid returns to take the basket of plums from the table and goes out again.*]

TRIGORIN [*returning*]: I forgot my walking-stick. I think it's out there on the terrace. [*Goes towards the left-hand door and meets* NINA *coming in.*] You here? We're leaving . . .

NINA: I felt we would see each other once more. [*Excitedly*] Boris Alekseyevich, I have taken an irrevocable decision, the die is cast, I'm going on the stage. Tomorrow I won't be here, I'm leaving my father, leaving everything and beginning a new life . . . I'm going like you . . . to Moscow. We'll see each other there.

TRIGORIN [*looking round*]: Stay at the Slavyansky Bazaar[4] . . . Get word to me at once . . . The Grokholsky Building on Molchanovka . . . I'm in a hurry.

[*A pause.*]

NINA: One minute more . . .

TRIGORIN [*in a low voice*]: You're so beautiful . . . Oh, the happiness of thinking that we shall soon see each other!

[*She rests her head on his breast.*]

I'll see those wonderful eyes again, that inexpressibly beautiful, tender smile . . . that gentle face, angelically pure expression . . . My darling . . .

[*A prolonged kiss.*]

[*Curtain.*]

[*Two years pass between Acts Three and Four.*]

Act Four

*One of the reception rooms in Sorin's house, which Konstantin Treplyov
has turned into a study. Right and left are doors leading to rooms inside the
house; at centre, French windows on to the terrace. Apart from the usual
drawing-room furniture, in the right-hand corner is a writing-desk, by the
left-hand door a Turkish divan; a bookcase, books on the windowsills and on
the chairs. Evening. A single lamp is burning under a shade. Semi-darkness.
The trees are groaning and the wind is howling in the chimneys. The
night-watchman knocks. Enter* MEDVEDENKO *and* MASHA.

MASHA [*calling*]: Konstantin Gavrilych! Konstantin Gavrilych!
   [*Looks around.*] There's no one. The old man asks every minute,
   where's Kostya, where's Kostya . . . He can't live without him . . .
MEDVEDENKO: He's frightened of being alone. [*Listening.*] What
   terrible weather. It's the second day now.
MASHA [*turning up the flame in the lamp*]: There are waves on the
   lake. Huge ones.
MEDVEDENKO: It's dark in the garden. We must tell them to pull
   down that theatre in the garden. It stands there like a skeleton,
   bare and ugly, and the curtain bangs in the wind. When I walked
   by it yesterday evening, it seemed to me as if someone was
   weeping there.
MASHA: Well, well . . .

   [*A pause.*]

MEDVEDENKO: Masha, let's go home.
MASHA [*shaking her head*]: I'm going to spend the night here.

MEDVEDENKO [*imploringly*]: Masha, let's go! The baby must be hungry.

MASHA: Nonsense. Matryona will feed him.

[*A pause.*]

MEDVEDENKO: Poor boy. It's the third night without his mother.

MASHA: You've become a bore. At least you once used to give us a bit of philosophy, but now it's just – the baby, home, the baby, home – and that's all anyone ever hears from you.

MEDVEDENKO: Let's go, Masha.

MASHA: Go yourself.

MEDVEDENKO: Your father won't give me a horse.

MASHA: He will. Ask him and he'll give you one.

MEDVEDENKO: I think I will ask. So you'll come home tomorrow?

MASHA [*taking snuff*]: Mm, tomorrow. You're nagging me . . .

[*Enter* TREPLYOV *and* POLINA ANDREYEVNA; TREPLYOV *has brought pillows and a blanket and* POLINA ANDREYEVNA *bed linen; they put them on the Turkish divan, then* TREPLYOV *goes to his writing-desk and sits down.*]

What's this for, Mama?

POLINA ANDREYEVNA: Pyotr Nikolayevich asked for his bed to be made up in Kostya's room.

MASHA: Let me . . . [*Makes the bed.*]

POLINA ANDREYEVNA [*sighing*]: An old man's the same as a child . . . [*Goes to the desk and, leaning on her elbows, looks at a manuscript; a pause.*]

MEDVEDENKO: So I'll go. Goodbye, Masha. [*Kisses his wife's hand.*] Goodbye, Mother. [*Tries to kiss his mother-in-law's hand.*]

POLINA ANDREYEVNA [*crossly*]: That's enough. Off you go, God bless.

MEDVEDENKO: Goodbye, Konstantin Gavrilych.

[TREPLYOV *silently gives his hand.* MEDVEDENKO *goes out.*]

POLINA ANDREYEVNA [*looking at the manuscript*]: No one thought or guessed, Kostya, that you would make a real writer. And now, thank God, magazines have begun to send you money. [*Strokes his hair.*] And you've become handsome . . . Dear, good Kostya, be a little nicer to my Mashenka . . .

MASHA [*making the bed*]: Let him be, Mama.

POLINA ANDREYEVNA [*to Treplyov*]: She's a dear.

[*A pause.*]

Kostya, a woman doesn't need much, only the odd tender look. I know that from my own experience.

[TREPLYOV *gets up from his desk and silently goes out.*]

MASHA: There, you've made him angry. You had to go and annoy him!

POLINA ANDREYEVNA: I'm sorry for you, Mashenka.

MASHA: Very helpful!

POLINA ANDREYEVNA: My heart has bled for you. I see everything, you know, I understand everything.

MASHA: It's all nonsense. Hopeless love only exists in novels. It's rubbish. Only you mustn't let yourself go and carry on waiting, waiting by the sea for the weather to change . . . Once love has flowered in your heart, out with it. They've promised to transfer my husband to another district. Once we move there I'll forget everything . . . I'll rip it out of my heart by the roots.

[*From two rooms away come the sounds of a melancholy waltz.*]

POLINA ANDREYEVNA: Kostya's playing. That means he's depressed.

MASHA [*silently making two or three turns of a waltz*]: The main thing, Mama, is not to have him in front of my eyes. If only my Semyon gets the transfer, believe me, I'll forget in a month. It's all rubbish.

[*The left-hand door opens.* DORN *and* MEDVEDENKO *wheel in* SORIN *in his chair.*]

MEDVEDENKO: I now have six people at home. And flour is seventy kopecks the *pud*.

DORN: So you must just try and get along.

MEDVEDENKO: It's all very well for you to laugh. You're rolling in money.

DORN: Money? My friend, in thirty years of practice, tireless practice when I didn't have day or night to myself, I only managed to save two thousand roubles – and that I spent abroad the other day. I've got nothing.

MASHA [*to her husband*]: Haven't you gone?

MEDVEDENKO [*guiltily*]: What do you expect? When I'm not given a horse!

MASHA [*in a low voice, in a bitter rage*]: Just get out of my sight!

[*The wheelchair comes to a stop in the left half of the room;* POLINA ANDREYEVNA, MASHA *and* DORN *sit down by it;* MEDVEDENKO *goes off to one side, in depression.*]

DORN: Well, what a lot of changes you've made! A study out of a drawing-room.

MASHA: It's easier for Konstantin Gavrilych to work here. He can go out into the garden and think there whenever he wants.

[*The watchman knocks.*]

SORIN: Where's my sister?

DORN: She's gone to the station to meet Trigorin. She'll be back right away.

SORIN: If you thought it necessary to write for my sister, I must be seriously ill. [*After a silence.*] Only here's a funny thing, I'm seriously ill but I'm still given no medicine.

DORN: Well, what do you want? Valerian drops? Bicarbonate of soda? Quinine?

SORIN: The philosophy lesson begins. What a punishment! [*Nodding at the divan.*] Is that made up for me?

POLINA ANDREYEVNA: For you, Pyotr Nikolayevich.

SORIN: Thank you.

DORIN [*sings*]: 'The moon she sails in the sky of night . . .'

SORIN: Now I want to give Kostya an idea for a story. It should be called 'The man who wanted to' – '*L'Homme qui a voulu*'. When I was young, at one time I wanted to become a writer – and didn't; I wanted to speak well – and spoke abominably [*mimics himself*]. 'And so on and so on, what with this and that . . .' I used to sum up, sum up till the sweat poured off me; I wanted to marry and didn't; I always wanted to live in town and here I am ending my life in the country, and so on and so on.

DORN: You wanted to become a Full State Councillor[1] – and did.

SORIN [*laughing*]: I didn't aim to. That just happened.

DORN: To express dissatisfaction with one's life at the age of sixty-two – you must agree – is small-minded.

SORIN: What a grouch you are. You must understand, I want to live.

DORN: That's silliness. By the laws of nature all forms of life must have an end.

SORIN: You are reasoning like a well-fed man. You're well-fed and therefore indifferent to life, it's all the same to you. But you too will be frightened of dying.

DORN: The fear of death is an animal fear . . . One must overcome it. Only those who believe in eternal life, who are fearful because of their sins, are consciously afraid of death. But firstly, you are a non-believer, and secondly, what are your sins? For twenty-five years you worked in the Department of Justice – that's all.

SORIN [*laughing*]: Twenty-eight . . .

[TREPLYOV *enters and sits down on a stool at Sorin's feet.* MASHA *doesn't take her eyes off him the whole time.*]

DORN: We're stopping Konstantin Gavrilovich working.

TREPLYOV: No, it doesn't matter.

[*A pause.*]

MEDVEDENKO: Can I ask you, doctor, which foreign city you liked most?

DORN: Genoa.[2]

MEDVEDENKO: Why Genoa?

DORN: It has an exceptional street crowd. When you go out of your hotel in the evening, the whole street is jammed with people. Then you move aimlessly in the crowd, this way, that way, zigzagging about, you live together with the crowd, you merge with it spiritually and you begin to believe in the possibility of a single universal spirit, like the one Nina Zarechnaya once acted in your play. By the way, where is Nina now? Where is she, and what's she doing?

TREPLYOV: I think she's well.

DORN: Someone told me she was leading an odd kind of life. What happened?

TREPLYOV: That, doctor, is a long story.

DORN: Then make it a short one.

[*A pause.*]

TREPLYOV: She ran away from home and took up with Trigorin. Did you know that?

DORN: I did.

TREPLYOV: She had a child. The child died. Trigorin lost his love for her and returned to his previous attachments, as one might have expected. He'd never really left them but, with true lack of character, sort of made do in both places. As far as I can understand from what I heard, Nina's personal life went completely wrong.

DORN: And the stage?

TREPLYOV: I think worse still. She made her debut in summer theatre outside Moscow, then went off to the provinces. At that time I kept my eye on her and for some while, wherever she went, I followed. She always went for big roles, but her acting was coarse, tasteless, full of noisy rhetoric and abrupt gestures. There were moments when she would show her talent in an exclamation or a death scene, but they were just moments.

DORN: So, she really has talent?

TREPLYOV: It was difficult to tell. She must have. I used to see her but she didn't want to see me and the maid wouldn't let me into her room. I understood her mood and didn't insist on our meeting.

[*A pause.*]

What more can I tell you? Later, when I'd returned home, I got letters from her. Letters that were intelligent, warm, interesting; she didn't complain but I felt she was deeply unhappy; every line was a painful nerve, stretched tight. And her imagination was rather deranged. She'd sign herself 'Seagull'. In *Rusalka*[3] the Miller says he is a raven, in the same way in her letters she kept on saying she was a seagull. She's here now.

DORN: What do you mean here?

TREPLYOV: At an inn in the town. She's been in a room there for the last five days. I would have gone to see her and Marya Ilyinichna did go, but she won't receive anyone. Semyon Semyonovich assures us he saw her yesterday in the fields two versts from here.

MEDVEDENKO: Yes, I did see her. She was walking in the other direction, towards the town. I bowed and asked her why she didn't pay us a visit. She said she would.

TREPLYOV: She won't come.

[*A pause.*]

Her father and stepmother don't want to know her. They've put guards everywhere to prevent her from coming anywhere near the house. [*Walks away with the doctor to the desk.*] How easy it is, doctor, to be a philosopher on paper, and how difficult in life!

SORIN: She was a delightful girl.

DORN: What?

SORIN: I said she was a delightful girl. Full State Councillor Sorin was even in love with her for a time.

DORN: You old goat.

[*Shamrayev's laugh is heard.*]

POLINA ANDREYEVNA: I think they've come from the station . . .

TREPLYOV: Yes, I can hear Mama.

[*Enter* ARKADINA *with* TRIGORIN, *followed by* SHAMRAYEV.]

SHAMRAYEV [*coming in*]: We all become old and weathered under the influence of the elements, but you, dear lady, are still young . . . A bright-coloured blouse, sparkle . . . grace . . .

ARKADINA: You want to bring me bad luck again, you boring man!

TRIGORIN [*to Sorin*]: Good evening, Pyotr Nikolayevich. So you're still poorly? That's not good. [*Seeing Masha, with pleasure*] Marya Ilyinichna!

MASHA: You recognized me? [*Shakes his hand.*]

TRIGORIN: Married?

MASHA: Long ago.

TRIGORIN: Are you happy? [*Exchanges bows with Dorn and Medvedenko, then hesitantly goes towards Treplyov.*] Irina Nikolayevna said you've forgotten the past now and have stopped being angry.

[TREPLYOV *extends him a hand.*]

ARKADINA [*to her son*]: Boris Alekseyevich has brought the magazine with your new story.

TREPLYOV [*taking it, to Trigorin*]: Thank you. You're very kind.

[*They sit down.*]

TRIGORIN: Your readers send you greetings . . . In Petersburg and Moscow there's a lot of interest in you and I'm always being asked about you. They ask what are you like, how old are you, are you dark or fair. Somehow everyone thinks you aren't young. And since you write under a pseudonym no one knows your real name. You're a mystery, like the Man in the Iron Mask.[4]

TREPLYOV: Are you here for a long stay?

TRIGORIN: No, tomorrow I think I'm going back to Moscow. I have to. I'm hurrying to finish a novel and then I've promised something for an anthology. In short – the same old story.

[*While they are talking* ARKADINA *and* POLINA ANDREYEVNA *put a card table in the middle of the room and open it;* SHAMRAYEV *lights candles and brings up chairs. They get a lotto[5] board from the cupboard.*]

The weather has given me an unfriendly welcome. The wind is cruel. Tomorrow morning if it drops I'll go down to the lake to fish. Incidentally, I must look at the garden and the place where your play was performed – do you remember? I've worked out a story, I just need to refresh the setting in my memory.

MASHA [*to her father*]: Papa, let Semyon take a horse. He has to get home.

SHAMRAYEV [*imitating her*]: A horse . . . get home . . . [*Sternly*] You saw yourself: they've just been sent to the station. They can't be driven again.

MASHA: But there are other horses . . . [*Seeing he is silent, throws up her hand.*] Having to deal with you . . .

MEDVEDENKO: Masha, I'll walk. Really . . .

POLINA ANDREYEVNA [*sighing*]: Walk, in weather like this . . . [*Sits down at the card table.*] Ladies and gentlemen, come on.

MEDVEDENKO: It's only six versts . . . Goodbye . . . [*Kisses his wife's hand.*] Goodbye, Mother.

[*His mother-in-law reluctantly gives him her hand to kiss.*]

I didn't want to bother anyone, but the baby . . . [*Bows to all.*] Goodbye . . . [*Goes out; his gait is apologetic.*]

SHAMRAYEV: He'll probably make it on his feet. He doesn't have to ride like a general.

POLINA ANDREYEVNA [*rapping on the table*]: Come on, ladies and gentlemen. Let's not waste time, soon we'll be called to supper.

[SHAMRAYEV, MASHA *and* DORN *sit down at the table*.]

ARKADINA [*to Trigorin*]: When the long autumn evenings come on, we play lotto here. Just look: the old lotto board on which my mother used to play with us when we were children. Won't you play a game with us before supper? [*She and* TRIGORIN *sit down at the table*.] It's a boring game but if you get used to it it's quite nice. [*Deals everyone three cards*.]

TREPLYOV [*turning the pages of the magazine*]: He read his own story but he didn't even cut the pages of mine. [*Puts the magazine on the desk, then moves towards the left-hand door; as he goes past his mother, kisses her on the head*.]

ARKADINA: What about you, Kostya?

TREPLYOV: I'm sorry, I don't really want to . . . I'll go for a walk. [*Goes out*.]

ARKADINA: The stake is ten kopecks. Will you ante for me, doctor?

DORN: At your command.

MASHA: Has everyone put down their stakes? I'm starting . . . Twenty-two!

ARKADINA: Yes.

MASHA: Three!

DORN: Yes.

MASHA: You've put down three? Eight! Eighty-one! Ten!

SHAMRAYEV: Don't go so fast.

ARKADINA: What a reception they gave me in Kharkov! Heavens, my head is still spinning.

MASHA: Thirty-four!

[*Offstage the strains of a melancholy waltz.*]

ARKADINA: The students gave me an ovation . . . Three baskets of flowers, two wreaths and this . . . [*Takes a brooch from her breast and throws it on the table.*]

SHAMRAYEV: Now, that's something . . .

MASHA: Fifty! . . .

DORN: Fifty exactly?

ARKADINA: I wore an amazing frock . . . Whatever else, I know how to dress.

POLINA ANDREYEVNA: Kostya's playing. The poor boy's depressed.

SHAMRAYEV: The papers are very rude about him.

MASHA: Seventy-seven!

ARKADINA: Why pay any attention?

TRIGORIN: He's unlucky. He still can't find his real voice. There's something strange, ill-defined, at times even like delirium. Not one live character.

MASHA: Eleven!

ARKADINA [*looking over at Sorin*]: Petrusha, are you bored?

[*A pause.*]

He's asleep.

DORN: The Full State Councillor is asleep.

MASHA: Seven! Ninety!

TRIGORIN: If I lived in a country house like this, by a lake, would I start writing? I'd overcome that urge and just go fishing.

MASHA: Twenty-eight!

TRIGORIN: To catch a ruff or perch – what bliss!

DORN: But I believe in Konstantin Gavrilych. There's something there. There really is. He thinks in images, his stories are vivid, brightly coloured . . . and I feel them strongly. It's just a pity he has no definite objectives. He makes an effect, that's all, and an effect on its own won't get you far. Irina Nikolayevna, are you glad your son's a writer?

ARKADINA: Can you imagine, I still haven't read him. I just have no time.

MASHA: Twenty-six!

[TREPLYOV *quietly comes in and goes to his desk.*]

SHAMRAYEV [*to Trigorin*]: We've still got that thing of yours, Boris
Alekseyevich.
TRIGORIN: What thing?
SHAMRAYEV: That time Konstantin Gavrilych shot a seagull and
you asked me to get it stuffed.
TRIGORIN: I don't remember. [*Thinking.*] I really don't.
MASHA: Sixty-six! One!
TREPLYOV [*throwing open a window and listening*]: It's so dark. I
don't understand why I feel so anxious.
ARKADINA: Shut the window, there's a draught.

[TREPLYOV *shuts the window.*]

MASHA: Eighty-eight!
TRIGORIN: Ladies and gentlemen, I've won.
ARKADINA [*merrily*]: Bravo! Bravo!
SHAMRAYEV: Bravo!
ARKADINA: This gentleman is always lucky, everywhere. [*Gets up.*]
And now let's go and have something to eat. Our great man has
had no dinner today. We'll go on playing after supper. [*To her
son*] Kostya, leave your manuscripts, let's go and eat.
TREPLYOV: I don't want to, Mama, I've had enough to eat.
ARKADINA: You know best. [*Wakes Sorin.*] Petrusha, supper!
[*Taking Shamrayev's arm.*] I shall tell you about my reception in
Kharkov . . .

[POLINA ANDREYEVNA *puts out the candles on the table, then she
and* DORN *wheel the chair out. All leave by the left-hand door; only*
TREPLYOV *is left on the stage, at his desk.*]

TREPLYOV [*getting ready to write; reads over what he has already
written*]: I've talked so much of new forms but now I feel I myself
am slowly slipping into a rut. [*Reading*] 'A poster on the wall
proclaimed . . . A pale face framed in dark tresses . . .' Proclaimed,

framed . . . that's poor stuff. [*Makes a deletion.*] I'll begin with the hero being woken by the noise of the rain, and everything else out. The description of the moonlit evening is long and forced. Trigorin has evolved his technique, it's easy for him . . . He has the neck of a broken bottle glistening on the sluice-gate and the darkling shadow of the mill wheel – there's his moonlit night; but I have tremulous light and the quiet blinking of the stars and the distant sounds of a piano dying in the quiet perfumed air . . . It's torture.

[*A pause.*]

Yes, increasingly I conclude that it's not a question of old and new forms but of a man writing without thinking of any forms, writing because it flows freely from his soul.

[*Someone knocks on the window nearest the desk.*]

What's that? [*Looks out of the window.*] I can't see anything. [*Opens the French windows and looks into the garden.*] Someone ran down the steps. [*Calls.*] Who's there? [*Goes out; he can be heard walking quickly along the terrace; in half a minute he returns with* NINA ZARECHNAYA.] Nina! Nina!

[NINA *puts her head on his breast and tries to control her sobbing.*]

[*With emotion*] Nina! Nina! It's you . . . you . . . I've been terribly low in spirit all day, as if I had a premonition. [*Takes off her hat and cloak.*] Oh my angel, my darling girl has come! We're not going to cry, no we aren't.

NINA: Someone's here.

TREPLYOV: There's no one.

NINA: Lock the doors or they'll come in.

TREPLYOV: No one will come in.

NINA: I know Irina Nikolayevna is here. Lock the doors.

TREPLYOV [*locking the right-hand door and going towards the left-hand one*]: There's no lock on this one. I'll block it with an armchair. [*Puts an armchair against the door.*] Don't be afraid. No one will come in.

NINA [*looking fixedly at his face*]: Let me look at you. [*Looking around.*] It's warm and nice . . . This was a drawing-room then. Have I changed a lot?

TREPLYOV: Yes . . . You're thinner and your eyes have become bigger. Nina, it's strange somehow that I'm seeing you now. Why wouldn't you let me come to you? Why haven't you come here before now? I know you've been here nearly a week. I've been to you several times every day. I've stood below your window like a beggar.

NINA: I was afraid you would hate me. Every night I dream that you're looking at me and don't recognize me. If you knew! Ever since I arrived I've been coming and walking here – by the lake. Many times I've been close to your house but I couldn't bring myself to go in. Let's sit down.

[*They sit.*]

We'll sit and talk and talk. It's nice here, warm and comfortable . . . Do you hear – the wind. Turgenev has a passage: 'Lucky is he who on such nights has the roof of a home above him, who has a warm nest.'⁶ I am a seagull . . . No, that's not right. [*Rubs her forehead.*] Where was I? Yes . . . Turgenev . . . 'And the Lord help all homeless wanderers . . .' Nothing's the matter. [*Sobs.*]

TREPLYOV: Nina, again you're . . . Nina!

NINA: Don't worry, I feel better for that . . . I haven't cried for two years. Late yesterday evening I went to look in the garden to see if our theatre was still there. And it's still standing. I cried for the first time in two years, and I got relief, things became clearer in my heart. You see, I'm no longer crying. [*Takes his hand.*] And so, you're a writer now . . . You're a writer, I'm an actress . . . We've both been sucked into the whirlpool . . . I used to live happily, like a child – I'd wake in the morning and start to sing; I loved you, I dreamed of being famous, but now? Off to Yelets early tomorrow morning, third class . . . with the peasants, and in Yelets merchants with a bit of education will make up to me with their compliments. Life is crude!

TREPLYOV: Why Yelets?

NINA: I've taken an engagement for the whole winter. It's time to leave.

TREPLYOV: Nina, I cursed you, I hated you, I tore up your letters and photographs, but I knew every moment that my spirit is bound to you for ever. Nina, it's beyond my power to stop loving you. Since I lost you and began to be published, life has been unbearable for me – I am suffering . . . It's as if my youth has been suddenly cut off and I feel as if I've lived out ninety years on this earth. I call you, I kiss the ground on which you've walked; wherever I look, everywhere I see your face, that tender smile which shone on me in the best years of my life . . .

NINA [*bewildered*]: Why is he talking like this, why is he talking like this?

TREPLYOV: I'm lonely, I have no one's affection to warm me, I'm cold as if I were in a cave underground, and whatever I write is all desiccated, stale, sombre. Stay here, Nina, I beg you, or let me go away with you!

[NINA *quickly puts on her hat and cloak*.]

Nina, why? Nina, for God's sake . . . [*Watches her dress; a pause*.]

NINA: My horses are at the gate. Don't see me off, I'll go by myself . . . [*With tears in her eyes*] Give me some water . . .

TREPLYOV [*giving her a drink*]: Where are you going now?

NINA: To town.

[*A pause*.]

Is Irina Nikolayevna here?

TREPLYOV: Yes . . . On Thursday my uncle felt ill, we telegraphed her to come.

NINA: Why do you say that you kissed the ground on which I

walked? You should kill me. [*Leans over the table.*] I'm so exhausted. If only I could rest . . . rest! [*Raises her head.*] I am a seagull
. . . That's not right. I am an actress. Yes! [*Hearing Arkadina and
Trigorin laugh, she listens, then runs to the left-hand door and
looks through the keyhole.*] And he's here . . . [*Returning towards
Treplyov.*] Yes . . . It doesn't matter . . . Yes . . . He didn't believe
in the theatre, he went on mocking my dreams, and little by little
I too stopped believing and lost heart . . . And then came the
troubles of love, jealousy, the constant fear for my child . . . I
became petty, worthless, I acted mindlessly . . . I didn't know
what to do with my hands, didn't know how to stand on the stage,
wasn't in control of my voice. You can't understand what it's like
to feel you're acting terribly. I am a seagull. No, that's not right
. . . Do you remember, you shot a seagull? A man just came
along, saw it and killed it from having nothing to do . . . A plot
for a short story. That's not right . . . [*Rubs her forehead.*] What
was I . . . ? I was talking about the stage. Now I am not so . . . I
am now a real actress, I act with enjoyment, with ecstasy, I get
intoxicated on the stage and feel that I'm beautiful. And now,
while I've been staying here, I've walked everywhere, I walk and
walk, and think, think and feel how every day my spiritual powers
grow . . . Kostya, I know now, I understand. In what we do –
whether we act on the stage or write – the most important thing
isn't fame or glory or anything I used to dream about – but the
ability to endure. To know how to bear your cross and have faith.
I have faith, and my pain is less, and when I think about my
vocation I'm not afraid of life.

TREPLYOV [*sadly*]: You have found your road, you know where
you're going, but I am still carried along in a chaos of dreams and
images, without knowing why and for whom they exist. I have
no faith and I don't know where my vocation lies.

NINA [*listening*]: Shh . . . I'm going. Goodbye. When I become a
great actress, come and watch me. Do you promise? And now
. . . [*Presses his hand.*] It's late. I can hardly stand on my feet . . .
I'm worn out, I'm hungry . . .

TREPLYOV: Stay, I'll give you some supper.

NINA: No, no . . . Don't see me off, I'll go by myself . . . My horses are near . . . So, she brought him with her? Well, it doesn't matter. When you see Trigorin, don't tell him anything . . . I love him, I love him even more than before . . . The plot for a short story . . . I love him, I love him passionately, I love him to desperation. It was good before, Kostya! Do you remember? What a clear, warm, joyful, pure life, what feelings – feelings like delicate, exquisite flowers . . . Do you remember? . . . [*Recites*] 'Men, lions, eagles and partridges, antlered deer, geese, spiders, silent fish which live in the water, starfish and organisms invisible to the eye – in short, all life, all life, all life has been extinguished after completing its sad cycle . . . For thousands of centuries the earth has not borne a single living being, and this poor moon lights her lantern to no purpose. In the meadow the cranes give their waking cry no more and in May the cockchafers are no longer heard in the lime groves . . .' [*Impulsively embraces Treplyov and runs out through the French windows.*]

TREPLYOV [*after a pause*]: It'll be awkward if someone meets her in the garden and then tells Mama. It could hurt Mama . . . [*For two whole minutes he silently tears up all his manuscripts and throws them under the desk, then he opens the right-hand door and goes out.*]

DORN [*from outside, trying to open the left-hand door*]: Funny. The door seems to be locked . . . [*Enters and puts the armchair in its place.*] It's an obstacle race.

[*Enter* ARKADINA *and* POLINA ANDREYEVNA, *followed by* YAKOV *carrying bottles and* MASHA, *then* SHAMRAYEV *and* TRIGORIN.]

ARKADINA: Put the red wine and the beer for Boris Alekseyevich here on the table. We're going to play cards and have a drink. Ladies and gentlemen, let's sit down.

POLINA ANDREYEVNA [*to Yakov*]: Serve the tea now too. [*Lights the candles and sits down at the card table.*]

SHAMRAYEV [*takes Trigorin to the cupboard*]: Here's the thing I was just telling you about . . . [*Out of the cupboard he produces the stuffed seagull.*] This is what you ordered.

TRIGORIN [*looking at the seagull*]: I don't remember. [*Thinking.*] I don't remember.

[*Offstage, right, a shot; everyone starts.*]

ARKADINA [*frightened*]: What's that?

DORN: Nothing. Something must have exploded in my travelling medicine chest. Don't worry. [*Goes out of the right-hand door and returns half a minute later.*] I was right. A bottle of ether went off. [*Sings.*] 'Again before thee I stand bewitched . . .'

ARKADINA [*sitting down at the table*]: Phew, I was frightened. It reminded me how . . . [*Covers her face with her hands.*] It even went dark before my eyes.

DORN [*turning the pages of a magazine, to Trigorin*]: They published an article here a couple of months ago . . . a letter from America, and I wanted to ask you, by the way . . . [*puts his arm round Trigorin's waist and takes him towards the footlights*] . . . as I'm very interested in this question . . . [*Quietly, dropping his voice*] Take Irina Nikolayevna somewhere away from here. The fact is, Konstantin Gavrilovich has shot himself . . .

[*Curtain.*]

Uncle Vanya

Scenes from Country Life in Four Acts

CHARACTERS

ALEKSANDR VLADIMIROVICH SEREBRYAKOV,
  an emeritus professor

YELENA ANDREYEVNA [*also* HÉLÈNE,
  LENOCHKA], *his wife, aged twenty-seven*

SOFYA ALEKSANDROVNA [*also* SONYA, SOPHIE],
  his daughter by his first marriage

MARIYA VASILYEVNA VOYNITSKAYA, *the widow
  of a Privy Councillor, mother of the Professor's first
  wife*

IVAN PETROVICH VOYNITSKY [*also* JEAN,
  VANYA], *her son*

MIKHAIL LVOVICH ASTROV, *a doctor*

ILYA ILYICH TELEGIN [*nicknamed* WAFFLE], *an
  impoverished landowner*

MARINA TIMOFEYEVNA, *an old* nyanya[1]

A WORKMAN

The action takes place in Serebryakov's country house.

Act One

The garden. Part of the house and the terrace are visible. A table is laid for tea under an old poplar in an avenue. Benches and chairs; on one of the benches lies a guitar. Near the table a swing. It is early afternoon. Overcast.

[MARINA, *a heavy, slow-moving old woman, sitting by the samovar and knitting a stocking, and* ASTROV, *walking by.*]

MARINA [*pouring a glass of tea*]: Have some, dear.
ASTROV [*unwillingly taking the glass*]: I don't really want it.
MARINA: Perhaps you'd like a little vodka?
ASTROV: No. I don't drink vodka every day. And it's so close today . . .

[*A pause.*]

Nyanya, how long have we known each other?
MARINA [*thinking*]: How long? Lord help me remember . . . You came here, to these parts . . . when was it? . . . Vera Petrovna, little Sonya's mother, was still alive. You visited us then for two winters . . . So that means eleven years have passed. [*Thinking.*] And maybe more . . .
ASTROV: Have I changed a lot since then?
MARINA: A lot. You were young and handsome then, and now you've aged. Also – you like your vodka.
ASTROV: Yes . . . In ten years I've become another person. And why? I've worn myself out, Nyanya. From morning to night I'm on my feet, I don't know the meaning of rest, and at night I lie under my blanket afraid of being called out to a patient. Over the

whole time we've known each other I haven't had one day off. How am I not going to age? Yes, and this life itself is boring, stupid, dirty . . . It drags one down. You're surrounded by eccentrics, nothing but eccentrics, and you live with them two or three years and you gradually become one yourself without noticing. An unavoidable fate. [*Twiddling his long moustaches.*] What a huge moustache I've grown . . . Stupid moustache. I've become an eccentric, Nyanya . . . I haven't yet become soft in the head, thank the Lord, my brain is in the right place, but my feelings have somehow got blunted. I don't want anything, I don't need anything, I don't love anyone . . . But I do love you. [*Kisses her on the head.*] As a child I had a *nyanya* like you.

MARINA: Do you want something to eat?

ASTROV: No. In the third week of Lent I went to Malitskoye where there was an epidemic . . . Typhus . . . They were crammed side by side in the huts . . . Filth, stench, smoke, calves on the ground by the sick . . . Little pigs too . . . I worked all day, didn't sit down, didn't have a poppy-seed to eat, and I came home – to find no rest – they brought me a railway pointsman; I put him on the table to operate and he goes and dies on me under the chloroform. And when there was absolutely no need, my feelings were aroused and conscience pricked me as if I'd killed him deliberately . . . I sat down, closed my eyes – like this – and thought: will those who will be living a hundred, two hundred years from now, those for whom we are now laying down the road to the future, will they remember us in their prayers? Nyanya, they won't!

MARINA: Man may not remember, but God will.

ASTROV: Thank you for that. It was well said.

[*Enter* VOYNITSKY.]

VOYNITSKY [*comes out of the house; he has had a sleep after lunch and has a crumpled look; sits down on a bench and straightens his stylish necktie*]: Yes . . .

[*A pause.*]

Yes . . .

ASTROV: Have you had enough sleep?

VOYNITSKY: Yes . . . Plenty. [*Yawns.*] Ever since the Professor came to live here with his wife, my life has left its track . . . I go to sleep at the wrong time, for lunch and dinner I eat all kinds of rich dishes, I drink wine – that's all unhealthy. I used not to have a spare minute, Sonya and I worked – my goodness, how we worked, and now only Sonya works and I sleep, eat and drink . . . That's no good!

MARINA [*shaking her head*]: What a way to live! The Professor gets up at noon, and the samovar has been going all morning, waiting for him. Before they came we always had dinner before one o'clock, like people everywhere else, but with them here it's after six. At night the Professor reads and writes, and suddenly he rings after one in the morning . . . I ask you, gentlemen. For tea! Wake the servants for him, put on the samovar . . . What a way to live!

ASTROV: And will they be staying here long?

VOYNITSKY [*whistling*]: A hundred years. The Professor has decided to settle here.

MARINA: And they've done it now. The samovar has been brewing on the table for two hours, and they've gone for a walk.

VOYNITSKY: They're coming, they're coming . . . Don't work yourself up.

[*Voices are heard;* SEREBRYAKOV, YELENA ANDREYEVNA, SONYA *and* TELEGIN *enter from the depths of the garden, returning from their walk.*]

SEREBRYAKOV: Lovely, lovely . . . Wonderful views.

TELEGIN: Exceptional, Your Excellency.[1]

SONYA: Tomorrow, Papa, we'll drive to the forestry station. Would you like that?

VOYNITSKY: Tea, ladies and gentlemen!

SEREBRYAKOV: My friends, would you be so kind as to send my tea over to my study? I've still got things to do today.

SONYA: You'll really like the forest . . .

[YELENA ANDREYEVNA, SEREBRYAKOV *and* SONYA *go into the house.* TELEGIN *goes to the table and sits down by Marina.*]

VOYNITSKY: It's hot and stuffy, and our great scholar has an overcoat, galoshes, gloves and an umbrella.

ASTROV: So he obviously has to look after himself.

VOYNITSKY: But how lovely she is! How lovely! In all my life I've never seen such a beautiful woman.

TELEGIN: Marina Timofeyevna, whether I'm driving in the fields or walking in the shade of the garden or looking at this table, I feel inexpressible happiness! The weather is delightful, the little birds are singing, we all live in peace and concord – what more could we want? [*Taking a glass of tea.*] That's very kind of you.

VOYNITSKY [*dreamily*]: What eyes . . . A wonderful woman!

ASTROV: Tell us something, Ivan Petrovich.

VOYNITSKY [*feebly*]: What can I tell you?

ASTROV: Anything new?

VOYNITSKY: No. Everything is as before. I am the same man that I was, probably a bit worse since I've got lazy, I do nothing and only complain like an old grouch. Maman,[2] our old tame jackdaw, still chatters on about the emancipation of women – one eye looking into her grave and the other searching her learned books for the dawn of a new life.

ASTROV: And the Professor?

VOYNITSKY: The Professor sits in his study as before, from morning to late at night, and writes. 'With straining mind, with wrinkled brow we write our odes interminably. They get no plaudits nor do we.'[3] I feel sorry for the paper! He'd do better to write his autobiography. What a wonderful plot! You've got a retired professor, a dried-up old crust, a scholarly fish . . . Gout, rheumatism, migraine, a liver bloated from jealousy and envy . . . This old fish is living on the estate of his first wife, he has to live there because he can't afford to live in the city. He's always complaining about his misfortunes though in fact his luck is exceptional. [*Irritably*] Just think what luck! The seminarist son of a humble sexton, he's got academic degrees and a chair, has become His

Excellency, the son-in-law of a senator, et cetera, et cetera. However, none of that is of any consequence. But think of this now. For exactly twenty-five years a man reads and writes about art, understanding precisely nothing about art. For twenty-five years he chews over other people's ideas about Realism, Naturalism and all manner of other rubbish; for twenty-five years he reads and writes about things long known to the wise and of no interest to the stupid: so for twenty-five years he has been pouring from one empty vessel into another. And combined with what conceit! What pretensions! He retires and not a living soul has heard of him, he is completely unknown; so, for twenty-five years, he has occupied a post which shouldn't have been his. And look at him: he strides about like a demigod!

ASTROV: Well, I think you're envious.

VOYNITSKY: Yes, I envy him! And he's so successful with women! No Don Juan has had such complete success! His first wife, my sister, a lovely meek creature, pure as that blue sky, noble, generous, with more admirers than he had students, loved him with the kind of love only pure angels have for those as pure and beautiful as themselves. His mother-in-law, my mother, still worships him and he still inspires her with a holy awe. His second wife, a beauty, a woman with a mind – you just saw her – married him when he was already old, gave him her youth, beauty, freedom, brightness. For what? Why?

ASTROV: Is she faithful to the Professor?

VOYNITSKY: Unfortunately, yes.

ASTROV: Why unfortunately?

VOYNITSKY: Because that 'fidelity' is false from start to finish. It's full of rhetoric but has no logic. To betray your old husband whom you can't stand – is immoral; but to try and stifle in yourself your wretched youth and your living feeling – is not.

TELEGIN [in a plaintive voice]: Vanya, I don't like it when you say that. Really . . . Someone who betrays wife or husband must be without faith and could betray our country!

VOYNITSKY [crossly]: Turn off the tap, Waffle.[4]

TELEGIN: Excuse me, Vanya. Because of my unprepossessing looks my wife ran off the day after our wedding with a man she loved. Since then I haven't abandoned my duty. I still love her and am faithful to her, I help with what I can and have given up my property for the education of the children she had by the man she loved. I lost my happiness but I kept my pride. And what became of her? Her youth has now gone, by the laws of nature her beauty has faded, the man she loved has passed on . . . What has she left?

[*Enter* SONYA *and* YELENA ANDREYEVNA; *a little later* MARIYA VASILYEVNA *enters with a book; she sits down and reads; she is served tea which she drinks without looking.*]

SONYA [*hurriedly, to the* nyanya]: Nyanya, the men from the village have come. Go and talk to them, and I'll do the tea . . . [*Pours tea.*]

[*The* nyanya *goes out.* YELENA ANDREYEVNA *takes her cup and drinks sitting on the swing.*]

ASTROV [*to Yelena Andreyevna*]: I actually came to see your husband. You wrote that he's very ill, rheumatism and something else, but he turns out to be pretty fit.

YELENA ANDREYEVNA: Yesterday evening he was depressed, complained of pains in the legs, but today he's all right.

ASTROV: And I killed myself galloping thirty versts. Well, no matter, it's not the first time. But I'll stay here till tomorrow and at least I'll sleep myself out *quantum satis.*[5]

SONYA: Excellent. It's so seldom you spend the night with us. You probably haven't had any dinner?

ASTROV: No, I haven't.

SONYA: So you'll have something to eat. We dine now after six. [*Drinks.*] The tea's cold!

TELEGIN: There has been a significant drop of temperature in the samovar.

YELENA ANDREYEVNA: Don't worry, Ivan Ivanych, we'll drink it cold.

TELEGIN: Excuse me . . . Not Ivan Ivanych, but Ilya Ilyich . . .

Ilya Ilyich Telegin, or, as some call me, Waffle, for my pitted complexion. I am Sonya's godfather and His Excellency your husband knows me very well. I now live here, on your estate . . . If you deigned to notice, I dine with you every day.

SONYA: Ilya Ilyich is our helper and right hand. [*With tenderness*] Let me pour you some more, dear godfather.

MARIYA VASILYEVNA: Ah!

SONYA: What's the matter, Granny?

MARIYA VASILYEVNA: I forgot to tell Aleksandr . . . I'm losing my memory . . . today I got a letter from Pavel Alekseyevich in Kharkov . . . He sent me his new pamphlet . . .

ASTROV: Is it interesting?

MARIYA VASILYEVNA: Interesting but rather strange. He rejects a position that seven years ago he himself was defending. It's disgraceful!

VOYNITSKY: There's nothing disgraceful about it. Drink your tea, Maman.

MARIYA VASILYEVNA: But I want to talk!

VOYNITSKY: You've been talking now for fifty years, talking and reading pamphlets. Time to stop.

MARIYA VASILYEVNA: For some reason you find it unpleasant to listen when I talk. I'm sorry, Jean,[6] but in the last year you've changed so that I just don't know you. You were a man of definite convictions, a man of enlightenment . . .

VOYNITSKY: Oh yes! I was a man of enlightenment, who gave no one any light . . .

[*A pause.*]

I was a man of enlightenment . . . You could not make a more poisonous joke! I am now forty-seven. Till last year, like you, I deliberately tried to cloud my eyes with your learned talk, so as not to see real life – and I thought I was doing right. And now if you only knew! At nights I don't sleep from vexation, from anger that I so foolishly lost the time when I could have had everything that my age now denies me!

SONYA: Uncle Vanya, you're being a bore!

MARIYA VASILYEVNA [*to her son*]: You're just blaming your former beliefs for something . . . But they're not to blame, you are. You forget that beliefs alone are nothing, a dead letter . . . What you needed was action.

VOYNITSKY: Action? Not everyone can be a scribbling perpetuum mobile like your Herr Professor.

MARIYA VASILYEVNA: What do you mean?

SONYA [*in a pleading voice*]: Granny! Uncle Vanya! I beg you!

VOYNITSKY: I'll shut up. I'll shut up and apologize.

[*A pause.*]

YELENA ANDREYEVNA: The weather is lovely today . . . It isn't hot . . .

[*A pause.*]

VOYNITSKY: Lovely weather for hanging oneself . . .

[TELEGIN *tunes the guitar.* MARINA *walks near the house and calls the chickens.*]

MARINA: *Tsyp, tsyp, tsyp* . . .[7]

SONYA: Nyanya dear, why did the men come? . . .

MARINA: The same thing, about the waste land again. *Tsyp, tsyp, tsyp.*

SONYA: Which one are you calling?

MARINA: The speckled one's gone off with her chicks . . . I'm worried the crows will get them . . . [*Exit.*]

[TELEGIN *plays a polka; they all listen in silence; enter a* WORKMAN.]

WORKMAN: Is the doctor gentleman here? [*To Astrov*] Please, Mikhail Lvovich, they've come for you.

ASTROV: Where from?

WORKMAN: The factory.

ASTROV [*crossly*]: Thank you so much. Well, I must go . . . [*Looks around for his cap.*] It makes me angry, damn it . . .

SONYA: It's really annoying . . . Come and have dinner, when you get back from the factory.

ASTROV: No, it'll be late. Where on earth . . . [*To the workman*] Be a good chap and bring me a glass of vodka. [*The* WORKMAN *goes out.*] Where on earth . . . [*Finds his cap.*] In some play of Ostrovsky's there's a character[8] with a big moustache and small gifts . . . Like me. Well, my friends, goodbye . . . [*To Yelena Andreyevna*] I'll be really pleased if you and Sofya Aleksandrovna come and see me some time. I've a little place, just thirty *desyatinas*, but if you're interested, I have a first-rate garden and you won't find a nursery like mine within a thousand versts. Next door is the state forest . . . The forester there is old and always ill, so in practice I run it all.

YELENA ANDREYEVNA: I've already been told that you really love the forests. Of course, that can be very useful, but doesn't it get in the way of your true calling? You're a doctor.

ASTROV: Only God knows where our true calling lies.

YELENA ANDREYEVNA: And is forestry interesting?

ASTROV: Yes, it's interesting work.

VOYNITSKY [*sarcastically*]: Most interesting!

YELENA ANDREYEVNA [*to Astrov*]: You're still a young man, you look – well, thirty-six, thirty-seven – and it can't be as interesting as you say. Just trees and trees. Monotonous, I would think.

SONYA: No, it's extraordinarily interesting. Every year Mikhail Lvovich plants new woods and he's already been given a bronze medal and a diploma. He campaigns against the destruction of old forests. If you listen to him you'll find yourself in complete agreement with him. He says that forests embellish the earth, they teach man to understand beauty, they inspire ideals in him. Forests alleviate a climate's harshness. In countries with a gentle climate less energy is spent on the struggle with nature, and so man is gentler there, more delicate; people are handsome, versatile, easily aroused, their speech is refined, their movements graceful. The arts and sciences flourish among them, their philosophy isn't gloomy, their attitude to women is fine and noble . . .

VOYNITSKY [*laughing*]: Bravo, bravo! . . . All that is charming but unconvincing, so [*to Astrov*], my friend, you must let me go on stoking stoves with logs and building sheds of wood.

ASTROV: You can burn peat in your stoves and build your sheds of stone. Well, I grant you can cut down forests out of need, but why destroy them? The forests of Russia are being wiped out by the axe, thousands of millions of trees are dying, the homes of animals and birds are being laid waste, river levels are dropping and drying up, wonderful scenery vanishes for ever, and all because lazy man hasn't the sense to bend down and pick up fuel from the ground. [*To Yelena Andreyevna*] Am I not right, Madame? One has to be a mindless barbarian to burn such beauty in a stove, to destroy what we cannot create. Man is endowed with reason and creative power in order to increase what he is given, but hitherto he has not created but destroyed. There are fewer and fewer forests . . . rivers are drying up, game is becoming extinct, the climate is damaged and every day the earth is becoming poorer and uglier. [*To Voynitsky*] You're looking at me ironically and think all I'm saying isn't serious, and . . . and perhaps this really is just craziness, but when I go past the peasants' woods, which I saved from destruction, or when I hear the hum of my young trees, which I planted with my own hands, I know the climate is a little in my control and that if in a thousand years man is happy, the responsibility for that will in a small way be mine. When I plant a birch and then watch it come into leaf and sway in the wind, my spirit fills with pride and I . . . [*Seeing the* WORKMAN, *who has brought in a glass of vodka on a tray*] However . . . [*drinking*] I must go. All this is probably craziness, after all. I bid you farewell! [*Goes towards the house.*]

SONYA [*taking his arm and walking with him*]: When will you be back?

ASTROV: I don't know.

SONYA: In another month's time? . . .

[ASTROV *and* SONYA *go into the house;* MARIYA VASILYEVNA *and* TELEGIN *remain by the table;* YELENA ANDREYEVNA *and* VOYNITSKY *go towards the terrace.*]

YELENA ANDREYEVNA: Ivan Petrovich, you again behaved impossibly. You had to go and annoy your mother and talk of the perpetuum mobile. And today at lunch you quarrelled again with Aleksandr. How petty you are!

VOYNITSKY: But if I hate him?

YELENA ANDREYEVNA: There's no reason to hate Aleksandr, he's the same as everyone else. No worse than you.

VOYNITSKY: If you could see your face, your movements . . . What indolence you have towards life! Ah, what indolence!

YELENA ANDREYEVNA: Ah yes, indolence and boredom! Everyone criticizes my husband, everyone looks at me with pity: unhappy woman, she has an old husband! That sympathy – I understand it well! As Astrov said just now: all of you are mindlessly destroying the forests and soon there'll be nothing left on earth. In the same way you mindlessly destroy a man, and soon thanks to you the earth will have neither loyalty, nor purity, nor the capacity for self-sacrifice. Why can't you look at a woman neutrally if she isn't yours? Because – that doctor is right – in all of you sits a devil of destruction. You have no pity for the forests or the birds or each other.

VOYNITSKY: I don't like this philosophy!

[*A pause.*]

YELENA ANDREYEVNA: The Doctor has a nervous, exhausted face. An interesting face. Sonya is obviously attracted by him; she is in love with him and I understand her. Since I came he's already been here three times, but I'm shy and I haven't talked with him as I should, I haven't been nice to him. He thinks I'm ill-natured. Ivan Petrovich, we are probably such friends because we're both tiresome, boring people! Tiresome! Don't look at me like that, I don't like it.

VOYNITSKY: Can I look at you otherwise, if I love you? You are my happiness, my life, my youth! I know my chances of your reciprocating are negligible, next to nothing, but I don't need anything, just let me look at you, hear your voice.

YELENA ANDREYEVNA: Quiet, someone might hear you!

[*They go into the house.*]

VOYNITSKY [*following her*]: Allow me to speak of my love, don't drive me away — just that will be the greatest happiness for me . . .

YELENA ANDREYEVNA: This is agonizing . . .

[TELEGIN *plucks the strings and plays a polka;* MARIYA VASIL-YEVNA *makes some notes in the margins of her pamphlet.*]

[*Curtain.*]

Act Two

The dining-room in Serebryakov's house. Night. The night-watchman can be heard knocking in the garden.

[SEREBRYAKOV *sitting in an armchair in front of an open window and dozing, and* YELENA ANDREYEVNA *sitting by him, also dozing.*]

SEREBRYAKOV [*waking up*]: Who's that? Is that you, Sonya?

YELENA ANDREYEVNA: It's me.

SEREBRYAKOV: Lenochka . . . The pain's intolerable!

YELENA ANDREYEVNA: Your rug's fallen on the floor. [*Wraps his legs.*] I'll shut the window, Aleksandr.

SEREBRYAKOV: No, it's stuffy . . . I just dropped off and I dreamt my left leg was someone else's. I woke from excruciating pain. No, it's not gout, more like rheumatism. What time is it now?

YELENA ANDREYEVNA: Twenty past midnight.

[*A pause.*]

SEREBRYAKOV: In the morning would you find Batyushkov[1] in the library. I think we have him.

YELENA ANDREYEVNA: What?

SEREBRYAKOV: Find the Batyushkov in the morning. I remember, we did have him. But why do I find it so hard to breathe?

YELENA ANDREYEVNA: You're tired. It's the second night you haven't slept.

SEREBRYAKOV: They say Turgenev[2] developed angina from gout.

I'm afraid that might happen to me. Cursed and disgusting old age. To hell with it. When I got old, I became repulsive to myself. And all of you must find me repulsive to look at.

YELENA ANDREYEVNA: When you speak of your age your tone is as if we were all to blame for your being old.

SEREBRYAKOV: You are the first to find me repulsive.

[YELENA ANDREYEVNA *moves away and sits down at a distance.*]

Of course, you're right. I'm not stupid and I understand. You are young, healthy, beautiful, you want to live, and I am an old man, almost a corpse. Well? Do you think I don't understand? And of course it's absurd that I'm still alive. But wait a little and I'll soon set all of you free, I won't hold out much longer.

YELENA ANDREYEVNA: I'm getting exhausted . . . For God's sake, stop.

SEREBRYAKOV: It turns out that thanks to me, everyone is exhausted and bored and wasting their youth, while I'm the only one to enjoy life and have satisfaction. Of course.

YELENA ANDREYEVNA: Oh, be quiet! You've worn me down!

SEREBRYAKOV: I've worn you all down. Of course.

YELENA ANDREYEVNA [*with tears in her eyes*]: It's intolerable! Tell me, what do you want from me?

SEREBRYAKOV: Nothing.

YELENA ANDREYEVNA: Then be quiet. I beg you.

SEREBRYAKOV: It's a funny thing, if Ivan Petrovich or that old idiot Mariya Vasilyevna start talking — it's all right, everyone listens, but if I so much as say one word, then everyone begins to feel unhappy. Even the sound of my voice you find repulsive. Well, I may be repulsive, egotistical, a tyrant, but don't I even, in my old age, have some right to egotism? Don't I deserve that? I ask you, do I not have the right to a peaceful old age, to people's consideration?

YELENA ANDREYEVNA: No one is disputing your rights.

[*The window bangs in the wind.*]

The wind's risen, I'll shut the window. [*Shuts it.*] It'll rain now. No one is disputing your rights.

[*A pause; the watchman in the garden knocks and sings a song.*]

SEREBRYAKOV: I work all my life for learning, I'm used to my study, the lecture hall, colleagues I esteem – and then, I end up for no good reason in this tomb, see fools here every day, listen to worthless conversations . . . I want to live, I like success, I like fame, making a noise, and here it's like being in exile. To pine every minute for the past, to watch the success of others, to be afraid of death . . . I can't! I haven't the strength! And they won't even excuse me my age here!

YELENA ANDREYEVNA: Wait, be patient: in five or six years' time I too am going to be old.

[*Enter* SONYA.]

SONYA: Papa, you yourself sent for Dr Astrov, but when he came you refused to see him. It's bad manners. To put someone to trouble just for nothing . . .

SEREBRYAKOV: What use is your Astrov to me? He knows as much about medicine as I do about astronomy.

SONYA: We can't call in the whole faculty of medicine here for your gout.

SEREBRYAKOV: I won't even talk to that holy fool.[3]

SONYA: As you please. [*Sits down.*] It's all the same to me.

SEREBRYAKOV: What time is it?

YELENA ANDREYEVNA: After midnight.

SEREBRYAKOV: It's stuffy . . . Sonya, give me the drops on the table!

SONYA: Here. [*Gives him the drops.*]

SEREBRYAKOV [*crossly*]: No, not these! One can't ask for anything!

SONYA: Please don't be difficult. Maybe some people like it, but kindly spare me! I don't. And I have no taste, tomorrow I have to get up early, it's haymaking.

[*Enter* VOYNITSKY, *wearing a dressing-gown and with a candle.*]

VOYNITSKY: There's a storm brewing outside.

[*Lightning.*]

There! Hélène, Sonya, go to bed, I've come to take over from you.

SEREBRYAKOV [*nervously*]: No, no! Don't leave me with him! No. He'll wear me out with his talk!

VOYNITSKY: But you must give them some rest. It's the second night they haven't slept.

SEREBRYAKOV: Let them go to bed, but you go off too. I'd be grateful. I beg you. In the name of our former friendship, don't protest. We'll talk later.

VOYNITSKY [*with irony*]: Our former friendship . . . Former . . .

SONYA: Shut up, Uncle Vanya.

SEREBRYAKOV [*to his wife*]: My dear, don't leave me with him! He'll wear me out.

VOYNITSKY: It's even becoming funny.

[MARINA *enters with a candle.*]

SONYA: You should go to bed, Nyanya dear. It's late.

MARINA: The samovar hasn't been cleared from the table. How can I go to bed?

SEREBRYAKOV: No one can sleep, everyone's exhausted, I'm the only one who's happy.

MARINA [*going to Serebryakov, affectionately*]: Master, what's the matter? Does it hurt? My own legs ache and ache. [*Adjusts the rug.*] It's your old trouble. Vera Petrovna, your late wife, little Sonya's mother, used not to sleep at nights, she used to worry . . . She loved you very much . . .

[*A pause.*]

Old people are like children, they want somebody to be sorry for them, but no one is sorry for the old. [*Kisses Serebryakov on the shoulder.*[4]] Master, come to bed . . . Come, dear . . . I'll make you some lime tea and warm up your feet . . . I'll say a prayer to God for you . . .

SEREBRYAKOV [*touched*]: Let's go, Marina.

MARINA: My own legs ache and ache! [*She and* SONYA *lead him together.*] Vera Petrovna used to get so upset, she used to cry . . . Sonya, you were still a little girl then, didn't know . . . Come, master, come . . .

[*Exeunt* SEREBRYAKOV, SONYA *and* MARINA.]

YELENA ANDREYEVNA: I'm worn out by him. I can hardly keep on my feet.

VOYNITSKY: You're worn out by him, and I by my own self. It's the third night I haven't slept.

YELENA ANDREYEVNA: This house is troubled. Your mother hates everything except her pamphlets and the Professor; the Professor is angry, he doesn't trust me and is frightened of you; Sonya is cross with her father, is cross with me and hasn't talked to me now for two weeks; you hate my husband and openly despise your mother; I'm angry and today I've started to cry twenty times . . . This house is troubled.

VOYNITSKY: Let's stop philosophizing!

YELENA ANDREYEVNA: Ivan Petrovich, you are educated and clever and I think you must understand that the world is being destroyed, not by bandits, not by fires, but by hatred, enmity, and all these petty squabbles . . . Instead of grumbling you should reconcile everyone.

VOYNITSKY: First reconcile me with myself! My dearest . . . [*Stoops to kiss her hand.*]

YELENA ANDREYEVNA: Stop it. [*Takes away her hand.*] Go to bed!

VOYNITSKY: The rain will pass now and all nature will be refreshed and give a gentle sigh. I alone will not be refreshed by the storm. Day and night I am weighed down, as if by some devil,[5] by the thought that my life is irrevocably gone. I have no past, it has been stupidly squandered on rubbish, and the present is terrible in its absurdity. You have here my life and my love; where am I to put them, what am I to do with them? My feelings are going to waste, like a ray of sunshine falling into a chasm, and I myself am going to waste.

YELENA ANDREYEVNA: When you speak to me of your love, I somehow go numb and don't know what to say. I'm sorry, I can't say anything to you. [*Moves towards door.*] Goodnight.

VOYNITSKY [*blocking her way*]: And if you knew how I suffer from the thought that next to me in this house another life is going to waste — your life! What are you waiting for? What cursed philosophy is stopping you? You must understand, understand . . .

YELENA ANDREYEVNA [*looking hard at him*]: Ivan Petrovich, you are drunk!

VOYNITSKY: It's possible . . .

YELENA ANDREYEVNA: Where's the Doctor?

VOYNITSKY: He's there . . . spending the night in my room. It's possible . . . Anything is possible!

YELENA ANDREYEVNA: So you've been drinking again today? Why?

VOYNITSKY: At least it offers one something like life . . . Don't stop me, Hélène!

YELENA ANDREYEVNA: You never used to drink, and you never used to talk so much . . . Go to bed! I'm bored with you.

VOYNITSKY [*kissing her hand*]: My darling . . . wonderful woman!

YELENA ANDREYEVNA [*angrily*]: Leave me alone! It's disgusting. [*Goes out.*]

VOYNITSKY [*alone*]: She's gone . . .

[*A pause.*]

I used to meet her ten years ago at my sister's. She was seventeen then and I was thirty-seven. Why didn't I fall in love with her then and propose to her? I could have — quite easily! And she would now be my wife . . . Yes . . . We would both now have been woken by the storm, she would be frightened by the thunder and I would hold her in my arms and whisper, 'Don't be afraid, I'm here.' Oh, wonderful thoughts, so good I'm even laughing . . . but, God, my thoughts are confused in my head . . . Why am I old? Why doesn't she understand me? Her rhetoric, her lazy moral strictures, her pointless, lazy thinking about the end of the world – I find all that deeply hateful.

[*A pause.*]

How deceived I was! I worshipped the Professor, that pathetic victim of gout, I worked for him like an ox! Sonya and I squeezed the last juice out of this estate; we traded like kulaks[6] in vegetable oil and dried peas and curd cheese, we ourselves hardly had enough to eat in order to make the pennies and kopecks into thousands and send them to him. I was proud of him and his scholarship, I lived and breathed him! Every word he wrote and uttered seemed to me to come from genius . . . God, and now? Here he is in retirement, and now one can see the sum total of his life: not a single page of his labours will survive him, he's completely unknown, he's nothing! A soap bubble! I was deceived . . . I see it – deeply deceived . . .

[*Enter* ASTROV *in his coat, without waistcoat and tie; tipsy; followed by* TELEGIN *with a guitar.*]

ASTROV: Play!
TELEGIN: Everyone's asleep!
ASTROV: Play!

[TELEGIN *plays quietly.*]

[*To Voynitsky*] Are you alone here? No ladies? [*Puts his arms akimbo and sings softly*] 'No home, no stove for a bed, where's a man to lay his head . . .' The storm woke me. That's real rain. What time is it?

VOYNITSKY: God only knows.

ASTROV: I thought I heard Yelena Andreyevna's voice.

VOYNITSKY: She was in here just now.

ASTROV: A gorgeous woman. [*Inspects the bottles on the table.*] Medicines. What a lot of prescriptions! From Kharkov and Moscow and Tula . . . He's plagued every city with his gout. Is he ill or malingering?

VOYNITSKY: He's ill.

[*A pause.*]

ASTROV: Why are you so gloomy today? Are you sorry for the Professor or something?

VOYNITSKY: Leave me alone.

ASTROV: Or perhaps you're in love with the Professor's wife?

VOYNITSKY: She is my good friend.

ASTROV: Really?

VOYNITSKY: What does that 'really' mean?

ASTROV: A woman can be a man's good friend only in the following sequence of events: first friend, then mistress, then good friend.

VOYNITSKY: A coarse philosophy.

ASTROV: What? Yes . . . I must admit, I am becoming coarse. You see, I'm drunk too. I usually get this drunk once a month. When I'm in this condition, I become extremely aggressive and ambitious. I can do anything then! I take on the most difficult operations and do them perfectly; I draw up the grandest plans for the future; I don't then think myself an eccentric, and I can believe I am bringing colossal benefits to mankind – colossal! Also at these times I have my own system of philosophy, and all of you, my friends, appear to me as just so many insects – microbes. [*To Telegin*] Waffle, play something!

TELEGIN: For you, dear fellow, I'd be glad to, with all my heart, but you must understand – people are sleeping in this house!

ASTROV: Play!

[TELEGIN *plays quietly.*]

We need a drink. Come on, I think we've still got some brandy left in there. And when it gets light, we'll drive to my house. Do you *loik* the idea? I have an assistant who never says 'like' but 'loik'. A terrible crook. So do you *loik* it? [*Seeing* SONYA *come in.*] I'm sorry, I haven't got a tie on. [*Quickly goes out, followed by* TELEGIN.]

SONYA: Uncle Vanya, you've got drunk with the doctor again. All boys together. Well, he's always like that, but why must you be? At your age it doesn't suit you at all . . .

VOYNITSKY: Age is neither here nor there. When one has no real life, one lives by mirages. It's still better than nothing.

SONYA: The hay is all cut, it rains every day, everything is rotting – and you're occupied with mirages. You've completely given up the estate . . . I work alone, I've worn out my strength . . . [*Frightened*] Uncle, you have tears in your eyes!

VOYNITSKY: Tears? There's nothing . . . nonsense . . . You just looked at me like your dead mother. My darling . . . [*Hungrily kisses her hands and face.*] My sister . . . my dear sister . . . where is she now? If she knew! Oh, if she only knew!

SONYA: What? Uncle, knew what?

VOYNITSKY: It's not easy, not right . . . It's nothing . . . Later . . . Nothing . . . I'm going . . . [*Exit.*]

SONYA [*knocking on the door*]: Mikhail Lvovich! Are you awake? Just for a minute!

ASTROV [*through the door*]: Coming! [*After a moment he enters, now wearing a waistcoat and tie.*] What do you want?

SONYA: Drink yourself, if it doesn't revolt you, but I beg you, don't let my uncle drink. It's bad for him.

ASTROV: All right. We won't drink any more.

[*A pause.*]

I'm just going home. All signed and sealed. The sun'll be up by the time they harness the horses.

SONYA: It's raining. Wait till morning.

ASTROV: The storm is passing us by, we'll only get the edge of it.

I'll go. And please don't ask me over for your father again. I tell him it's gout, but he says rheumatism; I ask him to lie down, he sits up. And today he wouldn't speak to me at all.

SONYA: He's been spoilt. [*Looks in the sideboard.*] Would you like something to eat?

ASTROV: Why not, give me something.

SONYA: I like to have a snack at night. I think there's something in the sideboard. People say he had a lot of success with women in his life, and the ladies pampered him. Have some cheese.

[*They both stand by the sideboard and eat.*]

ASTROV: I haven't had anything to eat today, I've only been drinking. Your father has a difficult character. [*Gets a bottle out of the sideboard.*] May I? [*Drinks down a glass.*] There's no one here and I can speak frankly. You know, I think I wouldn't last one month in this house, I'd suffocate in this atmosphere ... Your father taken up with his gout and books, Uncle Vanya with his depression, your grandmother, finally your stepmother ...

SONYA: What about my stepmother?

ASTROV: A human being should be beautiful all through: face and clothes and spirit and thoughts. She is beautiful, no question about that, but ... she just eats, sleeps, walks, enchants us all with her beauty – and that's all. She has no responsibilities, others work for her ... It's true, isn't it? And an idle life can't be a virtuous one.

[*A pause.*]

But perhaps I'm judging too harshly. Like your Uncle Vanya I'm dissatisfied with life, and we're both becoming grouches.

SONYA: So you don't like life?

ASTROV: I love life in general, but I can't stand our narrow Russian provincial life, and I despise it with all the strength of my soul. And as far as my own personal life is concerned, Lord, there's really nothing good there. You know, when you walk in the forest on a dark night and if you then see a tiny light in the distance, you don't notice exhaustion or darkness or the brambles hitting you in the face. As you know I work harder than anyone in the district, I am unremittingly knocked about by fate, from time to time I suffer unbearably, but there's no tiny light in the distance for me. I now expect nothing for myself, I don't love humanity ... It's a long time since I loved anyone.

SONYA: Anyone?

ASTROV: Anyone. I only feel a certain affection for your Nyanya – for old times' sake. The muzhiks are dull, uneducated, live in squalor, and it's difficult to get on with the intelligentsia. They're exhausting. All of them, all our good friends, have petty thoughts and petty feelings, and they see no further than the end of their nose – they're simply stupid. And those who are a bit cleverer, a bit more significant, are hysterics, eaten up by analysis and introspection ... They whine and hate and utter their morbid gossip, they sidle up to a man and look at him sideways and decide 'Oh, he's a psychopath!' or 'He's a phrasemonger!' And when they don't know what label to stick to my forehead, they say 'He's a strange man, strange!' I love forests – that's strange; I don't eat meat – that's strange too. They have no direct, clean, free relationship with nature and with people ... None, none! [*He is about to drink.*]

SONYA [*stopping him*]: No, please, I beg you, don't drink any more.

ASTROV: Why?

SONYA: It really doesn't suit you. You're cultured, you have such a gentle voice ... More than that, unlike anyone I know, you are a fine man. Why do you want to be like ordinary men who drink and play cards? Don't, I beg you! You're always saying that people don't create but only destroy what is given them from on high. Why, why do you destroy yourself? You mustn't, you mustn't, I beg, I entreat you.

ASTROV [*giving her his hand*]: I won't drink any more.

SONYA: Give me your word.

ASTROV: My word of honour.

SONYA [*shaking his hand firmly*]: Thank you!

ASTROV: *Basta.*[7] I've sobered up. You see, I am now completely sober and will stay so to the end of my days. [*Looks at his watch.*] And so we'll continue. This is what I say: my time is now past, it's late for me . . . I am old, I've worked myself to the bone, I've coarsened, all my feelings are blunted and I don't think now I could become attached to a human being. I love no one and . . . now I won't love. What still excites me is beauty. I am not indifferent to that. I think that if Yelena Andreyevna wanted to, she could turn my head in a day . . . But that's not love, that's not affection . . . [*Covers his eyes with a hand and shudders.*]

SONYA: What's the matter?

ASTROV: Don't worry . . . During Lent one of my patients died under chloroform.

SONYA: It's time to forget about that.

[*A pause.*]

Tell me, Mikhail Lvovich . . . If I had a friend or a younger sister and if you learnt that she . . . well, let's say, loved you, how would you react to that?

ASTROV [*shrugging*]: I don't know. I suppose, not at all. I would let her know that I could not love her . . . but my thoughts are elsewhere. If I'm really going to leave, it's now time. Goodbye, my dear, otherwise we'll be at it till morning. [*Shakes her hand.*] I'll go out through the drawing-room if I may, otherwise I'm afraid your uncle will keep me. [*Goes out.*]

SONYA [*alone*]: He said nothing to me . . . His heart and soul are still hidden from me, but why do I feel so happy? [*Laughs with happiness.*] I said to him, you are cultured, noble, you have such a gentle voice . . . Did that come out wrong? His voice trembles, caresses . . . I can feel it in the air. But when I talked to him about a younger sister, he didn't understand. [*Wringing her hands.*] Oh how I hate being plain! It's dreadful! And I know I'm plain, I know it, I know it . . . Last Sunday when we were leaving church, I heard people talking about me, and one woman said, 'She's kind and generous, but it's a pity that she's so plain.' Plain . . .

[*Enter* YELENA ANDREYEVNA.]

YELENA ANDREYEVNA [*opening the window*]: The storm has passed. What wonderful air!

[*A pause.*]

Where's the Doctor?
SONYA: He's gone.

[*A pause.*]

YELENA ANDREYEVNA: Sophie.
SONYA: What?
YELENA ANDREYEVNA: How long are you going to be offended with me? We've done no harm to one another. Why be enemies? Let's stop it . . .
SONYA: I wanted to myself . . . [*Hugs her.*] Let's stop being angry.
YELENA ANDREYEVNA: That's wonderful.

[*Both are emotional.*]

SONYA: Has Papa gone to bed?
YELENA ANDREYEVNA: No, he's sitting in the drawing-room . . . We don't speak to one another for weeks at a time, God knows why . . . [*Seeing the sideboard is open.*] What's that?
SONYA: Mikhail Lvovich had supper.
YELENA ANDREYEVNA: And there's some wine . . . Let's drink and be friends.
SONYA: Let's.
YELENA ANDREYEVNA: From one glass . . . [*Pours.*] That's better. So, it's *ty*?[8]
SONYA: *Ty.*

[*They drink and kiss.*]

I've wanted to make up for a long time, but I was always sort of ashamed . . . [*Cries*.]

YELENA ANDREYEVNA: Why are you crying?

SONYA: It's nothing, I just am.

YELENA ANDREYEVNA: There, there . . . [*Cries*.] You funny girl, I've started crying too . . .

[*A pause*.]

You were angry with me because you thought I married your father for ulterior motives . . . If you believe oaths, then I swear to you that I married him for love. I was attracted to this famous scholar. My love was not real, it was artificial, but I thought it was real then. I'm not to blame. But from the day of our marriage you never stopped punishing me with your clever, suspicious eyes.

SONYA: Pax, pax. Let's forget.

YELENA ANDREYEVNA: You mustn't look at people like that – it doesn't suit you. You must trust everyone, otherwise life is impossible.

[*A pause*.]

SONYA: Tell me honestly, as a friend . . . Are you happy?

YELENA ANDREYEVNA: No.

SONYA: I knew it. One more question. Tell me frankly – would you like to have had a young husband?

YELENA ANDREYEVNA: What a little girl you are still. Of course I would. [*Laughs*.] Well, ask me something else, ask . . .

SONYA: Do you find the Doctor attractive?

YELENA ANDREYEVNA: Yes, very.

SONYA [*laughing*]: I've got a stupid face . . . don't you think? He's gone and I still hear his voice and his footsteps, and I look at the dark window and I see his face there. Let me have my say . . . But I can't talk so loudly, I'm ashamed. Let's go to my room and talk there. Do you find me silly? Admit it . . . Say something to me about him . . .

YELENA ANDREYEVNA: What?

SONYA: He's clever. He knows how to do everything, he's able to do everything . . . He heals the sick and he plants trees . . .

YELENA ANDREYEVNA: It's not a question of trees, or medicine . . . You see, my dear, it's talent! And do you know what talent means? Courage, a free mind, a broad sweep . . . He plants a little tree and he can foretell what will come of it in a thousand years, he's already dreaming of the happiness of mankind. Such men are rare, to be loved . . . He drinks, he's often a bit coarse – but what harm in that? A man with talent in Russia can't be nice and clean. Think yourself what kind of life this doctor has! Impassable mud on the roads, frosts, snow-storms, huge distances, crude and primitive people, everywhere poverty, disease, and in these circumstances it's hard for someone struggling and fighting from day to day to get to forty and remain nice and sober . . . [*Kisses Sonya.*] I wish you happiness with all my heart, you deserve it . . . [*Gets up.*] But I'm a boring incidental character . . . In my music and in my husband's house, in all my romances – in a word, in everything, I've always just been an incidental character. In truth, Sonya, if I think about it, I'm very, very unhappy! [*In her emotion, walks about the stage.*] There's no happiness for me on this earth. None! Why are you laughing?

SONYA [*laughing, covering her face*]: I'm so happy . . . so happy!

YELENA ANDREYEVNA: I want to play the piano . . . to play something now.

SONYA: Play. [*Embraces her.*] I can't sleep . . . Play!

YELENA ANDREYEVNA: In a minute. Your father isn't asleep. When he's ill, music irritates him. Go and ask him. If he doesn't mind, I'll play. Go.

SONYA: I'm going. [*Goes out.*]

[*The night-watchman knocks in the garden.*]

YELENA ANDREYEVNA: I haven't played for years. I shall play and cry, cry like an idiot. [*Through the window*] Is that you knocking, Yefim?

WATCHMAN'S VOICE: Yes, it's me!

YELENA ANDREYEVNA: Don't knock, the master's not well.

WATCHMAN'S VOICE: I'll go now. [*Whistles.*] Hey, come on, Zhuchka, Malchik![9] Zhuchka!

[*A pause.*]

SONYA [*coming back*]: The answer's no.

[*Curtain.*]

Act Three

A drawing-room in Serebryakov's house. Three doors, left, right and centre. Daytime.

[VOYNITSKY *and* SONYA, *seated, and* YELENA ANDREYEVNA, *walking about the stage, thinking of something.*]

VOYNITSKY: The Herr Professor has expressed a wish that all of us assemble here in this drawing-room today at one p.m. [*Looks at his watch.*] Quarter to one. He wants to tell the world something.

YELENA ANDREYEVNA: Probably some matter of business.

VOYNITSKY: He has none. He writes rubbish, grumbles and is jealous, that's all.

SONYA [*in a reproachful tone*]: Uncle!

VOYNITSKY: Yes, yes, I'm sorry. [*Points at Yelena Andreyevna.*] Just look at her: she walks about reeling with indolence. Very nice! Very!

YELENA ANDREYEVNA: You've been droning and droning all day long – haven't you had enough! [*In an anguished voice*] I'm dying of boredom, I don't know what to do.

SONYA [*shrugging her shoulders*]: There's plenty to do. You just need to want to.

YELENA ANDREYEVNA: For instance?

SONYA: Help run the estate, teach, treat the sick. Is that not enough? When Papa and you weren't here, Uncle Vanya and I ourselves went to market to sell the flour.

YELENA ANDREYEVNA: I can't. And it isn't interesting. It's only in novels of ideas that people teach the peasants or treat them –

how can I all of a sudden go and give them medical treatment or lessons?

SONYA: But I don't understand why you don't go and teach. Just wait a bit and you'll get the habit. [*Embraces her.*] Don't be bored, dearest. [*Laughing*] You're bored, you can't find a role for yourself, and boredom and inactivity are infectious. Look: Uncle Vanya does nothing and just follows you round like a shadow, I've left my work and come running to you to talk. I've got lazy, I can't do it! Doctor Mikhail Lvovich used to visit us very seldom, once a month, it was difficult to persuade him, but now he drives over here every day, he's left his woods and his practice. You must be a sorceress.

VOYNITSKY: Why languish? [*Animatedly*] Well, my dear, splendid creature, do something clever! In your veins flows a mermaid's blood, so be a mermaid. For once in your life let yourself go, fall head over heels in love with some water sprite — and plop, head first, into a whirlpool, so the Herr Professor and all of us just raise our hands in amazement!

YELENA ANDREYEVNA [*in anger*]: Leave me in peace! You're so cruel! [*Starts to go.*]

VOYNITSKY [*preventing her*]: There, there, joy of my heart, forgive me . . . I apologize. [*Kisses her hand.*] Peace.

YELENA ANDREYEVNA: You must agree, you'd try the patience of an angel.

VOYNITSKY: As a sign of peace and concord I'll now bring you a bouquet of roses; I made it for you this morning . . . Autumn roses — lovely melancholy roses . . . [*Exit.*]

SONYA: Autumn roses — lovely melancholy roses . . .

[*Both of them look out of the window.*]

YELENA ANDREYEVNA: It's already September. Somehow we'll get through the winter here.

[*A pause.*]

Where's the Doctor?

SONYA: In Uncle Vanya's room. He's writing something. I'm glad Uncle Vanya's gone, I need to talk to you.

YELENA ANDREYEVNA: What about?

SONYA: What about? [*Lays her head on Yelena Andreyevna's breast.*]

YELENA ANDREYEVNA: There, there ... [*Strokes Sonya's hair.*] There.

SONYA: I'm so plain.

YELENA ANDREYEVNA: You have lovely hair.

SONYA: No! [*Turns round to look at herself in a mirror.*] No! When a woman is plain, people say to her, 'You have lovely eyes, you have lovely hair' ... I've loved him for six years now, I love him more than my mother; every minute I hear him, I feel the pressure of his handshake; and I look at the door, I wait, I always think he's about to walk in. And, you see, I keep on coming to you to talk about him. Now he's here every day, but he doesn't look at me, he doesn't see me ... It's such torment! I have no hope, none, none! [*Desperately*] O God, send me strength ... I prayed all night ... I often go up to him, I open conversations with him, I look him in the eye ... I've no pride now, no strength for self-control ... I gave in and yesterday I confessed to Uncle Vanya that I love ... And all the servants know that I love him. Everyone knows.

YELENA ANDREYEVNA: And what about him?

SONYA: No. He doesn't notice me.

YELENA ANDREYEVNA [*thinking*]: He's a strange man ... Do you know what? Let me talk to him ... I'll do it carefully, obliquely ...

[*A pause.*]

How long can you remain in uncertainty ... Let me!

[SONYA *nods her head in affirmation.*]

Excellent. It won't be hard to find out whether he loves you or not. Don't be embarrassed, my dear, don't worry ... I'll question him carefully, he won't even notice. We only need to find out: is it yes or no?

[*A pause.*]

If it's no, then he shouldn't be here, should he?

[SONYA *nods her head in affirmation.*]

It's easier if you don't see him. We won't put it off, we'll question him now. He was going to show me some plans . . . Go and tell him that I want to see him.

SONYA [*in great agitation*]: You will tell me the whole truth, won't you?

YELENA ANDREYEVNA: Yes, of course. I think that the truth, whatever it is, is not as frightening as uncertainty. Rely on me, my dear.

SONYA: Yes . . . yes . . . I'll say that you want to see his plans . . . [*Goes and stops by the door.*] No, uncertainty is better . . . There's still hope . . .

YELENA ANDREYEVNA: What *are* you saying?

SONYA: Nothing. [*Exit.*]

YELENA ANDREYEVNA [*alone*]: There's nothing worse than knowing someone else's secret and being unable to help. [*Reflecting*] He isn't in love with her – that's clear, but why shouldn't he marry her? She's plain, but for a country doctor, at his age, she would be a splendid wife. She's a clever girl, so kind, so pure . . . No, that's not it, that's not it at all . . .

[*A pause.*]

I understand the poor girl. In the midst of this desperate boredom, where some kind of grey blobs wander about instead of human beings, where you only hear vulgarity and where people do nothing but eat, drink and sleep, sometimes there comes this man, a man unlike others, handsome, interesting, attractive, like a bright moon rising in the darkness . . . To give in to the charm of such a man and to forget yourself . . . I think I myself have been a little carried away . . . Yes, I'm bored when he isn't around, I'm smiling now I'm thinking of him . . . That Uncle Vanya says I have a mermaid's blood in my veins. 'For once in your life let yourself go' . . . So? Perhaps I should . . . Should fly away from all of you free as a bird, away from your sleepy faces, your conversations, should forget that all of you exist on the earth . . . But I am cowardly, timid . . . I'm tormented by conscience . . . He's here every day, I guess why he's here and now I feel guilty, ready to fall on my knees before Sonya and apologize and weep . . .

ASTROV [*coming in with a map*]: Good afternoon. [*Shakes her hand.*] Do you want to look at my picture?

YELENA ANDREYEVNA: Yesterday you promised to show me your work . . . Are you free?

ASTROV: Oh, of course. [*Spreads out the map on a card table and fixes it with drawing-pins.*] Where were you born?

YELENA ANDREYEVNA [*helping him*]: In Petersburg.

ASTROV: And educated?

YELENA ANDREYEVNA: At the Conservatoire.[1]

ASTROV: So this probably isn't very interesting for you.

YELENA ANDREYEVNA: Why? It's true I don't know about the countryside but I've read a lot about it.

ASTROV: I have my own desk here in the house . . . In Ivan Petrovich's room. When I'm worn out, in a complete stupor, I drop everything and escape here and amuse myself with this thing for an hour or two . . . Ivan Petrovich and Sofya Aleksandrovna click away on the abacus,[2] and I sit by them at my desk and daub away – and I'm warm and at peace, and the cricket chirps. But I don't allow myself this pleasure often, just once a month . . . [*Pointing to the map.*] Now look here. A portrait of our district as it was fifty years ago. The dark and light green indicate forest; half of the whole area is covered by forest. Where there's a red grid over the green, there were elk and wild goats . . . I show here both flora and fauna . . . This lake had swans, geese, duck, and as old folk say, a mighty eyeful of all kinds of wildfowl, which used to take off in a great storm cloud. Besides villages and hamlets, you can see scattered here and there various settlements, farmsteads, schismatic monasteries, watermills . . . There were a lot of cattle and horses. You can tell that by the blue colour. For example, this unit of land has a thick layer of blue: here there were whole herds of horses and every household had three.

[*A pause.*]

Now let's look lower down, that's as it was twenty-five years ago. There's only a third of the whole area under forest. No more goats, but there are still elk. The green and blue are paler. And so on and so forth. Let's move on to the third part: the district today. There's green here and there, but not all over, just in patches; the swans and elk and wood grouse have disappeared . . . There isn't a trace of the settlements, farms, monasteries, mills there once were. In general terms a picture of gradual and definite decline, which clearly will take some ten to fifteen years to become total. You may say that these are cultural influences, that the old life was naturally bound to give way to the new. Yes, I understand that: if in place of these destroyed forests they had laid highways and railroads, if we had here factories, mills, schools, the people would be healthier, richer, better educated – but there's nothing of the kind! The district has the same swamps and mosquitoes, the same lack of roads, poverty, typhus, diphtheria, fires . . . We have here a decline which is the consequence of an impossible struggle for existence; a degeneration arising from stagnation, ignorance, a total lack of self-awareness, when a frozen, hungry, sick man, in order to preserve the remnants of life, to protect his children, instinctively, unconsciously grasps at anything to relieve his hunger and get warm, and destroys everything around without a thought for tomorrow. Now almost everything is destroyed, but nothing has yet been created to take its place. [*Coldly*] I see by your expression this doesn't interest you.

YELENA ANDREYEVNA: But I understand so little of it . . .

ASTROV: There's nothing here to understand, it's simply not interesting you.

YELENA ANDREYEVNA: To be frank, my mind is elsewhere. I'm sorry. I need to give you a little interrogation, and I'm embarrassed, I don't know how to begin.

ASTROV: An interrogation?

YELENA ANDREYEVNA: Yes, an interrogation, but . . . a quite harmless one. Let's sit down.

[*They sit down.*]

It concerns a young person. We will speak in plain terms, like honest people, like friends. We will talk and forget what we talked about. Yes?

ASTROV: Yes.

YELENA ANDREYEVNA: It concerns my stepdaughter Sonya. Do you like her?

ASTROV: Yes, I respect her.

YELENA ANDREYEVNA: Are you attracted to her as a woman?

ASTROV [*after a pause*]: No.

YELENA ANDREYEVNA: Just two or three words more – and that's it. Haven't you noticed anything?

ASTROV: No, I haven't.

YELENA ANDREYEVNA [*taking him by the hand*]: You don't love her, I can see it in your eyes . . . She is suffering . . . You must understand that and . . . stop coming here.

ASTROV [*getting up*]: My time's up . . . I'm too busy . . . [*Shrugging his shoulders.*] When can I? [*He is embarrassed.*]

YELENA ANDREYEVNA: Phew, what an unpleasant conversation! I'm in such a state I feel I've been carrying a thousand *pud* load. Well, thank God, it's over. We will forget, as if we hadn't talked at all, and . . . now leave. You're an intelligent man, you will understand . . .

[*A pause.*]

I'm blushing all over.

ASTROV: If you'd said this to me a month or two ago, I probably would still have thought about it, but now . . . [*Shrugs.*] But if she is suffering, then of course . . . Only I don't understand one thing: why did you need to have this interrogation? [*Looks her in the eye and wags his finger at her.*] You're a sly one!

YELENA ANDREYEVNA: What does that mean?

ASTROV [*laughing*]: Sly! We say Sonya is suffering, I readily admit that, but why these questions of yours? [*Stopping her speaking, animatedly*] Please don't look surprised, you know very well why I come here every day . . . Why and for whom I come, you know full well. Dear predator, don't look at me like that, I'm an old sparrow . . .

YELENA ANDREYEVNA [*bewildered*]: Predator? I don't understand.

ASTROV: Beautiful fluffy polecat . . . You need victims! For a whole month I've been idle, I've dropped everything, I hungrily look for you . . . and you're terribly pleased by that, terribly . . . So? I am conquered, you knew that without any questions. [*Crossing his arms and bowing his head*] I submit. There, eat me up!

YELENA ANDREYEVNA: You've gone out of your mind!

ASTROV [*laughing through clenched teeth*]: You're being coy . . .

YELENA ANDREYEVNA: Oh, I'm better and more principled than you think! I swear to you! [*Tries to go.*]

ASTROV [*blocking her way*]: I will leave today, I won't come here, but . . . [*Takes her by the hand and looks round.*] Where shall we meet? Tell me quickly, where? Tell me quickly, someone might come in. [*Passionately*] What a marvellous voluptuous woman . . . One kiss . . . Let me just kiss your scented hair . . .

YELENA ANDREYEVNA: I swear to you . . .

ASTROV [*stopping her from speaking*]: Why swear? No need to swear. You mustn't swear. No need for superfluous words. What beauty! What hands! [*Kisses her hands.*]

YELENA ANDREYEVNA: Stop, enough . . . go away . . . [*Pulls away her hands.*] You've forgotten yourself.

ASTROV: Tell me, tell me where we'll meet tomorrow. [*Puts his arm round her waist.*] You see, it can't be avoided, we must see one another. [*Kisses her; at this moment* VOYNITSKY *enters with a bouquet of flowers and stops by the door*.]

YELENA ANDREYEVNA [*not seeing Voynitsky*]: Spare me . . . leave me . . . [*Lays her head on Astrov's breast*.] No! [*Tries to leave*.]

ASTROV [*holding her by the waist*]: Come tomorrow to the forestry station . . . about two . . . Yes? Yes? You'll come?

YELENA ANDREYEVNA [*seeing Voynitsky*]: Let me go! [*Overcome by embarrassment, moves away towards the window*.] This is dreadful.

VOYNITSKY [*puts the bouquet on a chair; in his agitation wipes his face and inside his collar with a handkerchief*]: Don't worry . . . No . . . It doesn't matter . . .

ASTROV [*sulkily*]: My dear Ivan Petrovich, the weather isn't too bad today. The morning was overcast, as if it was going to rain, but now there's sunshine. It really has turned out to be a beautiful autumn . . . and the winter crop is all right. [*Rolls up the map*.] The only thing is the days have become short . . . [*Goes out*.]

YELENA ANDREYEVNA [*quickly going towards Voynitsky*]: Try and use all your influence to see that I and my husband leave today! Do you hear? Today!

VOYNITSKY [*wiping his face*]: Ah? Yes . . . very well . . . Hélène, I saw everything, everything . . .

YELENA ANDREYEVNA [*irritably*]: Do you hear! I must leave here today!

[*Enter* SEREBRYAKOV, SONYA, TELEGIN *and* MARINA]

TELEGIN: I myself am not very well, Your Excellency. It's the second day now that I've been feeling ill. My head sort of . .

SEREBRYAKOV: Where are the others? I don't like this house. It's like a maze. Twenty-six huge rooms, everyone wanders off and you never find them. [*Rings*.] Ask Mariya Vasilyevna and Yelena Andreyevna to come here!

YELENA ANDREYEVNA: I'm here.

SEREBRYAKOV: Please sit down, ladies and gentlemen.

SONYA [*going up to Yelena Andreyevna, impatiently*]: What did he say?

YELENA ANDREYEVNA: Later.

SONYA: Are you shivering? You're upset? [*Looks inquiringly into her face.*] I understand . . . He said that he won't come here any more . . . yes?

[*A pause.*]

Tell me, did he?

[YELENA ANDREYEVNA *nods her head.*]

SEREBRYAKOV [*to Telegin*]: Whatever the circumstances, one can accommodate oneself to ill health, but I can't cope with this way of life in the country. I feel as if I'd fallen from earth onto another planet. Please sit down, ladies and gentlemen. Sonya!

[SONYA *doesn't hear him, and stands sadly hanging her head.*]

Sonya!

[*A pause.*]

She's deaf. [*To Marina*] Nyanya, you sit down too.

[*The* nyanya *sits down and knits a stocking.*]

Please, ladies and gentlemen. Hang up your ears, so to speak, on a peg of attention. [*Laughs.*]

VOYNITSKY [*agitated*]: Perhaps you don't need me? Can I go?

SEREBRYAKOV: No, you're needed here more than anyone.

VOYNITSKY: What do you want from me, Serebryakov?

SEREBRYAKOV: 'Serebryakov' . . . ? Why are you angry, Vanya?³

[*A pause.*]

If I've offended you in anything, please forgive me.

VOYNITSKY: Do drop that tone. Let's move on to business. What do you want?

[*Enter* MARIYA VASILYEVNA.]

SEREBRYAKOV: Here's Maman. I shall start.

[*A pause.*]

I've asked you to come here, ladies and gentlemen, to make an announcement to you, the Inspector-General is coming to us.[4] But jokes aside. The matter is a serious one. I have assembled you, my friends, to ask for your help and advice, and knowing your continued indulgence I hope that I will receive them. I am a scholar, a man of books, and have always been a stranger to the practical life. I cannot do without the views of well-informed people, and so I am asking you, Ivan Petrovich, you, Ilya Ilyich, you, Maman . . . The fact is that *manet omnes una nox*,[5] that is, we are all God's creatures; I am old and sick, and so I find it timely to regulate my property arrangements insofar as they affect my family. My life is now over, I'm not thinking of myself, but I have a young wife and an unmarried daughter.

[*A pause.*]

I cannot go on living in the country. We are not made for the country. But we cannot live in the city on the income we receive from this estate. Were we to sell, say, the forest, that would be an extraordinary measure which we could not utilize every year. We must find ways of guaranteeing a more or less fixed sum of income. I have thought of one such and humbly submit it for your consideration. I shall pass over the details and outline it in general terms. Our estate produces on average not more than two per cent. I propose to sell it. If we convert the receipts into interest-bearing bonds, then we shall receive four to five per cent, and I think there will be a surplus of several thousand roubles which will allow us to buy a small dacha[6] in Finland.[7]

VOYNITSKY: Wait . . . I think my ears are failing me. Repeat what you said.

SEREBRYAKOV: Convert the monies into interest-bearing bonds and buy a dacha in Finland with the surplus.

VOYNITSKY: Not Finland . . . You said something else too.

SEREBRYAKOV: I'm proposing selling the estate.

VOYNITSKY: Exactly. You'll sell the estate, excellent, a splendid idea . . . And where would you like me and my old mother and Sonya here to go?

SEREBRYAKOV: We will discuss all that at the appropriate time. Not now.

VOYNITSKY: Wait a minute. Clearly until now I haven't had an ounce of common sense. Until now I've been stupid enough to think this estate belongs to Sonya. My late father bought this estate as a dowry for my sister. Up till now I've been naïve, I assumed we weren't living under Turkish law and I thought the estate had passed from my sister to Sonya.

SEREBRYAKOV: Yes, the estate belongs to Sonya. Who is disputing that? Without Sonya's consent I would not decide to sell it. Furthermore, I am proposing to do this in Sonya's interest.

VOYNITSKY: This is incomprehensible, incomprehensible! Either I have gone mad, or . . . or . . .

MARIYA VASILYEVNA: Jean, don't contradict Aleksandr. Believe me, he knows what's good and what's bad for us better than we do.

VOYNITSKY: No, give me some water. [*Drinks the water.*] Say whatever you want, whatever you want!

SEREBRYAKOV: I do not understand why you're upset. I don't say that my plan is ideal. If everyone finds it inappropriate, then I won't insist on it.

[*A pause.*]

TELEGIN [*embarrassed*]: Your Excellency, for scholarship I have not just reverence but feelings of kinship. My brother Grigory Ilyich's wife's brother – perhaps you know him – Konstantin Trofimovich Lakedemonov, had a master's degree . . .

VOYNITSKY: Waffle, do stop, we're talking business . . . Wait a moment, later . . . [*To Serebryakov*] Now ask him. This estate was bought from his uncle.

SEREBRYAKOV: Oh, why should I ask him? To what end?

VOYNITSKY: This estate was bought then for ninety-five thousand roubles. My father only paid down seventy and had a mortgage for twenty-five thousand. Now listen . . . This estate would not have been bought if I had not given up my inheritance in favour of my sister, whom I dearly loved. What's more, I worked like an ox for ten years and paid off the entire mortgage . . .

SEREBRYAKOV: I regret having started this conversation.

VOYNITSKY: The estate is free of debt and in good order only thanks to my personal efforts. And now in my old age I'm to be thrown out of here on my neck!

SEREBRYAKOV: I don't understand what you're getting at!

VOYNITSKY: For twenty-five years I've managed this estate, worked, sent you money like the most conscientious steward and over that whole time you haven't thanked me once. The whole time – both when I was young and now – I've been getting a salary of five hundred roubles a year from you – a beggar's wage – and you haven't once thought of increasing my salary by a single rouble!

SEREBRYAKOV: Ivan Petrovich, how should I have known? I am not a practical man and don't understand anything. You could have added as much as you wanted.

VOYNITSKY: Why didn't I steal, you mean? Why don't you all despise me for not stealing? It would have been fair, and today I wouldn't be a pauper!

MARIYA VASILYEVNA [*sternly*]: Jean!

TELEGIN [*upset*]: Vanya, dear friend, you mustn't, you mustn't . . . I'm trembling . . . Why spoil good relations? [*Kisses him.*] You mustn't.

VOYNITSKY: For twenty-five years I've sat with my mother here within these four walls – like a mole . . . All our thoughts and feelings belonged to you alone. By day we talked about you, about your work, we were proud of you, we uttered your name with reverence: we ruined our nights reading magazines and books which I now deeply despise!

TELEGIN: You mustn't, Vanya, you mustn't . . . I can't . . .

SEREBRYAKOV [*angrily*]: I do not understand what you want.

VOYNITSKY: For us you were a being of a higher order, and we knew your articles by heart . . . But now my eyes have been opened! I see it all! You write about art but you understand nothing about art! All your works, which I used to love, are not worth a brass farthing! You fooled us!

SEREBRYAKOV: All of you, stop him now! I am going!

YELENA ANDREYEVNA: Ivan Petrovich, I insist you stop! Do you hear?

VOYNITSKY: I will not be silent! [*Blocking Serebryakov's way.*] Stay here, I haven't finished! You have destroyed my life! I haven't lived, I haven't lived! Thanks to you I wasted, I destroyed the best years of my life! You are my worst enemy!

TELEGIN: I can't . . . I can't . . . I'm going . . . [*Goes out in great agitation.*]

SEREBRYAKOV: What do you want of me? And what right do you have to speak to me in this tone? You are nothing! If the estate is yours, take it, I don't need it!

YELENA ANDREYEVNA: I am leaving this hell this very minute. [*She is shouting.*] I can't stand it any longer!

VOYNITSKY: My life is over! I am talented, clever, ambitious . . . If I'd lived normally, I might have been a Schopenhauer, a Dostoyevsky . . . I'm babbling! I'm losing my mind . . . Mother, I'm desperate! Mother!

MARIYA VASILYEVNA [*sternly*]: Listen to Aleksandr!

SONYA [*kneeling in front of the* nyanya *and clinging to her*]: Nyanya! Dearest Nyanya!

VOYNITSKY: Mother! What am I to do! No, don't speak. I know myself what I must do! [*To Serebryakov*] You will remember me! [*Goes out of the middle door.*]

[MARIYA VASILYEVNA *follows him.*]

SEREBRYAKOV: Ladies and gentlemen, what on earth is all this? Take this madman away from me! I cannot live under the same roof as him! He is there [*points at the middle door*], almost in the next room to me . . . Let him move into the village or the wing, or else I'll move out of here, but I cannot remain in the same house as him . . .

YELENA ANDREYEVNA [*to her husband*]: We will leave here today! You must give the instructions this minute.

SEREBRYAKOV: What a worthless fellow!

SONYA [*on her knees, turns to her father; nervously, with tears in her eyes*]: You must be merciful, Papa! Uncle Vanya and I are so unhappy! [*Trying to control her despair*] You must be merciful! Do you remember, when you were younger, Uncle Vanya and Grandmother used to translate books for you at night, used to transcribe your papers . . . every night, every night! I and Uncle Vanya worked without any rest, we were afraid to spend a kopeck on ourselves and sent everything to you . . . We earned our keep! I don't mean that, I'm not saying it right, but you must understand us, Papa. You must be merciful!

YELENA ANDREYEVNA [*in distress, to her husband*]: Aleksandr, for God's sake have a talk to him . . . I beseech you.

SEREBRYAKOV: Very well, I will have it out with him . . . I am not accusing him of anything, I am not angry, but you must admit his behaviour is strange at the very least. All right, I will go to him. [*Goes out by the middle door.*]

YELENA ANDREYEVNA: Be gentle with him, calm him . . . [*Goes out after him.*]

SONYA [*clinging to the* nyanya]: Nyanya! Dearest Nyanya!

MARINA: It's all right, darling. Just geese – they'll cackle away a bit – and then stop . . . Cackle away – and then stop . . .

SONYA: Nyanya!

MARINA [*stroking her head*]: You're shivering like when there's a frost. There, there, my motherless child, God is merciful. Some lime or raspberry tea, and it'll go . . . Don't get upset, my little motherless girl . . . [*Looking at the middle door, with feeling*] How those wretched geese got going!

[*Offstage a shot;* YELENA ANDREYEVNA *is heard to cry out;* SONYA *shudders.*]

Oh, curse you!

SEREBRYAKOV [*running in, stumbling in fright*]: Hold him! Hold him! He's gone mad!

[YELENA ANDREYEVNA *and* VOYNITSKY *are struggling in the doorway.*]

YELENA ANDREYEVNA [*trying to take a revolver from him*]: Give it to me! Give it to me, I order you!

VOYNITSKY: Let me go, Hélène! Let me go! [*Freeing himself, he runs in and looks for Serebryakov.*] Where is he? There he is! [*Shoots at him.*] Bang!

[*A pause.*]

Haven't I hit him? Missed again? [*Angrily*] The devil, devil . . . devil take you. [*Hurls the revolver on the floor and sits down on a chair exhausted.* SEREBRYAKOV *is in shock;* YELENA ANDREYEVNA *leans against a wall, she is feeling faint.*]

YELENA ANDREYEVNA: Take me away from here! Take me, kill me, but . . . I can't stay here, I can't.

VOYNITSKY [*desperately*]: Oh what am I doing! What am I doing!

SONYA [*quietly*]: Nyanya! Dearest Nyanya!

[*Curtain.*]

Act Four

Voynitsky's room, which is where he sleeps but is also the estate office. By the window is a large table with ledgers and papers of all kinds on it, a bureau, cupboards and a pair of scales. There is a smaller table for Astrov; on it are drawing materials and paints; by it is a portfolio. A cage with a starling. On the wall is a map of Africa, obviously not needed by anyone here. An outsize sofa covered in oilcloth. Left — an internal door; right — a door to the outside lobby; by the right-hand door a mat is laid so that the peasants don't bring in mud. An autumn evening. Quiet.

[TELEGIN *and* MARINA: *they are sitting opposite one another, winding wool for stockings.*]

TELEGIN: You must go a bit quicker, Marina Timofeyevna, they'll be calling us to say goodbye any minute. They've already asked for the horses.

MARINA [*trying to wind faster*]: There's not much left.

TELEGIN: They're leaving for Kharkov. They're going to live there.

MARINA: That'll be better.

TELEGIN: They got frightened . . . Yelena Andreyevna was saying, 'I don't want to live here one single hour more . . . let's just go . . . We'll stay a while in Kharkov,' she said, 'and take stock, and then send for our things . . .' They're leaving with no luggage. So, Marina Timofeyevna, they were fated not to live here. Fated . . . A disposition of fate.

MARINA: It'll be better. They were making such a row, and shooting . . . A disgrace!

TELEGIN: Yes, a subject for the brush of Ayvazovsky.[1]
MARINA: I wish I hadn't seen it.

[*A pause.*]

We'll live again as we used to, in the old days. Tea at eight in the morning, dinner at one, sitting down to supper in the evening; everything in its proper order, just as people do it . . . Christian people. [*With a sigh*] It's been a long time, for my sins, since I've eaten noodles.
TELEGIN: Yes, it's a while since we had noodles.

[*A pause.*]

Quite a while . . . This morning, Marina Timofeyevna, I was walking in the village, and a shopkeeper called out after me, 'You old sponger!' And I was upset!
MARINA: Don't you take any notice, dear. We are all spongers on God. You and Sonya and Ivan Petrovich – none of you sit with nothing to do, we all work! All of us . . . Where's Sonya?
TELEGIN: In the garden. She's still with the Doctor. She's looking for Ivan Petrovich. They're afraid he might do something to himself.
MARINA: But where's his gun?
TELEGIN [*in a whisper*]: I hid it in the cellar.
MARINA [*with a smile*]: Naughty!

[*Enter* VOYNITSKY *and* ASTROV *from outside.*]

VOYNITSKY: Leave me. [*To Marina and Telegin*] Go away from here, leave me alone for just one hour! I can't stand this supervision.
TELEGIN: At once, Vanya. [*Goes out on tiptoe.*]
MARINA: Old goose! *Go-go-go!* [*Gathers up the wool and goes out.*]
VOYNITSKY: Leave me!

ASTROV: With great pleasure, I should have gone hours ago, but, I repeat, I will not go until you return what you've taken from me.

VOYNITSKY: I've taken nothing from you.

ASTROV: I'm being serious – don't make me late. I should have left long ago.

VOYNITSKY: I've taken nothing from you.

[*Both sit down.*]

ASTROV: Really? Well, I'll wait a little longer, and then, I'm sorry, I'll have to use force. We'll tie you up and search you. I mean that quite seriously.

VOYNITSKY: As you please.

[*A pause.*]

What a fool – to shoot twice and not score a single hit! I'll never forgive myself for that!

ASTROV: If you had the urge to shoot, why didn't you put a bullet through your own head?

VOYNITSKY [*shrugging*]: It's odd. I attempted murder but no one is arresting me or going to prosecute me. So they must think I'm mad. [*A sour laugh.*] I'm mad, unlike those who hide their lack of talent, their dullness, their crying heartlessness under the mask of professors, wise men. Unlike those who marry old men and then deceive them under the eyes of everyone. I saw, I saw you embracing her!

ASTROV: Yes, I embraced her. And this is for you. [*Thumbs his nose at him.*]

VOYNITSKY [*looking at the door*]: No, it's a mad world, with all of you in it!

ASTROV: That's silly.

VOYNITSKY: Well, I'm mad, I have no responsibility for my actions, I have the right to say silly things.

ASTROV: An old trick. You aren't mad but simply an eccentric. A buffoon. I used to consider all eccentrics sick, abnormal, but I'm now of the opinion that the normal condition of man is to be eccentric. You're quite normal.

VOYNITSKY [*covering his face with his hands*]: I'm ashamed! If you knew how ashamed I am! This sharp feeling of shame can't be compared with any pain. [*Anguished*] It's unbearable! [*Bows his head over the table.*] What am I to do? What am I to do?

ASTROV: Nothing.

VOYNITSKY: Give me something! Oh my God . . . I'm forty-seven; if I live, say, to sixty, I've still got thirteen years. A long time! How will I get through those thirteen years? What shall I do, how will I fill them? Oh, you have to understand . . . [*convulsively shakes Astrov's hand*] you have to understand, if only I could live the rest of my life somehow afresh. Could wake to a bright calm morning and feel that I'd begun to live anew, that all the past was forgotten, dissolved like smoke. [*Weeps.*] Begin a new life . . . Advise me how to begin . . . where to begin . . .

ASTROV [*irritatedly*]: What a fool you are! What new life out there! Our situation, yours and mine, is hopeless.

VOYNITSKY: Is it?

ASTROV: I'm sure of it.

VOYNITSKY: Give me something . . . [*Pointing to his heart.*] There's a burning feeling here.

ASTROV [*shouting angrily*]: Stop it! [*Calming down.*] Those who will live after us in a hundred or two hundred years' time and who will despise us for living our lives so foolishly and with such a lack of taste – they may find a way of being happy, but we . . . You and I have only one hope. The hope that when we lie in our coffins we'll be visited by visions, perhaps even agreeable ones. [*Sighing.*] Yes, my friend. In the whole District there used to be only two decent intelligent human beings – myself and you. But in the space of ten years or so the ordinary life we despise has dragged us down; it has poisoned our blood with its putrid exhalations and we've become as commonplace as everyone else. [*Animatedly*] But don't try and get round me. Give me back what you took from me.

VOYNITSKY: I've taken nothing from you.

ASTROV: You took a jar of morphine from my travelling medicine chest.

[*A pause.*]

Look, if you are absolutely set on committing suicide, then go into the woods and shoot yourself. But give back the morphine or there'll be talk and conjecture and people will think that I gave it to you . . . It'll be quite enough having to do your autopsy . . . Do you think I'll find that interesting?

[*Enter* SONYA.]

VOYNITSKY: Leave me alone!

ASTROV [*to Sonya*]: Sofya Aleksandrovna, your uncle has taken a jar of morphine from my travelling medicine chest and won't give it back. Tell him that it's . . . actually, not very clever. And I have no more time. I must leave.

SONYA: Uncle Vanya, did you take the morphine?

[*A pause.*]

ASTROV: He took it. I'm sure of it.

SONYA: Give it back. Why do you frighten us? [*Tenderly*] Give it back, Uncle Vanya! I may be no less unhappy than you, but I don't become desperate. I endure and will endure until my life comes to a natural end . . . You must endure.

[*A pause.*]

Give it back! [*Kisses his hands.*] Dear, wonderful, sweet Uncle, give it back! [*Cries.*] You are kind, you'll feel sorry for us and give it back. You must endure, Uncle! Endure!

VOYNITSKY [*getting the jar out of a table drawer and giving it to Astrov*]: There, take it! [*To Sonya*] But we must quickly get to work, do something, otherwise I can't . . . I can't . . .

SONYA: Yes, yes, work. As soon as we've said goodbye to them, we'll sit down and work ... [*Nervously turns over papers on the table.*] We've let everything get into a mess.

ASTROV [*putting the jar into his medicine chest and tightening the straps*]: Now I can get on the road.

YELENA ANDREYEVNA [*entering*]: Ivan Petrovich, are you here? We're leaving now ... Go in to Aleksandr, he wants to say something to you.

SONYA: Go, Uncle Vanya. [*Taking Voynitsky by the arm*] Let's go. You and Papa must make it up. It's essential.

[*Exeunt* SONYA *and* VOYNITSKY.]

YELENA ANDREYEVNA: I'm leaving. [*Giving Astrov her hand.*] Goodbye.

ASTROV: So soon?

YELENA ANDREYEVNA: They've already brought the horses.

ASTROV: Goodbye.

YELENA ANDREYEVNA: You promised me today you would leave here.

ASTROV: I remember. I'm going now.

[*A pause.*]

Were you frightened? [*Taking her hand.*] Was it so frightening?

YELENA ANDREYEVNA: Yes.

ASTROV: Otherwise you might have stayed! So? Tomorrow at the forestry station ...

YELENA ANDREYEVNA: No ... It's decided now ... And I'm brave enough to look at you because our departure is now settled ... I ask you one thing: think better of me. I want you to respect me.

ASTROV: Oh! [*with an impatient gesture*]. Stay, please. Admit it, you have nothing to do on this earth, you have no goal in life, you have nothing to hold your interest, and sooner or later you will surrender to feeling – it's inevitable. So rather than doing that in

Kharkov or somewhere in Kursk, do it here in the bosom of nature ... It's at least poetic, even the autumn is beautiful ... Here we have forestry plantations, crumbling country houses à la Turgenev ...

YELENA ANDREYEVNA: What an amusing man you are ... I'm angry with you, but still ... I shall remember you with pleasure. You are interesting and original. We shall never see one another again, so – why not be open about it? – I even fell for you a little. Well, let's shake hands and part friends. Don't think badly of me.

ASTROV [*shaking her hand*]: Yes, go ... [*Reflectively*] I think you are a good, sincere person but there's also something strange in your whole being. You came here with your husband and everyone who was busily working here and creating something had to drop what they were doing and devote the whole summer to looking after your husband's gout and you yourself. Both of you – he and you – infected all of us with your idleness. I was attracted and did nothing for a whole month, and during that time people were ill, and the peasants put their cattle out to feed in my woods with their young trees ... And so, wherever you and your husband tread, you bring destruction. I'm joking of course, but still ... it's strange, and I'm convinced that if you had stayed, the devastation would have been enormous. And I would have been lost, and you ... it wouldn't have been good for you. So, leave. *Finita la commedia!*[2]

YELENA ANDREYEVNA [*taking a pencil from his table and quickly putting it away*]: I'm taking this pencil as a souvenir.

ASTROV: Isn't it strange ... We were friends and suddenly, for some reason ... we won't ever see each other again. It's like everything in the world ... While there's no one here, before Uncle Vanya comes in with a bunch of flowers, allow me to ... kiss you ... To say goodbye ... Yes? [*Kisses her on the cheek.*] So ... good.

YELENA ANDREYEVNA: I wish you all the best! [*Having looked round.*] Just once in my life, come what may. [*Impulsively embraces him and both immediately separate.*] We must leave.

ASTROV: Leave quickly. If the horses are ready, then go.
YELENA ANDREYEVNA: I think someone's coming.

[*Both listen.*]

ASTROV: *Finita!*

[*Enter* SEREBRYAKOV, VOYNITSKY, MARIYA VASILYEVNA *with a book,* TELEGIN *and* SONYA.]

SEREBRYAKOV [*to Voynitsky*]: A curse on anyone who brings up the past. After what happened, in these last few hours I've experienced so much and changed my thinking so much that I think I could write a whole treatise on how to live for the edification of posterity. I willingly accept your apologies and I myself ask you to forgive me. Goodbye. [*He and* VOYNITSKY *kiss three times.*]
VOYNITSKY: You will receive exactly what you used to receive. Everything will be as before.

[YELENA ANDREYEVNA *embraces Sonya.*]

SEREBRYAKOV [*kissing Mariya Vasilyevna's hand*]: Maman . . .
MARIYA VASILYEVNA [*kissing him*]: Aleksandr, get your photograph taken again and send it to me. You know how dear you are to me.
TELEGIN: Goodbye, Your Excellency! Don't forget us!
SEREBRYAKOV [*kissing his daughter*]: Goodbye . . . Goodbye to you all! [*Giving his hand to Astrov.*] Thank you for your pleasant company . . . I respect your way of thinking, your enthusiasms, your impulses, but let an old man include just one observation in his farewell greetings: my friends, one must do a job of work! One must do a job of work! [*A bow to everyone.*] All the best! [*Goes out followed by* MARIYA VASILYEVNA *and* SONYA.]
VOYNITSKY [*firmly kissing Yelena Andreyevna's hand*]: Goodbye . . . Forgive me . . . We'll never see each other again.

YELENA ANDREYEVNA [*touched*]: Goodbye, my dear. [*Kisses him on the head and goes out.*]

ASTROV [*to Telegin*]: Waffle, tell them to bring my horses round at the same time.

TELEGIN: I hear and obey, old chap. [*Goes out.*]

[*Only* ASTROV *and* VOYNITSKY *remain.*]

ASTROV [*clearing the paints from the table and packing them into his suitcase*]: Why don't you go and see them off?

VOYNITSKY: Let them leave, I . . . I can't. I feel wretched. I must quickly occupy myself with something . . . To work, to work! [*Rummages in the papers on the table.*]

[*A pause; the sound of harness bells.*]

ASTROV: They've gone. The Professor's probably pleased. Wild horses wouldn't get him back here.

MARINA [*entering*]: They've gone. [*Sits down in an armchair and knits a stocking.*]

SONYA [*entering*]: They've gone. [*Wiping her eyes.*] God grant them a safe journey. [*To her uncle*] Well, Uncle Vanya, let's do something.

VOYNITSKY: To work, to work . . .

SONYA: It's a long, long time since we sat together at this table. [*Lights the lamp on the table.*] I don't think there's any ink . . . [*Takes the inkpot, goes to the cupboard and pours in ink.*] But I'm sad they've gone.

MARIYA VASILYEVNA [*entering slowly*]: They've gone. [*Sits down and absorbs herself in reading.*]

SONYA [*sitting down at the table and leafing through an account book*]: Uncle Vanya, first of all let's write out the bills. We've let things go dreadfully. Today someone sent a reminder. Start writing. You write out one bill, I'll do another . . .

VOYNITSKY [*writing*]: 'Account for Mr . . .'

[*Both write in silence.*]

MARINA [*yawning*]: Bedtime calls . . .

ASTROV: It's quiet. The pens are scratching, the cricket's chirping. It's warm, cosy . . . I don't want to leave here.

[*The sound of harness bells.*]

There, they're bringing the horses . . . So, my friends, it remains for me to say goodbye to you, to say goodbye to my table, and — we're off! [*He puts the maps away in the portfolio.*]

MARINA: Why have you started fussing? You should sit down.

ASTROV: I mustn't.

VOYNITSKY: 'Two seventy-five outstanding . . .'

[*Enter a* WORKMAN.]

WORKMAN: Mikhail Lvovich, the horses are ready.

ASTROV: Right. [*Gives him the medicine chest, the suitcase and the portfolio.*] Take these. Watch out you don't crush the portfolio.

WORKMAN: Yes, sir. [*Goes out.*]

ASTROV: Well . . . [*Moves to say goodbye.*]

SONYA: When shall we meet again?

ASTROV: It won't be before the summer. Unlikely in the winter . . . Of course, if something happens, then let me know — I'll come. [*Shakes hands.*] Thank you for your hospitality, for looking after me . . . in short, for everything. [*Goes to the* nyanya *and kisses her on the head.*] Goodbye, my old dear.

MARINA: So you're going without having tea?

ASTROV: I don't want any, Nyanya.

MARINA: Perhaps you'd like some vodka?

ASTROV [*indecisively*]: Maybe . . .

[MARINA *goes out.*]

[*After a pause.*] My trace-horse has gone a bit lame. I noticed it when Petrushka took them to drink.

VOYNITSKY: You need new shoes.

ASTROV: I'll have to go to the blacksmith at Rozhdestvennoye. I've no choice. [*Goes up to the map of Africa.*] It must be boiling now there in Africa – terrible!

VOYNITSKY: Yes, it probably is.

MARINA [*returning with a tray on which are a glass of vodka and a piece of bread*]: Eat.

[ASTROV *drinks the vodka.*]

Your good health, my dear. [*Bows low.*] And send it down with a little bit of bread.

ASTROV: No, I'll have it without . . . Good luck then! [*To Marina*] Don't see me off, Nyanya. You mustn't. [*Goes out.* SONYA *follows him with a candle to see him off;* MARINA *sits down in her armchair.*]

VOYNITSKY [*writing*]: '2nd February vegetable oil twenty pounds . . . 16th February vegetable oil again twenty pounds . . . Buckwheat . . .'

[*A pause. The sound of harness bells.*]

MARINA: He's gone.

[*A pause.*]

SONYA [*returning and putting the candle on the table*]: He's gone.

VOYNITSKY [*counting up on the abacus and writing down*]: 'Total . . . fifteen . . . twenty-five . . .'

[SONYA *sits down and writes.*]

MARINA [*yawning*]: Oh, forgive us our trespasses . . .

[*Enter* TELEGIN *on tiptoe. Sits down by the door and quietly tunes his guitar.*]

VOYNITSKY [*to Sonya, stroking her hair*]: My child, how heavy my heart is. If you only knew how heavy.

SONYA: What can we do, we've got to live!

[*A pause.*]

We shall live, Uncle Vanya. We shall live out many, many days and long evenings; we shall patiently bear the trials fate sends us; we shall labour for others both now and in our old age, knowing no rest, and when our time comes, we shall meekly die, and there beyond the grave we shall say that we suffered, that we wept, that we were sorrowful, and God will have pity on us, and you and I, dear Uncle, shall see a life that is bright and beautiful and full of grace, we shall rejoice and look back on our present woes with tenderness, with a smile – and we shall rest. I believe that, Uncle, I believe fervently, passionately . . . [*Kneels before him and lays her head on his hands; in an exhausted voice*] We shall rest!

[TELEGIN *quietly plays his guitar.*]

We shall rest! We shall hear the angels, we shall see the whole sky paved with diamonds, we shall see all earthly evil, all our sufferings covered by the sea of mercy which shall fill the whole earth, and our life will become quiet, tender, sweet as a caress. I believe, I believe . . . [*Wipes away his tears with a handkerchief.*] Poor, poor Uncle Vanya, you're crying. [*With tears in her eyes*] You've known no joys in your life, but wait, Uncle Vanya, wait . . . We shall rest . . . [*Hugs him.*] We shall rest!

[*The night-watchman knocks.* TELEGIN *plays quietly;* MARIYA VASILYEVNA *makes notes in the margins of a pamphlet;* MARINA *knits a stocking.*]

We shall rest!

[*The curtain slowly falls.*]

Three Sisters

A Drama in Four Acts

CHARACTERS

ANDREY SERGEYEVICH PROZOROV [*also*
ANDRYUSHA, ANDRYUSHANCHIK]

NATALYA IVANOVNA [*also* NATASHA], *his* fiancée,
later his wife

OLGA [*also* OLECHKA, OLYA, OLYUSHKA] ⎫
MASHA [*also* MARIYA, MARYA, MASHKA, ⎬ *his*
  MASHENKA] │ *sisters*
IRINA [*also* ARINUSHKA, ARISHA] ⎭

FYODOR ILYICH KULYGIN [*also* FEDYA], *a teacher
in a Gymnasium,*[1] *Masha's husband*

ALEKSANDR IGNATYEVICH VERSHININ,
  Lieutenant-Colonel and battery commander

BARON NIKOLAY LVOVICH TUZENBAKH,
  Lieutenant

VASILY VASILYEVICH SOLYONY, *Staff Captain*

IVAN ROMANOVICH CHEBUTYKIN, *an army doctor*

ALEKSEY PETROVICH FEDOTIK, *Second Lieutenant*

VLADIMIR KARLOVICH RODE, *Second Lieutenant*

FERAPONT, *an old man, a District Council watchman*

ANFISA, *an eighty-year-old* nyanya[2]

A MAID

The action takes place in a provincial capital.[3]

Act One

The Prozorovs' house. A drawing-room with columns, beyond which a large reception hall is visible. Midday; outside it is sunny and cheerful. In the hall a table is being laid for lunch. OLGA, *wearing the dark blue uniform dress of a teacher in a Girls' Gymnasium, carries on correcting pupils' exercise books as she stands and walks about;* MASHA *in a black dress is sitting with a hat on her knees and reading a book;* IRINA *is standing lost in thought.*

OLGA: Father died exactly a year ago, on this very day, the fifth of May, your name-day,[1] Irina. It was very cold, it was snowing then. I thought I wouldn't live through it, you lay in a faint as if you were dead. But now a year has passed and we're remembering it without pain, you're wearing white again, your face is radiant . . . [*The clock strikes twelve.*] The clock struck that noon too.

[*A pause.*]

I remember a band played at Father's funeral and they fired a salute at the graveside. He was a general, in command of a brigade, but there weren't many people there. However, it was raining that day. Heavy rain and snow.

IRINA: Why bring it all back!

[BARON TUZENBAKH, CHEBUTYKIN *and* SOLYONY *appear beyond the columns, by the table in the hall.*]

OLGA: Today it's warm, we can keep the windows open, but the birches aren't in leaf yet. Father got his brigade and we left Moscow eleven years ago, and I remember very well, at the beginning of May just now in Moscow everything is already in bloom, it's warm, everything's bathed in sunshine. Eleven years have passed and I remember it all there as if we'd left yesterday. My God! This morning I woke up, I saw a mass of light, I saw the spring, and joy welled up in my soul and I had a huge longing for home.

CHEBUTYKIN: The devil it is!

TUZENBAKH: Of course, that's nonsense.

[MASHA, *lost in thought over her book, quietly whistles a song.*]

OLGA: Don't whistle, Masha. How can you!

[*A pause.*]

Every day I teach at the Gymnasium and afterwards I give lessons until evening, and so I've got a constant headache and my thoughts are those of an old woman. And indeed, during these four years I've been teaching at the Gymnasium, I've felt my strength and my youth draining from me every day, drop by drop. And one single thought grows stronger and stronger . . .

IRINA: To leave for Moscow. To sell the house, finish with everything here and – to Moscow . . .

OLGA: Yes! To Moscow, soon.

[CHEBUTYKIN *and* TUZENBAKH *laugh.*]

IRINA: Andrey will probably get a professor's chair and in any case he won't live here. The only problem is poor Masha.

OLGA: Masha will come to Moscow for the whole summer, every year.

[MASHA *quietly whistles a song.*]

IRINA: Everything will come out all right, God willing. [*Looking out of the window.*] The weather's good today. I don't know why I feel so radiant. This morning I remembered it's my name-day, and suddenly I felt joy and I remembered my childhood when Mama was still alive. And what wonderful thoughts stirred me, what thoughts!

OLGA: Today you're all aglow, you look exceptionally beautiful. And Masha is beautiful too. Andrey could be good-looking, only he's filled out a lot and it doesn't suit him. But I've become old, I've got very thin, I suppose because I lose my temper with the girls at the Gymnasium. Today I'm free, I'm at home and I have no head-ache, I feel younger than yesterday. I'm only twenty-eight . . . Life is good, everything in life comes from God, but I think it would be better if I were to marry and be sitting at home all day.

[*A pause.*]

I'd love my husband.

TUZENBAKH [*to Solyony*]: You talk such rubbish, I'm fed up listening to you. [*Entering the drawing-room.*] I forgot to say. Today our new battery commander Vershinin will be paying a call on you. [*Sits down at the piano.*]

OLGA: Really! I'm so pleased.

IRINA: Is he old?

TUZENBAKH: No. Not very. At most, forty, forty-five. [*Plays quietly.*] He seems a good fellow. He's not stupid – there's no doubt about that. Only he talks a lot.

IRINA: Is he an interesting man?

TUZENBAKH: Yes, quite, only he has a wife, a mother-in-law and two little girls. And it's his second marriage. He pays calls and says everywhere that he has a wife and two little girls. And he'll say it here. His wife is sort of crazy, she has a long plait of hair like a young girl, she dabbles in philosophy, only talking about high-flown things, and often attempts suicide, clearly to spite her husband. I would have left a woman like that long ago, but he bears it and only complains about it.

SOLYONY [*coming into the drawing-room from the hall with Chebu-tykin*]: With one hand I can only lift one and a half *puds*, but with two I can do five or even six. From that I conclude that two men are stronger than one by a factor not of two but of three or even more . . .

CHEBUTYKIN [*reading the newspaper as he walks*]: For falling hair, two *zolotniks* of naphthaline to half a bottle of spirit . . . dissolve and use daily . . . [*Makes a note in a notebook.*] We'll make a note of that. [*To Solyony*] So, as I was saying to you, you put a cork into a little bottle with a glass tube stuck through it . . . Then you take a pinch of simple, ordinary alum . . .

IRINA: Ivan Romanych, dear Ivan Romanych!

CHEBUTYKIN: What is it, dear girl, my joy?

IRINA: Tell me why I'm so happy today. It's as if I had sails and above me great white birds were flying in the wide blue sky. Why is this? Why?

CHEBUTYKIN [*kissing both her hands, tenderly*]: My white bird . . .

IRINA: When I woke today and got up and washed, I suddenly started to think that everything in this world is clear to me, and that I know the way to live. Dear Ivan Romanych, I know everything. A man, whoever he may be, must work, must toil by the sweat of his brow, and in that alone lie the sense and the goal of our life, its happiness, its joys. How good to be a labourer who gets up at dawn and breaks stones on the street, or a shepherd, or a schoolteacher teaching children, or an engine-driver on the railway . . . My God, better even not to be a man, better to be an ox, a simple horse, if only to work, than a young woman who gets up at midday, then drinks coffee in bed, then spends two hours dressing . . . Oh, how awful that is! Sometimes, in hot weather, you long for a drink – that's how I long to work. And if I don't get up early and work hard, then, Ivan Romanych, you must refuse me your friendship . . .

CHEBUTYKIN [*tenderly*]: I will refuse it, I will . . .

OLGA: Father taught us to get up at seven. Now Irina wakes at seven and lies there till nine at least, thinking about something. And her expression is so serious! [*Laughs.*]

IRINA: You've got accustomed to seeing me as a little girl and you find it strange when I have a serious expression. I'm twenty years old!

TUZENBAKH: God, how I understand the longing for work! I've never worked in my life, not once. I was born in cold and empty Petersburg, in a family which didn't know about work, didn't know about worries. I remember, when I came home from cadet school,[2] a footman used to pull off my boots. I was difficult at that time but my mother revered me and was surprised when others had a different view of me. I was protected from work. Only not wholly successfully, not wholly! This time has come, a great mass is moving towards all of us, a mighty, healthy storm is rising, it's coming, it's already near, and soon it will blow sloth, indifference, contempt for work, this festering boredom right out of our society. I will work and in some twenty-five or thirty years' time everyone will work. Everyone!

CHEBUTYKIN: I won't work.

TUZENBAKH: You don't count.

SOLYONY: In twenty-five years you won't be in this world, thank God. In two or three years you'll die of a stroke, or else I shall lose my temper, dear boy, and put a bullet through your forehead. [*He takes a scent bottle out of his pocket and sprinkles his chest and hands.*]

CHEBUTYKIN [*laughing*]: But I've really never done anything. Since I finished university I haven't lifted a finger, I haven't even read a single book, I've just read the newspapers . . . [*Takes another paper out of his pocket.*] Here . . . I know from the papers that a writer called Dobrolyubov,[3] say, existed, but what he wrote – I've no idea . . . God knows . . .

[*There's the sound of banging on the ceiling of the floor below.*]

There . . . They're calling me downstairs, someone has come to see me. I'm coming right away . . . wait a moment . . . [*Hurriedly goes out combing his beard.*]

IRINA: He's made that up.

TUZENBAKH: Yes. He went out with a solemn expression. He's obviously now going to bring you a present.

IRINA: How tiresome!

OLGA: Yes, it's terrible. He's always doing silly things.

MASHA: 'An oak in leaf beside the seashore, upon that oak a chain of gold' . . . 'upon that oak a chain of gold'⁴ . . . [*Gets up and sings softly.*]

OLGA: You're not very cheerful today, Masha.

[MASHA *puts on her hat, still singing.*]

Where are you going?

MASHA: Home.

IRINA: Odd . . .

TUZENBAKH: Leaving us on her name-day!

MASHA: It doesn't matter . . . I'll come back this evening. Goodbye, my dear . . . [*Kisses Irina.*] Let me again wish you health and happiness. In the old days, when Father was alive, thirty or forty officers used to come on each of our name-days, it was really noisy, but today there are only one and a half people and it's quiet as the desert . . . I'm going . . . Today I'm in a melancholy mood, I'm feeling depressed, so don't listen to me, Irina. [*Laughing with tears in her eyes.*] We'll talk later, but goodbye for now, my dear, I'm going somewhere.

IRINA [*crossly*]: Really, you are a . . .

OLGA [*in tears*]: I understand you, Masha.

SOLYONY: If a man talks philosophy, you get philosophistry, or at least sophistry; but if a woman talks philosophy, or two women, you'll end up with – I won't say it.

MASHA: What do you mean by that? You're being terribly scary.

SOLYONY: Nothing. 'He had no time his tale to tell before the bear upon him fell.'⁵

[*A pause.*]

MASHA [*to Olga, angrily*]: Do stop blubbing!

[*Enter* ANFISA *and* FERAPONT *with a cake.*]

ANFISA: In here, old man. Come in, your feet are clean. [*To Irina*] From the Council, from Mikhail Ivanych Protopopov . . . A cake.

IRINA: Thank you. Thank him for me. [*Takes the cake.*]

FERAPONT: What?

IRINA [*louder*]: Thank him!

OLGA: Nyanya dear, give him some cake. Ferapont, go, they'll give you some cake in there.

FERAPONT: What?

ANFISA: Let's go, old Ferapont Spiridonych. Let's go . . . [*She and* FERAPONT *go out.*]

MASHA: I don't like that Protopopov, that Mikhail Potapych or Ivanych. We shouldn't invite him.

IRINA: I haven't invited him.

MASHA: Well done.

[*Enter* CHEBUTYKIN, *followed by an orderly carrying a silver samovar; there's a buzz of surprise and annoyance.*]

OLGA [*covering her face with her hands*]: A samovar! It's terrible! [*Goes into the hall towards the table.*]

IRINA: Dear Ivan Romanych, what are you up to?

TUZENBAKH [*laughing*]: I told you.

MASHA: Ivan Romanych, you simply have no shame.

CHEBUTYKIN: My good girls, my dear girls, you are all I have, you are the dearest thing that exists in the world for me. I shall soon be sixty, I am an old man, a lonely, worthless old man . . . There's no good in me except for this love I have for you, and if it weren't for you, I would long ago have ceased to live in this world . . . [*To Irina*] My darling child, I've known you since the day you were born . . . I carried you in my arms . . . I loved your late mother . . .

IRINA: But why do you give such expensive presents?

CHEBUTYKIN [*angrily, with tears in his eyes*]: Expensive presents . . . Really! [*To the orderly*] Take the samovar in there . . . [*Mimics her.*] Expensive presents . . .

[*The orderly carries the samovar into the hall.*]

ANFISA [*passing through the drawing-room*]: My dears, there's a colonel we don't know! He's already taken his coat off, girls, he's coming in here. Arinushka, be nice and polite . . . [*Going out.*] And it's long past lunch time . . . heavens above . . .

TUZENBAKH: It must be Vershinin.

[*Enter* VERSHININ.]

Lieutenant-Colonel Vershinin!

VERSHININ [*to Masha and Irina*]: May I have the honour of introducing myself: Vershinin. I am very, very pleased to be in your house at last. How you've grown! Goodness!

IRINA: Sit down, please. We're delighted.

VERSHININ [*gaily*]: How pleased I am, how pleased! But you are three sisters. I remember – three little girls. I don't remember the faces any longer, but I do remember very well that your father, Colonel Prozorov, had three little girls and I saw them with my own eyes. How time passes! Oh yes, how time passes!

TUZENBAKH: Aleksandr Ignatyevich is from Moscow.

IRINA: From Moscow? You are from Moscow?

VERSHININ: Yes, from Moscow. Your late father commanded a battery there and I was an officer in the same brigade. [*To Masha*] Now I think I remember your face a little.

MASHA: But I don't remember you.

IRINA: Olya! Olya! [*Shouts to the hall*] Olya, come here!

[OLGA *comes from the hall into the drawing-room.*]

It turns out Colonel Vershinin is from Moscow.

VERSHININ: You must be Olga Sergeyevna, the eldest . . . And you Mariya . . . And you are Irina – the youngest . . .

OLGA: You're from Moscow?

VERSHININ: Yes. I studied in Moscow and I went into the army in Moscow, I served there a long time, finally I got a battery here – I've moved here as you can see. I don't remember you clearly, I remember only that you were three sisters. Your father has stayed in my memory, I just have to close my eyes and I see him as if he were alive. I used to come to your house in Moscow . . .

OLGA: I thought I remembered everyone, and now . . .

VERSHININ: My name is Aleksandr Ignatyevich . . .

IRINA: Aleksandr Ignatyevich, you are from Moscow . . . What a surprise!

OLGA: You see, we're moving there.

IRINA: We think we'll be there by the autumn. It's our home town, we were born there . . . In Staraya Basmannaya Street . . .

[*Both of them laugh with happiness.*]

MASHA: What a surprise to see someone else from Moscow. [*Animatedly*] Now I remember! Do you remember, Olya, we used to talk of 'the Lovesick Major'? You were a subaltern then and in love with someone, and everyone used to tease you for some reason as 'Major' . . .

VERSHININ [*laughing*]: Yes, yes . . . The Lovesick Major, exactly . . .

MASHA: Only then you had a moustache . . . Oh how you've aged! [*With tears in her eyes*] How you've aged!

VERSHININ: Yes, when you used to call me the Lovesick Major, I was still young, I was in love. It's different now.

OLGA: But still you don't have a single grey hair. You've aged but you're not yet old.

VERSHININ: However, I'm already forty-two. Did you leave Moscow a long time ago?

IRINA: Eleven years ago. Now, Masha, why are you crying, you funny thing? . . . [*With tears in her eyes*] I'm going to start crying too . . .

MASHA: It's nothing. And what street did you live in?

VERSHININ: Staraya Basmannaya.

OLGA: And so did we . . .

VERSHININ: At one time I lived in Nemetskaya Street. From Nemetskaya I used to walk to the Krasnye Barracks. There's a grim bridge on the way there, the water makes a noise under the bridge. A melancholy place for a man on his own.

[*A pause.*]

But what a wide, splendid river you have here! A wonderful river!

OLGA: Yes, only it's cold. It's cold here and there are mosquitoes . . .

VERSHININ: What! You've got such a good, healthy Slav climate here. The forest, the river . . . and there are birches here too. Dear humble birches, I love them best of all trees. It's good to live here. Only it's odd the railway station is twenty-five versts away . . . And no one knows why.

SOLYONY: But I do know why.

[*Everyone looks at him.*]

Because if the station were near by, it wouldn't be far away, and if it's far away that means it isn't near by.

[*An awkward silence.*]

TUZENBAKH: What a joker you are, Vasily Vasilyich.

OLGA: Now I've remembered you too. I remember.

VERSHININ: I knew your Mama.

CHEBUTYKIN: She was a good woman, God rest her soul.

IRINA: Mama is buried in Moscow.

OLGA: In the Novodevichy Cemetery[6] . . .

MASHA: Just think, I'm already beginning to forget her face. They won't remember us either. We'll be forgotten.

VERSHININ: Yes. We'll be forgotten. That's our destiny, we can't do anything about it. What seems to us serious and significant and really important – a time will come when it'll be forgotten or seem unimportant.

[*A pause.*]

And it's interesting that we absolutely can't know what exactly will be regarded as sublime and important and what will be thought pathetic and ridiculous. Didn't the discoveries of Copernicus or, say, Columbus, seem unnecessary at first, ridiculous, and didn't some vacuous nonsense written by a crank seem the truth? And maybe our life today, with which we are so comfortable, with the passage of time will come to seem strange, awkward, stupid, not pure enough, even sinful . . .

TUZENBAKH: Who knows? Perhaps people will talk about our lofty existence and recall it with reverence. There are no tortures now, no executions, no invasions, but all the same, how much suffering!

SOLYONY [*in a piping voice*]: Cluck, cluck, cluck . . . Don't give the Baron anything to eat, just let him talk philosophy.

TUZENBAKH: Vasily Vasilyich, I beg you to leave me in peace . . . [*Sits down in another place.*] It becomes a bore.

SOLYONY [*in a high-pitched voice*]: Cluck, cluck, cluck . . .

TUZENBAKH [*to Vershinin*]: But still, the suffering we see now – there's so much of it – shows that at this stage society has reached a certain moral development . . .

VERSHININ: Yes, yes, of course.

CHEBUTYKIN: You just said, Baron, that people will talk about our lofty existence; but men are still small . . . [*Gets up.*] Look how small I am. Of course, to console me people call my existence lofty.

[*Offstage someone is playing the violin.*]

MASHA: That's Andrey playing, our brother.

IRINA: He's our scholar. He'll probably get a university chair. Father was a soldier but his son chose an academic career.

MASHA: As Papa wanted.

OLGA: We teased him quite a lot today. I think he's a little in love.

IRINA: With a local young lady. She'll very probably be here today.

MASHA: Oh dear, her clothes! It's not that they're ugly or unfashionable, they're simply pathetic. Some odd, bright-coloured, yellowish skirt with a kind of horrid little fringe and a red blouse. And those cheeks scrubbed shiny clean! Andrey isn't in love – I won't admit that, he still has some taste, but he just seems to be teasing us, playing the fool. Yesterday I heard that she's marrying Protopopov, the chairman of the local Council. Just right . . .

[*Speaking through the side door*] Andrey, come in here! Only for a moment, dear.

[*Enter* ANDREY.]

OLGA: This is my brother Andrey Sergeich.

VERSHININ: Vershinin.

ANDREY: Prozorov. [*Wipes his perspiring face.*] Are you our new battery commander?

OLGA: Imagine, Aleksandr Ignatyich is from Moscow.

ANDREY: Really? Well, congratulations, now my sisters will give you no peace.

VERSHININ: I've already had time to bore your sisters.

IRINA: Look what a dear little portrait frame Andrey gave me today. [*Shows him the frame.*] He made it himself.

VERSHININ [*looking at the frame and not knowing what to say*]: Yes . . . that's something . . .

IRINA: And he also made that little frame above the piano.

[ANDREY *throws up a hand and moves off.*]

OLGA: Our brother is a scholar and plays the violin and makes all kinds of bits of woodwork – in short, he's master of all trades. Andrey, don't go off. He has a way of always walking off. Come here.

[MASHA *and* IRINA *take him by the arms and, laughing, bring him back.*]

MASHA: Come, come.

ANDREY: Leave me alone, please.

MASHA: What a funny man you are. Aleksandr Ignatyich once used to be called the Lovesick Major, and he wasn't cross at all.

VERSHININ: Not at all.

MASHA: And I'm going to call you the Lovesick Violinist.

IRINA: Or the Lovesick Professor . . .

OLGA: He's in love! Andryusha is in love!

CHEBUTYKIN [*coming up to Andrey from behind and taking him by the waist with both hands*]: 'For what does Nature bear us? For love, and love alone.' [*Roars with laughter; the whole time he is carrying his newspaper.*]

ANDREY: Well, that's enough, enough . . . [*Wiping his face.*] I didn't sleep all night and now, as people say, I'm not quite myself. I read until four, then I went to bed, but it was no good. I thought of this and that, and then it was early light, the sun really shines into my bedroom. While I'm here in the summer I want to translate a book from English.

VERSHININ: So you know English?

ANDREY: Yes. My father, God rest his soul, piled education onto us. It's funny and silly but I have to admit that after his death I began to fill out and in a year I've become fat, as if my body had been liberated. Thanks to my father, my sisters and I speak French, German and English, and Irina speaks Italian as well. But at what cost!

MASHA: In this town to know three languages is an unnecessary luxury. Not even a luxury but some kind of unnecessary append-age, like a sixth finger. We have a lot of superfluous knowledge.

VERSHININ: Well, well, well! [*Laughs.*] You have a lot of superfluous knowledge. I don't think there can be a town so boring and depressed that it has no need for an intelligent, educated person. Let us suppose that among the hundred thousand inhabitants of this town – which of course is backward and crude – there are only three like you. It goes without saying that you are not going to overcome the mass of ignorance surrounding you; in the course of your life, little by little, you are going to have to give ground and get lost in the crowd of the hundred thousand, life will stifle you, but you still won't disappear, you won't remain without influence; after you will come maybe six people like you, then twelve, and so on, until people like you become the majority. In two or three hundred years life on earth will be inexpressibly beautiful and amazing . . . Man needs that kind of life, and if he doesn't have it yet, then he must have some presentiment of it, must wait, dream, get ready for it, for this he must see and know more than his grandfather and father saw and knew. [*Laughs.*] And you complain that you have too much superfluous knowledge.

MASHA [*taking off her hat*]: I'm staying for lunch.

IRINA [*with a sigh*]: Someone really ought to write all this down . . .

[ANDREY *has left, unnoticed.*]

TUZENBAKH: In many years' time, you say, life on earth will be beautiful and amazing. That's true. But in order to take part in that life now, even if at a remove, one must prepare for it, one must work . . .

VERSHININ [*getting up*]: Yes. But what a lot of flowers you've got. [*Looking around.*] And a wonderful house. I envy you. My whole life I've been in quarters with two chairs and a sofa, and with stoves which always smoke. What I've lacked in my life is precisely flowers like these . . . [*Rubbing his hands.*] Aah! Never mind!

TUZENBAKH: Yes, one must work. You must be thinking the German is becoming sentimental. But I assure you I am Russian and don't even speak German. My father is Orthodox . . .

[*A pause.*]

VERSHININ [*walking about the stage*]: I often think, what if one were to begin life afresh but consciously? If one life, the life already lived, were so to speak a rough draft and the other one a fair copy? Then all of us, I think, would especially try not to repeat ourselves, we would at least create a different setting for our lives, would make a home like this for ourselves with flowers and a mass of light . . . I have a wife and two little girls, but my wife is a sick lady and so on and so forth, well, but if I were to begin life afresh, I wouldn't marry . . . No, no!

[*Enter* KULYGIN *wearing a uniform frock-coat.*⁷]

KULYGIN [*going up to Irina*]: Dear sister, let me congratulate you on your saint's day and wish you sincerely, from the bottom of my heart, good health and everything else one could wish a girl of your age. And then let me offer you this little book as a present. [*Gives her a book.*] The history of fifty years of our Gymnasium, written by me. A worthless little book, written out of idleness, but read it all the same. Good day, gentlemen. [*To Vershinin*] Kulygin, a master in the local Gymnasium. Court Councillor[8] Kulygin. [*To Irina*] In this little book you'll find a list of all those who have matriculated from our Gymnasium in the last fifty years. *Feci quod potui, faciant meliora potentes*.[9] [*Kisses Masha.*]

IRINA: But you've already given me this book for Easter.

KULYGIN [*laughing*]: I can't have! In that case give it back or, better, give it to the Colonel. Take it, Colonel. You'll read it one day out of boredom.

VERSHININ: Thank you. [*Gets ready to leave.*] I'm very glad indeed to have met you . . .

OLGA: Are you leaving? You can't!

IRINA: You'll stay and have lunch with us. Please.

OLGA: Let me press you.

VERSHININ [*bowing*]: I think I've intruded on a name-day. I'm sorry, I didn't know, I didn't congratulate you . . . [*Goes out into the hall with Olga.*]

KULYGIN: Today, my friends, is Sunday, the day of rest, and we will rest, we will make merry, each according to his or her age and position. We must take up the carpets for the summer and put them away till winter . . . With insect powder or mothballs . . . The Romans were healthy because they knew how to work and knew how to rest, they had *mens sana in corpore sano*.[10] Their life went on within definite forms. Our Principal says the important thing in every life is its form . . . What loses its form comes to an end – and the same in our everyday life. [*Takes Masha by the waist, laughing.*] Masha loves me. My wife loves me. And the window curtains too need to be put away with the carpets . . . Today I am happy, in an excellent mood. Masha, today at four we're going to the Principal's. They've arranged an excursion for the teachers and their families.

MASHA: I won't come.

KULYGIN [*upset*]: Masha dear, why not?

MASHA: I'll tell you afterwards . . . [*Angrily*] Very well, I'll go, only please leave me alone . . . [*Moves away.*]

KULYGIN: And afterwards we'll spend the evening at the Principal's. In spite of his poor state of health that man tries to be sociable above all else. An exceptional, luminous personality. Yesterday, after the meeting, he said to me, 'I'm tired, Fyodor Ilyich! I'm tired!' [*Looks at the wall clock, then at his own pocket watch.*] Your clock is seven minutes fast. Yes, he was tired, he said.

[*Offstage the sounds of a violin.*]

OLGA: Gentlemen, please, lunch is served. We're having a pie.

KULYGIN: Oh, my dear, dear Olga! Yesterday I worked from morning until eleven at night, I was tired, and today I feel happy. [*Goes out into the hall to the table*.] My dear . . .

CHEBUTYKIN [*putting his newspaper into his pocket and combing his beard*]: Are we having pie? Splendid!

MASHA [*sternly, to Chebutykin*]: Only see you don't drink anything today. Do you hear? It's bad for you to drink.

CHEBUTYKIN: Nonsense! All that's over for me. It's two years since I drank too much. [*Impatiently*] Besides, my dear girl, what does it matter!

MASHA: Still, don't you dare drink. Don't you dare. [*Angrily, but so her husband doesn't hear*] Again, damn it, a whole boring evening at the Principal's!

TUZENBAKH: In your place I wouldn't go. Very simply.

CHEBUTYKIN: Don't go, my darling.

MASHA: Oh, don't go . . . What a cursed, intolerable life . . . [*Goes into the hall.*]

CHEBUTYKIN [*going after her*]: There, there!

SOLYONY [*passing into the hall*]: Cluck, cluck, cluck . . .

TUZENBAKH: That's enough, Vasily Vasilyich. Stop it!

SOLYONY: Cluck, cluck, cluck . . .

KULYGIN [*cheerily*]: Your health, Colonel! I'm a schoolmaster and as Masha's husband I'm quite at home in this house . . . She is kind, very kind . . .

VERSHININ: I'll have some of that dark vodka. [*Drinks.*] Your health! [*To Olga*] I feel so at ease here! . . .

[*Only* IRINA *and* TUZENBAKH *are left in the drawing-room.*]

IRINA: Masha is out of sorts today. She got married at eighteen when he seemed to her a very intelligent man. And now it's different. He's the kindest of men but not the most intelligent.

OLGA [*impatiently*]: Andrey, come on now!

ANDREY [*offstage*]: I'm coming. [*Enters and goes to the table.*]

TUZENBAKH: What are you thinking about?

IRINA: Nothing. I don't like Solyony, he frightens me. He only talks nonsense . . .

TUZENBAKH: He's an odd man. I'm both sorry for him and annoyed by him, but more sorry. I think he's shy . . . When we're alone together, he's very clever and friendly, but in company he's a crude fellow, always picking quarrels. Don't go, let them sit at the table a moment. Let me be near you a bit. *t are you* thinking about?

[*A pause.*]

You're twenty, I'm not yet thirty. We've got so many years ahead of us, a long, long line of days, full of my love for you . . .

IRINA: Nikolay Lvovich, don't talk to me about love.

TUZENBAKH [*not listening*]: I have a passionate thirst for life, for the struggle, for work, and that thirst has merged in my soul with my love for you, Irina, and as if it were all planned, you are beautiful and life seems to me so beautiful. What are you thinking about?

IRINA: You say life is beautiful. Yes, but what if it only seems so! For us three sisters life has not yet been beautiful, it has choked us like a weed . . . My tears are streaming. We don't need that. [*Quickly wipes her face and smiles.*] We must work, work. We're gloomy and look at life so darkly because we don't know work. We were born to people who despised work . . .

[*Enter* NATALYA IVANOVNA; *she is wearing a pink dress with a green belt.*]

NATASHA: They're already sitting down to lunch in there . . . I'm late . . . [*Gives a passing glance at the mirror and arranges herself.*] I think my hair's all right . . . [*Seeing Irina.*] Dear Irina Sergeyevna, congratulations! [*Gives her a heavy and prolonged kiss.*] You have a lot of guests, I feel really guilty . . . Good afternoon, Baron.

OLGA [*coming into the drawing-room*]: And here is Natalya Ivanovna. How are you, my dear?

[*They kiss.*]

NATASHA: To the name-day girl. There're so many people, I'm terribly embarrassed . . .

OLGA: That's enough, they're all friends here. [*In a low voice, with an alarm*] You're wearing a green belt. It's not right, dear. . . . Is it bad luck?

OLGA: No, it simply doesn't go . . . and it's sort of odd . . .

NATASHA [*in a tearful voice*]: Really? But it's not green, more a sort of neutral colour. [*Follows Olga into the hall.*]

[*Everyone sits down to lunch in the hall; no one is left in the drawing-room.*]

KULYGIN: Irina, I wish you a good husband. It's time you got married.

CHEBUTYKIN: Natalya Ivanovna, I wish you too a nice young man.

KULYGIN: Natalya Ivanovna's already got a nice young man.

MASHA [*banging her plate with a fork*]: I am going to have a little glass of wine. Well, come what may life is still a bowl of cherries!

KULYGIN: Bad marks to you for behaviour.

VERSHININ: It's a delicious liqueur. What's it made of?

SOLYONY: Cockroaches.

IRINA [*in a plaintive voice*]: Ugh! How disgusting! . . .

OLGA: For supper there's going to be roast turkey and a sweet apple pie. Thank God, today I'm at home the entire day, at home in the evening . . . Gentlemen, come this evening . . .

VERSHININ: Can I come this evening too?

IRINA: Please do.

NATASHA: There's no formality in this house.

CHEBUTYKIN: 'For what does Nature bear us? For love, and love alone.' [*Laughs.*]

ANDREY [*crossly*]: Gentlemen, stop it! Haven't you had enough?

[*Enter* FEDOTIK *and* RODE *with a big basket of flowers.*]

FEDOTIK: But they're already having lunch.

RODE [*loudly and rolling his* rs[11]]: Are they having lunch? Yes, they're already having lunch . . .

FEDOTIK: Wait a moment! [*Takes a photograph.*] One! Wait a bit longer . . . [*Takes another photograph.*] Two! Now it's done!

[*They pick up the basket and go into the hall where they are greeted noisily.*]

RODE [*loudly*]: Congratulations and very best wishes! This weather is delicious, a glory. I walked all morning today with my Gymnasium pupils. I teach gymnastics at the Gymnasium . . .

FEDOTIK: You can move, Irina Sergeyevna, you can now! [*Taking a photograph.*] You're looking especially pretty today. [*Takes a spinning top from his pocket.*] By the way, here's a top . . . It makes an amazing sound . . .

IRINA: What a delightful thing.

MASHA: 'An oak in leaf beside the seashore, upon that oak a chain of gold . . . upon that oak a chain of gold . . .' [*In a melancholy voice*] Now why am I saying that? I've had that phrase on my mind the whole morning . . .

KULYGIN: We're thirteen at table.

RODE [*loudly*]: My friends, do you really attach any importance to superstitions?

[*Laughter.*]

KULYGIN: If there are thirteen at table it means there are lovers here. For all I know it may be you, Ivan Romanych . . .

[*Laughter.*]

CHEBUTYKIN: I'm an old sinner, but I really cannot understand why Natalya Ivanovna looks embarrassed.

[*Loud laughter.* NATASHA *runs out of the hall into the drawing-room,* ANDREY *follows her.*]

ANDREY: Don't, pay no attention! Wait . . . please stay . . .

NATASHA: I feel ashamed . . . I don't know what's the matter with me, but they're laughing at me. It's bad manners that I left the table just now, but I can't . . . I can't . . . [*Covers her face with her hands.*]

ANDREY: My darling, please, I beg you, don't get upset. I assure you they're joking, they don't mean it. My darling, my love, they are all kind, sincere people and they're fond of me and of you. Come here to the window, they can't see us here. [*Looks around.*]

NATASHA: I'm not used to going out! . . .

ANDREY: Your youth, your wonderful, beautiful youth! My darling, my love, don't get so upset! . . . Trust me, trust me . . . I feel so good, my soul is full of love and rapture . . . Oh, they can't see us! They can't see us! Why, why did I come to love you, when did I come to love you – oh, I don't understand anything. My darling, my pure love, be my wife! I love you, love you . . . as I've never loved anyone . . .

[*They kiss. Two officers come in and, seeing the couple embrace, stop dumbfounded.*]

[*Curtain.*]

Act Two

The set of Act One.[1] *Eight in the evening. Offstage the barely audible sound of an accordion in the street. There is no light. Enter* NATALYA IVANOVNA *wearing a housecoat, with a candle; she walks about and stops by the door which leads to Andrey's room.*

NATASHA: Andryusha, what are you doing? Are you reading? It isn't anything, I'm just . . . [*Goes to open another door, looks inside and shuts it.*] If anyone's left a light . . .

ANDREY [*entering with a book in his hand*]: Yes, Natasha?

NATASHA: I'm looking to see if there are any lights . . . It's Carnival now and the servants aren't themselves, one just has to keep one's eyes open for anything. Yesterday at midnight I was walking through the dining-room and a candle was burning there. I couldn't get to the bottom of who'd lit it. [*Puts down the candle.*] What time is it?

ANDREY [*looking at his pocket watch*]: A quarter past eight.

NATASHA: And Olga and Irina still aren't back. They haven't come in. They're still working, poor things. Olga at a teachers' meeting and Irina at the Telegraph Office . . . [*Sighs.*] This morning I was saying to your sister, 'Look after yourself a little, Irina love.' And she doesn't listen. Did you say it's quarter past eight? I'm afraid our Bobik isn't at all well. Why is he so cold? Yesterday he had a temperature and today he's cold all over . . . I'm so worried.

ANDREY: It's nothing, Natasha. The boy's healthy.

NATASHA: But still, we'd better put him on a diet. I'm scared. And they said today the mummers will be here after nine. It would be better if they didn't come, Andryusha.

223

ANDREY: I really don't know. They were asked to come.

NATASHA: This morning the little boy woke and looked at me and smiled suddenly; it means he recognized me. 'Bobik,' I said, 'Hello! Hello, darling!' And he laughed. Children understand, they understand very well. So, Andryusha, I'll tell them not to let the mummers in.

ANDREY [*indecisively*]: It really depends on whether my sisters agree. It's their house.

NATASHA: It is their house too. I'll tell them. They're kind ... [*Walks about.*] I've ordered yoghurt for supper. The doctor says you should only eat yoghurt, otherwise you won't lose weight. [*Stops.*] Bobik is cold. I'm afraid he's probably cold in his room. We should put him in another room at least until the warm weather comes. Irina's room, for example, is just right for a child: it's dry and there's sun the whole day. We must tell her, for the time being she can share a room with Olga ... In any case during the day she isn't at home, she just spends the night ...

[*A pause.*]

Andryushanchik, why don't you say anything?

ANDREY: I was thinking ... And there's nothing to say ...

NATASHA: Yes ... I wanted to tell you something ... Oh yes, Ferapont has come from the Council, he's asking for you.

ANDREY [*yawning*]: Tell him to come in.

[NATASHA *goes out;* ANDREY *reads a book, bending over the candle she has forgotten. Enter* FERAPONT; *he is wearing a shabby overcoat with the collar turned up and a scarf round his ears.*]

Good evening, old boy. What have you got to tell me?

FERAPONT: The Chairman has sent you a book and some sort of papers. Here they are ... [*Gives him a book and a package.*]

ANDREY: Thank you. Good. Why have you come so late? It's already after eight.

FERAPONT: What?

ANDREY [*louder*]: I said you've come late, it's already after eight.

FERAPONT: Yes, sir. When I came to your house it was still light, but they didn't let me in. They said the master's busy. Well, it doesn't matter. If he's busy he's busy, I'm in no hurry to go anywhere. [*Thinking that Andrey is asking him about something.*] What?

ANDREY: Nothing. [*Looking at the book.*] Tomorrow's Friday, there's no business but I'll go in all the same . . . I'll find something to do. It's boring at home . . .

[*A pause.*]

Dear old Ferapont, how strangely life changes, how it deceives us! Today out of boredom and having nothing to do I picked up this book – my old university lectures, and I began to laugh . . . My God, I'm the secretary of the District Council – and Protopopov's the chairman – and the most I can hope for is to be a member of that Council! To be a member of the local District Council, when every night I dream that I am a professor at Moscow University, a famous scholar who is Russia's pride!

FERAPONT: I don't really know . . . I don't hear very well . . .

ANDREY: If your hearing was all right, then perhaps I wouldn't be talking to you. I need to talk to someone but my wife doesn't understand me, and for some reason I'm afraid of my sisters, I'm afraid they'll laugh at me or make me feel ashamed . . . I don't drink, I don't like taverns, but, my dear old chap, with what pleasure I'd sit down now in Moscow at Testov's or the Bolshoy Moskovsky.[2]

FERAPONT: And in Moscow, a contractor was telling us the other day at the Council, some merchants were eating pancakes; one of them ate forty pancakes and died of it. Forty or fifty. I can't remember.

ANDREY: You're sitting in Moscow, in a big restaurant, you don't know anybody and nobody knows you, and at the same time you don't feel a stranger. Whereas here you know everybody and everybody knows you, but you're a stranger, a stranger . . . A stranger and lonely . . .

FERAPONT: What?

[*A pause.*]

And the same contractor said – maybe he's lying – that they're stretching a rope across the whole of Moscow.

ANDREY: What for?

FERAPONT: I don't know. That's what the contractor said.

ANDREY: What nonsense. [*Reads his book.*] Have you ever been to Moscow?

FERAPONT [*after a pause*]: I haven't. It hasn't been God's will.

[*A pause.*]

Can I go?

ANDREY: Yes, you can. Goodbye.

[FERAPONT *goes out.*]

Goodbye. [*Reading.*] Come tomorrow morning and pick up the papers from here . . . Off you go . . .

[*A pause.*]

He's gone.

[*A bell.*]

Yes, things to do . . . [*Stretches and unhurriedly goes to his own room.*]

[*Offstage a nursemaid is singing, rocking the baby to sleep. Enter* MASHA *and* VERSHININ. *While they talk, a maid lights the lamp and candles.*]

MASHA: I don't know.

[*A pause.*]

I don't know. Of course, habit counts for a lot. For instance, after our father's death it took us a long time to get accustomed to not having any orderlies to serve us. But apart from habit I think that what I said is quite right. Perhaps in other places it's different, but in our town the most decent, the finest, the most educated people are in the army.

VERSHININ: I'm thirsty. I'd like some tea.

MASHA [*glancing at her watch*]: They'll serve it soon. I was married when I was eighteen and I was frightened of my husband because he was a schoolmaster and I'd barely finished school. He seemed to me then terribly learned, clever and important. But now, unfortunately, it's rather different.

VERSHININ: I see . . . yes.

MASHA: I don't mean my husband, I've become accustomed to him, but among civilians generally there are so many coarse, unpleasant, uneducated people. Coarseness upsets and offends me, I suffer when I see a man without refinement, without gentleness and courtesy. When I happen to be among the schoolmasters who are my husband's colleagues, I simply suffer.

VERSHININ: Yes . . . But I think whether you're talking about civilians or soldiers, they're equally uninteresting, at any rate in this town. No difference! If you listen to an educated man in this town, civilian or soldier, he's got problems with his wife, problems with his house, he's got problems with his estate, problems with his horses . . . It's very typical of the Russian to have elevated thoughts, but tell me why he aims so low in life? Why?

MASHA: Why?

VERSHININ: Why does he have problems with his children, problems with his wife? And why do his wife and children have problems with him?

MASHA: You're not in a very good mood today.

VERSHININ: Maybe not. I've had no dinner today. I haven't had anything to eat since the morning. One of my daughters is a bit unwell, and when my little girls are ill, then I become worried, I feel guilty that their mother is like that. Oh, if you had seen her today! What a worthless person she is! We began to quarrel at seven in the morning, and at nine I slammed the door and went out.

[*A pause.*]

I never speak about this and, it's strange, I'm complaining just to you alone. [*Kisses her hand.*] Don't be angry with me. But for you I have no one, no one . . .

[*A pause.*]

MASHA: What a noise there is in the stove. Not long before Father's death there was a howling in the chimney. Just like that.

VERSHININ: Are you superstitious?

MASHA: Yes.

VERSHININ: That's strange. [*Kisses her hand.*] You're a splendid, wonderful woman. Splendid, wonderful! It's dark in here but I can see your eyes shining . . .

MASHA [*sitting down in another chair*]: It's lighter over here . . .

VERSHININ: I love, I love, I love . . . I love your eyes, your movements, which I see in my dreams . . . Splendid, wonderful woman!

MASHA [*laughing quietly*]: When you talk to me like that, then for some reason I laugh, although I'm frightened. Don't say it again, I beg you . . . [*In a low voice*] Or else go on talking, it's all the same to me . . . [*Covers her face with her hands.*] It's all the same to me . . . Someone is coming in here, talk about something else . . .

[*Enter* IRINA *and* TUZENBAKH, *through the hall.*]

TUZENBAKH: I have a triple-barrelled name. My name is Baron Tuzenbakh-Krone-Altschauer, but I am Russian and Orthodox like you. There's little of the German left in me except perhaps the patience and stubbornness with which I bore you . . . I see you home every evening.

IRINA: I'm so tired!

TUZENBAKH: And every day I'll come to the Telegraph Office and see you home, and I will do so for ten or twenty years until you chase me away . . . [*Seeing Irina and Vershinin, happily*] Are you here? Good evening.

IRINA: Now I'm home, at last. [*To Masha*] Just now a lady came and sent a telegram to her brother in Saratov to say that her son died today, and she just couldn't remember the address. In the end she sent it without an address, simply to Saratov. She was crying. And I was rude to her for no reason. 'I've no time,' I said. It sounded so stupid. Aren't the mummers coming today?

MASHA: Yes.

IRINA [*sitting down in an armchair*]: A rest. I'm tired.

TUZENBAKH [*with a smile*]: When you come home from work you look so small, such an unhappy little thing . . .

[*A pause.*]

IRINA: I'm tired. No, I don't like the Telegraph Office, I don't like it.

MASHA: You've become thinner . . . [*Whistles.*] And you look younger and your face looks like a boy's . . .

TUZENBAKH: That's the way she's done her hair.

IRINA: I must find another job, this one doesn't suit me. What I wanted, what I dreamed of, it definitely does not have. It's work with no poetry, no thinking . . .

[*A knock on the floor from below.*]

The Doctor's knocking. [*To Tuzenbakh*] Give a knock, dear friend . . . I can't . . . I'm tired.

[TUZENBAKH *knocks on the floor.*]

He'll come up right away. We must do something. Yesterday the Doctor and our Andrey were in the Club and lost again. They say Andrey lost two hundred roubles.

MASHA [*indifferently*]: Well, what can we do about it?

IRINA: He lost two weeks ago, he lost at the beginning of December. I wish he'd be quick and lose everything, perhaps we'd leave this town. Lord God in heaven, I dream of Moscow every night, I'm just like a madwoman. [*Laughs.*] We're moving there in June, and until June there's still . . . February, March, April, May . . . almost half a year!

MASHA: We must only see Natasha doesn't somehow hear of the losses.

IRINA: I don't think she cares.

[CHEBUTYKIN, *having only just got out of bed – he has had a rest after dinner – comes into the hall and combs his beard, then sits down at the table and takes a newspaper from his pocket.*]

MASHA: Here he is . . . Has he paid his rent?

IRINA [*laughing*]: No. Not a kopeck in eight months. He's obviously forgotten.

MASHA [*laughing*]: How important he looks sitting there!

[*Everyone laughs; a pause.*]

IRINA: Why aren't you saying anything, Aleksandr Ignatyevich?

VERSHININ: I don't know. I want some tea. Half my life for a glass of tea! I haven't had anything to eat since the morning . . .

CHEBUTYKIN: Irina Sergeyevna!

IRINA: What is it?

CHEBUTYKIN: Come here. *Venez ici.*[3]

[IRINA *goes and sits down at the table.*]

I can't be without you.

[IRINA *lays out a game of patience.*]

VERSHININ: Well? If they aren't serving tea, then at least let's talk a little philosophy.

TUZENBAKH: Let's. What shall we talk about?

VERSHININ: What about? Let's talk about our dreams ... for example, about the life which will come after us, two or three hundred years from now.

TUZENBAKH: Why not. After us men will fly in hot-air balloons, and jackets will change, and they'll discover, maybe, a sixth sense and develop it, but life will remain the same, difficult and full of secrets and happy. And in a thousand years man will still sigh, 'Ah, life is hard!' – and at the same time he will, as now, be afraid and not want to die.

VERSHININ [*after some thought*]: What shall I say to you? I think that everything on earth must gradually change, and already is changing before our eyes. In two or three hundred or even a thousand years – the point isn't in the precise period – a new, happy life will dawn. Of course we won't take part in that life, but we are living for it now, working, yes, suffering, we are creating that life – and in this alone lies the goal of our existence and, if you like, our happiness.

[MASHA *laughs quietly*.]

TUZENBAKH: What's the matter with you?

MASHA: I don't know. I've been laughing all day today, ever since morning.

VERSHININ: I went to the same cadet school as you, I didn't go on to the military academy; I read a lot but I don't know how to choose books and maybe I don't read quite what I ought to, but all the same the longer I live, the more I want to know. My hair is getting grey, I'm now nearly an old man, but I know very little, oh so little! But still I think I know, and know very well, what is most important and real. And how I would like to prove to you that for us there's no happiness, there can't be and there won't be ... We must just work and work, and happiness is something for our remote descendants.

[*A pause.*]

If I won't be happy, at least the descendants of my descendants will be.

[FEDOTIK *and* RODE *appear in the hall; they sit down and sing softly, playing the guitar.*]

TUZENBAKH: In your view we shouldn't even dream of happiness. But what if I am happy?

VERSHININ: No, you're not.

TUZENBAKH [*throwing up his hands and laughing*]: We clearly don't understand one another. Well, how can I convince you?

[MASHA *laughs quietly.*]

[*Wags a finger at her.*] Go on, laugh! [*To Vershinin*] Life will remain the same as ever not just in two hundred or three hundred years but even in a million; life doesn't change, it remains constant, following its own particular laws, which don't concern you, or which at least you will never know. Migratory birds, cranes for example, fly and fly, and whatever thoughts, big or little, stray through their heads, they will still fly on without knowing why or where to. They fly and they will go on flying, whatever philosophers are born among them; and they can talk philosophy as much as they like, only they must fly on . . .

MASHA: But what's the meaning of it?

TUZENBAKH: Meaning . . . Look, it's snowing. What meaning is there in that?

[*A pause.*]

MASHA: I think human beings must have faith or must look for faith, otherwise our life is empty, empty . . . To live and not to know why the cranes fly, why children are born, why there are stars in the sky . . . You must know why you are alive, or else everything is nonsense, just blowing in the wind.

[*A pause.*]

VERSHININ: It's still a pity one's young days have gone . . .

MASHA: Gogol said, 'Gentlemen, life on this earth is boring!'⁴

TUZENBAKH: And I say, gentlemen, it's tough to argue with you. So, enough of that . . .

CHEBUTYKIN [*reading his newspaper*]: Balzac was married in Berdichev.⁵

[IRINA *sings quietly*.]

I'll even write that down in my notebook. [*Makes a note*.] Balzac was married in Berdichev. [*Continuing to read his newspaper*.]

IRINA [*laying out a game of patience, pensively*]: Balzac was married in Berdichev.

TUZENBAKH: The die is cast. You know, Mariya Sergeyevna, I'm retiring.

MASHA: So I've heard. But I see nothing good in that. I don't like civilians.

TUZENBAKH: It doesn't matter . . . [*Gets up*.] I'm not good-looking, what kind of a soldier do I make? But it doesn't really matter . . . I shall work. Work for just one day in my life and come home in the evening, fall into bed with exhaustion and go to sleep right away. [*Going out into the hall*.] Workmen, I think, sleep soundly!

FEDOTIK [*to Irina*]: I just bought you some coloured pencils at Pyzhikov's in Moskovskaya. And this penknife . . .

IRINA: You're used to treating me like a little girl, but you know I'm now grown up . . . [*Happily takes the pencils and knife*.] How lovely!

FEDOTIK: And I bought a knife for myself . . . look . . . one blade, a second blade, a third, that's for scratching in your ears, that's a little pair of scissors, that's for cleaning your nails . . .

RODE [*loudly*]: Doctor, how old are you?

CHEBUTYKIN: Me? Thirty-two.

[*Laughter*.]

FEDOTIK: I'll show you another patience . . . [*Lays out a game of patience.*]

[*The samovar is brought in;* ANFISA *stands by the samovar; after a little* NATASHA *comes in and also fusses round the table;* SOLYONY *comes in and after greeting the others sits down at the table.*]

VERSHININ: Goodness, what a wind!

MASHA: Yes. I'm fed up with winter. I've now even forgotten what summer's like.

IRINA: The game will come out, I can see. We will be in Moscow.

FEDOTIK: No, it won't come out. Look, the eight was on the two of spades. [*Laughs.*] That means you won't get to Moscow.

CHEBUTYKIN [*reading his newspaper*]: Tsitsihar.[6] Smallpox is raging there.

ANFISA [*going up to Masha*]: Masha, come and have your tea, dear. [*To Vershinin*] Please come, Your Honour . . . forgive me, sir, I've forgotten your name . . .

MASHA: Bring it here, Nyanya. I won't go over there.

IRINA: Nyanya!

ANFISA: Co-o-oming!

NATASHA [*to Solyony*]: Babies understand everything. 'Good morning, Bobik,' I said. 'Good morning, darling.' He gave me a special kind of look. You're thinking it's just the mother in me speaking, but no, no, I assure you! This is an exceptional child.

SOLYONY: If that child were mine, I'd fry it in a pan and eat it up. [*Goes with a glass of tea into the drawing-room and sits down in a corner.*]

NATASHA [*covering her face with her hands*]: What a rude, vulgar man!

MASHA: Happy is the man who doesn't notice whether it's now summer or winter. I think that if I were in Moscow I wouldn't mind about the weather . . .

VERSHININ: The other day I was reading the diary of a French minister, written in prison. The minister had been sent there over the Panama affair.[7] With what delight, with what rapture he talks about the birds he sees from his prison window and which he never noticed before when he was a minister. Of course, now he's been released, he doesn't notice the birds, just as before. In the same way you too won't notice Moscow when you're living there. We have no happiness and it doesn't exist, we only desire it.

TUZENBAKH [*taking a box from the table*]: Where are the sweets?

IRINA: Solyony's eaten them.

TUZENBAKH: All of them?

ANFISA [*serving tea*]: There's a letter for you, sir.

VERSHININ: For me? [*Takes the letter.*] It's from my daughter. [*Reads.*] Yes, of course . . . Excuse me, Mariya Sergeyevna, I'll go off quietly. I won't have tea. [*Gets up in a state of agitation.*] These incidents are always happening . . .

MASHA: What is it? It's not a secret, is it?

VERSHININ [*quietly*]: My wife has taken poison again. I must go. I'll go out without anyone noticing. All this is terribly unpleasant. [*Kisses Masha's hand.*] My dear, you fine, good woman . . . I'll go out here very quietly . . . [*Exit.*]

ANFISA: Where's he gone? But I gave him tea . . . What an odd man!

MASHA [*getting angry*]: Go away! You pester us here, don't give us any peace . . . [*Goes to the table with her cup.*] I'm fed up with you, wretched old woman!

ANFISA: What's offended you? My darling!

ANDREY'S VOICE: Anfisa!

ANFISA [*imitating him*]: Anfisa! He sits in there . . . [*Exit.*]

MASHA [*by the table in the reception hall, angrily*]: Let me sit down! [*Mixes up the cards on the table.*] You've taken over the entire table with your cards. Drink your tea!

IRINA: You are in a bad mood, Mashka.

MASHA: Since I'm in a bad mood, don't speak to me. Don't touch me!

CHEBUTYKIN [*laughing*]: Don't touch her, don't touch her . . .

MASHA: You're sixty years old, but you're always talking some damn-fool nonsense, like a little boy.

NATASHA [*sighing*]: Dear Masha, why do you use such expressions in conversation? With your nice looks, I tell you frankly, you would be simply charming in good society if it weren't for those words of yours. *Je vous prie pardonnez moi, Marie, mais vous avez des manières un peu grossières.*[8]

TUZENBAKH [*holding back his laughter*]: Give me . . . give me . . . I think there's some brandy over there . . .

NATASHA: *Il parait, que mon Bobik déjà ne dort pas,*[9] he's woken up. My baby's not very well today. I'll go to him, excuse me . . . [*Exit.*]

IRINA: But where's Aleksandr Ignatyich gone?

MASHA: Home. There's another problem with his wife.

TUZENBAKH [*going up to Solyony, with the brandy decanter in his hand*]: You're always sitting by yourself, thinking about something – who knows what. So, let's make it up. Let's drink some brandy.

[*They drink.*]

Today I'll have to play the piano all night, probably have to play all kinds of stupid things . . . Well, it happens . . .

SOLYONY: What is there to make up? I haven't quarrelled with you.

TUZENBAKH: You always give off the feeling that something has happened between us. You must admit you have a strange character.

SOLYONY [*declaiming*]: I am strange, who is not! Be not angry, Aleko.[10]

TUZENBAKH: What's Aleko got to do with it . . .

[*A pause.*]

SOLYONY: When I'm alone with someone, then it's fine, I'm like everyone else, but in company I'm depressed, shy and . . . I talk all sorts of nonsense. But still I'm more honest and more decent than very, very many others. And I can prove that.

TUZENBAKH: I often get angry with you, you're constantly picking on me when we're in company, but still for some reason I find you sympathetic. Come what may, I'm going to get drunk today. Chin-chin!

SOLYONY: Chin-chin!

[*They drink.*]

I've never had anything against you, Baron. But I have Lermontov's character.[11] [*Quietly*] I even look a little like Lermontov . . . so people say . . . [*Takes a bottle of scent out of his pocket and puts some on his hands.*]

TUZENBAKH: I'm going to retire. *Basta!*[12] I've been thinking about it for five years and I've finally made up my mind. I shall work.

SOLYONY [*declaiming*]: Be not angry, Aleko . . . Forget, forget your dreams . . .

[*While they are talking* ANDREY *enters quietly with a book and sits down by the candle.*]

TUZENBAKH: I shall work . . .

CHEBUTYKIN [*coming into the drawing-room with* IRINA]: And they also gave us proper Caucasian food: soup with onion, and for the main course – *chekhartmá*, of meat.

SOLYONY: *Cheremshá* isn't meat at all but a plant like our onion.

CHEBUTYKIN: No, my friend. *Chekhartmá* isn't an onion but a meat dish of mutton.

SOLYONY: But I'm telling you, *cheremshá* is an onion.

CHEBUTYKIN: And I'm telling you, *chekhartmá* is mutton.

SOLYONY: But I'm telling you, *cheremshá* is an onion.

CHEBUTYKIN: Why am I having to argue with you? You've never been to the Caucasus and you haven't eaten *chekhartmá*.

SOLYONY: I haven't eaten it because I can't stand it. *Cheremshá* gives off the same smell as garlic.

ANDREY [*beseechingly*]: Gentlemen, enough! Please!

TUZENBAKH: When are the mummers coming?

IRINA: They promised towards nine; so, any minute.

TUZENBAKH [*hugging Andrey*]: 'Oh lobby, my lobby, my lob-lob-lobby . . .'[13]

ANDREY [*dancing and singing*]: 'My brand new lobby, my maple-wood lobby . . .'

CHEBUTYKIN [*dancing*]: 'My trellis-covered lobby!'

[*Laughter.*]

TUZENBAKH [*kissing Andrey*]: What the hell, let's drink, Andryusha, let's drink to brotherhood.[14] And I'm going to Moscow with you too, Andryusha, to the university.

SOLYONY: Which one? There are two universities in Moscow.

ANDREY: There's only one university in Moscow.

SOLYONY: And I tell you there are two.

ANDREY: How about three? All the better.

SOLYONY: There are two universities in Moscow.

[*Murmurs and booing.*]

There are two universities in Moscow, the old one and the new one. But if you don't want to listen, if what I say annoys you, then I can stop speaking. I can even go into another room. [*Goes out of one of the doors.*]

TUZENBAKH: Bravo, bravo! [*Laughs.*] My friends, let's begin, I'm sitting down to play! What a funny fellow that Solyony is . . . [*Sits down at the piano and plays a waltz.*]

MASHA [*waltzing alone*]: The Baron is drunk, is drunk, is drunk!

[*Enter* NATASHA.]

NATASHA [*to Chebutykin*]: Ivan Romanych! [*Says something to Chebutykin, then quietly goes out.*]

[CHEBUTYKIN *touches Tuzenbakh on the shoulder and whispers something to him.*]

IRINA: What is it?

CHEBUTYKIN: It's time for us to go. Goodbye.

TUZENBAKH: Good night. It's time to go.

IRINA: But . . . but what about the mummers? . . .

ANDREY [*embarrassed*]: There won't be any mummers. You see, my dear, Natasha says that Bobik isn't very well, and so . . . The fact is, I don't know, it's really all the same to me.

IRINA [*shrugging her shoulders*]: Bobik isn't well!

MASHA: Well, there we are! They're shooing us out, so we'd better go. [*To Irina*] It isn't Bobik who's sick but she herself . . . Here! [*Taps her forehead with her finger.*] Common little woman!¹⁵

[ANDREY *goes out of the right-hand door to his room,* CHEBUTYKIN *follows him; people say their goodbyes in the hall.*]

FEDOTIK: What a pity! I was counting on having a nice evening, but if the little boy is ill, then of course . . . Tomorrow I'll bring him some toys . . .

RODE [*loudly*]: I deliberately had a good sleep after dinner today, I thought I'd be dancing all night. It's only nine o'clock now!

MASHA: Let's go out in the street and talk there. We'll decide what to do.

['*Goodbye!*' *and* '*Good night!*' *can be heard. Also* TUZENBAKH'*s merry laugh. Everyone leaves.* ANFISA *and a* MAID *clear the table and put out the lights. There is the voice of the nursemaid singing.* ANDREY *wearing overcoat and hat and* CHEBUTYKIN *enter quietly.*]

CHEBUTYKIN: I didn't find time to marry because life flashed by, like lightning, and because I was madly in love with your mother, who was married . . .

ANDREY: We shouldn't get married. We shouldn't, because it's boring.

CHEBUTYKIN: Yes, that's true, but what about loneliness? However much philosophy one spouts, loneliness is a frightful thing, old chap . . . Although really . . . of course, it absolutely cannot matter!

ANDREY: Let's hurry up and go.

CHEBUTYKIN: What's the rush? We've got time.

ANDREY: I'm afraid my wife will stop us.

CHEBUTYKIN: Ah!

ANDREY: Today I'm not going to play, I'll just sit a bit. I don't feel well . . . Ivan Romanych, what can I do about shortness of breath?

CHEBUTYKIN: What a question! I don't remember, old chap. I don't know.

ANDREY: Let's go out through the kitchen.

[*The bell rings, then it rings again; there is the sound of voices and laughter. They go out.*]

IRINA [*entering*]: Who's that?

ANFISA [*in a whisper*]: The mummers!

[*A bell.*]

IRINA: Tell them, Nyanya dear, that there's no one at home. They must excuse us.

[ANFISA *goes out.* IRINA *walks about the room thinking. She is agitated. Enter* SOLYONY.]

SOLYONY [*nonplussed*]: There's no one here . . . Where is everybody?

IRINA: They've gone home.

SOLYONY: That's odd. Are you alone here?

IRINA: I am.

[*A pause.*]

Good night.

SOLYONY: Just now I behaved tactlessly, without self-control. But you're not like all the others, you are high-minded and pure, you can see the truth . . . You're the only, only one who can understand me. I love you, I love you deeply, infinitely . . .

IRINA: Good night! Go away.

SOLYONY: I can't live without you. [*Following her.*] Oh my happiness! [*With tears in his eyes*] Oh bliss! What magnificent, wonderful, astounding eyes, the like of which I've seen in no other woman . . .

IRINA [*coldly*]: Stop it, Vasily Vasilyich!

SOLYONY: I'm speaking of my love for you for the first time, and I feel as if I'm not on earth but another planet. [*Wipes his forehead.*] Well, it doesn't matter. Of course one can't make oneself loved . . . But I cannot have a successful rival . . . I cannot . . . I swear to you by all that's holy, I will kill any rival . . . You sublime woman!

[NATASHA *passes through with a candle.*]

NATASHA [*looks through one door, then another and walks past the door leading to her husband's room*]: Andrey's in there. Let him read. Forgive me, Vasily Vasilyich, I didn't know you were here, I'm not dressed . . .

SOLYONY: I don't care. Good night! [*Exit.*]

NATASHA: But you're tired, my poor dear girl! [*Kisses Irina.*] You should go to bed earlier.

IRINA: Is Bobik asleep?

NATASHA: He is. But his sleep is restless. By the way, dear, I wanted to say to you, but either you're not here or I haven't the time . . . I think that it's cold and damp for Bobik in the present nursery. But your room is such a nice one for a child. My darling, move in with Olya for the time being!

IRINA [*not understanding*]: Where?

[*The ring of the bells of a troika driving up to the house.*]

NATASHA: You'll be in one room with Olya, for the moment, and Bobik will have your room. He's such a sweetheart, today I was saying to him, 'Bobik, you're mine! Mine!' And he looked at me with his darling little eyes.

[*A bell.*]

That must be Olga. How late she is!

[*The maid goes up to Natasha and whispers in her ear.*]

NATASHA: Protopopov? What a funny man. Protopopov has come and is inviting me to go for a troika drive with him. [*Laughs.*] How strange these men are . . .

[*A bell.*]

Someone's there. Why not go for a drive just for a quarter of an hour . . . [*To the maid*] Tell him I'm coming.

[*A bell.*]

The bell . . . That must be Olga . . . [*Exit.*]

[*The maid runs off;* IRINA *sits thinking; enter* KULYGIN *and* OLGA, *followed by* VERSHININ.]

KULYGIN: What's going on? They said they were having a party.

VERSHININ: That's funny, I went away just now, half an hour ago, and they were expecting the mummers . . .

IRINA: Everyone's gone.

KULYGIN: Has Masha gone too? Where has she gone? And why is Protopopov waiting down there in a troika? Who's he waiting for?

IRINA: Don't ask questions . . . I'm tired.

KULYGIN: You are being difficult . . .

OLGA: The meeting has only just finished. I'm worn out. Our headmistress is ill and I'm now standing in for her. My head, I've got a headache, my head . . . [*Sits down.*] Andrey lost two hundred roubles yesterday at cards . . . The whole town is talking about it . . .

KULYGIN: Yes, I got tired at the meeting too. [*Sits down.*]

VERSHININ: My wife just now had the idea of giving me a fright and almost managed to poison herself. It's turned out all right, and I'm glad, I can rest now . . . So, we've got to go? Very well, let me wish you good night. Fyodor Ilyich, let's go somewhere! I can't stay at home, I really can't . . . Let's go!

KULYGIN: I'm tired. I won't. [*Gets up.*] I'm tired. Did my wife go home?

IRINA: I think so.

KULYGIN [*kisses Irina's hand*]: Good night. Tomorrow and the next day – a complete rest. Goodbye! [*Going.*] I really want some tea. I was expecting to spend the evening in agreeable company and – *O fallacem hominum spem!* [16] An example of the accusative case in an exclamation.

VERSHININ: So, I'll go off by myself. [*Goes out with Kulygin, whistling.*]

OLGA: My head aches, my head . . . Andrey lost . . . the whole town is talking . . . I'll go and lie down. [*Going.*] Tomorrow I'm free . . . Heavens, how good that is! Tomorrow I'm free, the day after tomorrow I'm free . . . My head aches, my head . . . [*Exit.*]

IRINA [*alone*]: They've all gone. There's nobody left.

[*An accordion is being played in the street; the nursemaid is singing a song.*]

NATASHA [*walks through the hall wearing a fur coat and hat; she is followed by the maid*]: I'll be back home in half an hour. I'm just going for a little drive. [*Exit.*]

IRINA [*left alone and overcome by longing*]: Moscow! Moscow! Moscow!

[*Curtain.*]

Act Three

Olga and Irina's room.[1] *Left and right are beds surrounded by screens. It is after two in the morning. Offstage the alarm is being sounded for a fire which has been raging for a long time. It is clear no one in the house has gone to bed.* MASHA *is lying on the divan dressed in her usual black dress. Enter* OLGA *and* ANFISA.

ANFISA: They're sitting down there by the stairs now . . . I told them, 'Come up,' I said, 'it's all right, come just as you are,' and they cried. They said, 'We don't know where Papa is. Pray God he isn't burnt,' they said. What a thing to imagine! And there are some people in the yard . . . they haven't any clothes either.

OLGA [*taking clothes out of the cupboard*]: Take this grey one . . . And this . . . The blouse too . . . And take this skirt, Nyanya . . . My God, what a business! It seems the whole of Kirsanov Lane has burnt down . . . Take this . . . Take this . . . [*Throws clothes into her arms.*] The Vershinins got a fright, poor things . . . Their house almost went up. They can spend the night here . . . we can't let them go home . . . Everything of poor Fedotik's is burnt, nothing's left . . .

ANFISA: Would you call Ferapont, Olechka, otherwise I won't be able to carry so much . . .

OLGA [*ringing*]: No one hears the bell . . . [*Through the door*] Come in here, anyone who's there!

[*Through the open door a window can be seen glowing red with the fire; the sound of a fire engine passing.*]

What a terrible thing! I've just had enough!

[*Enter* FERAPONT.]

Take these things and carry them downstairs . . . The Kolotilin young ladies are standing by the stairs . . . give them to them. And give them this . . .

FERAPONT: I will. In 1812 Moscow burnt down too.[2] Good Lord above! The French were amazed.

OLGA: Go down, get on.

FERAPONT: I will. [*Goes out.*]

OLGA: Nyanya dear, give everything away. We don't need anything, give it all away, Nyanya . . . I'm tired, I can hardly stand on my feet . . . We mustn't let the Vershinins go home . . . The girls can sleep in the drawing-room and Aleksandr Ignatyich can go downstairs with the Baron . . . Fedotik too can go with the Baron or we can have him in the reception hall . . . The Doctor is drunk, terribly drunk, it's as if he's done it deliberately, and no one can go to him. And Vershinin's wife can go in the drawing-room.

ANFISA [*exhaustedly*]: Olyushka dear, don't send me away! Don't!

OLGA: You're talking nonsense, Nyanya. No one is sending you away.

ANFISA [*putting her head on Olga's breast*]: My darling, my golden girl, I slave, I work . . . When I get weak, they'll all say, 'Get out!' But where will I go? Where? Eighty years old. Eighty-one . . .

OLGA: You sit down, Nyanya . . . You've got tired, poor thing . . . [*Makes her sit down.*] Have a rest, my dear. You're quite pale!

[*Enter* NATASHA.]

NATASHA: They're saying out there we must form an association to help the victims of the fire as soon as possible . . . It's an excellent idea, don't you think? One should always help poor people, that's a duty of the rich. Bobik and Sofochka are fast asleep, sleeping as if nothing had happened. We've got so many people everywhere, wherever you go, the house is full. There's a lot of influenza now in town, I'm frightened the children will catch it.

OLGA [*not listening to her*]: In this room you can't see the fire, it's quiet here . . .

NATASHA: Yes . . . I must look a mess. [*Looking in a mirror.*] Someone said I'd got fatter . . . that's just not true! Not true at all! Masha's sleeping, she's worn out, poor thing . . . [*Coldly, to Anfisa*] Don't you dare sit in my presence! Get up! Get out of here!

[ANFISA *goes out; a pause.*]

And why you keep on that old woman I just do not understand!

OLGA [*dumbfounded*]: I'm sorry, I don't understand either . . .

NATASHA: She's got nothing to do here. She's a peasant, she should live in her village . . . You're just pampering her! I like to have order in the house! There shouldn't be people with nothing to do in the house. [*Strokes Olga's cheek.*] You're tired, you poor dear! Our headmistress is tired! And when my Sofochka grows up and goes to the Gymnasium, I'll be frightened of you.

OLGA: I won't be headmistress.

NATASHA: They'll appoint you, Olechka. That's been decided.

OLGA: I'll refuse. I can't . . . I'm not strong enough . . . [*Drinks some water.*] Just now you were so rude to Nyanya . . . I'm sorry, I can't stand it . . . it went dark in front of my eyes . . .

NATASHA [*agitated*]: I'm sorry, Olya, I'm sorry . . . I didn't mean to upset you.

[MASHA *gets up, takes a pillow and goes out, angry.*]

OLGA: You must understand, my dear . . . perhaps we were brought up oddly but I can't stand it. Behaviour like that brings me down, I become ill . . . I simply give up! . . .

NATASHA: I'm sorry, I'm sorry . . . [*Kisses her.*]

OLGA: Any rudeness, even something small, a roughly spoken word upsets me . . .

NATASHA: I often say too much, that's true, but you must agree, my dear, she could live in her village.

OLGA: She's been with us for thirty years.

NATASHA: But now she can't work! Either I don't understand something or you don't want to understand me. She is not capable of working, she only sleeps or sits.

OLGA: Then let her sit.

NATASHA [*surprised*]: What do you mean let her sit? But she's a servant. [*With tears in her eyes*] I don't understand you, Olya. I have a nursemaid, a wet-nurse, we have a maid, a cook . . . why do we need that old woman as well? Why?

[*Offstage the fire alarm is sounded.*]

OLGA: Tonight I've aged ten years.

NATASHA: We must come to an understanding, Olya. You're at the Gymnasium, I'm in the house, you have teaching, I have the household. And if I say something about the servants, then I know what I'm saying; I know *what I am saying* . . . And tomorrow I want that old thief, that old hag out of the house . . . [*Stamps her feet.*] That old witch! . . . I will not be provoked! I will not! [*Pulling herself together.*] Really, if you don't move downstairs we're always going to be quarrelling. It's terrible.

[*Enter* KULYGIN.]

KULYGIN: Where's Masha? It's time for us to go home now. They say the fire is dying down. [*Stretches.*] Only one block has burnt down, but there was a wind and at first it seemed the whole town would go up. [*Sits down.*] I'm exhausted. My dear little Olga . . . I often think, if there hadn't been Masha, I would have married you, Olechka. You're very nice . . . I'm worn out. [*Listens.*]

OLGA: What?

KULYGIN: He had to go and do it, the Doctor went on a bender, he's got terribly drunk. He just had to go and do it! [*Gets up.*] I think he's coming in here . . . Can you hear? Yes, here . . .

[*Laughs.*] Really, what a funny fellow he is . . . I'm going to hide . . . [*Goes to the cupboard and stands in the corner.*] What a rascal!

OLGA: He hasn't drunk for two years and now he's suddenly gone and got drunk . . . [*Goes with* NATASHA *to the back of the room.*]

[*Enter* CHEBUTYKIN; *he crosses the room without reeling, like a man not drunk, stops, look about, then goes to the washstand and begins to wash his hands.*]

CHEBUTYKIN [*glumly*]: To hell with them all . . . all to hell . . . They think I'm a doctor, can treat all kinds of illnesses, but I know absolutely nothing, I've forgotten everything I knew, I remember nothing, absolutely nothing.

[OLGA *and* NATASHA *go out without his noticing.*]

To hell with them. Last Wednesday I had a patient at Zasyp, a woman – she died and it's my fault that she died. Yes . . . Twenty-five years ago I knew a few things but now I remember nothing. Nothing. Perhaps I am not a man but only look as if I have arms and legs and a head; perhaps I don't exist at all but only think that I walk, eat, sleep. [*Weeps.*] Oh if only I could just not exist! [*Stops weeping; gloomily*] Devil knows . . . A couple of days ago they were chatting in the Club; talking about Shakespeare, Voltaire . . . I haven't read them, haven't read them at all, but I tried to look as if I had. And the others did what I did. How cheap! How low! And I remembered the woman I murdered on Wednesday . . . and I remembered everything, and I felt I was morally deformed, vile, loathsome . . . I went off and hit the bottle . . .

[*Enter* IRINA, VERSHININ *and* TUZENBAKH; TUZENBAKH *is wearing new and smart civilian clothes.*]

IRINA: Let's sit a moment in here. No one will come in.

VERSHININ: If it hadn't been for the soldiers, the whole town would have burnt down. Good boys! [*Rubs his hands with pleasure.*] Pure gold! What good boys!

KULYGIN [*going up to them*]: What time is it, my friends?

TUZENBAKH: Already after three. It's getting light.

IRINA: They're all sitting in the hall, no one is leaving. And your friend Solyony is sitting there too . . . [*To Chebutykin*] You should go to bed, Doctor.

CHEBUTYKIN: It's all right . . . Thank you . . . [*Combs his beard.*]

KULYGIN [*laughs*]: Ivan Romanych has got quite tiddly! [*Claps him on the shoulder.*] Good chap! *In vino veritas*[3] – as the ancients said.

TUZENBAKH: People keep asking me to organize a concert for the benefit of the fire victims.

IRINA: Well, who could you have . . . ?

TUZENBAKH: With a bit of will it could be organized. I think Marya Sergeyevna plays the piano beautifully . . .

KULYGIN: She does play beautifully.

IRINA: She's forgotten it all now. She hasn't played for three years . . . or four.

TUZENBAKH: In this town absolutely no one understands music, not a soul, but I, I do understand it and I honestly assure you that Mariya Sergeyevna plays splendidly, she's almost got a real gift.

KULYGIN: You're right, Baron. I love Masha very much. She's lovely.

TUZENBAKH: To be able to play so superbly and at the same time to know that no one, no one appreciates you!

KULYGIN [*sighing*]: Yes . . . But is it proper for her to play at a public concert?

[*A pause.*]

You see, my friends, I don't know anything about these things. Maybe it will be all right. I have to admit our Principal is a good man, even a very good man, he's very clever, but he has such particular views . . . Of course it isn't anything to do with him, but still if you like, I'll have a word with him.

[CHEBUTYKIN *picks up a china clock and examines it.*]

VERSHININ: I've got quite filthy in the fire, I look like I don't know what.

[*A pause.*]

Yesterday I heard a rumour that they're planning to transfer our brigade somewhere far off. Some are saying to the Kingdom of Poland, others to Chita.[4]

TUZENBAKH: I heard that too. Well then! Then the town will be quite empty.

IRINA: And we will be leaving!

CHEBUTYKIN [*dropping the clock, which breaks*]: To smithereens!

[*A pause; everyone is annoyed and embarrassed.*]

KULYGIN [*picking up the bits*]: Really, Ivan Romanych, Ivan Romanych – breaking such a valuable object! Zero minus for behaviour!

IRINA: It was Mama's clock.

CHEBUTYKIN: Perhaps it was . . . Mama's clock was Mama's clock. Perhaps I didn't break it but it just looks as if I did. Perhaps we just think we exist but really we don't. I don't know anything, no one knows anything. [*By the door.*] What are you looking at? Natasha is having a little affair with Protopopov but you don't see anything . . . You just sit here and don't see anything, and Natasha is having a little affair with Protopopov . . . [*Sings*] 'Won't you sample a date from the palm-tree . . .'[5] [*Exit.*]

VERSHININ: Yes . . . [*Laughs.*] Really, how strange it all is!

[*A pause.*]

When the fire began, I quickly rushed home; I go up and look – our house is safe and sound and out of danger, but there are my two little girls standing on the doorstep in just their night clothes, their mother isn't there, people are rushing about, horses and dogs running free, and what a look of fright, terror, supplication, I don't know what, on those girls' faces; my heart was wrung when I saw those faces. My God, I thought, what will these girls still have to live through in the course of a long life! I grab them, I run and all the time I'm thinking one thing: what will they still have to live through in this world!

[*The alarm; a pause.*]

I come here and their mother is here, shouting, angry.

[MASHA *comes in with her cushion and sits down on the divan.*]

And when my girls were standing at the door in just their night clothes and the street was red from the fire and the noise was terrifying, I thought that it must have been something like this many years ago when an enemy attacked suddenly and pillaged and burned . . . At the same time what a difference there is in reality between what is now and what was! And when just a bit more time goes by, say two or three hundred years, people will look at our life today both with alarm and with mockery, everything we have now will seem clumsy and burdensome and very inconvenient and strange. Ah, what a life that will surely be, what a life! [*Laughs.*] I'm sorry, I've begun to talk philosophy again. Let me go on, my friends. I terribly want to talk philosophy, I'm in the mood for it.

[*A pause.*]

You all seem to have gone to sleep. I was saying, what a life it will be! You can just imagine . . . In this town now there are only three people like you, but in the generations to come there will be more, more and more, and a time will come when it'll all change your way, everyone will be living your way, and later still you too will become obsolete and people will be born who will be better than you ... [*Laughs.*] Today I'm in a strange kind of mood. I have a passionate longing to live ... [*Sings*] 'All to love the knee must bow, bounteously love's blessings flow ...'⁶ [*Laughs.*]

MASHA: *Tram-tam-tam* ...

VERSHININ: *Tram-tam* ...

MASHA: *Tra-ra-ra?*

VERSHININ: *Tra-ta-ta.* [*Laughs.*]

[*Enter* FEDOTIK.]

FEDOTIK [*dancing*]: Burnt, burnt! Quite cleaned out!

[*Laughter.*]

IRINA: There's not much to laugh at. Is everything burnt?

FEDOTIK [*laughing*]: Cleaned out. Nothing is left. My guitar is burnt and my photography things are burnt and all my letters ... And I'd got you a notebook as a present – that's gone too.

[*Enter* SOLYONY.]

IRINA: No, please go away, Vasily Vasilyich. You can't come in here.

SOLYONY: Why is the Baron allowed in and I am not?

VERSHININ: We really should be going. How is the fire?

SOLYONY: They're saying it's dying down. No, I find it decidedly strange that the Baron is allowed in and I am not. [*Takes out his bottle of scent and sprinkles himself.*]

VERSHININ: *Tram-tam-tam?*

MASHA: *Tram-tam.*

VERSHININ [*laughing, to Solyony*]: Let's go into the hall.

SOLYONY: Very well, I'll just make a note of this. 'My thought could well be made more clear, but that would scare the geese I fear ...'⁷ [*Looking at Tuẓenbakh*] Cluck, cluck, cluck ...

[*Goes out with* VERSHININ *and* FEDOTIK.]

IRINA: That Solyony has smoked the house out . . . [*In astonishment*] The Baron's asleep! Baron! Baron!

TUZENBAKH [*waking up*]: Actually I'm tired . . . The brick factory . . . I'm not talking in my sleep, I really will soon be going to a brick factory, I shall be starting work . . . I've already had a discussion with them. [*To Irina, tenderly*] You're so pale, so lovely, so entrancing . . . Your pallor seems to illumine the darkness like the light . . . You are sad, you're dissatisfied with life . . . Oh come with me, come away and let's work together!

MASHA: Nikolay Lvovich, go away.

TUZENBAKH [*laughing*]: Are you here? I can't see. [*Kisses Irina's hand.*] Goodbye, I'll go . . . I look at you now and I remember how, long ago, on your name-day, you were talking of the joys of work, full of enthusiasm and cheer . . . And what a vision I had then of a happy life! Where has it gone? [*Kisses her hand.*] You have tears in your eyes. Go to bed, it's already getting light . . . morning is coming . . . If only I were allowed to give up my life for you!

MASHA: Nikolay Lvovich, go away! Really . . .

TUZENBAKH: I'm going . . . [*Exit.*]

MASHA [*lying down*]: Are you asleep, Fyodor?

KULYGIN: What?

MASHA: You should go home.

KULYGIN: My sweet Masha, my darling Masha . . .

IRINA: She's exhausted. Let her have some rest, Fedya.

KULYGIN: I'm going right away . . . My good wife, my wonderful wife . . . I love you, my only . . .

MASHA [*crossly*]: *Amo, amas, amat, amamus, amatis, amant.*[8]

KULYGIN [*laughing*]: No, really, she's astonishing. I've been married to you for seven years, but it seems as if we only got married yesterday. I swear it. No, really, you're an astonishing woman. I'm happy, I'm happy, I'm happy!

MASHA: I'm fed up, fed up, fed up . . . [*Gets up and talks from a sitting position.*] I just can't get it out of my head . . . It's simply outrageous. It's a nail hammered into my head, I can't not say anything. I mean about Andrey . . . He's mortgaged this house to the bank and his wife has grabbed all the money, but the house doesn't belong just to him but to all four of us! He must know that if he's a decent man.

KULYGIN: You're really looking for trouble, Masha! Why, why? Andryusha is up to his neck in debt, so good luck to him.

MASHA: However you look at it, it's outrageous. [*Lies down.*]

KULYGIN: You and I aren't poor. I work, I go to the Gymnasium, then I give lessons . . . I am an honest man. A simple man . . . *Omnia mea mecum porto,*[9] as the saying goes.

MASHA: I don't need anything, but injustice outrages me.

[*A pause.*]

Fyodor, go.

KULYGIN [*kisses her*]: You're tired, have a little rest for half an hour, and I'll sit down at home and wait. Have some sleep . . . [*Walks off.*] I'm happy, I'm happy, I'm happy. [*Exit.*]

IRINA: Really, what a trivial man our Andrey has become, he has lost his way and become really old in the company of that woman! He was once aiming at a professor's chair, and yesterday he was boasting that finally he's become a member of the District Council. He's a member of the Council, and Protopopov chairman . . . The whole town is talking and laughing, and he's the only one who knows nothing and sees nothing . . . And now everyone has rushed off to the fire and he sits in his room and pays no attention. He just plays his violin. [*Fretfully*] Oh, it's terrible, terrible, terrible! [*Weeps.*] I can't, I can't stand any more! . . . I can't, I can't! . . .

[*Enter* OLGA *and tidies things up by her table.*]

[*Sobs loudly.*] Throw me out, throw me out, I can't stand any more! . . .

OLGA [*alarmed*]: What's the matter, what's the matter? Darling!

IRINA [*sobbing*]: Where, where has it all gone? Where is it? My God, my God! I've forgotten everything, everything . . . My head is all muddled . . . I don't remember 'window' in Italian, or 'ceiling' say . . . I forget everything, every day I forget something, and life slips away and will never come back, we will never, never go to Moscow . . . I can see we won't go . . .

OLGA: Darling, darling . . .

IRINA [*pulling herself together*]: I'm so unhappy . . . I can't work, I'm not going to work. I've had enough, enough! I used to be in the Telegraph Office, now I work in the Town Council and I hate and despise every single thing they give me to do . . . I'm already twenty-three, I've been working for a long time, and my brain is dried up, I've become thin and ugly and old, and nothing, nothing gives me any satisfaction, and time is going on, and I keep on thinking I'm moving away from any genuine, free life, moving further and further away, into some abyss. I'm in despair, and I can't understand how I'm alive, how I haven't yet killed myself . . .

OLGA: Don't cry, little sister, don't cry . . . it makes me wretched too.

IRINA: I'm not crying, I'm not crying . . . I've stopped . . . There, I'm not crying. I've stopped . . . Stopped!

OLGA: Darling, I tell you as a sister, as a friend, if you want my advice, marry the Baron!

[IRINA *is crying quietly.*]

I know you respect him and think highly of him . . . True, he's not good-looking, but he's so decent and honest . . . After all, we marry not for love but just to do our duty. At any rate that's what I think, and I would marry without being in love. I would accept whoever proposed, provided only he was a decent man. I would even marry someone old . . .

IRINA: I've been waiting. We were going to move to Moscow and there I would meet my true love, I dreamed of him, I loved him . . . But all that's turned out to be nonsense, all nonsense . . .

OLGA [*embracing her sister*]: My darling, lovely sister, I understand it all. When Baron Nikolay Lvovich left the army and visited us wearing a civilian jacket, I found him so ugly I even cried . . . He asked me, 'Why are you crying?' How could I tell him! But if God made him your husband, I'd be happy. You see that's something quite different, quite different.

[NATASHA *crosses the stage from the right-hand door to the left-hand one, carrying a candle and without saying anything.*]

MASHA [*sitting down*]: She's walking about as if she'd started the fire.
OLGA: You're silly, Masha. You're the silliest one in our family. I'm sorry.

[*A pause.*]

MASHA: My dear sisters, I want to confess. My spirit is heavy. I'll make my confession to you and then to no one else, ever . . . I'll say it right now. [*Quietly*] It's my secret, but you have to know everything . . . I cannot be silent . . .

[*A pause.*]

I love, I love . . . I love this man . . . You've just seen him . . . So. In a word, I love Vershinin . . .
OLGA [*going behind her screen*]: Stop it. I can't hear you, anyway.
MASHA: What can I do! [*Clutching her head.*] First I thought he was strange, then I was sorry for him . . . then I fell in love with him . . . I loved him for his voice, his speeches, his unhappinesses, his two little girls . . .
OLGA [*from behind the screen*]: I still can't hear you. Whatever silly things you may be saying, I still can't hear.
MASHA: Oh, you are strange, Olya. If I love him – that's my destiny. That is my fate . . . And he loves me . . . It's all terrifying, isn't it? And is it right? [*Pulls Irina by the hand and draws her to her.*] Oh my darling . . . How are we going to live out our lives, what will become of us . . . When you read some novel, you think it's all old stuff and all so easy to understand, but when you yourself love someone, then you can see that no one knows anything and

everybody has to decide for themselves . . . My darlings, my sisters . . . I have confessed to you, now I will be silent . . . Now I will be like Gogol's madman[10] . . . silence . . . silence . . .

[*Enter* ANDREY, *followed by* FERAPONT.]

ANDREY [*crossly*]: What do you want? I don't understand . . .

FERAPONT [*at the door, impatiently*]: Andrey Sergeich, I've already said it ten times.

ANDREY: First, to you I am not Andrey Sergeich but Your Honour!

FERAPONT: Your Honour, the firemen are asking, will you let them get down to the river through the garden? Otherwise they have to go all the way round – it's a terrible nuisance.

ANDREY: Fine. Tell them it's fine.

[*Exit* FERAPONT.]

I'm fed up with them. Where's Olga?

[OLGA *appears from behind her screen.*]

I've come to see you, give me the key to the cupboard, I've lost mine. You've got that little key.

[OLGA *gives him the key without saying anything.* IRINA *goes behind her screen; a pause.*]

What an enormous fire! It's now started to die down. What the devil, that Ferapont made me mad, I said something silly to him . . . Your Honour . . .

[*A pause.*]

Why aren't you saying anything, Olya?

[*A pause.*]

It's time now to stop being silly and sulking like this for no reason at all . . . Masha, you're here, Irina is here, that's perfect – we'll really have it out, once and for all. What have you got against me? What is it?

OLGA: Stop it, Andryusha. We'll have it out tomorrow. [*Becoming agitated.*] What an agony this night has been!

ANDREY [*very embarrassed*]: Don't get upset. I am asking you quite calmly – what have you got against me? Tell me straight.

[VERSHININ*'s voice: 'Tram-tam-tam!'*]

MASHA [*getting up, loudly*]: *Tra-ta-ta!* [*To Olga*] Good night, Olya, God bless. [*Goes behind the screen and kisses Irina.*] Sleep well . . . Good night, Andrey. Go away, they're exhausted . . . you can explain tomorrow . . . [*Exit.*]

OLGA: Really, Andryusha, let's leave it till tomorrow . . . [*Goes behind her screen.*] It's time to sleep.

ANDREY: I'll just say it and then go. Right . . . First, you've got something against my wife Natasha, and I've noticed that ever since my wedding-day. If you want to know, Natasha is a fine, honest human being, noble and direct – that's what I think. I love my wife and I respect her, you have to understand that, I respect her and I require others to respect her too. I repeat, she is an honest, noble human being, and all your dissatisfaction with her – I'm sorry – is just childish . . .

[*A pause.*]

Secondly, you seem to be angry that I am not a professor and don't do academic work. But I have a job in the District Council Office, I'm a member of the District Council and I consider that job of mine just as hallowed and elevated as an academic one. I'm a member of the District Council and I'm proud of it if you want to know . . .

[*A pause.*]

Thirdly . . . I have something else to say . . . I have mortgaged the house without asking your permission . . . In that I was wrong, I know, and I ask your forgiveness. Debts drove me to that . . . thirty-five thousand . . . I've stopped playing cards, I gave it up some while ago, but the chief thing I can say in my own defence is that you girls, you've been getting paid while I didn't have . . . any, as it were, earnings . . .

[*A pause.*]

KULYGIN [*at the door*]: Isn't Masha here? [*Anxiously*] Where is she? That's strange . . . [*Exit.*]

ANDREY: They're not listening. Natasha is an exceptional, honest human being. [*Walks about the stage in silence, then stops.*] When I married, I thought we would be happy . . . we would all be happy . . . But my God . . . [*Weeps.*] My darling sisters, dear sisters, don't believe me, don't believe me . . . [*Exit.*]

KULYGIN [*anxiously at the door*]: Where's Masha? Isn't Masha here? That's surprising. [*Exit.*]

[*The alarm sounds. The stage is empty.*]

IRINA [*from behind the screen*]: Olya! Who's that knocking on the floor?

OLGA: It's the Doctor, Ivan Romanych. He's drunk.

IRINA: What a nightmarish night!

[*A pause.*]

Olya! [*Looking out round the screen.*] Have you heard? The Brigade is to be taken away from us and transferred somewhere far off.

OLGA: That's just a rumour.

IRINA: Then we'll be left on our own . . . Olya!

OLGA: Yes?

IRINA: My darling love, I respect and I appreciate the Baron, he's an excellent person, I will marry him, yes I will, only let us go to Moscow! I beg you, let us go! There's nothing better than Moscow in the whole world! Let us go, Olya! Let us go!

[*Curtain.*]

Act Four

The old garden round the Prozorovs' house.[1] A long avenue of fir trees, at the end of which the river can be seen. On the far bank of the river is the forest. Right – the terrace of the house; here there are bottles and glasses on a table, the remains of champagne drinking. It is midday. From time to time passers-by go from the street to the river through the garden; five or six soldiers quickly walk down.

[CHEBUTYKIN, *in a euphoric mood which stays with him for the whole act, is sitting in the garden in an armchair waiting to be called; he is wearing his army cap and has a stick.* IRINA, KULYGIN, *clean-shaven and with a decoration round his neck, and* TUZENBAKH *are standing on the terrace and saying goodbye to* FEDOTIK *and* RODE *going down the steps; both officers are in field dress.*]

TUZENBAKH [*kissing Fedotik*]: You're a good man, we've been such friends. [*Kissing Rode.*] Once more . . . Goodbye, my dear fellow!

IRINA: Till we meet again!

FEDOTIK: No, no, it's adieu – we won't ever meet again!

KULYGIN: Who knows! [*Wipes his eyes and smiles.*] There, I started crying.

IRINA: We'll meet some day.

FEDOTIK: In ten or fifteen years? But then we'll hardly recognize one another, we'll greet each other coldly . . . [*Takes a photograph.*] Stand still . . . Once more, for the last time.

RODE [*embracing Tuzenbakh*]: We won't meet again . . . [*Kissing Irina's hand.*] Thank you for everything, everything!

FEDOTIK [*crossly*]: Can't you stand still!

TUZENBAKH: We will see each other, God willing. Write to us. Make sure you write.

RODE [*looking round the garden*]: Goodbye, trees! [*Shouting*] Ho-ho!

[*A pause.*]

Goodbye, echo!

KULYGIN: For all I know you'll get married over in Poland . . . Your Polish wife will put her arms round you and say, '*kochany*, my darling.'[2] [*Laughs.*]

FEDOTIK [*looking at his watch*]: We've got less than an hour left. In our battery only Solyony is taking the barge, we're marching with the troops. Today three batteries of the division are leaving, in battalion order. Tomorrow another three – and then peace and quiet will descend on the town.

TUZENBAKH: And a terrible boredom.

RODE: And where is Mariya Sergeyevna?

KULYGIN: Masha's in the garden.

FEDOTIK: I must say goodbye to her.

RODE: Goodbye, I must go or I'll start crying . . . [*Quickly hugs Tuzenbakh and Kulygin, and kisses Irina's hand.*] We had wonderful times here . . .

FEDOTIK [*to Kulygin*]: This is something for you to remember me by . . . a notebook with a pencil . . . We'll go down here to the river . . .

[*They go off and both look back.*]

RODE [*shouting*]: Ho-ho!

KULYGIN [*shouting*]: Goodbye!

[*At the back of the stage* FEDOTIK *and* RODE *meet* MASHA *and say goodbye to her; she goes out with them.*]

IRINA: They've gone . . . [*Sits down on the bottom step of the terrace.*]

CHEBUTYKIN: They forgot to say goodbye to me.

IRINA: What about you?

CHEBUTYKIN: And I kind of forgot. Besides, I'll soon be seeing them, I'm leaving tomorrow. Yes . . . I've got one little day left. In a year's time I'll be retired, I'll come here again and I'll live out my days near you. I've got just one short year till I get my pension . . . [*Puts a newspaper in his pocket and takes out another one*.] I'll come here and I'll change my lifestyle completely . . . I'll be so quiet, so very good and well-behaved . . .

IRINA: You need to change your lifestyle, my dear. You really must somehow.

CHEBUTYKIN: Yes. I see that. [*Sings quietly*] 'Ta-ra-ra . . . boom-de-ay . . . ta-ra-ra-boom-de-ay . . .'[3]

KULYGIN: You're incorrigible, Ivan Romanych! Incorrigible!

CHEBUTYKIN: I should become your pupil. Then I'd reform.

IRINA: Fyodor's shaved his moustache off. I can't bear to look!

KULYGIN: What's the matter?

CHEBUTYKIN: I'd like to say what your face looks like now, but I just can't.

KULYGIN: Why, it's the done thing, the *modus vivendi*.[4] Our Principal is clean-shaven, and I am too. I shaved my moustache off when I became an inspector. No one likes it but I don't care. I'm happy with it . . . Whether I have a moustache or not, it's all the same to me . . . [*Sits down*.]

[*At the back of the stage* ANDREY *wheels a sleeping baby in a pram*.]

IRINA: Sweet Ivan Romanych, my dear friend, I'm terribly worried. You were on the boulevard yesterday, tell me what happened there.

CHEBUTYKIN: What happened? Nothing. A lot of nonsense! [*Reads his paper*.] What can it matter!

KULYGIN: They're saying that Solyony and the Baron met yesterday on the boulevard by the theatre . . .

TUZENBAKH: Stop it! Really . . . [*Makes a gesture with his hand and goes into the house*.]

KULYGIN: By the theatre . . . Solyony started to needle the Baron and he lost his temper and said something offensive . . .

CHEBUTYKIN: I don't know. All nonsense.

KULYGIN: A teacher in a seminary wrote 'nonsense' in Russian on an essay, and the pupil read it as Latin script – '*renyxa*' – he thought it was written in Latin.[5] [*Laughs.*] Terribly funny. They say Solyony's in love with Irina and that he has developed a hatred for the Baron . . . One can understand that. Irina is a very attractive girl. She's even rather like Masha, she's the thoughtful type. Only, Irina, you have got a gentler character. Although Masha by the way has a very nice character. I love her, Masha.

[*In the depths of the garden, offstage: 'Hallo-o! Ho-ho!'*]

IRINA [*shuddering*]: Somehow everything scares me today.

[*A pause.*]

All my things are ready now, I'm sending them off after dinner. Tomorrow the Baron and I are getting married, and tomorrow too we're going off to the brick factory, and the day after tomorrow I'll be teaching, a new life is beginning. God will somehow help me! When I passed the teachers' examination, I even cried for joy and well-being . . .

[*A pause.*]

The cart will be coming now for my things.

KULYGIN: All very true of course, only somehow it's not very serious. Just ideas and not much serious stuff. But I wish you the best with all my heart.

CHEBUTYKIN [*overcome with emotion*]: My wonderful, fine girl . . . My golden girl . . . You've gone far, I can't catch up with you. I have remained behind like a migratory bird which has got old and can't fly. Fly on, my dears, fly on with God's blessing!

[*A pause.*]

Fyodor Ilyich, you made a mistake in shaving off your moustache.

KULYGIN: That'll do! [*Sighing.*] Today the Army is leaving and everything will go back to what it was. Whatever they say there, Masha is a fine, honest woman, I love her very much, and I thank my destiny. People have different destinies. There's a Kozyrev who works in the Excise Office here. He was at school with me, he was expelled from the fifth class of the Gymnasium for being quite unable to understand the consecutive *ut.*[6] Now he is terribly poor and ill, and whenever I meet him, I say to him, 'Hallo there, Consecutive Ut.' 'Yes,' he says, 'Consecutive it is . . .' and he coughs. But I've had luck all my life, I'm happy, I've now even got a second-class Stanislav[7] and I'm now myself teaching others that consecutive *ut.* Of course I am an intelligent man, more intelligent than very many, but happiness doesn't lie in that . . .

[*In the house someone is playing 'The Maiden's Prayer'*[8] *on the piano.*]

IRINA: And tomorrow I won't have to hear that 'Maiden's Prayer' any more and I won't keep bumping into Protopopov . . .

[*A pause.*]

But Protopopov is sitting there in the drawing-room; he's come again today . . .

KULYGIN: Hasn't our headmistress come yet?

[MASHA *quietly strolls across the back of the stage.*]

IRINA: No. She's been sent for. If only you knew how difficult it is for me to live here alone, without Olya . . . She lives at the Gymnasium; she's headmistress, she's busy all day with work, and I'm alone, I'm bored, I haven't got anything to do, and the room in which I live is hateful . . . So I decided: if I am fated not to live in Moscow, that's how it must be. It means it's destiny.

Nothing to be done . . . Everything is by God's will, true. Nikolay Lvovich proposed to me . . . Well, I thought and made a decision. He's a good man, it's really astonishing how good he is . . . And suddenly it was as if my spirit had grown wings, I cheered up, a weight was lifted from me and again I wanted to work, to work . . . Only yesterday something happened, some mystery is hanging over me . . .

CHEBUTYKIN: *Renyxa*. Nonsense.

NATASHA [*through the window*]: Our headmistress!

KULYGIN: The headmistress has arrived. Let's go in.

[*He and* IRINA *go into the house.*]

CHEBUTYKIN [*reads his paper and sings quietly*]: Ta-ra-ra . . . boom-de-ay . . . ta-ra-ra-boom-de-ay . . .

[MASHA *comes up;* ANDREY *wheels the pram across the back of the stage.*]

MASHA: He's sitting here nicely all by himself . . .

CHEBUTYKIN: Why not?

MASHA [*sitting down*]: No reason . . .

[*A pause.*]

Did you love my mother?

CHEBUTYKIN: Very much.

MASHA: And did she love you?

CHEBUTYKIN [*after a pause*]: That I can't remember.

MASHA: Is my fellow here? That's what our cook Marfa used to call her policeman in the old days – my fellow. Is my fellow here?

CHEBUTYKIN: Not yet.

MASHA: When you get happiness in snatches, in small pieces, and then lose it, like me, then little by little you become coarse and ill-tempered. [*Points to her breast.*] I'm seething right here . . . [*Looking at her brother Andrey who is wheeling the pram.*] There's our dear brother Andrey . . . All his hopes gone. Thousands of people raise a church bell, much labour and money have been spent, and suddenly it falls and smashes. Suddenly, just like that. That's what happened to Andrey . . .

ANDREY: And when will it be quiet at last in the house? There's so much noise.

CHEBUTYKIN: Soon. [*Looks at his watch, then winds it; the watch strikes.*] I have an old-fashioned watch, a repeater . . . The first, second and fifth batteries will leave at one precisely.

[*A pause.*]

And I'm leaving tomorrow.

ANDREY: For good?

CHEBUTYKIN: I don't know. Maybe I'll come back in a year. Although what the devil . . . what can it matter . . .

[*A harp and violin are being played somewhere in the distance.*]

ANDREY: The town will be emptied. Like someone snuffing out a candle.

[*A pause.*]

Something happened yesterday by the theatre; everyone is talking about it but I don't know anything.

CHEBUTYKIN: It's nothing. All nonsense. Solyony started to needle the Baron and he lost his temper and insulted him, and the consequence was that Solyony was obliged to challenge him. [*Looks at his watch.*] I think it's the time now . . . At half past twelve in the public woods, the ones you can see from here on the other side of the river . . . Bang-bang. [*Laughs.*] Solyony imagines he's Lermontov and he even writes poetry. But joking apart, it's already his third duel.

MASHA: Whose?

CHEBUTYKIN: Solyony's.

MASHA: And the Baron's?
CHEBUTYKIN: The Baron's what?

[*A pause.*]

MASHA: Everything has become muddled in my head . . . Anyway,
I say they shouldn't allow them. He could wound the Baron or
even kill him.
CHEBUTYKIN: The Baron is a good man, but one baron more or
one baron less – what can it matter? Let it be! What can it matter!

[*Beyond the garden is a cry: 'Hallo-o! Ho-ho!'*]

You can wait. That's Skvortsov shouting, the second. He's sitting
in a boat.

[*A pause.*]

ANDREY: In my opinion, taking part in a duel and being present at
one, even if in the capacity of a doctor, are both simply immoral.
CHEBUTYKIN: That's just appearances . . . There is nothing in the
world, there is no 'we', we don't exist, it just seems we do . . .
And what can it matter!
MASHA: That's how they go on talking and talking the whole day
long . . . [*Starts walking.*] We live in this climate, it'll snow any
moment, and on top of that we have these conversations . . .
[*Stops.*] I won't go into the house, I can't go in there . . . When
Vershinin comes, will you tell me . . . [*Walks down the avenue.*]
And the migrant birds are starting to fly . . . [*Looks up.*] Swans or
geese . . . Dear birds, happy birds . . . [*Exit.*]
ANDREY: Our house will be empty. The officers will leave, you will
leave, my sister will be married, and I will remain alone in the
house.
CHEBUTYKIN: What about your wife?

[FERAPONT *comes in with some papers.*]

ANDREY: My wife is my wife. She is honest, decent, yes, kind, but all the same there's something in her which brings her down to the level of a small, blind, horny-skinned animal. At all events, she isn't human. I'm talking to you as a friend, the only person I can open my soul to. I love Natasha, that is the truth, but sometimes I find her amazingly coarse, and then I get confused, I don't understand how or why I love her so, or at least did love her . . .

CHEBUTYKIN [*getting up*]: I, my friend, am going away tomorrow, maybe we shall never meet again, so this is my advice to you. Just put on your hat, take a stick in your hand and leave . . . leave and start walking, walk and don't look round. And the further you walk, the better.

[SOLYONY *walks across the back of the stage with two officers; seeing Chebutykin he turns to him; the officers walk on.*]

SOLYONY: Doctor, it's time! It's already half past twelve. [*Greets Andrey.*]

CHEBUTYKIN: I'm coming. I've had enough of all of you. [*To Andrey*] If anyone asks for me, Andryusha, tell them I'll be back soon . . . [*Sighing.*] Oh-oh-oh!

SOLYONY: 'He had no time his tale to tell before a bear upon him fell.'[9] [*Walks off with Chebutykin.*[10]] Why are you groaning, old boy?

CHEBUTYKIN: Really!

SOLYONY: How's the health?

CHEBUTYKIN [*angrily*]: Right as rain.

SOLYONY: There's no reason for an old chap to get worked up. I'll allow myself a little latitude, I'll just wing him like a woodcock. [*Takes out his scent and sprinkles some on his hands.*] I've used up a whole bottle today and my hands still smell. They smell of dead bodies.

[*A pause.*]

Yes . . . Do you remember Lermontov's lines, 'And he, so restless, seeks the storm clouds, as if the storm can offer calm' . . . ?[11]

CHEBUTYKIN: Yes. 'He had no time his tale to tell before a bear upon him fell.' [*Exit with Solyony.*]

[*Cries of 'Hallo-o!' can be heard. Enter* ANDREY *and* FERAPONT.]

FERAPONT: Here are some papers to sign . . .

ANDREY [*irritably*]: Leave me alone! Leave me! I implore you! [*Goes out with the pram.*]

FERAPONT: Papers are meant to be signed. [*Goes off to the back of the stage.*]

[*Enter* IRINA *and* TUZENBAKH *wearing a straw hat;* KULYGIN *walks across the stage shouting: 'Hallo-o, Masha, hallo-o!'*]

TUZENBAKH: I think that's the only man in the town who's glad that the Army is going.

IRINA: One can understand that.

[*A pause.*]

Our town will be empty now.

TUZENBAKH: My dear, I'll be back straight away.

IRINA: Where are you going?

TUZENBAKH: I must go into the town and then . . . say goodbye to friends.

IRINA: That's not true . . . Nikolay, why are you so distracted today?

[*A pause.*]

What happened yesterday by the theatre?

TUZENBAKH [*making an impatient movement*]: I'll be back in an hour and be with you again. [*Kissing her hands.*] My beloved . . . [*Looking into her face.*] It's already five years since I came to love

you and I still can't get accustomed to it, and you seem to me
more and more beautiful. What wonderful, lovely hair! What
eyes! Tomorrow I will take you away, we will work, we'll be
rich, my dreams will come true. You will be happy. There's just
one thing, only one – you don't love me!

IRINA: It's not in my power! I will be your wife, true and obedient,
but love – no, what can I do! [*Weeps.*] I've never loved once in
my life. Oh, how I dreamed of love, for a long time how I
dreamed, day and night, but my soul was like an expensive piano,
shut and its key lost.

[*A pause.*]

Your eyes are worried.

TUZENBAKH: I didn't sleep all night. In my life there's nothing so
terrible that it can frighten me and only that lost key torments my
spirit and stops me sleeping. Say something to me.

[*A pause.*]

Say something to me . . .

IRINA: What? Say what? Everything around us is so mysterious,
the old trees are standing there, silent . . . [*Puts her head on his
breast.*]

TUZENBAKH: Say something to me.

IRINA: What? Say what? What?

TUZENBAKH: Anything.

IRINA: That's enough! Enough!

[*A pause.*]

TUZENBAKH: Sometimes in life trifles, silly little things, all of a
sudden acquire significance, and for no good reason. You laugh
at them as before and think them trifling, and you just go on
because you feel you haven't the strength to stop. Oh, don't let's
talk about it! I feel happy. I'm seeing those firs and maples and

birches as if for the first time, and everything is watching me with curiosity and waiting. What beautiful trees, and, indeed, how beautiful life should be around them!

[*A shout of 'Hallo-o! Ho-ho!'*]

I must go, it's time now . . . That tree is withered but it still sways in the wind with the others. In the same way I think that if I die I'll still be taking part in life somehow or other. Goodbye, my darling . . . [*Kissing her hands.*] Your papers, the ones you gave me, are lying on my writing table under the calendar.

IRINA: I'll come with you.

TUZENBAKH [*in alarm*]: No, no! [*Quickly walks off, then stops in the avenue.*] Irina!

IRINA: What?

TUZENBAKH [*not knowing what to say*]: I didn't have any coffee this morning. Will you ask them to make me some . . . [*Quickly goes out.*]

[IRINA *stands thinking, then she goes to the back of the stage and sits down on a swing. Enter* ANDREY *with the pram,* FERAPONT *appears.*]

FERAPONT: Andrey Sergeich, these aren't my papers, they're from the Council. I didn't dream them up.

ANDREY: Oh where is it now, where has my past gone, the time when I was young, merry, clever, when I had fine thoughts, fine dreams, when my present and my future were lit up by hope? Why is it that no sooner have we begun to live, we become boring, grey, uninteresting, lazy, indifferent, useless, unhappy . . . Our town has existed now for two hundred years, it has a hundred thousand inhabitants – and not one of them who isn't exactly like the others, not one hero, not one scholar, not one artist, not one who stands out in the slightest bit, who might inspire envy or a passionate desire to emulate him. They just eat, drink, sleep, then they die . . . others are born and they too eat, drink, sleep, and in order not to be dulled by boredom, they diversify their life with vile gossip, vodka, cards, law suits, and the wives deceive their husbands and the husbands lie, pretend they see nothing and hear nothing, and an irremediably coarse influence weighs down on the children, and the spark of God's spirit dies in them and they become the same kind of pitiful corpses, one like another, as their mothers and fathers . . . [*Angrily, to Ferapont*] What do you want?

FERAPONT: What? Sign the papers.

ANDREY: I'm fed up with you.

FERAPONT [*handing him the papers*]: The porter at the Accounts Office was telling me just now . . . He said apparently last winter Petersburg had two hundred degrees of frost.

ANDREY: The present is repulsive, but when I think of the future how wonderful things become! There's a feeling of ease, of space; and in the distance there's a glimmer of the dawn, I see freedom, I see myself and my children freed from idleness, from kvass,[12] from goose with cabbage, from a nap after dinner, from the ignoble life of a parasite . . .

FERAPONT: Two thousand people froze to death. People were in a state of terror, he said. It was in Petersburg, or in Moscow – I can't quite remember.

ANDREY [*overcome by feelings of tenderness*]: My dear sisters, my wonderful sisters! [*With tears in his eyes*] Masha, my sister . . .

NATASHA [*through the window*]: Who is talking so loudly here? Is it you, Andryusha? You'll wake Sofochka. *Il ne faut pas faire du bruit, la Sophie est dormée déjà. Vous êtes un ours.*[13] [*Getting angry*] If you want to talk, then give the baby and her pram to someone else. Ferapont, take the pram from your master.

FERAPONT: Yes, madam. [*Takes the pram.*]

ANDREY [*embarrassed*]: I'm talking quietly.

NATASHA [*in the window, playing with her little son*]: Bobik! Naughty Bobik! Bad Bobik!

ANDREY [*examining the papers*]: Very well, I'll look through them and sign what I need to, and then you can take them back to the Council . . .

[*He goes into the house reading the papers;* FERAPONT *starts wheeling the pram.*]

NATASHA [*in the window*]: Bobik, what's your Mama's name? Darling, darling! And who's that? It's Auntie Olya. Say to Auntie: 'Hello, Olya!'

[*Travelling musicians come in, a man and a girl; they play the violin and the harp;* VERSHININ, OLGA *and* ANFISA *come out of the house and listen in silence for a moment;* IRINA *comes up.*]

OLGA: Our garden's like a public thoroughfare, people walk through it and drive through it. Nyanya, give those musicians something! . . .
ANFISA [*giving the musicians some money*]: Go with God, my friends. [*The musicians bow and go off.*] Wretched people. You don't play like that on a full stomach. [*To Irina*] Good day, Arisha! [*Kissing her.*] Life is good, my little girl, life is good! In a school apartment in the Gymnasium with Olyushka, my darling – God has granted me this in my old age. I haven't lived like this in all my born days, sinner that I am . . . A big apartment, nothing to pay, and I have a little room all to myself and a bed. All free. I wake up at night – and O Lord, Mother of God, there is no human being happier than me!
VERSHININ [*glancing at his watch*]: We're leaving now, Olga Sergeyevna. It's time for me to go.

[*A pause.*]

I wish you every, every . . . Where is Mariya Sergeyevna?
IRINA: She's somewhere in the garden. I'll go and look for her.
VERSHININ: That's kind of you. I'm in a hurry.
ANFISA: And I'll go and look for her too. [*Shouting*] Mashenka, Hallo-o!

[*She and* IRINA *go out together to the bottom of the garden.*]

Hallo-o, hallo-o!
VERSHININ: Everything comes to an end. So we too are parting. [*Looking at his watch.*] The town gave us a sort of luncheon, we drank champagne, the mayor made a speech, I ate and listened,

but my heart was here, with you . . . [*Looking round the garden.*]
I've got accustomed to you.

OLGA: Will we ever see each other again?

VERSHININ: Most probably not.

[*A pause.*]

My wife and both girls will stay on here two more months; please,
if anything happens or if anything is needed . . .

OLGA: Yes, yes, of course. Don't worry.

[*A pause.*]

Tomorrow there won't be a single soldier in the town, everything
will be a memory, and of course for us a new life will be beginning . . .

[*A pause.*]

Nothing happens as we want it. I didn't want to become headmistress and all the same I did. So I won't get to Moscow . . .

VERSHININ: Well . . . Thank you for everything. Forgive me if I
haven't quite . . . I've talked a great deal, a very great deal –
forgive me for that too, don't think ill of me.

OLGA [*wiping her eyes*]: Why isn't Masha coming? . . .

VERSHININ: What else can I say to you as a goodbye? What bit of
philosophy? . . . [*Laughs.*] Life is a heavy load. Many of us find it
blank, hopeless, but still one has to admit it is becoming brighter
and easier every day, and one can see the time is not far off when it
will be filled with light. [*Looking at his watch.*] I must go, I must!
Once humanity was occupied with wars, filling the whole of its
existence with campaigns, invasions, victories, all that has now had
its day, and left behind a huge empty space, which for the time being
there is nothing to fill; humanity is passionately seeking that and
of course will find it. Oh, if only it could be quick about it!

[*A pause.*]

If we could just combine education with hard work, and hard work with education. [*Looking at his watch.*] But I must go . . .

OLGA: She's coming now.

[*Enter* MASHA.]

VERSHININ: I've come to say goodbye . . .

[OLGA *moves a little away so as not to be in the way of their goodbyes.*]

MASHA [*looking into his eyes*]: Goodbye . . .

[*A long kiss.*]

OLGA: That'll do . . .

[MASHA *sobs loudly.*]

VERSHININ: Write to me . . . Don't forget me! Let go of me . . . I must go . . . Olga Sergeyevna, take her, now I have to . . . I must go . . . I'm late . . . [*Overcome by emotion, kisses Olga's hands, then embraces Masha once more and quickly goes out.*]

OLGA: That'll do, Masha! Stop it, darling . . .

[*Enter* KULYGIN.]

KULYGIN [*embarrassed*]: It doesn't matter, let her cry, just let her . . . My sweet Masha, my good Masha . . . You are my wife and I am happy in spite of everything . . . I'm not complaining, I'm not making one reproach to you . . . Olya is my witness . . . We will begin to live again as we used to and I won't say one word to you, not a hint . . .

MASHA [*holding back sobs*]: 'An oak in leaf beside the seashore, upon that oak a chain of gold . . . upon that oak a chain of gold . . .' I'm going out of my mind . . . 'An oak in leaf . . . beside the seashore . . .'

OLGA: Calm down, Masha . . . Calm down . . . Give her some water.

MASHA: I'm not crying any more . . .

KULYGIN: She's not crying any more . . . she's a good girl . . .

[*The sound of a muffled shot, far off.*]

MASHA: 'An oak in leaf beside the seashore, upon that oak a chain of gold . . . A cat in leaf[14] . . . an oak in leaf . . .' I'm muddling things . . . [*Drinks the water.*] My life is a failure . . . I don't need anything now . . . I'll calm down right away . . . It doesn't matter . . . What does 'beside the seashore' mean? Why is that sticking in my head? My thoughts are muddled.

[*Enter* IRINA.]

OLGA: Calm down, Masha. There, good girl . . . Let's go indoors.

MASHA [*angrily*]: I won't go in there. [*Sobs but stops at once.*] I don't go into the house any more and I won't now . . .

IRINA: Let's sit a moment together, without even talking. You realize I'm leaving tomorrow . . .

[*A pause.*]

KULYGIN: Yesterday I confiscated this moustache and beard from a little boy in the third form . . . [*Putting on the moustache and beard.*] Just like the German master . . . [*Laughing*] Isn't it? Those little boys make one laugh.

MASHA: It really is like your German.

OLGA [*laughing*]: Yes.

[MASHA *cries.*]

IRINA: Masha, that's enough!

KULYGIN: It's very like him . . .

[*Enter* NATASHA *and the* MAID.[15]]

NATASHA [*to the maid*]: What? Mr Protopopov, Mikhail Ivanych, will sit for a bit with Sofochka, and Andrey Sergeich can give Bobik a turn. Children are so much trouble ... [*To Irina*] You're going tomorrow, Irina ... such a pity. Stay just one week more. [*Seeing Kulygin, shrieks; then laughs and takes off his moustache and beard.*] Really, you scared me! [*To Irina*] I've got so accustomed to you, do you think it will be easy for me to lose you? I'm telling them to move Andrey and his violin into your room – let him scrape away in there! – and we'll put Sofochka in his room. She's a marvellous, wonderful baby! What a darling little girl! Today she looked at me with her little eyes and – 'Mama'!

KULYGIN: She's a lovely baby, that's true.

NATASHA: So tomorrow I'll be on my own here. [*Sighs.*] First I'll tell them to cut down that avenue of fir trees, and then that maple. In the evenings it's so frightening and ugly ... [*To Irina*] Dearest, that belt doesn't suit you at all ... It's really tasteless. You must wear something light and pretty. And here I'll have them plant flowers – flowers, and there'll be scent ... [*Sternly*] What is a fork doing here on the bench? [*To the maid as she goes into the house*] What is a fork doing here on the bench, I'm asking you that! [*Shouting*] Don't you say anything!

KULYGIN: She's off!

[*Offstage the band plays a march; everyone listens.*]

OLGA: They're going.

[*Enter* CHEBUTYKIN.]

MASHA: Our friends are leaving. Well, there we are ... I hope they have a good journey! [*To her husband*] We must go home ... Where are my hat and cloak?

KULYGIN: I took them into the house ... I'll fetch them right away. [*Goes out into the house.*]

OLGA: Yes, we can all go home now. It's time.

CHEBUTYKIN: Olga Sergeyevna!

OLGA: What?

[*A pause.*]

What is it?

CHEBUTYKIN: Nothing ... I don't know how to tell you ... [*Whispers in her ear.*]

OLGA [*in alarm*]: It's not possible!

CHEBUTYKIN: Yes ... that's how it is ... I'm worn out, I've had a terrible time, I don't want to say more ... [*With irritation*] Besides, what can it matter!

MASHA: What's happened?

OLGA [*embracing Irina*]: Today is a terrible day ... My darling, I don't know how to tell you ...

IRINA: What? Tell me quickly, what is it? For God's sake! [*Cries.*]

CHEBUTYKIN: The Baron was killed just now in a duel.

IRINA: I knew it, I knew it ...

CHEBUTYKIN [*sitting down on a bench at the back of the stage*]: I'm worn out ... [*Takes a newspaper out of his pocket.*] Let them have a little cry ... [*Singing softly*] Ta-ra-ra-boom-de-ay ... ta-ra-ra-boom-de-ay ... What can it all matter!

[*The three sisters stand clinging to one another.*]

MASHA: Listen to the band playing! They're leaving us, one of them has gone for good, for ever, we will be left alone to begin our life anew. We must live ... We must live ...

IRINA [*putting her head on Olga's breast*]: A time will come and everyone will know the reason for all of this, all this suffering, there will be no secrets, but for the time being we must live ... we must work, just work! Tomorrow I will leave alone, I will teach in the school, and I will give away my whole life to those who perhaps need it. It's autumn now, soon winter will come and cover everything with snow, and I will work, I will work ...

OLGA [*embracing both her sisters*]: The band is playing so gaily and cheerfully, it makes one want to live! My God! Time will pass and we will be gone for ever, they'll forget us, forget our faces, our voices and how many there were of us, but for those who live after us our sufferings will become joy – happiness and peace will come down on earth, and there'll be a kind word and a blessing for those who are living now. Dear sisters, our life is not yet over. We shall live! The band is playing so gaily, so joyfully, and I think in a little while we too will know why we live, why we suffer . . . If we only knew, if we only knew!

[*The music of the band comes more and more faintly;* KULYGIN, *smiling and cheerful, brings in Masha's hat and cloak,* ANDREY *wheels the pram with Bobik sitting in it.*]

CHEBUTYKIN [*sings softly*]: Ta-ra . . . ra . . . boom-de-ay . . . ta-ra-ra-boom-de-ay . . . [*Reads the paper.*] What can it matter! What can it matter!

OLGA: If we only knew, if we only knew!

[*Curtain.*]

The Cherry Orchard

A Comedy in Four Acts

CHARACTERS

LYUBOV ANDREYEVNA RANEVSKAYA [*also*
LYUBA], *a landowner*

ANYA [*also* ANECHKA], *her daughter, aged seventeen*

VARYA [*also* VARVARA MIKHAYLOVNA], *her
adopted daughter, aged twenty-four*

LEONID ANDREYEVICH GAYEV [*also* LYONYA],
Ranevskaya's brother

YERMOLAY ALEKSEYEVICH LOPAKHIN, *a
merchant*

PYOTR SERGEYEVICH TROFIMOV [*also* PETYA], *a
student*

BORIS BORISOVICH SIMEONOV-PISHCHIK, *a
landowner*

CHARLOTTA IVANOVNA, *a governess*

SEMYON PANTELEYEVICH YEPIKHODOV, *a clerk*

DUNYASHA [*also* AVDOTYA FYODOROVNA], *a
maid*

FIRS,[1] *a manservant, an old man of eighty-seven*

YASHA, *a young manservant*

A PASSER-BY

A STATION-MASTER

A Post Office official

Guests, servants

The action takes place on L. A. Ranevskaya's estate.

Act One

A room which is still called the 'nursery'. One of the doors leads to Anya's room. Dawn; it will soon be sunrise. It is May and the cherry trees are in bloom, but out in the orchard it is cold, with a morning frost. The windows of the room are shut.

[*Enter* DUNYASHA *with a candle and* LOPAKHIN *with a book in his hand.*]

LOPAKHIN: The train has come, thank God. What time is it?

DUNYASHA: It's almost two. [*Puts out the candle.*] It's light already.

LOPAKHIN: How late is the train? Two hours, at least. [*Yawns and stretches.*] I'm a fine example, what a stupid thing I've done! I came here specially to meet them at the station and then I went and overslept . . . I went to sleep sitting in a chair. How annoying . . . You could have woken me up.

DUNYASHA: I thought you'd left. [*Listens.*] I think they're coming now.

LOPAKHIN [*listening*]: No. They've got to get the luggage, and this and that . . .

[*A pause.*]

Lyubov Andreyevna has lived abroad for five years, I wonder what she's like now . . . She's a good person. An easy, simple person. I remember, when I was a lad of fifteen, my old father – he had a shop here in the village then – punched me in the face, my nose bled . . . We'd come here together for some reason, into the yard, and he was drunk. Lyubov Andreyevna, I remember, was still very young and so thin, she brought me to the washstand in this very room, in the nursery. 'Don't cry, little muzhik,'[1] she said, 'it'll be all right by your wedding-day . . .'

[*A pause.*]

Little muzhik . . . Yes, my father was a muzhik and here I am in white gloves and yellow shoes. A pig in a baker's shop . . . But though I'm rich and have a lot of money, if you think a moment and work it out, I'm muzhik through and through . . . [*Leafs through the pages of his book.*] I was reading this book and understood nothing. I read and I fell asleep.

[*A pause.*]

DUNYASHA: But the dogs didn't sleep all night, they sense their mistress is coming.
LOPAKHIN: What's the matter with you, Dunyasha . . .
DUNYASHA: My hands are shaking. I'm going to faint.
LOPAKHIN: What a very refined thing you are, Dunyasha. And you dress like a young lady, and do your hair like one too. You shouldn't. One should remember one's place.

[*Enter* YEPIKHODOV *with a bouquet of flowers; he is wearing a jacket and highly polished boots, which squeak loudly; as he comes in he drops the bouquet.*]

YEPIKHODOV [*picking up the bouquet*]: The gardener sent these in, he says to put them in the dining-room. [*Gives the bouquet to Dunyasha.*]
LOPAKHIN: And you'll bring me some kvass.[2]
DUNYASHA: Yes, sir. [*Exit.*]
YEPIKHODOV: There's a morning frost now, three degrees, and the cherry's all in blossom. I cannot approve of our climate. [*Sighs.*] I just can't. Our climate cannot be conducive to the moment.

Now, Yermolay Alekseich, may I also tell you, the day before yesterday I bought myself some boots, and I can assure you they squeak really quite impossibly. What should I put on them?

LOPAKHIN: Lay off. You're becoming a pest.

YEPIKHODOV: Every day I have some accident. And I don't complain, I've got accustomed to it and I even smile.

[*Enter* DUNYASHA, *she serves Lopakhin some kvass.*]

I'll go. [*Bumps into a chair, which falls over.*] There, you can see how I'm circumstanced, if you'll excuse the phrase . . . It's simply extraordinary, even! [*Goes out.*]

DUNYASHA: I have to tell you, Yermolay Alekseyich, Yepikhodov proposed to me.

LOPAKHIN: Oh!

DUNYASHA: I don't know quite . . . He's a quiet fellow, only sometimes when he begins to speak, you can't understand anything. He talks well, with feeling, only you can't understand. I sort of like him. He's madly in love with me. He's an unlucky fellow, there's something every day. To tease him we call him The Walking Accident . . .

LOPAKHIN [*listening*]: There, I think they're coming . . .

DUNYASHA: They're coming! What's the matter with me . . . I've gone all cold.

LOPAKHIN: They're coming, really. Let's go and meet them. Will she recognize me? We haven't met for five years.

DUNYASHA [*in a state of emotion*]: I'm going to faint now . . . Oh, I'm going to faint!

[*There is the sound of two carriages driving up to the house.* LOPAKHIN *and* DUNYASHA *quickly go out. The stage is empty. A noise starts in the rooms next door.* FIRS, *who has been to meet Lyubov Andreyevna, hurries across the stage, leaning on a stick; he is wearing an old-fashioned livery and a tall hat; he is saying something to himself but not a single word is intelligible. The noise offstage is increasing all the time. A voice says: 'Let's go in here . . .'*]

LYUBOV ANDREYEVNA, ANYA *and* CHARLOTTA IVANOVNA
with a little dog on a chain, all in travelling clothes, VARYA *in a coat
and headscarf,* GAYEV, SIMEONOV-PISHCHIK, LOPAKHIN,
DUNYASHA *with a package and an umbrella, servants with luggage
– all cross the room.*]

ANYA: Let's go in here. Mama, do you remember what room this
is?

LYUBOV ANDREYEVNA [*happily, with tears in her eyes*]: The
nursery!

VARYA: It's so cold, my hands have gone numb. [*To Lyubov Andreyevna*] Mamochka, your rooms, the white one and the violet, have
stayed just the same.

LYUBOV ANDREYEVNA: The nursery, my dear, is a lovely room
. . . I slept here when I was a little girl . . . [*Cries.*] And now I feel
like a little girl again . . . [*Kisses her brother, then Varya, then her
brother again.*] And Varya is just the same as before, she looks like
a nun . . . And I recognized Dunyasha . . . [*Kisses Dunyasha.*]

GAYEV: The train was two hours late. How on earth? What kind of
a system is that?

CHARLOTTA [*to Pishchik*]: My dog loves nuts.

PISHCHIK [*in astonishment*]: Imagine that!

[*All go out except* ANYA *and* DUNYASHA.]

DUNYASHA: We waited and waited . . . [*Takes off Anya's coat and
hat.*]

ANYA: I couldn't sleep on the journey, for four nights . . . I'm frozen
through.

DUNYASHA: You left during Lent. It was snowy and freezing then,
and now? My darling! [*Laughs and kisses her.*] I've been waiting a
long time for you, my joy, light of my life . . . I must tell you
now, I can't hold out one minute more . . .

ANYA [*feebly*]: Not more . . .

DUNYASHA: Just after Holy Week Yepikhodov the clerk proposed
to me.

ANYA: You're always on about the same thing . . . [*Adjusting her hair.*] I've lost all my hairpins . . . [*She is exhausted, to the point of tottering.*]

DUNYASHA: I don't really know what to think. He loves me, he loves me so much!

ANYA [*looking at the door of her room, tenderly*]: My room, my windows, just as if I'd never gone away. I'm home! Tomorrow morning I'll get up, I'll run into the orchard . . . Oh if only I could get to sleep! I didn't sleep the entire journey, I was worrying away.

DUNYASHA: The day before yesterday Pyotr Sergeich came.

ANYA [*joyfully*]: Petya!

DUNYASHA: He's sleeping in the bath-house, that's where he's staying. He says he's afraid of being in the way. [*Looking at her pocket watch.*] I should wake him up, only Varvara Mikhaylovna told me not to. Don't you go and wake him, she said.

[*Enter* VARYA; *on her belt is a bunch of keys.*]

VARYA: Dunyasha, coffee quickly . . . Mamochka is asking for coffee.

DUNYASHA: Right away. [*Goes out.*]

VARYA: Well, thank God, you've all got here. You're home again. [*Affectionately*] My darling has come! My beauty has come!

ANYA: What I've had to put up with.

VARYA: I can imagine!

ANYA: We left in Holy Week, it was cold then. Charlotta talked and did conjuring tricks the whole way. Why did you go and dump Charlotta on me . . .

VARYA: You can't travel alone, darling. Not at seventeen!

ANYA: We arrive in Paris, it's cold there, it's snowing. My French is terrible. Mama is living five floors up, I go to her, there are some Frenchmen with her, some ladies, an old Reverend Father with his little book, and it's all full of smoke and uncomfortable. I suddenly felt sorry for Mama, so sorry, I took her head in my arms, I held it, and I couldn't let go. Later Mama was very loving and cried . . .

VARYA [*with tears in her eyes*]: Don't, don't . . .

ANYA: She'd already sold her villa near Mentone, she had nothing left, nothing. I hadn't a kopeck left either, we barely got there. And Mama didn't understand! We'd sit down to dinner in the station and she'd order the most expensive thing and tip the waiters a rouble each. Charlotta the same. Yasha too ordered for himself, it was simply terrible. Mama has this manservant Yasha, we've brought him here . . .

VARYA: I saw the creature.

ANYA: So, how are things? Have you paid the interest?

VARYA: Of course not.

ANYA: My God, my God . . .

VARYA: The estate will be up for sale in August.

ANYA: My God . . .

LOPAKHIN [*looking in at the door and mooing like a cow*]: Meh-eh-eh . . . [*Goes out.*]

VARYA [*with tears in her eyes*]: I want to hit him like this . . . [*Shakes her fist.*]

ANYA [*hugging Varya, quietly*]: Varya, has he proposed? [VARYA *shakes her head.*] But he loves you . . . Why don't you have it out together, what are you waiting for?

VARYA: I don't think anything will work out for us. He's very busy, he hasn't time for me . . . and doesn't pay me any attention. Good luck to him, I can't stand seeing him . . . Everyone talks about our wedding, everyone offers their congratulations, and in fact there isn't anything, it's all like a dream . . . [*In a different tone of voice*] You've got a little brooch, a bee.

ANYA [*sadly*]: Mama bought it. [*Goes to her room, talking gaily, like a child.*] In Paris I went up in a hot-air balloon!

VARYA: My darling has come! My beauty has come!

[DUNYASHA *has already come back with the coffee-pot and is making coffee.*]

[*Stands by the door.*] Darling, all day I go about my work round the house and all the time I'm dreaming. Marry you to a rich man and then I'd be at peace, I'd go to a convent, then to Kiev . . . to Moscow, and so I'd go off round the holy places . . . From place to place. Bliss! . . .

ANYA: The birds are singing in the orchard. What's the time now?

VARYA: It must be after two. It's time for you to be asleep, darling. [*Going into Anya's room.*] Bliss!

[*Enter* YASHA *with a rug and travelling bag.*]

YASHA [*walking delicately across the stage*]: May I come through here?

DUNYASHA: No one would recognize you, Yasha. You have changed abroad.

YASHA: Hm . . . And who are you?

DUNYASHA: When you left here, I was that high . . . [*Shows the height from the floor.*] Dunyasha, Fyodor Kozoyedov's daughter. Don't you remember!

YASHA: Hm . . . My little pickle! [*Looks round and embraces her; she shrieks and drops a saucer.* YASHA *quickly goes out.*]

VARYA [*in the door, in a cross voice*]: What is it?

DUNYASHA [*with tears in her eyes*]: I've broken a saucer . . .

VARYA: That's good luck.

ANYA [*coming out of her room*]: We must warn Mama: Petya is here . . .

VARYA: I told them not to wake him.

ANYA [*pensively*]: Six years ago Father died, a month later my brother Grisha drowned in the river, a lovely boy of seven. Mama couldn't take it, she went off, went off without a backward glance . . . [*Shudders.*] I do understand her, if she only knew it!

[*A pause.*]

And Petya Trofimov was Grisha's tutor, he might remind her . . .

[*Enter* FIRS *in jacket and white waistcoat.*]

FIRS [*going to the coffee-pot, in a worried tone*]: The mistress will take her coffee here . . . [*Puts on white gloves.*] Is the coffee ready? [*To Dunyasha, sternly*] You! What about the cream?

DUNYASHA: Oh, my God! [*Goes out quickly.*]

FIRS [*fussing round the coffee-pot*]: Oh you booby . . . [*Mutters to himself*] They've come home from Paris . . . And the master used to go to Paris . . . by carriage and horses . . . [*Laughs.*]

VARYA: Firs, what is it?

FIRS: Please? [*Joyfully*] My lady has come! I've waited a long time! Now I can die . . . [*Cries for joy.*]

[*Enter* LYUBOV ANDREYEVNA, GAYEV, LOPAKHIN *and* SIMEONOV-PISHCHIK; SIMEONOV-PISHCHIK *is wearing a long, waisted coat of fine cloth and wide oriental-style trousers.* GAYEV *as he comes in moves his arms and trunk as if he is playing billiards.*]

LYUBOV ANDREYEVNA: How does one play? Let me try and remember . . . Yellow into the corner pocket! Double it into the middle!

GAYEV: I'm aiming for the corner! Sister, we once slept in this very room, and now I'm fifty-one, strange as that may seem . . .

LOPAKHIN: Yes, time passes.

GAYEV: What?

LOPAKHIN: I said time passes.

GAYEV: It smells of patchouli in here.

ANYA: I'm going to sleep. Good night, Mama. [*Kisses her mother.*]

LYUBOV ANDREYEVNA: My darling child. [*Kisses her hands.*] Are you glad you're home? I just can't get over it.

ANYA: Good night, Uncle.

GAYEV [*kissing her face and hands*]: Bless you. How like your mother you are. [*To his sister*] You were just like that at her age, Lyuba.

[ANYA *gives her hand to Lopakhin and Pishchik, goes out and shuts the door behind her.*]

LYUBOV ANDREYEVNA: She's quite worn out.

PISHCHIK: It was a long journey.

VARYA [to Lopakhin and Pishchik]: So, gentlemen. It's after two, time to go.

LYUBOV ANDREYEVNA [laughing]: You're still just the same, Varya. [Pulls Varya to her and kisses her.] I'll just have my coffee, then we'll all go.

[FIRS puts a cushion under her legs.]

Thank you, dear Firs. I've got the habit of coffee. I drink it day and night. Thank you, old thing. [Kisses Firs.]

VARYA: I'll have a look to see if they've brought everything . . . [Goes out.]

LYUBOV ANDREYEVNA: Is it really me sitting here? [Laughs.] I want to jump and wave my arms about. [Covers her face with her hands.] Or am I dreaming! God is my witness, I love my country, I love it dearly, I couldn't look out of the railway carriage, I was crying the whole time. [With tears in her eyes] But I must drink my coffee. Thank you, Firs, thank you, my dear old thing. I'm so glad you're still alive.

FIRS: The day before yesterday.

GAYEV: He doesn't hear well.

LOPAKHIN: It'll soon be five and I've got to leave right away for Kharkov. I'm really upset! I wanted to look at you and talk . . . You're still just as splendid.

PISHCHIK [breathing heavily]: You look even lovelier . . . That Paris frock . . . I can't control myself . . .

LOPAKHIN: Your brother, Leonid Andreich there, says I'm a lout, a kulak, but I really don't care. Let him. I would only like you to trust me as you used to, I want your amazing, touching eyes to look on me as they used to. Merciful God! My father was a serf of your grandfather's and your father's, but you, yes you, once did so much for me that I've forgotten everything and love you like one of my own family . . . more than one of my family.

LYUBOV ANDREYEVNA: I can't sit, I'm incapable of it . . . [Jumps up and walks about overcome with emotion.] I can't get over this joy

. . . Laugh at me, I'm silly . . . My dear little cupboard . . . [*Kisses the cupboard.*] My little table.

GAYEV: Nyanya died while you were away.

LYUBOV ANDREYEVNA [*sitting down and drinking her coffee*]: Yes, God rest her soul. They wrote to me.

GAYEV: And Anastasy is dead. Petrushka Kosoy has left me and is now working in town for the police chief. [*Takes a box of sweets out of his pocket and puts one in his mouth.*]

PISHCHIK: My daughter Dashenka . . . sends you her regards . . .

LOPAKHIN: I want to say something very nice and cheerful to you. [*Looking at his watch.*] I'll go now, there's no time to talk . . . well, I'll do it in two or three words. You already know that your cherry orchard is being sold to pay the debts, the sale is fixed for the twenty-second of August, but don't worry, my dear lady, there's a way out . . . Here is my plan. Listen! Your property is only twenty versts from the town, the railway has come near, and if you break up the cherry orchard and the land along the river into building plots and then lease them out for dachas, you'll have at least twenty-five thousand a year income.³

GAYEV: Excuse me, what rubbish!

LYUBOV ANDREYEVNA: I don't quite understand you, Yermolay Alekseich.

LOPAKHIN: You'll get at least twenty-five roubles a year from holiday visitors for a *desyatina* of land, and if you advertise now, I'll bet you anything, by autumn you won't have a scrap left over, they'll take it all up. In a word, congratulations, you are rescued. The situation is wonderful here, the river's deep. Only of course it needs tidying and cleaning up . . . say, for example, pull down all the old buildings like this house, which isn't good for anything now, cut down the old cherry orchard . . .

LYUBOV ANDREYEVNA: Cut it down? My dear man, forgive me, you don't understand anything. If there is anything interesting, even remarkable, in the whole of this province, it's our cherry orchard.

LOPAKHIN: The only thing remarkable about the orchard is that it's very big. The trees bear fruit every other year, and you can't do anything with the fruit, no one buys it.

GAYEV: And the orchard is mentioned in the *Encyclopaedia*.

LOPAKHIN [*looking at his watch*]: If we don't come up with anything and actually do something, on the twenty-second of August both the cherry orchard and the whole estate will be sold at auction. Make your decision! There's no other solution, I swear to you. Absolutely none.

FIRS: In the old days, forty or fifty years ago, they dried the cherries, soaked them, marinaded them, made jam, and they used to . . .

GAYEV: Be quiet, Firs.

FIRS: And they used to send the dried cherries, whole wagonloads of them, to Moscow and Kharkov. That brought in money! And the dried cherries then were soft, juicy, sweet, perfumed . . . They knew a recipe then . . .

LYUBOV ANDREYEVNA: And where's that recipe now?

FIRS: They forgot it. No one can remember it.

PISHCHIK [*to Lyubov Andreyevna*]: What did you do in Paris? How was it? Did you eat frogs?

LYUBOV ANDREYEVNA: I ate crocodile.

PISHCHIK: Imagine that . . .

LOPAKHIN: Till now there were just masters and muzhiks in the country, but now summer visitors have appeared as well. Every town, even the very smallest, is now surrounded by dachas. And one can say that in twenty years' time there'll be an extraordinary increase of summer visitors. Now they just drink tea on the veranda but it may well be that they'll work their single *desyatina* of land, and then your cherry orchard will become happy, wealthy, splendid . . .

GAYEV [*becoming indignant*]: What nonsense!

[*Enter* VARYA *and* YASHA.]

VARYA: Mama, there are two telegrams for you. [*Takes out a key and noisily unlocks the old cupboard.*] Here they are.

LYUBOV ANDREYEVNA: They're from Paris. [*Tears up the telegrams without having read them.*] I've finished with Paris . . .

GAYEV: Do you know, Lyuba, how old that cupboard is? A week

ago I opened the bottom drawer and looked in, and there are numbers burnt into the wood there. The cupboard was made exactly one hundred years ago. Can you imagine? Eh? We could celebrate its jubilee. An inanimate object, but still, for all that, a book cupboard.

PISHCHIK [*in astonishment*]: A hundred years . . . Imagine that! . . .

GAYEV: Yes . . . It is something . . . [*Feeling the cupboard.*] Dear, revered cupboard! I salute your existence which for more than a hundred years now has been directed towards the shining ideals of good and justice; your silent call to fruitful labour has not faltered in the course of a hundred years, preserving [*with tears in his eyes*] in generations of our family a good spirit, faith in a better future and fostering in us ideals of the good and of social consciousness.

[*A pause.*]

LOPAKHIN: Yes . . .

LYUBOV ANDREYEVNA: You're still just the same, Lyonya.

GAYEV [*a little embarrassed*]: Off the ball, right, into the corner! I'm aiming for the middle pocket!

LOPAKHIN [*looking at his watch*]: Well, I must be going.

YASHA [*giving medicines to Lyubov Andreyevna*]: Perhaps you should take your pills now . . .

PISHCHIK: You mustn't take medicines, dear lady . . . they do no harm or good . . . Give them here . . . Madame. [*Takes the pills, pours them out onto the palm of his hand, blows on them, puts them in his mouth and washes them down with some kvass.*] Like that!

LYUBOV ANDREYEVNA [*alarmedly*]: You've gone mad!

PISHCHIK: I took all the pills.

LOPAKHIN: Greedy.

[*Everyone laughs.*]

FIRS: When the gentleman was here in Holy Week, he ate half a bucket of gherkins . . . [*Mumbles his words.*]

LYUBOV ANDREYEVNA: What's he saying?

VARYA: He's been mumbling like that for the last three years. We've got used to it.

YASHA: He's getting senile.

[CHARLOTTA IVANOVNA *crosses the stage; wearing a white dress, very thin and tightly corseted, with a lorgnette at her waist.*]

LOPAKHIN: I'm sorry, Charlotta Ivanovna, I haven't yet managed to greet you. [*Tries to kiss her hand.*]

CHARLOTTA [*taking away her hand*]: If I let you kiss my hand, you'll want the elbow next, then the shoulder . . .

LOPAKHIN: It's not my lucky day.

[*Everyone laughs.*]

Charlotta Ivanovna, do a trick!

LYUBOV ANDREYEVNA: Charlotta, do a trick!

CHARLOTTA: Not now. I want to go to sleep. [*Exit.*]

LOPAKHIN: We'll see each other in three weeks. [*Kisses Lyubov Andreyevna's hand.*] Goodbye for now. I must go. [*To Gayev*] Goodbye. [*Kisses Pishchik.*] Goodbye. [*Shakes hands with Varya, then with Firs and Yasha.*] I don't want to go. [*To Lyubov Andreyevna*] If you make up your mind about the dachas and decide, let me know, I'll borrow fifty thousand. Think about it seriously.

VARYA [*angrily*]: Go off now!

LOPAKHIN: I'm going, I'm going . . . [*Leaves.*]

GAYEV: What a lout. Oh, *pardon* . . . Varya's going to marry him, he's Varya's intended.

VARYA: You're saying more than you should, Uncle.

LYUBOV ANDREYEVNA: Well, Varya, I'll be very pleased. He's a good man.

PISHCHIK: A man, if truth be told . . . a very worthy man . . . And my Dashenka . . . also says that . . . she says all kinds of things. [*Emits a snore but wakes up immediately.*] Anyway, dear lady, can you lend me . . . two hundred and forty roubles . . . tomorrow I have to pay my mortgage interest . . .

VARYA [*alarmed*]: We just haven't got it!

LYUBOV ANDREYEVNA: I really haven't got anything.

PISHCHIK: I'll find something. [*Laughs.*] I never lose hope. I thought everything was lost, I was ruined, and – there, the railway crossed my land and . . . they paid me. And here, see, something else will happen, if not today then tomorrow . . . Dashenka will win two hundred thousand . . . She has a lottery ticket.

LYUBOV ANDREYEVNA: We've had our coffee, we can go to bed.

FIRS [*brushing Gayev down, reprovingly*]: You've again put on the wrong trousers. What am I to do with you!

VARYA [*quietly*]: Anya is asleep. [*Quietly opens the window.*] The sun's already risen, it isn't cold. Look, Mama: what beautiful trees! My God, the air! The starlings are singing!

GAYEV [*opening another window*]: The orchard is all white. You haven't forgotten, Lyuba? That avenue goes straight, straight as a ribbon, it's all shining on moonlit nights. Do you remember? You haven't forgotten?

LYUBOV ANDREYEVNA [*looking at the orchard through the window*]: Oh my childhood, my innocence! I used to sleep in this nursery, I used to look at the orchard from here, happiness woke up with me every morning, and the orchard was just like this, nothing has changed. [*Laughs with joy.*] All white, all white! Oh my orchard! After the dark and overcast autumn and the cold winter you're young again, full of happiness, the angels in heaven have not forsaken you . . . If only I could take this heavy stone from my breast and shoulders, if I could forget my past!

GAYEV: Yes, and the orchard will be sold to pay off debts, strange though it is.

LYUBOV ANDREYEVNA: Look, our dead mother is walking in the orchard . . . in a white dress! [*Laughs with joy.*] It's her.

GAYEV: Where?

VARYA: Bless you, Mama.

LYUBOV ANDREYEVNA: There's no one, I was seeing things. On

the right there, at the turning to the summer-house, a white tree was bending, like a woman . . .

[*Enter* TROFIMOV *in an old student uniform, wearing glasses.*]

What a wonderful orchard! The white masses of flowers, the blue sky . . .

TROFIMOV: Lyubov Andreyevna!

[*She looks round at him.*]

I'll just greet you and go off right away. [*Kisses her hand warmly.*] I was told to wait till morning but I didn't have the patience . . .

[LYUBOV ANDREYEVNA *looks at him with bewilderment.*]

VARYA [*with tears in her eyes*]: It's Petya Trofimov . . .

TROFIMOV: Petya Trofimov, your Grisha's old tutor . . . Have I changed so much?

[LYUBOV ANDREYEVNA *embraces him and quietly weeps.*]

GAYEV [*embarrassedly*]: That'll do, Lyuba.

VARYA [*crying*]: I told you, Petya, to wait till tomorrow.

LYUBOV ANDREYEVNA: My Grisha . . . my boy . . . Grisha . . . my son . . .

VARYA: What can we do, Mama? It was God's will.

TROFIMOV [*gently, with tears in his eyes*]: There, there . . .

LYUBOV ANDREYEVNA [*crying softly*]: My little boy died, he drowned . . . Why? Why, my friend? [*More quietly*] Anya is sleeping there, and I'm talking loudly . . . I'm making a noise . . . So, Petya? Why've you lost your looks? Become so old?

TROFIMOV: A woman on the train called me a moth-eaten gentleman.

LYUBOV ANDREYEVNA: You were just a boy then, a dear little student, and now your hair is thin and you're wearing glasses. Are you really still a student? [*Goes to the door.*]

TROFIMOV: I suppose I'm going to be a perpetual student.

LYUBOV ANDREYEVNA [*kissing her brother, then Varya*]: Well, go to bed . . . You've aged too, Leonid.

PISHCHIK [*following her*]: So, now to bed . . . Oh, this gout of mine. I'll stay here with you . . . Lyubov Andreyevna, my dear, if I could have, tomorrow morning . . . two hundred and forty roubles . . .

GAYEV: He only thinks of himself.

PISHCHIK: Two hundred and forty roubles . . . to pay my mortgage interest.

LYUBOV ANDREYEVNA: I have no money, my love.

PISHCHIK: I'll pay it back, dear . . . It's a tiny amount . . .

LYUBOV ANDREYEVNA: Very well, Leonid will give it to you . . . Give it to him, Leonid.

GAYEV: Me give anything? No hope.

LYUBOV ANDREYEVNA: Don't worry, give it to him . . . He needs it . . . He'll pay it back.

[*Exeunt* LYUBOV ANDREYEVNA, TROFIMOV, PISHCHIK *and* FIRS. GAYEV, VARYA *and* YASHA *remain.*]

GAYEV: My sister still hasn't lost the habit of being extravagant. [*To Yasha*] Be a good chap and move away a little, you smell of chicken.

YASHA [*grinning*]: You haven't changed, Leonid Andreich.

GAYEV: What? [*To Varya*] What did he say?

VARYA [*to Yasha*]: Your mother has come from the village, she's been sitting since yesterday in the servants' hall, she wants to see you . . .

YASHA: Good luck to her!

VARYA: Oh, aren't you ashamed of yourself!

YASHA: That's just what I need. She could come tomorrow. [*Goes out.*]

VARYA: Mamochka is just the same, she hasn't changed at all. If it was up to her she would give it all away.

GAYEV: Yes . . .

[*A pause.*]

If a great many remedies are prescribed for some disease, that means the disease is incurable. I think, I rack my brain, I have many remedies, a very great many, and that means, in actual fact, not a single one. It would be good to inherit from somebody, it would be good to marry our Anya to a very rich man, it would be good to go to Yaroslavl and try our luck with our aunt, the Countess. Our aunt is a very, very rich woman.

VARYA [*weeping*]: If God would come to our help!

GAYEV: Stop crying. Our aunt is very rich but she doesn't like us. In the first place, my sister married a lawyer, not a nobleman . . .

[ANYA *appears in the doorway*.]

She married a commoner and it can't be said her behaviour has been very virtuous. She is good, kind, a fine person, I love her very much, but however much you make allowances for mitigating circumstances, you have to admit she's still an immoral woman. You can feel it in her slightest movement.

VARYA [*in a whisper*]: Anya is standing at the door.

GAYEV: What?

[*A pause*.]

Funny, I've got something in my right eye . . . I can't see very well. And on Thursday, when I was at the district court . . .

[*Enter* ANYA.]

VARYA: Why aren't you asleep, Anya?

ANYA: I can't sleep. I'm not sleepy.

GAYEV: My darling. [*Kisses Anya's face and hands*.] My child . . . [*With tears in his eyes*] You aren't my niece, you're my angel, you're everything to me. Believe me, believe . . .

ANYA: I believe you, Uncle. Everyone loves you, respects you . . . but dear Uncle, you mustn't say things, just keep your mouth shut. What did you say just now about my Mama, about your sister? Why did you say that?

GAYEV: Yes, yes ... [*Hides his face with her hand.*] Really, it's terrible! My God! God have mercy on me! And I made that speech today in front of the cupboard ... so stupid! And it was only when I'd finished that I understood it was stupid.

VARYA: It's true, dear Uncle, you should keep your mouth shut. Just be quiet, that's all.

ANYA: If you keep your mouth shut, you'll feel calmer.

GAYEV: I won't speak. [*Kisses Anya's and Varya's hands.*] I won't speak. Only about business. On Thursday I was at the district court, well, people came, we began to talk of this and that, a whole load of things, and it seems it might be possible to arrange a loan against promissory notes so that the bank can be paid the interest.

VARYA: If only God could come to our help!

GAYEV: I'll go on Tuesday, I'll talk to them again. [*To Varya*] Stop crying. [*To Anya*] Your Mama will talk to Lopakhin; he of course won't refuse her ... And when you've had a rest, you can go to Yaroslavl to the Countess, your great-aunt. In that way we'll act on three fronts – and our business will be settled. We'll pay off the interest, I'm sure of that ... [*Puts a sweet into his mouth.*] I swear on my honour, on whatever you like, the estate won't be sold! [*Excitedly*] I swear by my happiness! Here's my hand, you can call me a piece of trash, a man without honour, if I let things go to auction! I swear by my whole being!

ANYA [*her peace of mind has come back, she is happy*]: How good are you, Uncle, how clever! [*Embraces her uncle.*] I won't worry now! I won't worry! I'm happy!

[*Enter* FIRS.]

FIRS [*reproachfully*]: Leonid Andreich, have you no fear of God! When are you going to bed?

GAYEV: Right away. You go, Firs. If I have to, I'll undress by myself. Well, children, bedtime ... We'll go over the details tomorrow, but go to bed now. [*Kisses Anya and Varya.*] I am a man of the Eighties[4] . . . People don't speak well of that period, but all the same I can say that in my time I've had a lot of attacks for my convictions. The muzhik has good reason to love me. You have to know the muzhik! You have to know how . . .

ANYA: You're off again, Uncle!

VARYA: Uncle dear, be quiet.

FIRS [*crossly*]: Leonid Andreich!

GAYEV: I'm going, I'm going . . . Go to bed. Off two cushions into the middle! Straight in the pocket without touching the sides . . . [*Goes out,* FIRS *hobbles after him.*]

ANYA: I'm calm now. I don't want to go to Yaroslavl, I don't like Great-aunt, but all the same I'm calm. Thanks to Uncle. [*Sits down.*]

VARYA: I must get some sleep. I'm going to bed. We had a problem here when you were away. As you know, there are only old servants living in the old quarters: Yefimyushka, Polya, Yevstig-ney, and Karp too. They started letting some vagrants spend the night there – I didn't say anything. Only then I heard they spread a rumour I'd said to give them only dried peas to eat. Out of stinginess, you see . . . And that was all Yevstigney . . . Very well, I thought. If it's like that, I thought, wait a moment. I call in Yevstigney . . . [*Yawns.*] He comes . . . Yevstigney, I say, how can you . . . what a fool you are . . . [*Looking at Anya.*] Anechka! . . .

[*A pause.*]

She's gone to sleep! . . . [*Takes Anya by the arm.*] Come to your little bed . . . Come on! . . . [*Leads her.*] My little girl went to sleep! Come on . . .

[*They go off. A shepherd is playing his pipe in the distance, outside the garden.* TROFIMOV *walks across the stage and, seeing Varya and Anya, stops.*]

VARYA: Shh . . . She's asleep . . . asleep . . . Come, darling.

ANYA [*softly, half-asleep*]: I'm so tired . . . I can still hear the harness bells jingling . . . Dear . . . Uncle . . . and Mama and Uncle . . .

VARYA: Come on, darling, come . . . [*They go out into Anya's room.*]

TROFIMOV [*overcome by emotion*]: My sun! My springtime!

[*Curtain.*]

Act Two

The countryside. A little old wayside shrine, crooked and long abandoned, beside it a well, big stones, clearly tombstones, and an old bench. The road to Gayev's estate can be seen. At one side are the tall, dark shapes of poplars: that is where the cherry orchard begins. In the distance is a line of telegraph poles and far off on the horizon the blur of a big town, only visible in very fine, clear weather. It is soon going to be sunset.

[CHARLOTTA, YASHA *and* DUNYASHA *are sitting on the bench;* YEPIKHODOV *is standing by them and playing the guitar; they are all sitting thinking.* CHARLOTTA *is wearing an old peak-cap; she has taken a gun from her shoulder and is fixing a buckle on its strap.*]

CHARLOTTA [*musing*]: I have no proper passport, I don't know how old I am, so I always think I'm young. When I was a little girl my father and mother travelled round fairs and gave performances, very good ones. And I used to do the *salto mortale*[1] and all kinds of tricks. And when Papa and Mama died, a German lady took me in and began to teach me. Well, I grew up, then I became a governess. But where I'm from and who I am – I don't know . . . Who were my parents, were they married . . . I don't know. [*Takes a gherkin out of her pocket and eats it.*] I don't know anything.

[*A pause.*]

I so want to talk but there's no one . . . I haven't got anybody.

YEPIKHODOV [*playing the guitar and singing*]: 'What to me are the world and its roar, what to me are friend and foe . . .' How pleasant is it to play the mandolin!

DUNYASHA: That's a guitar, not a mandolin. [*Looks in a pocket mirror and powders her face.*]

YEPIKHODOV: For a madman in love it's a mandolin . . . [*Sings*] 'If my heart is warmed by a love that is shared . . .'

[YASHA *joins in.*]

CHARLOTTA: These people sing horribly . . . pfui! Like jackals.

DUNYASHA [*to Yasha*]: You are lucky to go abroad.

YASHA: Yes, of course. I have to agree with you. [*Yawns, then lights a cigar.*]

YEPIKHODOV: Naturally. Abroad everything has been fully developed for a long time.

YASHA: Absolutely.

YEPIKHODOV: I am a man of culture, I read a number of remarkable books, but I just can't understand the direction in which I actually want to go, whether I should live or shoot myself, honestly, but all the same I always carry a revolver on me. Here it is . . . [*Shows the revolver.*]

CHARLOTTA: I've finished. Now I'm off. [*Shoulders her gun.*] Yepikhodov, you're a very clever man and a very frightening one; women must love you madly. Brrr! [*Begins to walk off.*] These clever ones are all so stupid, there's no one for me to talk to . . . I'm all alone, alone, I have nobody and . . . who I am, what I am here for, no one knows . . . [*Walks off slowly.*]

YEPIKHODOV: Speaking honestly, without touching on other subjects, I must state regarding myself, among other things, that fate shows me no pity, like a tempest with a small boat. If, for the sake of argument, I am wrong, then why this morning do I wake up, for example, and on my chest is a spider of horrendous size . . . As big as that . . . [*Demonstrates with both hands.*] And again I take some kvass to have a drink, and I look and find in it something exceptionally unpleasing, something like a cockroach.

[*A pause.*]

Have you read Buckle?[2]

[*A pause.*]

Avdotya Fyodorovna, might I trouble you for a couple of words.
DUNYASHA: Speak.
YEPIKHODOV: I would prefer alone with you . . . [*Sighs.*]
DUNYASHA [*embarrassed*]: Very well . . . only first fetch me my little
cape . . . It's by the cupboard . . . it's a bit damp here . . .
YEPIKHODOV: Very well . . . I'll bring it . . . Now I know what I
have to do with my revolver . . .

[*Takes the guitar and goes out playing.*]

YASHA: The Walking Accident! Between you and me, a silly fellow.
[*Yawns.*]
DUNYASHA: I hope to God he doesn't shoot himself.

[*A pause.*]

I've become nervous, I worry all the time. They took me into
service when I was still a little girl, I'm now out of the habit of
the simple life, and I've got white, white hands, like a young
lady's. I've become delicate, so refined, so ladylike, everything
frightens me . . . It's terrible. And if you deceive me, Yasha, I
don't know what my nerves will do.
YASHA [*kissing her*]: My little pickle! Of course, a girl mustn't forget
herself, and there's nothing I dislike more than bad behaviour in
a girl.
DUNYASHA: I love you passionately, you've got education, you can
discuss anything.

[*A pause.*]

YASHA [*yawns*]: Ye-es . . . What I think is this: if a girl loves someone, that means she has no morals.

[*A pause.*]

It's nice to smoke a cigar in the open air . . . [*Listens.*] Someone's coming . . . It's the family . . .

[DUNYASHA *impulsively embraces him.*]

Go home as if you'd gone to the river to have a swim, go by that path, otherwise they'll meet you and think we've been going out together. I can't bear that idea.

DUNYASHA [*coughing quietly*]: I've got a headache from the cigar. [*Goes out.*]

[YASHA *stays and sits by the shrine. Enter* LYUBOV ANDRE-YEVNA, GAYEV *and* LOPAKHIN.]

LOPAKHIN: You have to make a final decision – time won't wait. The question's really straightforward. Do you agree to sell the land for dachas or not? Answer in one word: yes or no. Just the one word!

LYUBOV ANDREYEVNA: Who's been smoking disgusting cigars here . . . [*Sits down.*]

GAYEV: Now they've built the railway it's become so easy. [*Sits down.*] We went into town and had lunch . . . yellow into the middle pocket! I'd have liked to go to the house first and play one game . . .

LYUBOV ANDREYEVNA: You'll have time.

LOPAKHIN: Just the one word! [*Imploringly*] Give me an answer!

GAYEV [*yawning*]: To what?

LYUBOV ANDREYEVNA [*looking in her purse*]: Yesterday there was a lot of money and today there's very little. To economize my poor Varya feeds all of us on milk soup, she gives the old men in the kitchen nothing but dried peas, but I'm somehow spending like a madwoman . . . [*She has dropped her purse and scattered gold coins about.*] Well, there they go . . . [*She is cross.*]

YASHA: Let me, I'll pick them up right away. [*Picks up the coins.*]

LYUBOV ANDREYEVNA: Thank you, Yasha. And why did I go and have lunch . . . Your wretched restaurant with a band, where the tablecloths smell of soap . . . Why drink so much, Lyonya? Why eat so much? Why talk so much? Today in the restaurant again you talked a lot, and always off the mark. About the Seventies, the Decadents. And who to? Talking to waiters about the Decadents!

LOPAKHIN: Yes.

GAYEV [*waving his hand*]: I'm incorrigible, that's clear . . . [*Crossly to Yasha*] Why are you constantly getting under our feet . . .

YASHA [*laughs*]: I can't hear your voice without laughing.

GAYEV [*to his sister*]: It has to be either me or him . . .

LYUBOV ANDREYEVNA: Go away, Yasha, off . . .

YASHA [*giving back Lyubov Andreyevna her purse*]: I'll go right away. [*Can hardly hold back his laughter.*] This minute . . . [*Exit.*]

LOPAKHIN: That rich Deriganov intends to buy your estate. They say he'll come to the auction personally.

LYUBOV ANDREYEVNA: And where did you hear that?

LOPAKHIN: That's what they're saying in town.

GAYEV: Our aunt in Yaroslavl has promised to send something, but when and how much we don't know . . .

LOPAKHIN: How much will she send? A hundred thousand? Two hundred thousand?

LYUBOV ANDREYEVNA: Well . . . Ten or fifteen thousand, at least that will be something.

LOPAKHIN: I'm sorry, I've never yet come across such frivolous people as you, my friends, so unbusinesslike, so peculiar. You're told in plain Russian, your estate is being sold, and you just don't seem to understand.

LYUBOV ANDREYEVNA: What are we to do? Tell us, what?

LOPAKHIN: I tell you every day. Every day I say one and the same thing. You've got to lease out both the cherry orchard and the land for dacha plots, you've got to do that now, as quickly as possible – the auction is upon us! Understand that! Once you've finally made the decision to have dachas, you'll get as much money as you want, and then you're rescued.

LYUBOV ANDREYEVNA: Dachas and summer people – I'm sorry but it's so vulgar.

GAYEV: I quite agree with you.

LOPAKHIN: I'm going to break down in sobs or scream or pass out. I've had enough! You've worn me out! [*To Gayev*] You're an old woman!

GAYEV: What?

LOPAKHIN: Old woman! [*On the point of leaving.*]

LYUBOV ANDREYEVNA [*frightened*]: No, don't go away, stay, my dear. I beg you. Perhaps we'll think of something!

LOPAKHIN: What is there here to think about!

LYUBOV ANDREYEVNA: Don't go, I beg you. I must say it's more cheerful when you're here . . .

[*A pause.*]

I'm waiting for something to happen all the time, as if the house were going to fall down on top of us.

GAYEV [*deep in thought*]: Double it into the corner pocket . . . Cross shot into the centre . . .

LYUBOV ANDREYEVNA: We've sinned very greatly . . .

LOPAKHIN: What are these sins of yours? . . .

GAYEV [*putting a sweet in his mouth*]: They say I've eaten up my entire substance in sweets . . . [*Laughs.*]

LYUBOV ANDREYEVNA: Oh, my sins . . . I always threw money around like a madwoman, and I married a man who only ran up debts. My husband died of champagne – he was a terrible drinker – and I was unlucky enough to fall in love with another man, I went off to live with him, and just at that time – it was the first punishment, a blow to the head – right here in the river . . . my little boy drowned, and I went abroad, went away for good, in order never to come back and see this river . . . I closed my eyes, I fled, out of my mind, and *he* followed me – pitilessly, crudely. I bought a villa near Mentone because *he* fell ill there and for three years I had no rest day or night; the invalid wore me out, my soul dried up. And last year, when the villa was sold to pay my debts, I went off to Paris and there he robbed me, he abandoned me, lived with another woman, I tried to poison myself . . . So stupid, so shaming . . . And suddenly I felt a longing for Russia, for my country, for my little girl . . . [*Wipes away her tears.*] Lord, Lord, be merciful, forgive me my sins! Do not punish me any more! [*Takes a telegram from her pocket.*] I got this today from Paris . . . He asks forgiveness, he begs me to come back . . . [*Tears up the telegram.*] I think there's music somewhere. [*Listens.*]

GAYEV: That's our famous Jewish band. Do you remember, four violins, a flute and a double bass?

LYUBOV ANDREYEVNA: Are they still around? We should get them over somehow, give a dance.

LOPAKHIN [*listening*]: I can't hear anything . . . [*Sings quietly*] 'If you pay them well the Germans'll make a Frenchman of a Russian.' [*Laughs.*] I saw a good play yesterday at the theatre, very funny.

LYUBOV ANDREYEVNA: And very likely there was nothing funny. You shouldn't go to plays but look more often at yourselves. Your lives are all so grey, you say such a lot of unnecessary things.

LOPAKHIN: That's true. One must admit our life is idiotic . . .

[*A pause.*]

My dad was a muzhik, an idiot, he didn't understand anything, he didn't teach me, he only hit me when he was drunk, and always with a stick. In fact I'm just as much of a dolt and an idiot. I learnt nothing, my handwriting is awful, like a pig's, I'm ashamed when other people see it.

LYUBOV ANDREYEVNA: You ought to get married, my friend.

LOPAKHIN: Yes . . . That's true.

LYUBOV ANDREYEVNA: To your Varya. She's a good girl.

LOPAKHIN: Yes.

LYUBOV ANDREYEVNA: She came to me from a simple family, she works all day, but the important thing is she loves you. And you've liked her for a long time.

LOPAKHIN: Why not? I'm not against it . . . She's a good girl.

[*A pause.*]

GAYEV: They're offering me a job at the bank. Six thousand a year
. . . Have you heard?

LYUBOV ANDREYEVNA: You! Sit tight where you are . . .

[*Enter* FIRS; *he has brought an overcoat.*]

FIRS [*to Gayev*]: Please put it on, sir, it's getting damp.

GAYEV [*putting on the coat*]: You get on my nerves, old man.

FIRS: There's no need to . . . You went off in the morning without
telling me. [*Looks him over.*]

LYUBOV ANDREYEVNA: How old you've become, Firs!

FIRS: What is it you want?

LOPAKHIN: She says you've become very old!

FIRS: I've lived a long time. They were looking for a wife for me
when your papa wasn't yet on this earth . . . [*Laughs.*] And when
Emancipation[3] came, I was already first valet. I didn't accept full
freedom then, I stayed with the family . . .

[*A pause.*]

And I remember everyone was glad, but why they were glad they
didn't know themselves.

LOPAKHIN: It used to be a very good life in the old days. At least
they used to flog people.

FIRS [*who hasn't heard*]: Of course. The muzhiks had masters, the
masters had muzhiks, but now everything's all broken up, you
can't make sense of anything.

GAYEV: Be quiet, Firs. Tomorrow I have to go to town. They've
promised to introduce me to a general who may be able to give
me some money on a promissory note.

LOPAKHIN: You won't get it. So don't worry, you won't have to
pay interest.

LYUBOV ANDREYEVNA: He's fantasizing. There's no general.

[*Enter* TROFIMOV, ANYA *and* VARYA.]

GAYEV: And here come our girls.

ANYA: There's Mama.

LYUBOV ANDREYEVNA [*affectionately*]: Come, come . . . My darlings . . . [*Embracing Anya and Varya.*] If you both knew how I love you. Sit down next to me, there.

[*Everyone sits down.*]

LOPAKHIN: Our perpetual student is hanging round the young ladies.

TROFIMOV: None of your business.

LOPAKHIN: He'll soon be fifty but he's still a student.

TROFIMOV: Do stop your silly jokes.

LOPAKHIN: Why are you getting angry, you funny man?

TROFIMOV: Don't you get at me.

LOPAKHIN [*laughing*]: May I ask you what you think of me?

TROFIMOV: This is what I think of you, Yermolay Alekseich: you're a rich man, you'll soon be a millionaire. Just as the cycle of nature requires a predator, gobbling up everything in its path, in the same way you are necessary.

[*Everyone laughs.*]

VARYA: Petya, better tell us about the planets.

LYUBOV ANDREYEVNA: No, let's continue yesterday's conversation.

TROFIMOV: What was that about?

GAYEV: Man's pride.

TROFIMOV: We talked a long time yesterday but didn't come to any conclusion. Man's pride, as you understand it, has something mystical. Perhaps in your own way you're right, but reasoning straightforwardly, without fancy – what ground for pride is there, is there any sense in it, if man is poorly constructed physiologically, if in the huge majority of cases he is coarse, unintelligent, deeply unhappy? You have to stop being pleased with yourself. You must just work.

GAYEV: You'll die just the same.

TROFIMOV: Who knows? And what does it mean — you'll die? Perhaps man has a hundred senses and death eliminates only the five that are known to us, but the other ninety-five remain alive.

LYUBOV ANDREYEVNA: How clever you are, Petya! . . .

LOPAKHIN [*ironically*]: Frightfully clever!

TROFIMOV: Man goes forward, perfecting his skills. Everything that is now beyond his reach will one day become near and comprehensible, only we must work, we must with all our strength help those who are seeking the truth. In Russia as yet we have very few who do work. The huge majority of the intelligentsia I know seek nothing, do nothing and aren't yet capable of hard work. They call themselves intelligentsia, but they're rude to servants,[4] they treat peasants like animals, they are poor students, they read nothing seriously, they don't do a thing, they just talk about science, they understand little about art. They're all serious, they all have stern expressions, they all only talk about what is significant, they talk philosophy, but meanwhile in front of their eyes the workers eat disgusting food, sleep without pillows, thirty or forty to a room, everywhere fleas, stench, damp, immorality . . . And of course all our fine conversations are just to divert our own and others' attention. Show me where we have the crèches, which are talked of so much and so often, where are the reading rooms? They're just written about in novels, in fact they don't exist at all. There's only dirt, smallness of spirit, just Asia . . . I fear and dislike very serious expressions, I'm frightened of serious conversations. Better to be silent!

LOPAKHIN: You know, I get up before five in the morning, I work from morning to evening, well, I'm dealing the whole time with money, my own and others', and I see what people around me are like. You just have to start doing something to understand how few honest, decent people there are. Sometimes, when I can't sleep, I think, 'Lord, thou hast given us huge forests, immense fields, far, far horizons, and living here we ourselves really ought to be giants . . .'

LYUBOV ANDREYEVNA: So you need giants . . . They're only good in fairy tales, otherwise they're frightening.

[*At the back of the stage* YEPIKHODOV *walks by playing his guitar.*]

[*Pensively.*] There goes Yepikhodov . . .

ANYA [*pensively*]: There goes Yepikhodov . . .

GAYEV: The sun has set, my friends.

TROFIMOV: Yes.

GAYEV [*quietly as if reciting*]: O nature, wonderful nature, you shine with an eternal light, lovely and indifferent, you whom we call mother, you combine within yourself being and death, you give life and you destroy . . .

VARYA [*imploringly*]: Uncle!

ANYA: Uncle, you've done it again!

TROFIMOV: Better double the yellow into the middle.

GAYEV: I'll shut up, I'll shut up.

[*They are all sitting lost in thought. Silence. There is only the sound of* FIRS *gently muttering. Suddenly there is a distant noise, as if up in the sky, the sound of a broken string, a dying, sad sound.*]

LYUBOV ANDREYEVNA: What's that?

LOPAKHIN: I don't know. A bucket's fallen somewhere far away in the mines. But it's somewhere very far off.

GAYEV: Perhaps a bird . . . like a heron.

TROFIMOV: Or an owl . . .

LYUBOV ANDREYEVNA [*shivering*]: It was somehow unpleasant.

[*A pause.*]

FIRS: It was the same before the troubles: the owl hooted and the samovar wouldn't stop whistling.

GAYEV: Before what troubles?

FIRS: Before Emancipation, when we were freed.

[*A pause.*]

LYUBOV ANDREYEVNA: Well, my friends, let's go, it's now evening. [*To Anya*] You've tears in your eyes . . . What is it, my little girl? [*Embraces her.*]

ANYA: Just that, Mama. Nothing.

TROFIMOV: Someone's coming.

[*A passer-by appears wearing a shabby white peak-cap and an overcoat; he is a little drunk.*]

PASSER-BY: Excuse my asking, can I go directly through here to the station?

GAYEV: You can. Take this path.

PASSER-BY: I'm extremely grateful to you. [*Coughing.*] It's very fine weather . . . [*Recites*] 'My brother, my suffering brother . . . go range the Volga whose moan . . .'⁵ [*To Varya*] Mademoiselle, may a hungry Russian ask for thirty kopecks . . .

[VARYA *is frightened and cries out.*]

LOPAKHIN [*angrily*]: This is going too far!

LYUBOV ANDREYEVNA [*confused*]: Take this . . . here you are . . . [*Looks in her purse.*] I haven't any silver . . . It doesn't matter, here's a gold coin for you . . .

PASSER-BY: Grateful from the bottom of my heart! [*He goes out.*]

[*Laughter.*]

VARYA [*frightened*]: I want to go . . . I want to go . . . Oh, Mama, at home there's nothing for people to eat and you gave him a gold coin.

LYUBOV ANDREYEVNA: What's to be done with me, I'm a fool!

When we're home I'll give you everything I have. Yermolay Alekseich, lend me some more! . . .

LOPAKHIN: At your command.

LYUBOV ANDREYEVNA: Let's go, my friends, it's time. And, Varya, we've just about fixed up your marriage, congratulations.

VARYA [*with tears in her eyes*]: You mustn't joke about it, Mama.

LOPAKHIN: Intoxicating Okhmeliya, get thee to a nunnery . . .⁶

GAYEV: My hands are trembling; I haven't played billiards for a long time.

LOPAKHIN: Okhmeliya, nymph, remember me in thy orisons!

LYUBOV ANDREYEVNA: Come, friends. It'll soon be time for dinner.

VARYA: He frightened me. My heart's thumping.

LOPAKHIN: I remind you, ladies and gentlemen: on the twenty-second of August the cherry orchard is going to be sold. Think of that! . . . Think of it! . . .

[*All go out except* TROFIMOV *and* ANYA.]

ANYA: We must thank that passer-by, he scared Varya, now we're alone.

TROFIMOV: Varya is frightened we'll go and fall in love with each other and she doesn't leave us alone for days on end. With her narrow mind she can't understand that we are above love. Avoiding things that are petty and illusory, that prevent us being free and happy, there's the goal and the sense of our life. Onward! We are going irresistibly towards a bright star burning there in the distance! Onward! Don't fall back, my friends!

ANYA [*clapping her hands in excitement*]: How well you speak!

[*A pause.*]

It's wonderful here today!

TROFIMOV: Yes, the weather is amazing.

ANYA: What have you done with me, Petya, why don't I love the cherry orchard as I used to? I loved it so dearly, I thought there was no better place on earth than our orchard.

TROFIMOV: All Russia is our orchard. The land is great and beautiful, there are many wonderful places in it.

[*A pause.*]

Just think, Anya: your grandfather, your great-grandfather and all your ancestors were serf-owners who owned living souls, and those human beings must surely be looking at you from every cherry-tree in the orchard, from every leaf, from every trunk, don't you hear their voices . . . The ownership of living souls has formed all of you, those who lived before and those who are living now, so that your mother, you, your uncle, no longer notice that you are living in debt, at others' expense, at the expense of those people whom you don't let in further than your front hall . . . We've got at least two hundred years behind, we have nothing at all yet, no defined relationship to the past, we only talk philosophy, complain of boredom or drink vodka. It's so very clear that to begin to live in the present we must first redeem our past, finish with it, and we can redeem it only by suffering, only by exceptional, ceaseless labour. Understand that, Anya.

ANYA: The house in which we live hasn't been our house for a long time, and I will leave, I give you my word.

TROFIMOV: If you have the household keys, throw them in the well and leave. Be free as the wind.

ANYA [*ecstatically*]: How well you said that!

TROFIMOV: Believe me, Anya, believe me! I'm not yet thirty, I'm young, I am still a student, but I have already been through so much! When winter comes, then I am hungry, sick, anxious, poor as a beggar, and – where hasn't fate driven me, where haven't I been! And all the time, every minute, day and night, my spirit is full of premonitions I can't express. I have a premonition of happiness, Anya, I can already see it . . .

ANYA [*pensively*]: The moon is rising.

[YEPIKHODOV *can be heard playing his guitar, the same melancholy tune as before. The moon rises. Somewhere by the poplars* VARYA *is looking for Anya and is calling,* 'Anya! Where are you?']

TROFIMOV: Yes, the moon is rising.

[*A pause.*]

There it is, happiness, there it comes, nearer and nearer, I can already hear its steps. And if we don't see it, don't recognize it, it's not so terrible. Others will see it!

[VARYA'*s voice:* 'Anya! Where are you?']

Varya again! [*Angrily*] She drives me mad!

ANYA: Well then? Let's go to the river. It's nice there.

TROFIMOV: Let's go.

[*They go out.*]

[VARYA'*s voice:* 'Anya! Anya!']

[*Curtain.*]

Act Three

A drawing-room divided from a ballroom by an arch. A chandelier is lit. A Jewish band is heard playing in the hall, the one mentioned in Act Two. Evening. In the ballroom they are dancing the grand rond. SIMEONOV-PISHCHIK's *voice:* 'Promenade à une paire!' *They come out into the drawing-room: the first couple is* PISHCHIK *and* CHARLOTTA IVANOVNA, *the second* TROFIMOV *and* LYUBOV ANDREYEVNA, *the third* ANYA *with a Post Office official, the fourth* VARYA *with the station-master, etc.* VARYA *is crying gently and wipes her tears as she dances.* DUNYASHA *is in the last couple. They dance through the drawing-room.* PISHCHIK *calls out,* 'Grand rond, balancez!' *and* 'Les cavaliers à genoux et remerciez vos dames.'[1]

[FIRS, *wearing a tail-coat, brings in soda water on a tray.* PISHCHIK *and* TROFIMOV *enter the drawing-room.*]

PISHCHIK: I have high blood-pressure, I've already had two strokes, it's hard for me to dance, but as the saying goes, once you're one of the pack, if you can't bark then you've got to wag your tail. I have the constitution of a horse. My late father, who liked a joke, God rest his soul, used to say of our origins that our ancient line of Simeonov-Pishchiks apparently comes from the horse that Caligula put in the Senate[2] . . . [*Sits down.*] But here's the problem: we've no money! A hungry dog only thinks about meat . . . [*Starts to snore and immediately wakes up.*] In the same way I . . . can only talk about money . . .

TROFIMOV: Your figure really does have something horsy about it.

PISHCHIK: Well . . . the horse is a good animal . . . you can sell a horse . . .

[*A game of billiards can be heard in the next room.* VARYA *appears in the ballroom under the arch.*]

TROFIMOV [*teasing her*]: Madame Lopakhina! Madame Lopakhina! . . .

VARYA [*angrily*]: Moth-eaten gentleman!

TROFIMOV: Yes, I'm a moth-eaten gentleman and proud of it!

VARYA [*after bitter reflection*]: We've hired a band, but what will we pay them with? [*Exit.*]

TROFIMOV [*to Pishchik*]: If the energy you've expended in the course of your whole life on the search for money to pay interest had gone on something else, you could very well have ended up being able to turn the world upside down.

PISHCHIK: Nietzsche[3] . . . the philosopher . . . the greatest, the most famous . . . a man of huge intellect, says in his writings that we have the right to forge banknotes.

TROFIMOV: Have you read Nietzsche?

PISHCHIK: Well . . . Dashenka told me that. And I'm now in a position where all I've got left to do is forge banknotes . . . The day after tomorrow I have to pay three hundred and ten roubles . . . I've already got hold of a hundred and thirty . . . [*Feels in his pockets, anxiously.*] My money's gone! I've lost my money! [*With tears in his eyes*] Where's my money? [*With joy*] Here it is, in the lining . . . I'd even started sweating . . .

[*Enter* LYUBOV ANDREYEVNA *and* CHARLOTTA IVANOVNA.]

LYUBOV ANDREYEVNA [*humming a* lezginka[4]]: Why is Leonid taking so long? What's he doing in town? [*To Dunyasha*] Dunyasha, offer the band some tea . . .

TROFIMOV: Probably the auction didn't take place . . .

LYUBOV ANDREYEVNA: And the band shouldn't have come, and we were wrong to give a dance . . . Well, it doesn't matter . . . [*Sits down and hums softly.*]

CHARLOTTA [*offering Pishchik a pack of cards*]: Here's a pack of cards, think of any one card.

PISHCHIK: I've thought of one.

CHARLOTTA: Now shuffle the pack. Very good. Give it here, my dear Mr Pishchik. *Eins, zwei, drei.*[5] Now look for it, it's in your side pocket . . .

PISHCHIK [*taking the card out of his side pocket*]: The eight of spades, absolutely right! [*In amazement*] Imagine that!

CHARLOTTA [*holding the pack of cards on the palm of her hand, to Trofimov*]: Tell me quickly, what card is on top?

TROFIMOV: What? Well, the queen of spades.

CHARLOTTA: Right! [*To Pishchik*] Well? What card is on top?

PISHCHIK: The ace of hearts.

CHARLOTTA: Right! [*Claps her hands, the pack of cards disappears.*] What lovely weather it is today!

[*She is answered by a mysterious female voice which seems to come from under the floor: 'Oh yes, madam, it's wonderful weather.'*]

You are my beau idéal . . .

[*The voice: 'I too, madam, find you most attractive.'*[6]]

STATION-MASTER [*clapping*]: Bravo, madam ventriloquist!

PISHCHIK [*in amazement*]: Imagine that! Most enchanting Charlotta Ivanovna, I'm simply in love . . .

CHARLOTTA: In love? [*Shrugging her shoulders*] Can you really love? *Guter Mensch, aber schlechter Musikant.*[7]

TROFIMOV [*clapping Pishchik on the shoulder*]: You're a real horse . . .

CHARLOTTA: Pay attention, one more trick. [*Picks up a rug from a chair.*] Here's a very good rug, I want to sell it . . . [*Shakes it out.*] Won't anyone buy it?

PISHCHIK [*in amazement*]: Imagine that!

CHARLOTTA: *Eins, zwei, drei!* [*Lowers the rug and quickly raises it again; ANYA is standing behind the rug; she makes a curtsy, runs to her mother, embraces her and runs back into the ballroom – to general delight.*]

LYUBOV ANDREYEVNA [*clapping*]: Bravo, bravo! . . .

CHARLOTTA: Once more now! *Eins, zwei, drei!* [*Raises the rug; VARYA is standing behind the rug, and bows.*]

PISHCHIK [*in amazement*]: Imagine that!

CHARLOTTA: That's all! [*Throws the rug over Pishchik, makes a curtsey and runs off into the ballroom.*]

PISHCHIK [*running after her*]: Wicked . . . what a woman! What a woman! [*Goes out.*]

LYUBOV ANDREYEVNA: Leonid still isn't here. I don't understand what he's doing in town for so long! Everything there has to be over by now, the estate is sold or else the auction didn't happen, why keep us so long without knowing!

VARYA [*trying to calm her*]: I'm sure Uncle has bought it.

TROFIMOV [*mocking*]: Right.

VARYA: Great-aunt sent him power of attorney so he could buy it in her name with the debt being transferred. She did that for Anya. And I'm sure that with God's help Uncle will have bought it.

LYUBOV ANDREYEVNA: Your old aunt in Yaroslavl sent fifteen thousand to buy the property in her name – she doesn't trust us – but that money wouldn't even be enough to pay the interest. [*Covers her face with her hands.*] Today my fate is being decided, my fate . . .

TROFIMOV [*teasing Varya*]: Madame Lopakhina!

VARYA [*angrily*]: You perpetual student! You've already been expelled twice from university.

LYUBOV ANDREYEVNA: Why are you getting angry, Varya? He's teasing you about Lopakhin, what does it matter? Marry Lopakhin if you want to, he's a good, interesting man. If you don't want to, don't; no one is forcing you, darling . . .

VARYA: I take the matter seriously, Mama, I must tell you that straight. He's a good man, I find him attractive.

LYUBOV ANDREYEVNA: So marry him. I don't understand, why wait!

VARYA: Mama, I can't propose to him myself. For two years now everyone has been talking to me about him, everyone talks, but he's either silent or makes jokes. I understand. He's getting rich, he's tied up with business, he has no time for me. If I had money, just a little, even a hundred roubles, I'd give it all up, I'd go off far away. I'd go into a convent.

TROFIMOV: Splendid!

VARYA [*to Trofimov*]: A student ought to be intelligent! [*In a gentle voice and tearfully*] How ugly you've become, Petya, how old! [*To Lyubov Andreyevna, no longer crying*] Only I can't stand it, Mama, unless I have something to do. I have to be doing something every minute.

[*Enter* YASHA.]

YASHA [*barely able to hold back his laughter*]: Yepikhodov has broken a billiard cue! . . . [*Goes out.*]

VARYA: Why is Yepikhodov here? Who let him play billiards? I don't understand these people . . . [*Goes out.*]

LYUBOV ANDREYEVNA: Don't tease her, Petya, you can see that she's upset as it is.

TROFIMOV: She's too eager, she meddles in other people's business. All summer she gave me and Anya no peace, she was afraid we would have a romance. What's it to do with her? What's more, there wasn't a sign from me of any such thing, I have nothing to do with any such vulgarity. We are above love!

LYUBOV ANDREYEVNA: And I suppose I must be below love. [*Very anxious*] Why hasn't Leonid come? If I could just know: is the estate sold or not? I find such a disaster so incredible that I somehow don't even know what to think, I'm getting confused . . . I might shriek out loud at any moment . . . I might do something stupid. Save me, Petya. Say something, say something . . .

TROFIMOV: Isn't it all the same whether the estate has been sold today or not? It's long been over, there's no turning back, the path's got overgrown. Calm down, my dear. You mustn't deceive yourself, for once in your life you must look the truth straight in the eye.

LYUBOV ANDREYEVNA: What truth? You can see where truth is and where falsehood is, but I have really lost my sight, I can't see anything. You're boldly solving all the important questions, but tell me, my dear, isn't that because you are young, because you haven't had time to suffer as a result of a single one of your questions? You look ahead boldly, and isn't that because you don't see and don't expect anything terrifying, as life is still hidden from your young eyes? You're bolder, more honest, you have greater depth than any of us, but just think, be generous just with the tip of a finger, spare me. After all I was born here, here lived my father and mother, my grandfather, I love this house, I can't understand my life without the cherry orchard, and if it's now so necessary to sell, then sell me along with the orchard . . . [*Embraces Trofimov, kisses him on the forehead.*] And my son was drowned here . . . [*Weeps.*] You good, kind man, have pity for me.

TROFIMOV: You know I sympathize with you with all my soul.

LYUBOV ANDREYEVNA: But you must say it in other words, other words . . . [*Takes out her handkerchief, a telegram falls on the floor.*] You can't imagine how heavy my heart is today. I find it noisy here, my spirit shudders at every sound, I shudder all over, but I can't go to my room, I'm frightened alone in the silence. Don't condemn me, Petya . . . I love you like one of my family. I would gladly let Anya marry you, I swear it to you, only you must study, my dear, you must finish your degree. You don't do anything, you're just tossed from place to place by fate, it's so strange . . . Isn't that the truth? Isn't it? And you must do something about your beard so it somehow grows . . . [*Laughs.*] You are a funny man!

TROFIMOV [*picking up the telegram*]: I don't want to be good-looking.

LYUBOV ANDREYEVNA: The telegram is from Paris. I get one every day. Yesterday and today. That wild man is ill again, again there's something wrong with him . . . He asks my forgiveness, begs me to come, and really I ought to travel to Paris, to be near him. You look stern, Petya, but what can I do, my dear, what can I do, he is ill, lonely, unhappy, and who is there to look after him, to keep him out of mischief, to give him his medicine on time? And why conceal things or say nothing, I love him, that's obvious. I love him, love him . . . It's a stone round my neck, I'm going down with it to the bottom, but I love this stone and I can't live without it. [*Shakes Trofimov's hand.*] Petya, don't think ill of me, don't say anything to me, don't say anything.

TROFIMOV [*with tears in his eyes*]: Forgive my frankness, for God's sake: but he robbed you!

LYUBOV ANDREYEVNA: No, no, no, you mustn't say that . . . [*Blocks her ears.*]

TROFIMOV: But he's a criminal, you're the only one who doesn't know that! He's a petty criminal, a nothing . . .

LYUBOV ANDREYEVNA [*getting angry, but controlling herself*]: You're twenty-six or twenty-seven, but you're still a second-year schoolboy!

TROFIMOV: Fine!

LYUBOV ANDREYEVNA: You must be a man, at your age you should understand those who love. And you must yourself love . . . you must fall in love! [*Angrily*] Yes, yes! And you're not pure, you just like being clean, you're a ridiculous character, a freak . . .

TROFIMOV [*appalled*]: What is she saying?

LYUBOV ANDREYEVNA: 'I am above love.' You're not above love, but simply a big booby, as our Firs says. At your age, not to have a mistress! . . .

TROFIMOV [*appalled*]: This is dreadful! What is she saying? [*Walks quickly into the ballroom, clutching his head.*] This is dreadful . . . I can't bear it, I'm leaving . . . [*Goes out, but comes back at once.*] It's all over between us! [*Goes out into the hall.*]

LYUBOV ANDREYEVNA [*calling after him*]: Petya, wait a minute! You funny man, I was joking! Petya!

[*There is the sound of someone in the hall running down the stairs and suddenly falling down with a crash.* ANYA *and* VARYA *shriek, but immediately laughter is heard.*]

What's happening out there?

[ANYA *runs in.*]

ANYA [*laughing*]: Petya fell down the stairs! [*Runs out.*]

LYUBOV ANDREYEVNA: What a strange man Petya is . . .

[*The* STATION-MASTER *stands in the middle of the ballroom and starts reciting A. Tolstoy's 'The woman who was a sinner'.*[8] *People listen to him but after only a few lines the sounds of a waltz come from the hall and his recitation is interrupted. Everyone dances.* TROFIMOV, ANYA, VARYA *and* LYUBOV ANDREYEVNA *come in from the hall.*]

There, Petya . . . there, pure spirit . . . I ask your forgiveness . . . Let's go and dance . . . [*Dances with Petya.*]

[ANYA *and* VARYA *dance.* FIRS *comes in and places his stick by the side door.* YASHA *too has come in from the drawing-room and is watching the dancing.*]

YASHA: What is it, old man?

FIRS: I don't feel well. In the old days we had generals, barons, admirals dancing at our balls, but now we send out for a Post Office clerk and the station-master, and even they don't come very willingly. I somehow feel weaker. The late master, the grandfather, used to treat everyone with sealing wax, for every illness. I've been taking sealing wax every day for twenty years, and more; perhaps that's why I'm still alive.

YASHA: I've had enough of you, old man. [*Yawning.*] The quicker you drop dead . . .

FIRS: You . . . big booby! [*Mumbles.*]

[TROFIMOV *and* LYUBOV ANDREYEVNA *are dancing in the ballroom, then in the drawing-room.*]

LYUBOV ANDREYEVNA: *Merci.* I'm going to sit down a moment . . . [*Sits down.*] I'm tired.

[*Enter* ANYA.]

ANYA [*agitatedly*]: Just now in the kitchen some man was saying that the cherry orchard was sold today.

LYUBOV ANDREYEVNA: Who to?

ANYA: He didn't say who to. He's left. [*Dances with Trofimov, both go out into the ballroom.*]

YASHA: It was just some old man drivelling. No one from here.

FIRS: And there's still no Leonid Andreich, he hasn't come. He's wearing his light autumn coat, he's going to catch a chill. Oh, young people!

LYUBOV ANDREYEVNA: I'm going to die, right now. Yasha, go and find out who it's been sold to.

YASHA: But the old man went off a long time ago. [*Laughs.*]

LYUBOV ANDREYEVNA [*with slight irritation*]: Well, what are you laughing at? What do you find to make you cheerful?

YASHA: It's Yepikhodov, he's very funny. Not a serious person. The Walking Accident!

LYUBOV ANDREYEVNA: Firs, if they sell the estate, where will you go?

FIRS: I'll go where you tell me to.

LYUBOV ANDREYEVNA: Why are you looking like that? Are you unwell? You know, you should go to bed . . .

FIRS: Yes . . . [*With a wry smile*] I'll go to bed, but without me here who will serve, who will look after things? There's just the one me for the whole house.

YASHA [*to Lyubov Andreyevna*]: Lyubov Andreyevna! May I come to you with a request, please! If you go to Paris again, take me with you, do me the favour. It is positively impossible for me to stay here. [*Looking round, in a low voice*] I don't need to say it, you can see yourself, this is a country without education, a people without morals, and there's the boredom, the food in the kitchen is disgusting, and then that Firs goes round here, mumbling all sorts of words that make no sense. Take me with you, please!

[*Enter* PISHCHIK.]

PISHCHIK: May I ask you . . . for a little waltz, fair one . . . [LYUBOV ANDREYEVNA *goes off with him.*] Enchantress, I'm still going to take a hundred and eighty roubles off you . . . I am . . . [*Dances.*] A hundred and eighty roubles . . .

[*They have moved off into the ballroom.*]

YASHA [*singing softly*]: 'Can you see my soul's agitation . . .'

[*In the ballroom a figure wearing a grey top-hat and checked trousers is waving arms and jumping about; there are shouts of 'Bravo, Charlotta Ivanovna!'*]

DUNYASHA [*stopping to powder her face*]: Miss Anya told me to dance – there are a lot of gentlemen but too few ladies – but the dancing has made me giddy, my heart is beating, and just now the clerk from the Post Office said something that took my breath away.

[*The music dies down.*]

FIRS: What did he say to you?
DUNYASHA: He said, you are like a flower.
YASHA [*yawning*]: What ignorance . . . [*Exit.*]
DUNYASHA: Like a flower . . . I'm such a sensitive girl, I'm terribly fond of tender words.
FIRS: Your head'll be turned.

[*Enter* YEPIKHODOV.]

YEPIKHODOV: Avdotya Fyodorovna, you don't want to see me . . . it's as if I were some kind of insect. [*Sighs.*] Ah, life!
DUNYASHA: What do you want?
YEPIKHODOV: Doubtless, you're perhaps right. [*Sighs.*] But of course if one takes a point of view, you, if I may say so, excuse my frankness, you have completely brought me to a state of mind. I know my fortune, every day I have an accident, and I've long

got accustomed to that so I regard my fate with a smile. You gave me your word and although I . . .

DUNYASHA: Please let's talk later but now leave me in peace. I'm having a reverie now. [*Plays with her fan.*]

YEPIKHODOV: I have an accident every day and if I may say so, I only smile, I even laugh.

[VARYA *comes in from the ballroom.*]

VARYA: You still haven't gone, Semyon? You really are a man with no sense of respect. [*To Dunyasha*] Get out of here, Dunyasha. [*To Yepikhodov*] One moment you're playing billiards and breaking a cue, now you're pacing the drawing-room like a guest.

YEPIKHODOV: If I may say so to you, you can't take it out on me.

VARYA: I'm not taking it out on you, I'm telling you. You do nothing but go about from place to place and you don't get on with your work. We keep an office clerk but I don't know why.

YEPIKHODOV [*offended*]: Whether I work or go about or eat or play billiards are matters to be discussed only by persons of understanding and seniority.

VARYA: You dare say that to me! [*Losing her temper*] You dare? So I have no understanding? Get out of here! This minute!

YEPIKHODOV [*taking fright*]: I must ask you to use nicer expressions.

VARYA [*beside herself*]: Out of here this minute! Out!

[YEPIKHODOV *goes to the door, she follows him.*]

The Walking Accident! Don't set foot in here again! Get out of my sight!

[YEPIKHODOV *has gone out; his voice outside the door: 'I'm going to make a complaint about you.'*]

Ah, are you coming back? [*Takes the stick which Firs has put by the door.*] Come on . . . Come on . . . Come, I'll show you . . .

Ah, are you coming? Coming in? Take that ... [*Brings down the stick at the moment* LOPAKHIN *enters.*]

LOPAKHIN: My humble thanks.

VARYA [*with angry sarcasm*]: I beg your pardon!

LOPAKHIN: Not at all. My humble thanks for the pleasant welcome.

VARYA: It's not worth the thanks. [*Walks away, then looks round and asks gently*] Did I hurt you?

LOPAKHIN: No, it's nothing. However, a huge bump'll come up.

[*Voices in the ballroom: 'Lopakhin has come! Yermolay Alekseich!'*]

PISHCHIK: My eyes have seen, my ears have heard ... [*He and* LOPAKHIN *kiss.*] There's a little smell of brandy about you, my dear fellow, friend of my heart. And we're having a good time here too.

[*Enter* LYUBOV ANDREYEVNA.]

LYUBOV ANDREYEVNA: Is that you, Yermolay Alekseich? Why have you been so long? Where's Leonid?

LOPAKHIN: Leonid Andreich came with me, he's coming ...

LYUBOV ANDREYEVNA [*getting agitated*]: Well, what happened? Was there an auction? Tell us!

LOPAKHIN [*with embarrassment, afraid of showing his happiness*]: The auction ended towards four o'clock ... We were late for the train, we had to wait till half past nine. [*With a heavy sigh*] Ouf! My head is going round a bit ...

[*Enter* GAYEV; *in his right hand are parcels, with his left he is wiping away tears.*]

LYUBOV ANDREYEVNA: Lyonya, what happened? Well, Lyonya? [*Impatiently, with tears in her eyes*] Quickly, for God's sake ...

GAYEV [*doesn't answer her, only waves his hand; weeping, to Firs*]: Take them ... I've got some anchovies and Kerch herrings ... I haven't had anything to eat today ... I've been through so much!

[*The door to the billiard-room is open; the click of balls is heard, and* YASHA's *voice, 'Seven and eighteen.' Gayev's expression changes, he is no longer crying.*]

I'm terribly tired. Firs, get me a change of clothes. [*Crosses the ballroom to his own room followed by* FIRS.]

PISHCHIK: What happened at the auction? Tell us!

LYUBOV ANDREYEVNA: Is the cherry orchard sold?

LOPAKHIN: It's sold.

LYUBOV ANDREYEVNA: Who bought it?

LOPAKHIN: I did.

[*A pause.* LYUBOV ANDREYEVNA *is overwhelmed; she would have fallen if she were not standing next to an armchair and table.* VARYA *takes the keys off her belt, throws them on the floor in the middle of the drawing-room and goes out.*]

I bought it! Wait a moment, my friends, if you please, my head is going round, I can't speak . . . [*Laughs.*] We arrived at the auction, Deriganov was already there. Leonid Andreich only had fifteen thousand but Deriganov put in thirty on top of the mortgage. I see how things are, so I take him on, I put in forty. He bid forty-five. I bid fifty-five. So he's going up in fives and I in tens . . . Well, it came to an end. I gave ninety over and above the mortgage, I got it. The cherry orchard is now mine! Mine! [*Laughs loudly.*] My God, Lord above, the cherry orchard is mine! Tell me I'm drunk, out of my mind, that all this is my imagination . . . [*Stamps his feet.*] Don't laugh at me! If only my father and grandfather could rise from their graves and see all that has come to pass, see their Yermolay, their beaten, barely literate Yermolay, who used to run about in winter barefoot, see that same Yermolay buy the estate, the fairest thing on earth. I have bought the estate where my grandfather and father were slaves, where they weren't even allowed into the kitchen. I am asleep, I'm only dreaming this, it's only illusion . . . It's the fruit of your imagination, shrouded in a mist of uncertainty . . . [*Picks up the keys, with a tender smile.*] She threw down the keys to show that she's no longer the mistress here ... [*Jiggles the keys.*] Well, it doesn't matter.

[*The sound of the band tuning up.*]

Hey, band, play, I want to listen to you! Everyone come and watch Yermolay Lopakhin bringing the axe to the cherry orchard and the trees falling to the ground! We'll build the dachas, and our grandchildren and great-grandchildren will see a new life here ... Band, play!

[*The band plays.* LYUBOV ANDREYEVNA *has fallen into a chair and is weeping bitterly.*]

[*Reproachfully*] Why, why didn't you listen to me? My poor, good friend, you won't get it back. [*In tears*] Oh, if only all this could quickly pass, if only our incoherent, unhappy life could somehow be transformed.

PISHCHIK [*taking him by the arm, in a low voice*]: She's crying. Let's go into the ballroom, let her be on her own ... Let's go ... [*Takes him by the arm and leads him into the ballroom.*]

LOPAKHIN: What's going on? Band, play up! Everything is going to be as I want it! [*With irony*] Here comes the new squire, the owner of the cherry orchard! [*Accidentally bumps into a small table and almost upsets a candelabrum.*] I can pay for everything! [*He and* PISHCHIK *go out.*]

[*In the ballroom and drawing-room there is no one apart from* LYUBOV ANDREYEVNA, *who is sitting all huddled up, crying bitterly. The band is playing softly.* ANYA *and* TROFIMOV *hurry in.* ANYA *goes up to her mother and kneels before her.* TROFIMOV *stays by the entrance to the ballroom.*]

ANYA: Mama! ... Mama, are you crying? My darling, kind, good Mama, my beautiful Mama, I love you, I bless you. The cherry orchard is sold, it's no longer there, that's the truth, the truth, but don't cry, Mama, you have your life ahead of you, you still have your good, pure spirit . . . Come with me, come away from here, darling, come! . . . We will plant a new orchard, more splendid than this one, you will see it, you will understand, and joy, a quiet, deep joy, will settle on your spirit like the sun in the evening, and Mama, you will smile! Come, darling! Come! . . .

[*Curtain.*]

Act Four

The set of Act One. There are no curtains on the windows or pictures, a little furniture remains piled up in one corner as if to be sold. The emptiness is palpable. By the entrance door and backstage are piles of suitcases, travelling bundles, etc.

[*On the left a door is open and through it comes the sound of the voices of* ANYA *and* VARYA. LOPAKHIN *is standing, waiting.* YASHA *is holding a tray of small glasses filled with champagne. In the hall* YEPIKHODOV *is tying up a chest. Offstage there is a distance hum. It is the peasants who have come to say goodbye.* GAYEV's *voice: 'Thank you, my men, thank you.'*]

YASHA: The village has come to say goodbye. If you ask me, Yermolay Alekseich, the people mean well but don't understand much.

[*The hum dies down.* LYUBOV ANDREYEVNA *and* GAYEV *come in through the hallway; she isn't crying but she is pale, her face is trembling, she cannot speak.*]

GAYEV: You gave them your purse, Lyuba. You shouldn't have done that! You shouldn't!

LYUBOV ANDREYEVNA: I couldn't stop myself doing it! I just couldn't!

[*Both go out.*]

LOPAKHIN [*through the door after them*]: Have something, please do! A little glass to say goodbye. I didn't have the sense to bring some from town but I found just one bottle at the station. Please!

[*A pause.*]

Well, my friends! Don't you want any? [*Moves away from the door.*] If I'd known I wouldn't have bought it. I'm not going to drink either.

[YASHA *carefully puts the tray on a chair.*]

Yasha, at least you have a drink.

YASHA: To the travellers! Good luck to those who stay behind! [*Drinks.*] This isn't real champagne, I can tell you that.

LOPAKHIN: Eight roubles a bottle.

[*A pause.*]

It's devilish cold in here.

YASHA: They didn't light the stoves today since we're leaving. [*Laughs.*]

LOPAKHIN: What's the matter with you?

YASHA: Pure pleasure.

LOPAKHIN: It's October outside but it's sunny and calm as summer. Good for building. [*Looking at his watch and speaking through the door.*] Ladies and gentlemen, remember you've only got forty-six minutes left before the train! That means we should leave for the station in twenty minutes. Hurry up.

[TROFIMOV *comes in from outside wearing an overcoat.*]

TROFIMOV: I think it's time to go now. The horses have been brought round. Where the devil are my galoshes? They've gone missing. [*Through the door*] Anya, my galoshes aren't here! I can't find them!

LOPAKHIN: And I've got to go to Kharkov. I'll take the same train as you. I'm going to spend the whole winter in Kharkov. I've wasted time with you, I'm fed up with having no work. I can't manage without work, I don't know what to do with my hands; they just hang down oddly as if they were someone else's.

TROFIMOV: We'll go away now and you can take up useful work again.

LOPAKHIN: Have a little glass.

TROFIMOV: I won't.

LOPAKHIN: So now you're off to Moscow?

TROFIMOV: Yes, I'll see them to town and tomorrow I go to Moscow.

LOPAKHIN: Yes . . . Well, I suppose the professors aren't giving their lectures, they're all waiting for you to come!

TROFIMOV: None of your business.

LOPAKHIN: How many years have you been studying at university?

TROFIMOV: Do think of something a little more original. That one's old and feeble. [*Hunts for his galoshes.*] You know, we probably won't meet again, so let me give you one piece of advice as a farewell gift: don't wave your arms about! Get rid of that habit of waving them about. And also this building of dachas, thinking that time will make smallholders out of the dacha people – that sort of thinking, again, is just like waving your arms about . . . All the same, I like you. You have fine, delicate fingers, like an artist's, you have a fine, delicate spirit.

LOPAKHIN [*embracing him*]: Goodbye, old chap. Thank you for everything. If you need it, take some money from me for the journey.

TROFIMOV: Why should I? I don't need it.

LOPAKHIN: But you haven't got any!

TROFIMOV: Yes, I have. Thank you. I got something for a translation. It's here, in my pocket. [*Anxiously*] My galoshes aren't here!

VARYA [*from the other room*]: Take your disgusting things! [*Throws a pair of rubber galoshes out onto the stage.*]

TROFIMOV: Why are you angry, Varya? Hm . . . But these aren't my galoshes!

LOPAKHIN: In the spring I sowed a thousand acres of poppy seed and now I've made forty thousand, net. And when my poppies were in bloom, what a sight it was! Well, I'm telling you I made forty thousand and so I'm offering you a loan because I can. Why turn up your nose at it? I'm a muzhik . . . it's as simple as that.

TROFIMOV: Your father was a muzhik, mine had a chemist's shop, and from that follows precisely nothing.

[LOPAKHIN *takes out his wallet.*]

Put it away, put it away . . . Even if you were to give me two hundred thousand, I wouldn't take it. I am a free man. And everything all of you, rich and poor, hold so high and dear – none of it has the slightest hold over me, it's all just like thistledown floating in the air. I can do without you, I can walk past you, I am strong and proud. Mankind is moving towards the greatest truth, towards the greatest happiness possible on earth, and I am in the front ranks!

LOPAKHIN: Will you get there?

TROFIMOV: I will.

[*A pause.*]

I will get there or I will show others the way there.

[*The distant sound of axe-strokes on a tree.*]

LOPAKHIN: Well, goodbye, old man. It's time to go. We turn up our noses at each other and life goes by regardless. When I work for a long time, tirelessly, then my thoughts are easier and I think I too know why I exist. But, my friend, how many people there are in Russia who exist without knowing why. Well, it doesn't matter, the world goes on working regardless. They say Leonid Andreich has taken a job, he'll be in a bank, six thousand a year . . . Only he won't stick at it, he's very lazy . . .

ANYA [*in the door*]: Mama asks you not to cut down the orchard until she's gone.

TROFIMOV: Really, can anyone be that tactless . . . [*Goes out through the hall.*]

LOPAKHIN: All right, all right . . . These people, really. [*Goes out after him.*]

ANYA: Have they sent Firs to the hospital?

YASHA: I told them to this morning. One must assume they did.

ANYA [*to* YEPIKHODOV, *who is passing through the room*]: Semyon Panteleich, can you find out please if they took Firs to the hospital.

YASHA [*offended*]: I told Yegor this morning. Why ask ten times!

YEPIKHODOV: In my definite opinion, that ancient Firs can't be mended, he should join his fathers. And I can only envy him. [*Has put a suitcase on a cardboard hatbox and squashes it.*] Well, of course. I knew that would happen. [*Exit.*]

YASHA [*mockingly*]: The Walking Accident.

VARYA [*outside the door*]: Have they taken Firs to the hospital?

ANYA: They have.

VARYA: Why didn't they take the letter to the doctor?

ANYA: We'll have to send it after him . . . [*Exit.*]

VARYA [*in the other room*]: Where's Yasha? Tell him his mother has come and wants to say goodbye to him.

YASHA [*throwing up his hand*]: They just wear out your patience.

[*All this time* DUNYASHA *has been busy with the luggage; now* YASHA *has been left alone, she goes up to him.*]

DUNYASHA: If you would just give me one little look, Yasha. You're going away . . . leaving me . . . [*Weeps and drapes herself round his neck.*]

YASHA: Why are you crying? [*Drinks some champagne.*] In six days I'll be in Paris again. Tomorrow we'll be getting into the express and we'll be off in a flash. Somehow I can't believe it. *Vive la France!* . . . It doesn't suit me here, I can't live . . . I can't help it. I've had my fill of looking at ignorance — that's enough for me.

[*Drinks champagne.*] Why are you crying? Behave properly and then you won't cry.

DUNYASHA [*powdering her face, looking in a hand mirror*]: Send me a letter from Paris. You know I loved you, Yasha, I loved you so! I'm a delicate being, Yasha!

YASHA: They're coming in here. [*Gets busy with the suitcases and hums quietly.*]

[*Enter* LYUBOV ANDREYEVNA, GAYEV, ANYA *and* CHARLOTTA IVANOVNA.]

GAYEV: We should go. There's not much time left. [*Looking at Yasha*] Someone smells of herring!

LYUBOV ANDREYEVNA: We should get in the carriages in ten minutes ... [*Looks round the room.*] Goodbye, dear house, old grandfather. Winter will pass, spring will come and you won't be there any more, they'll have pulled you down. How much these walls have seen! [*Kisses her daughter with passion.*] My treasure, you are just radiant, your little eyes are sparkling like two diamonds. Are you pleased? Are you very pleased?

ANYA: Very! A new life is beginning, Mama!

GAYEV [*cheerfully*]: Indeed, everything is all right now. Before the cherry orchard was sold we were all worried, we were suffering, and then, once the matter was finally and irrevocably settled, we all calmed down, we even cheered up ... I am a bank official, I am a financier now ... yellow ball into the middle, and you, Lyuba, you really are looking better, no doubt about it.

LYUBOV ANDREYEVNA: Yes. My nerves are better, that's true.

[*She is brought her hat and coat.*]

I'm sleeping well. Carry my things out, Yasha. It's time to go. [*To Anya*] My little girl, we'll see each other soon ... I'm off to Paris, I will live there on the money which your great-aunt in Yaroslavl sent to buy the property – three cheers for Auntie! – but that money won't last very long.

ANYA: Mama, you'll come back soon, soon ... won't you? I'm going to study, I'll pass the Gymnasium examination and then I will work, I'll help you. Mama, we'll read all sorts of books together ... Won't we? [*Kisses her mother's hands.*] We'll read on autumn evenings, we'll read a lot of books and a new, wonderful world will open up before us ... [*She falls into thought.*] Mama, come back ...

LYUBOV ANDREYEVNA: I will come back, my treasure. [*Embraces her daughter.*]

[*Enter* LOPAKHIN. CHARLOTTA *quietly sings a song.*]

GAYEV: Happy Charlotta: she's singing!

CHARLOTTA [*picking up a bundle which looks like a swaddled child*]: Hushaby, baby ...

[*The sound of a baby's cry: 'Wah, wah!'*]

Sleep, my good, darling boy!

[*'Wah! ... Wah!'*]

I'm so sorry for you! [*Throws down the bundle where it was.*] So please find me a job. I can't be like this.

LOPAKHIN: We will find you one, Charlotta Ivanovna, don't worry.

GAYEV: They're all abandoning us, Varya is leaving ... we've suddenly become unnecessary.

CHARLOTTA: I have nowhere to live in the town. I must leave ... [*Sings.*] It's all the same to me ...

[*Enter* PISHCHIK.]

LOPAKHIN: Wonder of nature! ...

PISHCHIK [*out of breath*]: Oh, let me get my breath back ... I'm exhausted ... My most revered friends ... Give me some water ...

GAYEV: I suppose you've come for some money? Your humble servant, I'll get myself out of harm's way . . . [*Exit.*]

PISHCHIK: It's a little while since I was here . . . lovely lady . . . [*To Lopakhin*] You're here . . . I'm glad to see you . . . a man of most enormous intelligence . . . here . . . take this . . . [*Gives Lopakhin some money.*] Four hundred roubles . . . I still owe you eight hundred and forty . . .

LOPAKHIN [*shrugging his shoulders in bewilderment*]: Am I dreaming . . . Where did you get it?

PISHCHIK: Wait a moment . . . I'm feeling hot . . . Something most extraordinary happened. Some Englishmen came to my property and discovered a kind of white clay in the soil . . . [*To Lyubov Andreyevna*] And four hundred for you . . . lovely, amazing woman . . . [*Gives her the money.*] The rest later. [*Drinks some water.*] Just now a young man in the train was telling how apparently some . . . great philosopher advises one to jump off the roof . . . 'Jump!' he says, and that's our whole mission. [*In astonishment*] Imagine that! Some water! . . .

LOPAKHIN: Who were these Englishmen?

PISHCHIK: I gave them a twenty-four-year lease on the land with the clay . . . And now, excuse me, I've no time . . . I must get on . . . I have to go to Znoykov . . . to Kardamonov . . . I owe everyone . . . [*Drinks.*] Your good health . . . I'll come round on Thursday . . .

LYUBOV ANDREYEVNA: We're moving out to town now and tomorrow I'm going abroad . . .

PISHCHIK: What? [*Anxiously*] Why are you going to town? Oh, that's why I can see the furniture . . . the suitcases . . . Well, it doesn't matter . . . [*With tears in his eyes*] It doesn't matter . . . People of the greatest intelligence . . . these Englishmen . . . It doesn't matter . . . Good luck . . . God will give you his aid . . . It doesn't matter . . . Everything on this earth comes to an end . . . [*Kisses Lyubov Andreyevna's hand.*] And if it comes to your ears that my end has come, remember this old . . . horse and say, 'Once there walked the earth one . . . Simeonov-Pishchik . . . God rest his soul' . . . Most remarkable weather . . . Yes . . . [*Goes out

in great confusion but returns immediately and speaks from the door.]
Dashenka sends you her greetings! [*Exit.*]

LYUBOV ANDREYEVNA: Now we can go. I'm leaving with two
worries. The first is Firs being ill. [*Looking at her watch.*] We can
have five minutes more . . .

ANYA: Mama, they've already sent Firs to the hospital. Yasha sent
him this morning.

LYUBOV ANDREYEVNA: My second anxiety is Varya. She's got
into the habit of getting up early and working, and now without
work she's like a fish out of water. She's become thin and pale,
and the poor girl keeps crying . . .

[*A pause.*]

You know this very well, Yermolay Alekseich; I dreamed . . . of
having Varya married to you and indeed there was every indication that you would marry her. [*Whispers to* ANYA, *who nods to
Charlotta and both go out*.] She loves you, you're fond of her, and
I do not know, I just do not know why you seem to avoid one
another. I don't understand!

LOPAKHIN: I have to say I don't understand, either. It's all somehow
strange . . . If there's still time, then I'm ready now . . . Let's get
it done right away, and *basta*[1] – without you I feel I'll never
propose.

LYUBOV ANDREYEVNA: Excellent. You really only need one
minute. I'll call her at once . . .

LOPAKHIN: And luckily there's champagne. [*Looking at the glasses.*]
They're empty, somebody's already drunk it.

[YASHA *coughs.*]

Lapped it up, I should say.

LYUBOV ANDREYEVNA [*animatedly*]: Splendid. We'll go out . . .
Yasha, *allez!*[2] I'll call her . . . [*Through the door*] Varya, leave all
that, come in here. Come! [*Goes out with Yasha.*]

LOPAKHIN [*looking at his watch*]: Yes . . .

[*A pause. On the other side of the door suppressed laughter and whispering; eventually* VARYA *enters.*]

VARYA [*inspecting the luggage for a long time*]: Strange, I just can't find it . . .
LOPAKHIN: What are you looking for?
VARYA: I packed it myself and I can't remember.

[*A pause.*]

LOPAKHIN: Where are you going now, Varvara Mikhaylovna?
VARYA: Me? To the Ragulins' . . . I've agreed to look after his estate . . . as a kind of housekeeper.
LOPAKHIN: You mean Yashnevo? That'll be seventy versts from here.

[*A pause.*]

Now life in this house is over . . .
VARYA [*looking over the luggage*]: Where is it . . . Or perhaps I packed it in the trunk . . . Yes, life in this house is over . . . there won't be any more . . .
LOPAKHIN: And I'm off to Kharkov now . . . on the same train. I have a lot of work. And I'm leaving Yepikhodov here in the yard . . . I've taken him on.
VARYA: Well, why not!
LOPAKHIN: At this time last year, if you remember, it was already snowing, but now it's calm and sunny. Only it's cold . . . Three degrees of frost.
VARYA: I didn't look.

[*A pause.*]

Anyway, our thermometer's broken . . .

[*A pause. A voice through the door to the outside: 'Yermolay Alekseich! . . .'*]

LOPAKHIN [*as if he has been awaiting this summons for a long time*]: Coming! [*Goes out quickly.*]

[VARYA, *sitting on the floor and laying her head against a bundle of clothes, sobs quietly. The door opens and* LYUBOV ANDREYEVNA *comes in cautiously.*]

LYUBOV ANDREYEVNA: Well?

[*A pause.*]

We must go.

VARYA [*no longer crying, wiping her eyes*]: Yes, it's time, Mama dear. I'll manage to get to the Ragulins' today, only I mustn't be late for the train . . .

LYUBOV ANDREYEVNA [*in the doorway*]: Anya, put your coat on!

[*Enter* ANYA, *then* GAYEV *and* CHARLOTTA IVANOVNA. GAYEV *is wearing a warm coat with a hood. The servants and drivers gather.* YEPIKHODOV *is busy around the luggage.*]

Now we can begin our journey!

ANYA [*joyously*]: Our journey!

GAYEV: My friends, my dear, cherished friends! As I leave this house for ever, how can I be silent, how can I restrain myself from expressing, in farewell, the feelings which now fill all my being . . .

ANYA [*in a pleading tone*]: Uncle!

VARYA: Dear Uncle, you mustn't!

GAYEV [*gloomily*]: Double the yellow into the middle pocket . . . I won't say anything . . .

[*Enter* TROFIMOV, *then* LOPAKHIN.]

TROFIMOV: Well, ladies and gentlemen, time to go!

LOPAKHIN: Yepikhodov, my coat!

LYUBOV ANDREYEVNA: I'll sit just a moment more.[3] It's as if I've never seen before what kind of walls this house has, what kind of ceilings, and now I look at them hungrily, with such tender love . . .

GAYEV: I remember when I was six, on Trinity Sunday I sat in this window and watched my father walk to church . . .

LYUBOV ANDREYEVNA: Have they taken all the luggage?

LOPAKHIN: Everything, I think. [*To Yepikhodov, who is helping him into his coat*] Yepikhodov, you see that everything's all right.

YEPIKHODOV [*speaking in a hoarse voice*]: Don't worry, Yermolay Alekseich!

LOPAKHIN: Why is your voice like that?

YEPIKHODOV: I drank some water just now, I swallowed something.

YASHA [*scornfully*]: What ignorance . . .

LYUBOV ANDREYEVNA: We'll go – and there won't be a soul left here . . .

LOPAKHIN: No one, till the spring.

VARYA [*pulling an umbrella out of a bundle with a movement as if she's going to hit someone;* LOPAKHIN *pretends to be frightened.*] There, there . . . I wasn't going to.

TROFIMOV: Ladies and gentlemen, let's go and get in the carriages . . . It's time now! The train will be coming!

VARYA: Petya, here are your galoshes, by the suitcase. [*In tears*] And what dirty, old ones you have . . .

TROFIMOV [*putting on the galoshes*]: Let's go, ladies and gentlemen! . . .

GAYEV [*very upset, afraid of crying*]: The train . . . the station . . . Cross shot into the centre, double the white into the corner pocket . . .

LYUBOV ANDREYEVNA: Let's go!

LOPAKHIN: Is everyone here? Is there anyone in there? [*Locks the side door on the left.*] Things are stored there, we must lock up. Let's go! . . .

ANYA: Farewell, house! Farewell, old life!

TROFIMOV: Hail, new life! . . . [*Goes out with Anya.*]

[VARYA *looks round the room and slowly goes out.* YASHA *and* CHARLOTTA *with the little dog go out.*]

LOPAKHIN: So, till the spring. Come on out . . . Goodbye! . . . [*Exit.*]

[LYUBOV ANDREYEVNA *and* GAYEV *are left alone together. As if they had been waiting for it, they fall on each other's necks and sob gently and quietly, afraid of being heard.*]

GAYEV [*desperately*]: My sister, my sister . . .

LYUBOV ANDREYEVNA: Oh my darling, my sweet, beautiful orchard! . . . My life, my youth, my happiness, farewell! . . . farewell! . . .

[ANYA's *voice, cheerfully calling:* 'Mama! . . .' TROFIMOV's *voice, cheerful and excited:* 'Hallo-o! . . .']

To look at these walls, these windows one last time . . . Our mother used to love walking about this room . . .

GAYEV: My sister, my sister! . . .

[ANYA's *voice:* 'Mama! . . .' TROFIMOV's *voice:* 'Hallo-o! . . .']

LYUBOV ANDREYEVNA: We're coming! . . .

[*Exeunt.*]

[*The stage is empty. There is the sound of all the doors being locked with keys, then the carriages leaving. It becomes quiet. The silence is broken by the hollow striking of an axe against a tree, sounding solitary and sad. There are footsteps.* FIRS *appears at the right-hand door. He is dressed as usual in a jacket and white waistcoat and slippers. He is ill.*]

FIRS [*going to the door, trying the handle*]: Locked. They've gone . . . [*Sits down on the sofa.*] They've forgotten about me . . . It doesn't matter . . . I'll sit here a moment . . . And Leonid Andreich probably didn't put on his fur coat but went off in his light one

... [*Sighs worriedly.*] I didn't look ... Young people! [*Mumbles something unintelligible.*] Life has gone by, as if I hadn't lived. [*Lies down.*] I'll lie down a moment ... You've got no strength, nothing is left, nothing ... Oh you ... big booby! ... [*Lies motionless.*]

[*There is the distant sound of a string breaking, as if in the sky, a dying, melancholy sound. Silence falls, and the only thing to be heard is a tree being struck with an axe far off in the orchard.*]

[*Curtain.*]

NOTES

Ivanov

CHARACTERS

1. *Sara Abramson*: These names indicate, without its being spelt out, that Anna Petrovna is a Jew who has converted to Christianity and been given a Christian first name and patronymic.

2. *District Council*: The *zemstvo*, the regional council in Russia which was the main unit of local government from 1864 to 1917.

3. *landowner*: This word (*pomeshchik*, masculine, *pomeshchitsa*, feminine) is as much an indication of class as a statement of fact. Merchants (*kuptsy*) were members of one of the classes (others being nobles and peasants) in a class system defined by law: while merchants very largely led Russia's business and also artistic expansion at the turn of the nineteenth century, they were also popularly regarded as embodiments of reaction and vulgarity.

4. *hanger-on*: The size of Russian country houses and the poor communications of the country attracted a population of resident *nakhlebniki* (hangers-on), a word difficult to translate since there isn't an English-language social parallel.

5. *Districts*: Imperial Russia was divided into *gubernii* (governments or provinces), which were subdivided in turn into *uyezdy* (districts).

ACT ONE

1. *troika*: A carriage or sleigh, drawn by three horses.

2. *Nicolas-voilà*: 'Nikolay here he is' (French) – from a popular ditty of the 1880s. The conversation of the upper classes in Chekhov's plays, as in life, was peppered with French names and words.

3. *papers*: Scented papers were chewed to sweeten the breath.

4. *melanchondria*: An attempt at a concocted word of Chekhov's – *merlekhlyundiya*.

5. *Kommen Sie hier*: 'Come here' (German).

6. *Madame Angot or Ophelia*: Heroines from C. Lecoq's operetta *La Fille de Madame Angot* and Shakespeare's *Hamlet*.

7. *Qui est-ce que c'est*: 'Who is this . . .' (inaccurate French).

8. *swine in a skullcap*: An allusion to the corrupt officials of *The Government Inspector*, V.8, by Nikolay Vasilevich Gogol (1809–52). His satiric comedy of 1836 is probably the most famous Russian play.

9. *Tartuffe*: The eponymous hero of Molière's comedy of 1664, the archetype of lust masked by hypocritical piety and virtue.

10. *Nicolas*: The aristocratic Count uses the French form of the name.

11. *Yes, sir*: *Slushayu*, literally 'I listen' – the standard response of military subordinates.

12. *Gevalt!*: Yiddish exclamation, expressing astonishment, protest, fear, from the German *Gewalt*, 'force'.

13. *The knock of the watchman*: Nightwatchmen in big houses and country estates knocked on a piece of wood as they did their rounds to indicate their passing.

ACT TWO

1. *covers*: In pre-revolutionary Russia furniture of all kinds in rooms that received little use was kept under covers against light and dirt. That the furniture in the Lebedevs' house was kept thus during a party is a tribute to the miserliness of the hostess.

2. *lottery issues*: In 1887 there had been a significant increase in the stock market prices for the Government lottery issues of 1864 and 1866.

3. *Flicks his throat with a finger*: Signifying that they would get drunk.

4. *entre nous*: 'Between ourselves' (French).

5. *. . . my dead youth . . .*: He is quoting (slightly inaccurately) from a famous poem by Mikhail Yurevich Lermontov (1814–41), later set to music, 'No, it's not you I love so ardently . . .' (1841).

6. *plumper*: The ideal of merchant beauty, indeed often of Russian beauty during the period, inclined towards the plump.

7. *Your Highness*: Counts and princes were entitled to be addressed as 'Your Highness'.

8. *Aesculapius*: Latin form of Asclepius, the Greek god of medicine.

9. *Dobrolyubov*: Nikolay Aleksandrovich Dobrolyubov (1836–61), radical social and literary critic.

10. *kulak*: Free, sometimes wealthy farmers, kulaks were often resented and

had the reputation of exploiting poorer peasants –one that Stalin made use of in the repressions of the 1920s.

11. *serfdom*: This had been abolished in 1861, to the distress of many nobles. Of course, Shabelsky and the other older characters in this play had grown up with it.

12. *Chatsky*: The outspoken hero of A. S. Griboyedov's comedy *Woe from Wit* (1822–23).

13. *Hegelian*: Influenced, like many Russians, by the ideas of the German idealist philosopher Georg Hegel (1770–1831).

14. *Francis Bacon*: English politician, philosopher and essayist (1561–1626).

15. *Michel Michelich*: A French version of Borkin's first name and patronymic.

16. *Manfred*: Byron's romantic hero, from his poem of that name (1817).

17. *'superfluous man'*: The classic hero of much Russian nineteenth-century literature, from Pushkin's Eugene Onegin and Lermontov's Pechorin onward.

ACT THREE

1. *Germany ... France*: The German Empire's aggressive policies at this time had led to a deterioration in its relations with France, bad in any case ever since the Franco-Prussian War.

2. *rabies*: In 1880 Louis Pasteur (1822–95) had begun his experiments on rabies which culminated in his development of an anti-rabies vaccine in 1885.

3. *'Jomini ... vodka'*: A quotation from the romantic poet Denis Davydov's 'Song of an Old Hussar' (it is also the epigraph to Tolstoy's novella *Two Hussars*, 1855). H. Jomini (1779–1869) was a French general and military theorist.

4. *Repetatur*: 'Let it be repeated' – so, 'again' (Latin).

5. *zakuski*: The Russian *hors d'oeuvres* served with vodka to introduce a meal, sometimes in a separate dining-room.

6. *Aesculapius*: See note 8 to Act Two.

7. *whist*: Actually *vint*, a whist-related game.

8. *alma mater*: 'Dear mother' – Latin cliché for 'university'.

9. *George Sand*: Pseudonym of Aurore Dupin, French writer and feminist (1804–76).

10. *Gymnasium*: High school or grammar school modelled on the German *Gymnasium*.

11. *old man*: Perceptions of age change. Ivanov is only in his middle thirties!

12. *house goblin*: The guardian house-spirit of Russian folklore.

ACT FOUR

1. *blessing*: A Russian Orthodox marriage involves a blessing that is separate from the actual wedding ceremony.

2. *In Gogol the two rats . . .* : In Gogol's *The Government Inspector* (I.1) the Mayor says he's had a dream about two black rats 'who came, sniffed – and went off'.

3. *yellow house*: A lunatic asylum in pre-revolutionary Russia was colloquially known as 'the yellow house'.

4. *Schopenhauer*: Arthur Schopenhauer (1788–1860), German philosopher.

5. *best man*: In a Russian Orthodox wedding both bride and groom have 'best men' who escort them and hold the crowns above the couple in church.

The Seagull

ACT ONE

1. *Nekrasov*: Nikolay Alekseyevich Nekrasov (1821–77), Russian lyric poet and radical.

2. *Duse*: Eleonora Duse (1858–1924), famous Italian classical actress who toured in Russia in the 1890s.

3. *La Dame aux Camélias*: A play of 1852 by Alexandre Dumas, *fils* (1824–95) and a dramatization of his novel of the same title (1848), which also provided the storyline of Verdi's opera *La Traviata* (1853), of the film *Camille* with Greta Garbo (1937), and of Frederick Ashton's ballet *Marguerite and Armand* (1963).

4. *Life's Hell*: *Chad zhizni*, a play by B. M. Markevich (1822–84).

5. *Maupassant*: Guy de Maupassant (1850–93), French short-story writer and novelist.

6. *petty bourgeois*: a *meshchanin*, a member of the *meshchanstvo*, the lower urban bourgeoisie, one of the social estates defined by law.

7. *Tolstoy*: Count Lev Nikolayevich Tolstoy (1828–1910), Russian novelist and thinker.

8. *Zola*: Emile Zola (1840–1902), French Naturalist novelist and journalist.

9. *'To France two grenadiers . . .'*: A setting by Schumann of the poem 'The Grenadiers' (1827) by Heinrich Heine (1797–1856).

10. *Rasplyuyev*: A leading role in A. V. Sukhovo-Kobylin's *Krechinsky's Wedding*, a popular play of the 1850s.

11. *De gustibus . . . nihil*: Literally, 'About taste, either good or nothing.' Shamrayev has got confused between two Latin tags.

12. *'O Hamlet . . .'*: From Hamlet's exchange with his mother Gertrude, *Hamlet* III.4. The Russians have long been obsessed with *Hamlet*.

13. *jeune premier*: 'romantic lead' (French).

ACT TWO

1. *'Tell her, flowers mine . . .'*: The opening words of Siebel's aria from Gounod's opera *Faust* (1859), III.1.

2. *comme il faut*: 'Proper', 'properly done' (French).

3. *Maupassant's 'Sur l'eau'*: Arkadina is reading Maupassant's non-fictional account of a boat journey, *On the Water*, which had been translated into Russian in 1896.

4. *valerian drops*: From the plant, much prescribed as a stimulant among other uses in early medicine.

5. *Your Excellency*: Having reached a rank in the higher reaches of the civil service, Sorin is entitled to the title of Excellency which went with it.

6. *'Words, words, words . . .'*: *Hamlet* II.2.

7. *. . . post-horses*: i.e. with relays of horses which served the post and also express travellers.

8. *Poprishchin*: The crazy civil servant narrator of Gogol's *Notes of a Madman* (1835). See also note 10 to *Three Sisters*, Act Three.

9. *Fathers and Sons*: The most famous novel (1862) of Ivan Sergeyevich Turgenev (1818–83).

ACT THREE

1. *decoration*: As a Full State Councillor (see note 1 to Act 4) Sorin will have been awarded an imperial order (conceivably of St Anna); he will be wearing its cross on a ribbon round his neck.

2. *Zemstvo*: See note 2 to *Ivanov*, Characters.

3. *The Post Office Robbery*: A popular French play.

4. *Slavyansky Bazaar*: One of the best Moscow hotels.

ACT FOUR

1. *Full State Councillor*: Sorin was a civil servant in Grade 4 of the Table of Ranks originally instituted by Peter the Great in 1722 and modified over the next two centuries. This established a formal hierarchy for the civil service, the armed services, the imperial court and the clergy. So Sorin was equivalent in rank to a rear-admiral and an archimandrite.

2. *Genoa*: Chekhov had visited the Italian city in the autumn of 1894.

3. *Rusalka*: Treplyov is referring to the Miller's aria in A. S. Dargomyzhsky's opera *Rusalka* (after Pushkin).

4. *the Man in the Iron Mask*: A political prisoner in the reign of Louis XIV of France who always wore a mask when being transferred from one prison to another; the mystery was the subject of one of Dumas *père*'s novels.

5. *lotto*: A board game played with cards and numbered discs drawn on the principle of a lottery – a domestic ancestor of bingo.

6. *'Lucky is he . . . warm nest'*: The quotation is from the epilogue to Turgenev's novel *Rudin* (1856).

Uncle Vanya

CHARACTERS

1. *nyanya*: 'Nanny' or 'nurse' is an inadequate translation for the *nyanyas* attached to Russian households in pre-revolutionary Russia who played a significant role in literature and in life; cf. Pushkin's attachment to his old *nyanya*.

ACT ONE

1. *Your Excellency*: Serebryakov is a retired Professor. His rank in the civilian grades of the Table of Ranks (see note 1 to *The Seagull*, Act Four) gave him the right to be addressed as Your Excellency.

2. *Maman*: 'Mama' or 'Mother' (French).

3. *'With straining mind . . . nor do we'*: From a satire by the classical poet and satirist Ivan Ivanovich Dimitriyev (1760–1837).

4. *Turn off the tap . . .*: Voynitsky is adapting a well-known Russian aphorism: 'If you have a fountain, put a tap on it.'

5. *quantum satis*: 'As much as I need' (Latin).

6. *Jean*: French for Ivan or John.

7. *Tsyp, tsyp, tsyp*: The Russian version of 'cluck, cluck, cluck'.

8. *In some play of Ostrovsky's there's a character*: Paratov in *The Girl with No Dowry* (1879) by Nikolay Aleksandrovich Ostrovsky (1823–86).

ACT TWO

1. *Batyushkov*: Konstantin Nikolayevich Batyushkov (1787–1855), lyric poet of the so-called 'Anacreontic' school.

2. *Turgenev*: See note 9 to *The Seagull*, Act Two.

3. *holy fool*: 'Holy fools' – the mentally retarded, often tramps – were traditionally regarded in Russia as touched by God and founts of wisdom.

4. *Kisses . . . on the shoulder*: To kiss someone on the shoulder was an antiquated form of greeting, the salutation of a superior by a social inferior.

5. *devil*: More precisely, a house goblin. See note 12 to *Ivanov*, Act Three.

6. *kulaks*: See note 10 to *Ivanov*, Act Two.

7. *Basta*: 'That's enough' (Italian).

8. *ty*: 'Thou'. They are now on the intimate terms of using the second person singular to one another.

9. *Zhuchka, Malchik*: Dogs' names – literally Beetle and Boy.

ACT THREE

1. *the Conservatoire*: The St Petersburg Conservatoire, founded in 1862.

2. *abacus*: As used for accounts and by cashiers in Russia until very recently, perhaps still in remote areas.

3. *'Serebryakov' . . . Vanya*: These forms here correspond to the use of the formal second person plural and the intimate 'thou' respectively.

4. *I've asked you to come here . . . coming to us*: Serebryakov is quoting here, somewhat inaccurately, the opening sentence of Gogol's famous play *The Government Inspector*.

5. *manet omnes una nox*: 'One night awaits all': from an ode of Horace (I.28).

6. *dacha*: The traditional Russian summer villa, usually within reach of towns and built of wood.

7. *Finland*: Part of the Russian Empire until 1917. The Finnish countryside near St Petersburg was classic dacha country (it is now again part of Russia – since the war of 1939/40).

ACT FOUR

1. *Ayvazovsky*: Ivan Ayvazovsky (1817–1900), a popular nineteenth-century artist, who painted an astonishing number of pictures, mostly of marine subjects. An obviously fatuous remark.

2. *Finita la commedia!*: 'The comedy [or play] is over' – an Italian phrase often used ironically.

Three Sisters

CHARACTERS

1. *Gymnasium*: See note 10 to *Ivanov*, Act Three.
2. *nyanya*: See note 1 to *Uncle Vanya*, Characters.
3. *provincial capital*: Seat of the governor of a province or *guberniya*, and of many institutions of local government; the town in which *Three Sisters* is set is loosely modelled on Perm, a remote city in the Urals.

ACT ONE

1. *name-day*: Day of the saint after whom a person is named in the Orthodox calendar – often celebrated more than a birthday. St Irina's day is 5 May in the Orthodox calendar (17 May in the Western).
2. *Cadet school*: A secondary stream of military high schools.
3. *Dobrolyubov*: See note 9 to *Ivanov*, Act Two.
4. *'An oak in leaf . . . a chain of gold'*: From the Prologue to Pushkin's fairy-tale poem *Ruslan and Lyudmila* (1820), known to every Russian schoolchild.
5. *'He had no time . . . upon him fell'*: Quotation from Krylov's fable 'The Peasant and the Labourer' (1815). The Aesopian fables of Ivan Aleksandrovich Krylov (1769–1844) were classics of the schoolroom.
6. *Novodevichy Cemetery*: The old cemetery attached to the Novodevichy Convent in south-western Moscow, where many famous Russians are buried (including Chekhov and his wife).
7. *uniform frock-coat*: Kulygin as a civil servant wears uniform.
8. *Court Councillor*: The seventh civilian grade in the Table of Ranks, see note 1 to *The Seagull*, Act Four.
9. *Feci quod potui . . . potentes*: 'I have done what I can. Let those who are able do better' (Latin). The words spoken by the Consuls of ancient Rome in handing over to their successors.
10. *mens sana in corpore sano*: 'A healthy mind in a healthy body' – Latin tag from Juvenal, *Satires*, X.356.
11. *rolling his rs*: Rode is probably of foreign (French or German) origin.

ACT TWO

1. *The set of Act One*: It is some twenty-one months later. The coming of the mummers indicates that it is Carnival time – Shrovetide.

2. *Testov's . . . Bolshoy Moskovsky*: Among Moscow's better restaurants. The Baedeker guidebook of 1914 still lists both these and gives the latter a star.

3. *Venez ici*: 'Come here' (French).

4. *'Gentlemen . . . boring!'*: The last sentence of 'The story of how Ivan Ivanovich quarrelled with Ivan Nikiforovich' (1832).

5. *Berdichev*: Balzac indeed got married in Berdichev in the Ukraine – to his mistress Madame Hanska, who had estates nearby, a few months before his death in 1850.

6. *Tsitsihar*: A city in Manchuria, north-east China (Qiqihar).

7. *the Panama affair*: The French Minister of Public Works Charles Baïhot (1843–1905) was sentenced to five years' imprisonment for accepting a substantial bribe in connection with the construction of the Panama Canal. After his release he published a diary, *Impressions cellulaires* (1898).

8. *Je vous prie . . . grossières*: 'Please forgive me, Marie, but your manners are a little crude' (French).

9. *Il paraît . . . pas*: 'It seems my Bobik isn't asleep yet' (French).

10. *I am strange . . . Aleko*: Solyony's first remark is a quotation of Chatsky's words from Griboyedov's *Woe from Wit*, III.1. Aleko is the hero of Pushkin's poem *The Gypsies* (1824), but the words declaimed by Solyony here and later are made up. More recently, the poem had been adapted into the libretto of Rachmaninov's one-act opera *Aleko*, written when he was nineteen (1892). That too may have been on Chekhov's mind.

11. *Lermontov's character*: Touchy and quarrelsome, Lermontov was killed in a duel.

12. *Basta!*: 'Enough!' (Italian).

13. *'Oh lobby . . .'*: A traditional folksong with a lively dance-tune but near-nonsense words.

14. *drink to brotherhood*: I.e. they will use the familiar forms of address to one another.

15. *Common little woman!*: The original here is *meshchanka*, a *petite bourgeoise*.

16. *O fallacem . . . spem!*: 'O illusory hope of mankind!' – Latin tag from Cicero.

ACT THREE

1. *Olga and Irina's room*: Another year has passed. Natasha has had a second child.

2. *In 1812 Moscow burnt down too*: Much of Moscow was destroyed in 1812 by fires, both deliberate and accidental, after Napoleon's occupation of the city.

3. *In vino veritas*: 'In wine is truth' – another Latin tag, a cliché even in antiquity.

4. *Poland . . . Chita*: I.e. to the opposite ends of the Russian Empire: to Poland, last an independent kingdom in 1795, or to Chita in eastern Siberia, virtually at the Chinese frontier, on the recently opened Trans-Siberian Railway.

5. *'Won't you sample a date from the palm-tree'*: Snatch from an operetta, but Chekhov when asked could not remember which.

6. *'All to love . . . blessings flow . . .'*: From Prince Gremin's aria in the third act of Tchaikovsky's opera *Yevgeny Onegin* (1879), after Pushkin's verse novel (VIII, 29: 1–3).

7. *'My thought could well . . . the geese I fear'*: An inexact quotation from Krylov's fable 'The Geese' (1811). See also note 5 to *Three Sisters*, Act One.

8. *Amo, amas . . . amant*: 'I love, thou lovest, he/she loves,' etc. – the conjugation of the present tense of the Latin verb *amare*, 'to love'.

9. *Omnia mea mecum porto*: 'All my goods I carry with me' – Latin tag.

10. *Gogol's madman*: Poprishchin in Gogol's *Notes of a Madman* (1835). His narration is characteristically broken by exclamations of 'silence!'

ACT FOUR

1. *The old garden . . .* : It is summer and rather more than a year later. The action of the whole play takes place over approximately four years.

2. *kochany*: 'Beloved, darling' (Polish).

3. *Ta-ra-ra-boom-de-ay*: The title and refrain of an American music hall song by Henry J. Sayers of 1891. It quickly crossed the Atlantic and caught on all over Europe. (The Russian refrain is *ta-ra-ra-bum-bi-ya*!)

4. *modus vivendi*: 'Way of living' (Latin).

5. *he thought it was written in Latin*: To spell this out – *chepukha* (nonsense) as handwritten in Russian could be read as the meaningless *renyxa* in Latin script.

6. *the consecutive ut*: I.e. *ut* meaning 'so that' in Latin.

7. *Stanislav*: The Tsarist decoration of the Order of St Stanislav. Chekhov

himself in 1899 had been awarded a third-class Stanislav for his 'outstanding work in the field of popular education'.

8. *'The Maiden's Prayer'*: *'La prière d'une vierge'*, a popular piano piece.

9. *'He had no time . . . upon him fell'*: See note 5 to Act One.

10. *Walks off with Chebutykin*: Andrey too must have left the stage. An oversight of Chekhov's.

11. *'And he, so restless . . . can offer calm'*: The concluding two lines, slightly misquoted in the Russian, of Lermontov's poem 'The Sail' (1832).

12. *kvass*: See note 2 to *The Cherry Orchard*, Act One.

13. *Il ne faut pas . . . Vous êtes un ours*: 'You mustn't make a noise, Sophie has already gone to sleep. You are a bear' (French). Natasha's French is not quite accurate, as one might expect.

14. *'An oak in leaf . . .'*: Masha is still quoting the opening of Pushkin's *Ruslan and Lyudmila* (see note 4 to Act One). The cat appears in the next two lines – thus: 'An oak in leaf beside the seashore, upon that oak a chain of gold, and day and night the chain a-circling, a learned cat stalks round and round.'

15. *and the maid*: Chekhov forgets to mention the entry of the maid in his stage direction.

The Cherry Orchard

CHARACTERS

1. *Firs*: The old ex-serf is named after the obscure Orthodox Saint Thyrsus, martyred in 251 (rendered yet more obscure by transliteration).

ACT ONE

1. *muzhik*: Male Russian peasant, a word which can bear literal, affectionate or derogatory meanings.

2. *kvass*: As much the national drink as vodka, a 'beer', sweet, mildly acid and mildly alcoholic, made from fermenting grain with water and sugar.

3. *twenty-five thousand a year income*: Maxim Gorky's play *Summerfolk* examines critically just such a colony of dachas and its summer population. The first draft was finished a month after *The Cherry Orchard* opened on 20 January 1904. Did Gorky conceivably intend his play as some kind of comment on Chekhov's?

4. *the Eighties*: The period of the reactionary governments of Alexander III.

ACT TWO

1. *salto mortale*: cartwheel or somersault (Italian).

2. *Buckle*: Henry Buckle (1821–62), English social historian, whose *History of English Civilization* was translated into Russian in 1861.

3. *Emancipation*: The Emancipation of the serfs had come in 1861. Before that most domestic servants were owned and tied serfs. After Emancipation they had freedom of movement.

4. *rude to servants*: I.e. they call servants by the familiar 'thou'.

5. *'My brother . . . whose moan . . .'*: The passer-by is quoting (inaccurately) the opening of a poem by the hugely popular Semyon Yakovlevich Nadson (1862–87) – literally, 'My friend, my brother, tired, suffering brother' (1881). And the second phrase is a snatch from a poem by Nikolay Alekseyevich Nekrasov (1821–77), 'Thoughts by a main entrance' (1858).

6. *. . . Okhmeliya . . .*: Here and in his next line Lopakhin is roughly quoting Hamlet's words to Ophelia (*Hamlet*, III.1) and is making a heavy-handed play on the name of Ophelia and the verb *okhmelyat'*, to intoxicate. See also note 12 to *The Seagull*, Act One.

ACT THREE

1. *Promenade . . . vos dames*: Pishchik's calls during the dance are: 'Partners, promenade!', 'Grand circle, get set!' and 'Gentlemen, on your knees and thank your partners.'

2. *horse . . . in the Senate*: The unstable Roman Emperor Gaius, nicknamed Caligula (12–41), was said to have intended to make his favourite horse Incitatus Consul (and therefore a Senator).

3. *Nietzsche*: Friedrich Wilhelm Nietzsche (1844–1900), German philosopher.

4. *lezginka*: A dance tune from the Caucasus.

5. *Eins, zwei, drei!*: 'One, two, three!' (German).

6. *'I too . . . attractive'*: It is impossible to translate the voice's, that is Charlotta's, mistake here with Russian gender – the verb which should be plural and feminine is singular and masculine.

7. *Guter Mensch . . .*: 'A good man but a bad musician' (German) – a phrase from Clemens Brentano's comedy *Ponce de Leon* (1804).

8. *'The woman who was a sinner'*: A poem of 1857 by Count Aleksey Konstantinovich Tolstoy (poet, novelist and dramatist, 1817–75) on the subject of Mary Magdalene, which opens with a feast in a rich man's house. It was a popular subject for recital at literary soirées.

ACT FOUR

1. *basta*: Enough (Italian).
2. *allez*: Go (French).
3. *sit . . . a moment more*: It is a Russian custom to sit down for a moment before embarking on a journey.

PENGUIN ONLINE

READ MORE IN PENGUIN

In every corner of the world, on every subject under the sun, Penguin represents quality and variety – the very best in publishing today.

For complete information about books available from Penguin – including Puffins, Penguin Classics and Arkana – and how to order them, write to us at the appropriate address below. Please note that for copyright reasons the selection of books varies from country to country.

In the United Kingdom: Please write to *Dept. EP, Penguin Books Ltd, Bath Road, Harmondsworth, West Drayton, Middlesex UB7 0DA*

In the United States: Please write to *Consumer Services, Penguin Putnam Inc., 405 Murray Hill Parkway, East Rutherford, New Jersey 07073-2136.* VISA and MasterCard holders call 1-800-631-8571 to order Penguin titles

In Canada: Please write to *Penguin Books Canada Ltd, 10 Alcorn Avenue, Suite 300, Toronto, Ontario M4V 3B2*

In Australia: Please write to *Penguin Books Australia Ltd, 487 Maroondah Highway, Ringwood, Victoria 3134*

In New Zealand: Please write to *Penguin Books (NZ) Ltd, Private Bag 102902, North Shore Mail Centre, Auckland 10*

In India: Please write to *Penguin Books India Pvt Ltd, 11 Community Centre, Panchsheel Park, New Delhi 110017*

In the Netherlands: Please write to *Penguin Books Netherlands bv, Postbus 3507, NL-1001 AH Amsterdam*

In Germany: Please write to *Penguin Books Deutschland GmbH, Metzlerstrasse 26, 60594 Frankfurt am Main*

In Spain: Please write to *Penguin Books S. A., Bravo Murillo 19, 1°B, 28015 Madrid*

In Italy: Please write to *Penguin Italia s.r.l., Via Vittorio Emanuele 45/a, 20094 Corsico, Milano*

In France: Please write to *Penguin France, 12, Rue Prosper Ferradou, 31700 Blagnac*

In Japan: Please write to *Penguin Books Japan Ltd, Iidabashi KM-Bldg, 2-23-9 Koraku, Bunkyo-Ku, Tokyo 112-0004*

In South Africa: Please write to *Penguin Books South Africa (Pty) Ltd, P.O. Box 751093, Gardenview, 2047 Johannesburg*